CONAN DOYLE

PIERRE NORDON

Conan Doyle

A BIOGRAPHY

HOLT,
RINEHART AND WINSTON

New York   Chicago   San Francisco

Library of Congress Catalog Card Number: 67-10075

Translated from the French by Frances Partridge

8602054
Printed in the United States of America

TO THE MEMORY OF MY MOTHER
MARGUERITE NORDON
AND
TO MY WIFE

CONTENTS

PART I: THE MAN

PART II: THE WRITER

Contents

ILLUSTRATIONS

Illustrated letter from Richard Doyle

Conan Doyle at Edinburgh University

Sir Arthur Conan Doyle at his desk in Southsea, writing *A Study in Scarlet*

Sir Arthur Conan Doyle from a portrait by Sidney Paget, 1897

Jean Conan Doyle, 1910

Sir Arthur Conan Doyle towards the end of his life. *Photo: Paul Thomson. Copyright: Paul Popper*

'The Old Horse' drawn by Sir Arthur Conan Doyle

A Study in Scarlet: the first manuscript conception of Sherlock Holmes

The first appearance of *A Study in Scarlet*

ABBREVIATIONS

C.D.B.A. The Conan Doyle Biographical Archives
AUT.   *Memories and Adventures* (autobiography)
CHA.   *The Professor Challenger Stories*
HIS.   *The Conan Doyle Historical Romances*
HOL. I   *The Sherlock Holmes Long Stories*
HOL. II *The Sherlock Holmes Short Stories*
NAP.   *The Napoleonic Stories*

ACKNOWLEDGEMENTS

This book owes much to the example set by John Dickson Carr. His acute and sympathetic biography of Sir Arthur Conan Doyle was the first serious attempt to separate the figure of Sherlock Holmes's creator from the detective myth.

For permission to print hitherto unpublished material I am particularly grateful to the Public Trustee and the Society of Authors (George Bernard Shaw); Mr. Randolph Churchill; Hodder & Stoughton Ltd. (Jerome K. Jerome); Mrs. George Bambridge (Rudyard Kipling) and the Trustees of the Chamberlain Estate.

I wish to express my gratitude also to my correspondents in America: Mr. Joseph Baylen, Mr. Morton N. Cohen, Mr. William Lindsay Gresham, Mr. James Keddie Jr. and Dr. C. F. Kittle; in Australia: Mrs. Marjorie Hancock, assistant librarian, and Mr. G. D. Richardson, librarian, of the Library of Sydney; in Holland: Mr. Cornelis Helling; in Great Britain: Miss Mary Louise Conan Doyle, Group Officer Jean Conan Doyle, Mr. C. A. Gordon, Mr. James E. Holroyd and Mr. John G. Murray. I would like to pay my respects to the memory of M. Corneille Benoist, whose kindness and help were invaluable during my visits to the Conan Doyle Biographical Archives between 1956 and 1958; and lastly, above all, express my gratitude to Mr. Adrian Conan Doyle, the most privileged of witnesses, and a generous and tactful host, from whose impartiality, objectivity and critical intuition I have had the unusual good fortune to benefit.

PART I
The Man

Chapter 1

LIGHT FROM THE PAST

Several essentially modern factors have helped to establish Sir Arthur Conan Doyle's immense reputation—first and foremost the boom enjoyed by the detective story. But Conan Doyle was very far from being the self-made man whose image emerges from the misleading publicity he has sometimes received. The social, religious and racial traditions he inherited all tell a different story. So that to devote a few pages to his origins is not merely a formal concession to biographical conventions; it is absolutely necessary. Looking backwards beyond the historical vicissitudes natural to a Catholic and Anglo-Norman minority, we find the cradle of the Doyle family in France. Traces both of their name and their coat of arms exist in the village of Pont d'Ouilly-sur-l'Orne, eighteen kilometres from Falaise. According to Sir Francis Hastings Doyle the family arms used to figure on the walls of the village church. Sir Francis was writing three-quarters of a century ago and the walls have been restored several times since then, but one can still see on the altar screen the buck's head belonging to the arms of Sir Arthur's Doyle ancestors. D'Ouilly, D'Oyly, D'Oel, Doyle—the armorial bearings must have been registered in France, for they were already being used in the twelfth century by the Anglo-Norman family of D'Oel. By the beginning of the fourteenth century this branch was established in Ireland, along with other aristocratic Norman families such as the Burkes and the Fitzgeralds. Their coat of arms was ratified at Arklow in County Wicklow in 1618. Adrian Conan Doyle, Sir Arthur's third son, recalls a family tradition that their earliest known Doyle ancestor was Foulkes D'Oyley, comrade in arms of Richard Cœur de Lion.

It is also worth remarking that the coat of arms of Sir Baldwin D'Oyley, godson of Baldwin of Redvers, Earl of Devon, who in Sir Walter Scott's *Ivanhoe* offers to ransom Brian de Bois-Guilbert from the Disinherited Knight, is similar to that on the death certificate of Sir Arthur's ancestor James Doyle, dated 1638. Between the Squire in Walter Scott's novel and James Doyle, we find Sir Alexander D'Oyly, grandson of Baldwin, on whom Edward III bestowed property in County Wexford in 1333. Drawing up their genealogical tree presented almost insuperable difficulties to the Doyles, as it did to most Irish Catholic families; their history had been punctuated by wars, insurrections, looting, destruction and religious persecution, including the long martyrdom inflicted on them by the enforcement of the penal laws against the Catholic landed gentry. In a very restrained passage of his autobiography, Sir Arthur reminds us: 'My forbears, like most old Irish families in the south, kept to the old faith at the Reformation and fell victims to the penal laws in consequence.' Not until the seventeenth century does it become possible to trace Arthur Conan Doyle's line of descent without a break. The Doyles had settled successively at Arklow and at Ballyteige in County Wexford. But in 1668 John Doyle was dispossessed of almost all his Irish land in favour of the Duke of York; only the small estate of Barracurra was left him, and his grandson Richard was forced to leave even this in 1762. By way of literary amends, his descendant Sir Arthur described in *Sir Nigel* the regeneration of the Loring family after a long period of decadence: he was thinking of the Doyles when he wrote of the Lorings, and in the character of Nigel he expresses his own sense of staunch participation in the fate of his ancestors. After being uprooted from his home, Richard went to Dublin and set up as a silk merchant. His son James Doyle had two sons, of whom the elder, John, was born in 1797.

With John Doyle the family makes its entry into English history by the front door; he and four of his descendants, including his grandson Arthur Conan Doyle, appear in the *Dictionary of National Biography*. John Doyle learnt drawing from an Italian landscape-painter called Gabrielli, and afterwards studied art at the Royal Dublin Society's school under John Comerford, the miniaturist. In 1817, when he was just twenty, he left Dublin and his father (who lived to be over ninety); and, more significantly still, he definitely decided against returning to the land, even though the clouds of suspicion surrounding Catholics were beginning to dissolve. His contemporaries describe him as a rather austere and very stand-offish man. However, the young artist did not hesitate to follow his vocation and try his luck in London; he must already have found its call impossible to resist. To encourage him in his venture, he took with him two treasures showing how faithful the Doyles were to their family traditions: one was a sixteenth-century medical mortar with the Doyle arms embossed on it, the other was a portrait of Lord Stafford, afterwards attributed to Van Dyck. John Doyle went to live at 17 Cambridge Terrace, near Hyde Park. His name may hardly have been known outside the limits of a small circle, but that circle was a magic one, including the élite of political, literary and artistic London. And this made it possible for him to observe and perpetuate in hundreds of sketches the appearance, gestures, expressions and frowns of the individuals caricatured by 'H.B.' For, under the disguise of these initials, he soon became generally known as the best caricaturist of his day.

According to an enthusiastic witness, whenever a new set of caricatures by 'H.B.' were published there were traffic jams in the London streets. They even penetrated as far as Downing Street, and one day in 1830 the young Macaulay whiled away the time of waiting to be received by Wellington in studying 'H.B.'s innumerable versions of Grey's features.[1]

The first caricatures had been published in about 1827. Two years later Thomas Maclean, a printer in the Haymarket, was publishing them regularly at the rate of four or five sets at a time. They were sought after by collectors, and *The Times* published a descriptive catalogue of his lithographs, without revealing the true identity of 'H.B.'

In fact they became an institution, a document of political and afterwards historical value.[2] For contemporary observers they were a source of information, perhaps sometimes a weapon. We have mentioned Wellington, but Metternich's passion for John Doyle's engravings was even more conspicuous. After his death his collection of several hundred examples went to join the already large number in the Print Room of the British Museum. Their value must be considerable today, since four drawings by John Doyle were bought for a thousand guineas in 1880, and twelve years later three more were acquired for the same sum. Their purely artistic merit has been generally recognised, and from a sheaf of tributes two may be selected— Benjamin Haydon emphasised the suppleness and skill of 'H.B.'s art, and Thackeray praised the urbanity of his wit.

The terms on which Samuel Rogers corresponded with John

[1] Letter from Lord Macaulay to his sister, quoted by Austin Dobson in the *Dictionary of National Biography*.

[2] In 1952 Macaulay's descendant G. M. Trevelyan published reproductions of a series of sixty-two engravings by John Doyie, under the title *The Seven Years of William IV; a Reign cartooned by John Doyle*.

Doyle from 1829 onwards make it clear that the artist had quickly been accepted by the literary society of his day.

He went out very little, and according to chance references in his sons' letters his majestic solemnity was scarcely that of a very hospitable man. His dining-table is still treasured by his descendants, but the brilliance of the guests who were invited to it was more remarkable than their numbers: Sir Walter Scott of course as well as Landseer, Holman Hunt, Millais, John Leech, Sir Richard Owen, Newman, Disraeli, De Quincey, Samuel Lover, Thackeray and Dickens.

John Doyle's talent alone did not justify the consideration he received. Another reason for the respect shown him was probably the loyalty, sometimes tinged with intransigence, with which he clung to his Catholic faith. It was not so much a question of religious mysticism as of militant conservatism, and an untiring devotion to the family beliefs. The sufferings they had entailed may have seemed to justify them in some mysterious way. In fact his fidelity to the rites of his chosen religion was symbolic of his desire to keep his family traditions and history as much alive in London as they had been in Ireland—symbolic in just the same way as the medical mortar or the portrait of Lord Stafford. The calm but masterful patrician revealed in every feature of the bust made of him by Christopher Moore in 1849 would certainly have insisted on the same fidelity from his sons. But what is really remarkable is that he succeeded in enforcing it, and that none of them failed him. How could the world be indifferent to such heroic if absurd loyalty? The best Roman Catholic families opened their arms to John Doyle and afterwards to his sons. Thus James and his young wife spent their honeymoon as guests of the Duke of Norfolk, premier Catholic peer of the realm, at Arundel Castle.[1]

[1] This same James Doyle would, much later, have the opportunity to judge the esteem in which his father's memory was held. In 1875, in a letter to Charles, he remarked: '. . . I went a few days ago to see Sir Duffus Hardy, the Keeper of the Records, and had a long interview, in the course of which he said that whenever I wished "the experience of fifty years was at my service". He also said—and this I repeat because it applies to all of us—"you bear a very distinguished name, and as a son of so eminent a man as your father, you enjoy a great advantage over most people". What made his kindness more impressive was that he seemed naturally rather a dry, stern, kind of man, not given to speechifying. Finally he said that everything under his care was at my service "not as a favour, but as a right", and that any day I liked he would introduce me to his subordinates.' (Unpublished, C.D.B.A.)

It was because *The Official Baronage of England*, published in 1886, was being prepared that James Doyle had to visit the Record Office where Sir Thomas Duffus Hardy was Keeper until 1876.

John Doyle had married Marianna Conan, sister of Michael Conan, an artist and journalist with connections in both France and England, who was dramatic critic of *The Morning Herald* and Paris correspondent for *The Art Journal* edited by Marcus Huish. One daughter, Annette, was born of the marriage, and five sons, one of whom—Francis—died before he was sixteen but already having shown great talent as an artist.

His four surviving sons followed in John Doyle's footsteps, each in his own particular vein but all four with success. James, who has been mentioned already, was the eldest. His personality and career remain veiled in a certain amount of obscurity. He was evidently a frequent visitor at Holland House, where his tall, rather stooping figure, long black beard, discreet behaviour and pensive expression earned him the nickname of 'The Priest'. Arthur Conan Doyle was inclined to be reserved about 'Uncle James'. It is easy to guess that he was the chief obstacle to any rapprochement between Arthur and his uncles after he had told them he was an agnostic. Before taking to genealogy, this austere man gained a certain reputation as a painter, his best work being *A Literary Party at Sir Joshua Reynolds's*.

He also edited and illustrated a history of England up to the accession of the Tudors, under the title *Chronicles of England*. This triple orientation as artist, historian and genealogist was also apparent in varying degrees in the careers of his brothers, and—as we shall see—in that of their nephew the creator of Sherlock Holmes.

There was some conflict between the artist and the archivist in Henry's character. His output was more considerable than that of James, and his activities were more various. He began as an art critic and painter. He specialised in portraits, two of which—of his brother Richard and his friend Cardinal Wiseman—he bequeathed to the National Gallery of Ireland, where they hang beside John Doyle's portrait of Christopher Moore. He decorated the walls of the Roman Catholic Church at Lancaster with frescoes of the Last Judgement, and in 1862 Wiseman commissioned him to represent the Papal States for the International Exhibition.

When George Mulvaney died in 1869, Henry was appointed Director of the National Gallery of Ireland, and devoted himself entirely to this new occupation. In 1884, after twelve years hard work, he founded the National Historical and Portrait Gallery. Under his régime a great many Flemish and Dutch paintings were acquired,

notably Rembrandt's *Sleeping Shepherds*, for which he paid £514 in
1883. In 1886 he bought Fra Angelico's *Martyrdom of Saint Cosmo
and Saint Damien* for the modest sum of £73.

Neither James nor Henry seem to have had much imagination.
Richard and Charles on the other hand shared an aptitude for dream-
ing and communicating their dreams. But whereas Charles's fantasies
were melancholy, Richard's bubbled over with mischievous, almost
dionysiac high spirits. As precocious as Francis, he was only fifteen
when he published his first series of caricatures: *The Eglinton Tournament; or the Days of Chivalry Revived*. It attracted some notice, and
the Comte d'Orsay wrote to Henry Chorley that young Doyle seemed
to him 'a genius of the first order':

> My dear Chorley,
>   Will you thank for me Mr. Doyle for the extraordinary drawings he
> sent me. They are remarkably clever, and I venture to say that I would
> be embarrassed to find any old artist capable to enter into competition
> with this young one. He is undoubtedly a genius of the first order, and
> from this moment I will back him against any one. Give my best com-
> pliments to the father and believe me yours most faithfully,
>
> Cte d'Orsay[1]

But the most remarkable work of Richard's youth, *Dicky Doyle's
Journal*, was not published until 1885; the manuscript is in the British
Museum. The pen drawings show a bold and flexible talent full of
fresh inspiration, and foreshadow the style of the future chronicler of
Punch. Here we see Liszt playing the piano, but it is to the besotted
admiration of the audience that Richard mischievously draws our
attention. It is the same when he shows us a recital by Braham the
tenor (probably singing 'The Death of Nelson') or Eliasson the
violinist. A few pages further on we see Queen Victoria driving in her
carriage or visiting the National Gallery. These delicate drawings are
alive with a precocious, spontaneous mastery that arouses a sort of
fearful admiration. As well as worldly subjects such as these, Richard
presents us with a few scenes of family life, treated with the same
imperturbable humour as we see in his father's work. Sometimes he
includes himself in the picture and the drawings can be read conse-
cutively as a story. Here he is, determined to produce an important painting, unrolling before his brothers and sister a piece of
paper larger than himself but still virgin. Farther on we see the family

[1] Unpublished (C.D.B.A.).

having a private view; do they really like it or are they simply being indulgent? Richard knows exactly how to suggest this uncertainty. From his arm-chair, 'H.B.' is studying the picture with a non-committal expression. However Annette sits in the middle of the scene, with her elbows on the table and chin in her hands, apparently absorbed in quite unmixed admiration. Her brothers seem to be chiefly impressed by the contrast in size between the painting and the artist, whose slight body has been fitted out with an enormous head for the occasion. This *Journal* may be compared to Richard's illustrated letters to his father, only half a dozen pages of which have been published by Mr. Peter Quennell.[1]

These are less 'finished' but just as lively; the drawings overflow with youthful exuberance. Incongruous incidents of every description follow one another higgledy-piggledy: a review in Hyde Park, Richard's despair at having his pocket picked, walks with his brothers and Annette, exhibitions of painting. Judgements and reflections match the style of the drawings and the same mixture of seriousness and buffoonery emanates from them.

It is not without interest that stories and legends from French history had a particular charm for his imagination. This was an element of the Doyle tradition which we shall find later on in Sir Arthur.

'After all', writes Richard, 'fiction is nothing compared to reality. The Histories of England and France are full of the most romantic incidents, and the only doubt is as to which is the best. After due consideration and a patient investigation of both sides of the subject, I have come to the conclusion that the latter is the most fertile, not, of course, as to grand historical subjects, but in those interesting, picturesque and poetical passages, so delightful to meet, such as Joan of Arc . . .'[2]

John Doyle chose a French artist, Horace Vernet, as a model for his son to follow. It was said that Vernet had a gift of drawing from memory with extraordinary accuracy, and John Doyle had tried to imitate him with a certain amount of success. Richard does not seem to have succeeded so well in developing his visual memory, but his admiration for the French artist is more apparent in his letters than in his art. On 24 July 1842 he wrote to his father: '. . . I have just seen an engraving after Horace Vernet, illustrative of a ballad of Bürger,

---

[1] *The Cornhill Magazine*, Nos. 963 and 964, 1945.
[2] Letter to John Doyle, 12 November 1843, unpublished (C.D.B.A.).

the German poet, so striking in its design, so powerfully worked out and so original withal, that I am quite lost in admiration of the genius that conceived it.'

Towards the end of 1843, Mark Lemon, who was a friend of Michael Conan's, invited Richard Doyle to join the youthful staff of *Punch*. Richard's first drawing—signed 'Dick Kitcat'—appeared in the number for 16 March 1844. It represented Sir Robert Peel as Sisyphus pushing O'Connell in the shape of a rock, and watched by Furies one of whom is curiously like Lord John Russell. During the six years he worked on this famous paper, Richard Doyle imprinted it with his own special brand of quiet geniality, and a breath of fantasy began to blow through the pages of the magazine. In his hands Mr. Punch became a milder character in spite of his celebrated truncheon, and Richard was responsible for the long nose and upturned chin that regularly appeared on the cover of *Punch* after 1849, but had figured in the corners of Richard's letters to his father as early as 1843. For many years *Punch* was published with the cover designed by 'Dicky' Doyle.

De Quincey describes the pleasure he got from the young caricaturist's inventions, particularly from their mischievous, ingenuous and original freshness. Most of Richard Doyle's work was done between 1848 and 1855. In 1849 he collaborated with Percival Leigh in the remarkable series called *Pip's Diary: Ye Manners and Customs of Ye Englyshe*, in the same vein as Thackeray's *Snobs of England* published two years earlier by *Punch*, and just as successful. But while Thackeray generally wrote with identifiable models in mind, Leigh and Doyle gave their satire a more general though just as characteristic documentation. The style of the drawings suggests the artist's detachment, but also that he was less sceptical and more indulgent than Thackeray. Soon afterwards Richard and Thackeray were to collaborate outside the pages of *Punch*. For the time being they were occasional boon companions: '. . . I committed a terrible piece of dissipation on Saturday, after *Punch* dinner by going with Thackeray and Leech to the Cider Cellar to hear the famous song of "Jack Hall" and "damn his eyes" which is not edifying but wonderfully got up as a dramatic performance.'

Early in 1850 the Doyle brothers made the 'grand tour' together, taking a boat up the Rhine, and afterwards visiting Switzerland, Italy and Bohemia. Dickens wrote a letter of welcome to Dick when he returned with his luggage full of sketches for the unforgettable *Foreign Tour of Brown, Jones and Robinson:*

> Devonshire Terrace, 3rd April 1850.
>
> My Dear Doyle, Welcome to your native land! You will find us all a good deal changed since you went away on that long voyage. I am very rheumatic, and Leech (you recollect him?) uses a tin trumpet, but we are still good for a bowl of broth, or a social glass of punch.
>
> Several expeditions to the North Pole having taken place since you left us, they never found poor Franklin. You will be sorry to hear that Dr. Wiseman has been dead these many years. He made a decent end. Ever faithfully,
>
> Charles Dickens.[1]

Afterwards the artist renewed the collaboration with Thackeray that had begun with his illustrations for *Our Street*. This time it was *The Kickleburys on the Rhine*, followed by *Rebecca and Rowena* and finally *The Newcomes*. Here Doyle's talent in illustrating fiction is shown at its best; but his difficulty in adapting the drawings to the words, and the irritation he caused Thackeray by his delays in carrying them out (the two friends nearly quarrelled over Richard's slowness) throw an interesting light on Thackeray's methods as a writer: '. . . The first No. of *The Newcomes* is out,' Doyle wrote to his father in 1853. 'You must not judge of the next by it. It was done in great hurry. In fact Thackeray sent sketches for some of them which he had already done intending to illustrate it himself, and I adopted them considerably for safety not knowing anything about the characters or what he intended. In fact it is quite guess work now, for Thackeray scarcely ever describes a character as Dickens does, all at once—he leaves them to work themselves out by degrees, so that after reading the M.S. of a couple of numbers, one really knows scarcely anything about the story.'[2]

After this experimental period, Doyle became as we know the successful portraitist of such characters as Lady Kew, Honeyman and the Colonel. In an unpublished study of Richard Doyle, the critic whose identity was concealed under the pseudonym of Lewis Lusk suggests that Doyle may have been the original of J. J. Ridley in Thackeray's novel. It is more probable that this character is a cross between Richard Doyle and the painter David Roberts. J.J.'s humble origins, perseverance and financial caution suggest Roberts, but

[1] Unpublished (C.D.B.A.) [2] (C.D.B.A.).

Doyle was the original for his amiability, youthful charm and way of forgetting himself in his devotion to his art. Lewis Lusk consulted Lady Ritchie (Anne Thackeray), who remembered Richard Doyle very well but protested against Lusk's interpretation, saying it was contrary to her father's views of art.[1]

However, in spite of the apparent differences between J.J. and Richard Doyle, one cannot help detecting an underlying similarity between the character in Thackeray's novel and his friend. Doyle's modesty and quiet amiability were qualities Thackeray particularly appreciated, and he gave them to J.J. Moreover the phrases he uses about J.J.'s art and his descriptions of individual examples of it could all be applied to particular works by Doyle, such as *The Fairy Ring*, a copy of which Thackeray begged Doyle to lend him so that he could show it to his guests. This is how he describes J.J. in *The Newcomes:* '. . . Study was his chief amusement. Self-denial came easily to him. Pleasure or what is generally called so, had little charm for him. His ordinary companions were pure and sweet thoughts; his outdoor enjoyment the contemplation of natural beauty; for recreation the hundred pleasant dexterities and manipulations of his craft were ceaselessly interesting to him: he would draw every knot in an oak panel, or every leaf in an orange-tree, smiling and taking a gay delight over the simple feats of skill: whenever you found him he seemed watchful and serene, his modest virgin-lamp always lighted and trim. No gusts of passion extinguished it; no hopeless wandering in the darkness afterwards led him astray. Wayfarers through the world, we meet now and again with such purity; and salute it, and hush whilst it passes on.'

[1] Lewis Lusk (unpublished MS., C.D.B.A.) quotes the following letter from Mrs. Ritchie. He gives no date, but from the context we can place it in 1897 or 1898, when Anne Thackeray Ritchie was working on the biographical edition of her father's works: 'Dear Sir, Your note has just reached me . . . I am finishing *The Newcomes* and have been once more admiring Mr. Doyle's drawings. I never thought of it before:—his beautiful fanciful art was certainly akin to J.J.'s, but his personality was so homogeneous, his gentle confidence was so sympathetic, that it never occurred to me to think of him as anybody but himself,—charming, exceptional, dignified and gentle. Indeed, my Father always said that to imitate people and write them down was bad art. Mr. Roberts had absolutely nothing of J.J. He was more like James Binnie—hospitable, a man of the world, and a club-goer. His drawing was perfectly lovely and like a flash of lightning; and he was very kind to us as girls. I don't think Mr. Doyle's work is appreciated seriously enough, and I am always glad to hear him praised. How people admire Fra Angelico! But Dicky Doyle's fancy and beauty are as great, and his fun is perfectly irresistible. I was laughing again only yesterday over the Brighton scenes in *The Newcomes*.'

It is impossible for anyone who has examined Richard Doyle's work or got the flavour of his simple, sensitive personality from his letters, not to find it conjured up in this passage. One may also suppose that Thackeray knew of Richard's lifelong secret passion, platonic but faithful, for one of the daughters of the famous Lady Henrietta Stanley. This sheds a new light on the enigmatic words with which he takes farewell of J.J. in the last chapter of *The Newcomes:* 'J.J.'s history, let me confidentially state, has been revealed to me too, and may be told some of these fine summer months, or Christmas evenings, when the kind reader has leisure to hear.'

In 1850 Richard was given the chance to show a seldom seen but important side of his character by an event in home politics. This was what was known at the time as the 'papal aggression'. Pius IX's decision to create an archbishopric and twelve bishoprics in England was treated as a provocative act by a section of the newspapers and public. Some of the reactions to it took a violent form—processions, broken windows, looting of Catholic churches—and *Punch* stood in the front rank of the opposition as champion of the Protestant cause. Richard had not hitherto made any show of his religious beliefs and practices, but he now took a very simple decision: on 27 November he wrote Mark Lemon a letter resigning from the paper. Lemon realised too late that a valued contributor and friend had been badly treated. Jerrold, who had reason to regret his own violent words, and also Thackeray tried in vain to get Doyle to reverse his decision. They drew his attention to the fact that although *The Times* had also published a violent criticism of the Pope's decision, no Catholic journalist had found it necessary to resign. 'That is all very well in *The Times*,' said Richard Doyle, 'but not in *Punch*. For *The Times* is a monarchy whereas *Punch* is a republic.'[1] Doyle was alluding to the egalitarian methods adopted by his colleagues ever since the paper's foundation, and also to the spirit of free speech prevailing at *Punch* dinners. There was another reason for Richard's intransigence. The man Pius IX had chosen as head of the Catholic Church in England was John Doyle's friend and fellow-Irishman, Nicholas Wiseman, future cardinal and patron of Henry Doyle. The controversy aroused by the papal aggression was therefore of special interest to the Doyle family. However, by taking the decision to leave *Punch* against the advice of his friends, Richard sacrificed at a moment's notice the very

---

[1] Cf. Spielmann. *The History of Punch*, p. 456.

real material advantages and prospects he had earned by his great talent and long years of work. *Punch* had given him a safe income of £800 a year, representing £4,000 today. In 1852 Mark Lemon invited Doyle to rejoin the staff of *Punch*, but without success.

Which of those involved had most reason to deplore the breach? It is difficult to say. Of course *Punch* had lost an important contributor. But on the other hand Richard was now excluded from the brilliant group which met every week at the *Punch* dinners, as well as from the stimulating company of other artists. In *The Quarterly Review* for December 1854, Thackeray publicly regretted his friend's decision, while at the same time saluting the moral standards which had made it irrevocable. However Richard did not cut himself off completely from the literary and artistic world and still frequented circles where he met some of his friends from *Punch*. Matthew Higgins's house was a case in point. Better known under the pseudonym 'Jacob Omnium', he was a contributor to *The Times* and *Punch*, and later joined *The Cornhill Magazine* at Thackeray's invitation. And in April 1856 he invited Richard Doyle to dinner. It was Lent, and we can see what a reputation as a touchy Catholic the *Punch* affair had given Doyle from the fact that, in honour of his visitor, Higgins forced all his other guests to abstain from meat!

In his father's house at Cambridge Terrace, Richard had the opportunity of meeting Landseer, Millais, Holman Hunt, Rossetti and Ruskin, whose *The King of the Golden River* he illustrated in 1851. And he was often a guest of Lord Ashburton (William Baring), the scientist and politician. It was at his house that he met Thiers and heard him heap abuse on Napoleon III.

Towards the end of 1851, Thackeray gave a series of lectures on eighteenth-century humorists in Edinburgh. There he met Richard's younger brother Charles, the Benjamin of the Doyle family, who had left home two years before to take up a good administrative job in the Scottish capital. He was assistant to Robert Mathieson in the Office of Works—a very responsible post for a young architect. Those who had suggested to John Doyle that his son should apply for it implied that he would be on trial. Charles was not best pleased at the idea of leaving London, but he was told it might lead to something nearer home later on, with the Commissioners of Woods and Forests. However, six months after his arrival in Edinburgh something happened which altered his plans. While looking for new lodgings, Charles was welcomed by an Irish family living in Scotland, the Foleys. There was one daughter, Mary, and five years later she became Mrs. Charles Doyle. Under the circumstances, Charles decided to settle in Edinburgh. He was probably one of those who easily come to terms with life, either through a naturally philosophic outlook or mere indifference. We get this impression from the few lines devoted to him in his eldest son's autobiography: 'His thoughts were always in the clouds, and he had no appreciation of the realities of life'. The other side of this contemplative, apathetic nature was to be seen in an imagination expressed less perhaps in the architectural works he left behind (such as the fountain at Holyrood and the great window of Glasgow cathedral) than in a series of extremely original paintings. Their capricious spontaneity and often childish subjects remind one of Richard's work. But they often evoke the supernatural or fantastic in a way that is all his own. Compositions with such significant titles as 'Revels in the Sea', 'The Drowning Seaman', 'An Oriental Dream' and 'The Death Coach' secrete an atmosphere of subtle hallucination linking them with the work of Blake and the Pre-Raphaelites. In 1924 Sir Arthur organised an exhibition of his father's paintings, and Bernard Shaw told him that if he had his way they should be hung in a special room in one of the national museums.

Charles Doyle's young wife—she was only just seventeen—had received an Anglo-French education, and perhaps more French than English, since she spent five years in France and went to school there. She always thought of France as her second home and had no difficulty later on in cultivating in her children francophile interests, which were already traditional in the Doyle family. Mary Doyle was an ideal mother for a literary man. Cultivated and sensitive, she developed her eldest son's taste for reading and the art of self-expression while he was still very young. Her great passion was for legends and history, and her pride of race and lineage had much less to do with vanity than with romantic nostalgia for the past. She was delighted to recall that through her cousins the Scotts of Nurley she was a distant relative of Sir Walter Scott, and that as a member of a younger branch of the noble family of Percy through her great-grandmother Mary Percy of Ballintemple, she was descended from the Plantagenet kings. Later on she encouraged a taste for genealogical research in Arthur.[1]

[1] As is shown by the following MS. note: 'The Percies of our family have been traced

The Pack family tree, as well as the Percy's had plenty in it to stimulate the imagination of the young Conan Doyles, and perhaps explains why many of them and their descendants went into the army. Their great-great-grandmother, Mary Percy, had married Richard Pack of Kilkenny. We are concerned here with two of their sons: William, Sir Arthur's great-grandfather, and Sir Denis, who was general in command of the Scottish brigade at Waterloo. Three other Packs fought on this same battlefield; one had part of his skull shot away. The family historian, Pack Beresford, states that the military tradition can be traced back to Major Pack, an officer in Cromwell's army who settled in Ireland, and writes thus of the battle of Quatre Bras:

> The gallant, the brilliant, the heroic manner in which the remnants of Kempt's and Pack's brigades held their ground, of which they surrendered not a single inch throughout the terrible struggle of that day, must ever stand preeminent in the records of the triumphs and prowess of British infantry.[1]

If there were fewer military traditions on the Foley side, we find some very picturesque figures among them. The family had been living at Lismore in County Waterford ever since the reign of Queen Elizabeth, when they accompanied the Earl of Devonshire to Ireland, and had acquired a reputation for a rugged feudalism. In the eighteenth century a certain Thomas Foley, known as 'Black Tom' ruled over his domain of Bally Inn like an absolute monarch, and was specially remembered for his 'three hundred gallon pot', an immense cauldron always kept in the kitchen of the Manor full of some sort of soup for the benefit of the poor or any passing travellers. In 1761, Tom's son Patrick led a party against the 'Whiteboys' and killed one of them in single combat.

What is to be gleaned from this brief excursion into genealogy?

---

back through the Cork Municipal Records. The original Percy in Ireland was Carew's Lieutenant in Munster and Governor of Kinsale for Queen Elizabeth (see the Pacification of Ireland and Cork records). Richard Percy of Ballin Temple in King's County came to Ireland as a Colonel in the army. My mother heard Dame Eliza Pack say to her mother: "We trace back to Plantagenet blood through the Louvain Percies. My sister, Mrs. Oldham has the Percy tree made out." My mother adds: "We are descended from these old Packs, Percies, Parsons, Kinsleys by her mother Catherine Pack. They are the best Norman blood in Ireland." Documentary evidence is scarce owing to the great misfortunes of owners of great names and the countless laying waste and burning of old homes.' (C.D.B.A.)

[1] R. Pack Beresford, *A Memoir of Major General Sir Denis Pack*, 1908, p. 82.

Firstly the existence of a great many ancient, varied and potently attractive family traditions: these are the key to Conan Doyle's complex character. An Irish, Catholic tradition, associated with the arts for two generations came from the Doyles. An Irish, military and nationalist tradition, associated with legends and a passionate interest in history, came from the Packs and the Foleys. Conan Doyle could neither relegate these traditions completely to the past, nor integrate them wholly in the present; but we cannot understand him if we ignore them. They explain his vocation as an artist and the impulse that urged him to other activities beyond literature. They explain the shadows surrounding his work—about whose modernity there is much to be said—and his reputation. It remains to be seen how much the latter rests on the books themselves and how much on his moral authority.

Chapter 2

THE FIRST FORTY YEARS

A plate on the walls of No. 11 Picardy Place, Edinburgh, reminds us that this was Conan Doyle's birthplace, and that he was the creator of Sherlock Holmes.[1] 'I was born on May 22, 1859, at Picardy Place, Edinburgh,' he tells us in his autobiography, 'so named because in old days a colony of French Huguenots had settled there. At the time of their coming it was a village outside the City walls, but now it is at the end of Queen Street, abutting upon Leith Walk. When last I visited it, it seemed to have degenerated, but at that time the flats were of good repute.' He was the second child of Charles and Mary Doyle; like his elder sister Annette he had his father's uncle, Michael Conan, for godfather, and both children took the name of Conan Doyle. Michael Conan had no heir, and his name was thus carried on by his nephew and niece. Though he had no children, Michael Conan had very fixed ideas about bringing them up; he took his responsibilities very seriously and tried to influence his godson's education from Paris, where he lived. Charles's interest in such problems was relatively slight, it must be admitted, and he was glad to leave his wife to deal with Michael Conan's letters. So that at first the little boy's godfather had some influence over the direction of his mind. He even chose his first name, Arthur, from a definitely prophetic motive: he wanted to combine a reference to the child's Breton ancestry, already suggested by the surname, with those associations with chivalry which excited his imagination. A whole programme was contained in the significant christening-present he gave the baby—a book called *Arthur de Bretagne*, by C. Fallet. In his letters to Mary Doyle, Michael Conan often described the sort of influence he wanted her to have on her child. Mary was Arthur's first teacher and soon succeeded in implanting in him various characteristics based on knightly values: moral initiative, desire to do good, romantic worship of the Middle Ages, of his ancestors and France, and above all repudiation

---

[1] 'Creator of Sherlock Holmes, Arthur Conan Doyle was born here, 22nd May, 1859.' This plaque was put up on 22 April 1949 by the *Edinburgh Evening News*.

of all that was materialistic, utilitarian and cynical in the present age. Conan Doyle said later that he owed to his mother all those qualities on which his literary career was founded. In 1907, he told a representative of *The New York World*: '. . . My real love for letters, my instinct for story-telling, springs, I believe, from my mother, who is of Anglo-Celtic stock, with the glamour and romance of the Celt very strongly marked . . . In my early childhood, as far back as I can remember anything at all, the vivid stories which she would tell me stand out so clearly that they obscure the real facts of my life. It is not only that she was—is still—a wonderful story-teller, but she had, I remember, an art of sinking her voice to a horror-stricken whisper when she came to a crisis in her narrative, which makes me goose-fleshy now when I think of it. I am sure, looking back, that it was in attempting to emulate these stories of my childhood that I first began weaving dreams myself.'

When he was about six or eight years old, the little boy wrote and illustrated a story about a Bengal tiger. He was going at the time to a day school in Edinburgh, of which he retained only unpleasant memories, but the time was coming to decide where his serious education should take place. It was not a simple question. Nothing but the best was good enough for Arthur, yet Charles's small income would barely pay for him to go to a public school. There was no question of breaking with the Catholic influences traditional in the Doyle family, and there were only two large Catholic public schools: Downside and Stonyhurst, the former kept by Benedictines, the latter by Jesuits. Michael Conan recommended the Jesuits, but not unreservedly. Of course their standard of teaching could not be beaten, but might they perhaps one day entice the boy away towards a too specialised career? Meanwhile the idea of sending their son to Stonyhurst was gradually gaining ground in his parents' minds, in spite of Michael Conan's repeated warnings, which were not however without effect.

The principals of Stonyhurst showed their grasp of the situation by offering the parents a completely free education for their son if they would agree—and it amounted to a contract—to dedicate him to a career in the church. This proposal clarified the situation, and it must be admitted that after Mary Doyle had definitely rejected it the Fathers never once tried to bring pressure to bear on Arthur Conan Doyle during the seven years he spent as their pupil.

Founded in 1794, Stonyhurst had by now about two hundred and fifty boys in two houses; they spent two years at the preparatory school of Hodder, which Arthur entered early in 1868, and five more in the 'big school'.

The school provided a scholastically dogmatic education and severe discipline. Classes were divided up in a very archaic manner into 'elements', 'figures', 'rudiments', 'grammar', 'syntax', 'poetry' and 'rhetoric'. Perhaps these antiquated concepts and methods laid the foundation for Conan Doyle's subsequent reaction towards scepticism, and his abandonment of Catholicism when he had finished his medical studies. Day and night, the boys were subjected to vigilant, jealous supervision. Arthur endured this severity and the fear of corporal punishment—especially beating on the hands—with a calm stoicism which however never turned into tolerant acceptance, as sometimes happens. '. . . I am bound to say,' he wrote to his friends the Ryans, 'that I don't, looking back, consider the Stonyhurst system a good one, nor would I send a son there if I had one. They try to rule too much by fear—too little by love or reason. However, perhaps it is only because I was such an obstinate little mule that the place has not left a pleasant impression on my mind . . .'[1]

While he was at Stonyhurst Conan Doyle began corresponding regularly with his mother, and perhaps this was one of the most important consequences of his stay there. He went on writing long after his schooldays were over, so that the letters cover more than half a century. They help to fill in many important details of his life and also to give us a picture of him that is perhaps even more revealing than a diary. And they prove what a major part was played in his life by the loving concern of this formidably moral woman—'The Ma'am' as her children always called her.

At Hodder the boy's character began to unfold and take shape: physically at first, for games and sport obviously interested him more than lessons. Perhaps this helped him come safe and sound through a violent epidemic of diphtheria, which carried off several of his fellow-pupils during the winter of 1869. It may have been because of his sense of escape from danger, or because of this premature experience of death in a particularly painful and horrifying form, that he took his first communion the following spring in a state of inexpressible exaltation: '. . . My dear Mamma, I hope you are quite

---

[1] Unpublished, April 1889 (C.D.B.A.).

well. I am glad to say that I have made my first communion. Oh mama, I cannot express the joy that I felt on the happy day to receive my creator into my breast. I shall never though I live a hundred years, I shall never forget that day.'[1]

Up till now the boy had grown up in an exclusively feminine atmosphere, among his sisters and under the jealous supervision of his mother. Charles was a rather remote father, and his only brother Innes was not born until 1873. Arthur's sudden transplantation to Stonyhurst had the effect of stimulating his emotional development, instead of cramping it, as might have happened to someone less robust.

He plunged into work with characteristic enthusiasm, and a sort of intoxication in which the satisfaction of doing better than other boys played little part. Soon his letters began giving regular reports on his studies, and notes for essays. He admitted that he was doing better than he had expected or hoped: it was a sign of his natural modesty. Better still he never mentioned the names of his rivals and seemed to attach very little importance to his place in class. It was as if he had too much confidence in his own powers to need to assert himself at the expense of his fellows, and this was probably the secret of his popularity. He divided his time equally between the cricket-field and the library. What did he read? The adventures of Arthur and Lancelot, already told him by Mary Doyle; *The Cloister and the Hearth*, which he always rated among the best historical novels. He was delighted when new books were bought for the library and haunted it assiduously.

In 1870 Conan Doyle entered the upper school, where for five years he was to receive a solid education based on the classics. Science was a poor relation; Latin and German took the lion's share. The future writer made a respectable showing, but his greatest efforts were reserved for the playing-fields.

The classical writers figuring in the syllabus for the upper forms were either historians or rhetoricians: Sallust, Cicero, Caesar and Xenophon, but no poets or dramatists. The French syllabus for the last year included Fénelon's *Télémaque*, perhaps a surprising choice for Jesuit Fathers. In the last year less time was given to German, which was taught according to the direct method as it has since been called. It was an education based partly on strict discipline—as we have already seen—partly on a régime and time-table that was truly

---

[1] Letter to Mary Doyle, 30 May 1869 (C.D.B.A.).

spartan. The boys had too little to eat, got up at five o'clock in the morning winter and summer, and washed in icy water. A little poem written by Conan Doyle at the time he left Hodder and went to Stonyhurst speaks volumes about the difficulties of getting used to his new surroundings in the first months:

THE STUDENT'S DREAM

The Student he lay on his narrow bed
He dreamt not of the morrow
Confused thoughts they filled his head
And he dreamt of his home with sorrow . . .

He thought of the birches stinging stroke
And he thought with fear of the morrow
He wriggled and tumbled and nearly awoke
And again he sighed with sorrow.

Apart from the summer holidays, the school year was dominated by two happy events: Christmas and the opening of the cricket season. The boys usually stayed at Stonyhurst over Christmas, as travel was often difficult at that time of year, and there were only twelve days' holiday. These were given over to plays acted and produced by the boys, usually several in each season. Conan Doyle mentions *Macbeth*, *Rob Roy* and *Le Courrier de Lyon*, all in a single winter. Then, if there was a spell of cold, dry sunny weather, there would be skating on the school pond, and the boys stayed awake at nights amusing themselves by telling stories, often ghost stories. Mid-Lent was celebrated with another performance, and each of the amateur actors had to sing a comic song at the excellent supper which followed. Then came summer. At Corpus Christi they set up triumphal arches, and the boys marched through them with a band at their head and the bells pealing their loudest. But the best thing about this day was that it marked the beginning of the cricket season. Now Conan Doyle became the uncontested leader and hero of Stonyhurst; as captain of one or other of the two elevens he spent most of the Whitsun holidays on the cricket-field. But his studies were not neglected. For instance, in the summer of 1873, we see him possessed of a sudden passion for the French language, which he studied by reading Jules Verne. He soon began to find it easy to slip from one language into the other. He read *Vingt Mille Lieues sous les Mers*, *Cinq Semaines en Ballon*, *De la Terre à la Lune* and *Aventures de Trois Russes et de Trois Anglais*. 'I am getting to relish them quite as well as English books,' he wrote to Mary Doyle in June 1873. It was in fact at about this time that he began to be aware that he had certain literary gifts. Gifts of oratory—the Fathers usually chose him to read aloud in the refectory, because of his good elocution and strong dramatic sense; gifts of imagination and composition, as several poems written in different moods bear witness. The most convincing of these early efforts is *The Passage of the Red Sea*, a poem of fifty lines in rhymed pentameters, written in a conventional but strict and scholarly epic style which suggests that the young author practised this form of exercise for his own pleasure. It shows an influence very different from Jules Verne's: Michael Conan had just sent his godson a copy of *The Lays of Ancient Rome*. Later on Conan Doyle took Macaulay's prose as his model, but he first became acquainted with him as a poet, and we see this influence in *The Passage of the Red Sea*.

In the summer of 1875 Conan Doyle took his Matriculation, and did very well. He passed with honours with 70%—as embarrassing a success in its way as that of the Sherlock Holmes stories later on! Far from confident of the results, the boy had hardly given a thought to his future career, but had been too much involved in the whirl of school life, essay-writing, sports and games at Stonyhurst to realise that it must come to an end. The Jesuits quite understood this, and found a tactful means of helping him put off his decision for a year more. They suggested to Charles and Mary Doyle that their son would benefit from spending some time in Austria at the Jesuit school of Feldkirch in the Tyrol. It was intended as a favour but it meant some sacrifice for Mary Doyle. This extra year of schooling deferred the moment when her eldest son could start his chosen career, just at a time when Charles Doyle's health was beginning to cause anxiety. She never regretted the sacrifice, because Arthur's year at Feldkirch was a happy one, active and profitable. He divided his time between learning German, walking—and music. For he learned to play the bombardon or bass tuba. This huge instrument suited the size of his thorax, if not his feeling for music. He wrote a poem about it which reflects the comic side of his musical activities:

> There is an instrument whose power
> Does all the others far surpass.
> Far o'er the rest one sees him tower,
> A mighty instrument of brass.

The soundest sleeper, far or near,
I think would scarcely slumber on,
If close to his unconscious ear
You played upon the Bombardon.

He sent a whole series of poems in the same humorous vein to his uncle Michael, who wrote to Mary Doyle that he had received a regular volume of poetry, and also a prose journal which seemed to him very promising.

Does this mean that Michael Conan already envisaged a literary career for his nephew, perhaps beginning with journalism?

It seems likely. He was never much in favour of his godson's studying medicine. This was the question that came up in discussion between the two at the end of June 1876, when Arthur spent a few days in Paris on his way back to Edinburgh. Michael Conan's impartial views were counteracted by those of Dr. Waller, a friend of the Doyle family. And whereas a medical career was not in the family tradition, and he appeared to have no very definite vocation for it, there were none the less practical reasons which made it necessary for him to come to some decision quickly.

At the time, a medical career perhaps offered more attractive prospects than it does today, and Conan Doyle seems from every point of view to have been destined to succeed in it. He was patient, observant, and above all full of humanity, and therefore naturally inclined to serve other people. Finally, the Faculty of Medicine at Edinburgh was said to be one of the best in the world. Arthur could save money by living at home, and at the same time keep an eye on his brother's education. As soon as he got back from Feldkirch he began to study for the bursary examination. Dr. Waller coached him efficiently and he was successful; but disappointment and injustice followed, for owing to a clerical error the prize-winner was completely overlooked, the bursary given to another candidate and the victim unable to get any practical redress. This was a very depressing beginning. The next five years, normally ending with the title of M.B., were remembered by Conan Doyle chiefly for their tedium. He was not good at adapting himself to what seemed to him the too theoretical teaching he received.

It was 'one long weary grind at botany, chemistry, anatomy, physiology and a whole list of compulsory subjects, many of which have a very indirect bearing upon the art of curing. The whole system of teaching, as I look back upon it, seems far too oblique and not nearly practical enough for the purpose in view.'[1]

There was another contrast between university and school which Conan Doyle found hard to accept. There was no community life at Edinburgh whatever. The very free régime was more like that of a French than an English university, and left a student entirely responsible for arranging how he spent his time. The drawback of this was that he had few human contacts with other members of the University. Other students were strangers or very nearly so, and there was often an unbridgeable gulf between students and their teachers. However there were two who left permanent impressions on Conan Doyle's mind. The first was Rutherford, the anatomist, whose impressive figure, bushy beard, thunderous voice and eccentric manner were revived thirty-five years later in the character of Professor Challenger. Less remote, less imposing, but just as disconcerting, Joseph Bell the surgeon exercised a proverbial fascination on all who attended his lectures in the hospital wards. R. L. Stevenson was not a medical student, but he knew Bell by reputation, as did all the undergraduates at Edinburgh, and the connection between Sherlock Holmes and 'Joe' Bell did not escape him. On 5 April 1893, he wrote to Conan Doyle: 'Only the one thing troubles me: can this be my old friend Joe Bell?'[2] There is no doubt that Bell's almost clairvoyant powers of diagnosis, and his skill in making the most of them, played a part in the creation of the character of Sherlock Holmes. Like so many others, Conan Doyle was fascinated by Dr. Bell's personality, but there was still at the moment no question of turning it to literary account. Too many worries darkened the horizon, most of them family ones. His eldest sister Annette had gone to Portugal, but the education of his four other sisters and his younger brother had still to be thought of. Meanwhile in 1879 Charles Doyle had been obliged to retire into a nursing-home, and so become a burden to his family. Obviously therefore his undergraduate son would have to pay his own expenses if he wanted to finish his education. At the end of his second year he began looking for a job as assistant to a doctor. His first venture that summer was with a Dr. Richardson at Sheffield, and a few months later he was taken on by Dr. Elliot at Ruyton in Shropshire. Difficulties and obstacles of every description were a stimulus to this obstinate Celt. He now felt sure of his medical vocation and

[1] AUT., p. 30.   [2] Correspondence, edited Colvin, Vol. II, p. 287.

while with Dr. Elliot he took part in a medico-literary competition
for the best essay on the evil effects of alcohol and drugs in general.
Dr. Elliot glanced through his assistant's effort and seemed doubtful
of his success: 'I told Elliot I wouldn't sell my chance for £5', Conan
Doyle wrote to his mother. 'He said I had the bump of self-esteem
largely developed but that he didn't like men who hadn't.'[1]

As he approached his twentieth birthday he began to believe that
fortune would favour him if only he took a chance:

> ... I am beginning to see that I have certain advantages which, if
> properly directed and given a fair chance might lead to great success,
> but which it would be a thousand pities to nullify aboard ship or in
> a country practice. Let me once get my footing in a good hospital and
> my game is clear. Observe cases minutely, improve in my profession,
> write to the *Lancet*, supplement my income by literature, make friends
> and conciliate everyone I meet, wait ten years if need be, and then when
> my chance comes be prompt and decisive in stepping into an honorary
> surgeonship. I see there is a vacancy at the Queen's which I am going
> up to Gainger to consult about today. We'll aim high, old lady, and
> consider the success of a lifetime, rather than the difference of a fifty
> pound note in an annual screw ...[2]

Already he seems to have decided which were the essentials to be
aimed at: literature was to be a leisure activity, or at least a secondary
one, a hobby to fill out his small income. In his spare time—though
one may well wonder how he found any—Conan Doyle amused himself by writing three or four short stories. He sent them to various
magazines and had very little difficulty in placing them. *Chambers'
Journal* published *The Mystery of Sasassa Valley* in October 1879,
and *London Society* accepted *The American's Tale*. These successes
gave the undergraduate author some satisfaction, but the stories were
published anonymously and did not advance him on the course he
had chosen. At the beginning of 1880 he was offered a marvellous
opportunity to travel at small expense, perhaps even to earn a little
money. There was a vacancy for a doctor on a whaler sailing from
Peterhead to the Arctic. Another of the medical students had been
given the post, and finding himself unable to go at the last moment
asked his friend Conan Doyle to take his place. Eight days later he
was on board the *Hope* and the next seven months were spent as a
member of her crew of about fifty. Conan Doyle was soon at his ease

[1] Letter to Mary Doyle, 23 August 1878 (C.D.B.A.).
[2] Letter to Mary Doyle, n.d., (1879) (C.D.B.A.).

with them all, sharing their work and simple amusements. It was a tremendous change, and there is no doubt it transformed and matured his character considerably. The memory of marvellous things seen, the exhilaration of the essentially physical pleasures of a life lived to the full on board ship, all combined to give colour to the adventure stories he was to write later on. As he says in his autobiography: 'The perpetual light, the glare of the white ice, the deep blue of the water, these are the things which one remembers most clearly, and the dry crisp exhilarating air, which makes mere life the keenest of pleasures.'[1]

He was intoxicated by his own energy, by the joys of the chase and of finding himself in a real but primitive world even more beautiful than that described in the books he had read. The harpoon fishing itself made an indelible impression on him, and he wrote of it in his autobiography: 'Who would swap that moment for any other triumph that sport can give?'[2] The violent change from the lecture-room to the open sea, from the world of study to the world of action (conjured up later in *The White Company*), the revelation of the un-suspected beauty of nature when unspoiled by human intrusion, all this precipitated a spiritual revolution which had probably been secretly working in him since his school days and now emerged in the light of day as rejection of his Catholic faith. So that as well as speed-ing up his intellectual development his voyage provided him with an almost mystical experience; both were necessary, just as a long period of reflection had to be confirmed by an incommunicable experience before his subsequent conversion to spiritualism could take place. His change of heart did not exactly declare itself as agnostic doubt; on the contrary it could be better described as a form of romantic deism, transcending the narrow bounds of the traditional belief he had hitherto passively accepted. 'Nature is the true revelation of the Deity to man,' he was to write soon afterwards.[3]

His return to Edinburgh plunged him again among academic realities: the final examinations were approaching. During his last term, a Birmingham friend, Dr. Hoare, took him on as his assistant. However neither his patients nor the imminence of the exams pre-vented him from writing three adventure stories at this time: *The Gully of Bluemansdyke, Bones* and *Our Derby Sweepstakes*. The two first were published in *London Society*; it was by his own wish, so he

[1] AUT., p. 54.   [2] AUT., p. 53.   [3] *The Stark Munro Letters*, 1895, p. 46.

said afterwards, that the third never appeared in print. Hogg, the editor of the magazine, seriously advised him to give up medicine and take to literature.

'I called on Hogg in London, he was very polite and flattering, said that he and many of his friends looked upon me as one of the coming men in literature.'[1]

But greater satisfactions were in store for him. First, he heard that he had passed his finals. Here he was, not yet twenty-three, Bachelor of Medicine and Master of Surgery. And another chapter seemed to be beginning for him when, during his vacations at Lismore, he fell in love with a Miss Welden. It was a short but violent passion, not really important and with no future. He was still, and remained for a long time afterwards, too much of a bachelor by inclination for any woman to play a significant part in his life. A few weeks after this idyll—it was not finally broken off until the beginning of 1882 and then apparently by common consent—he was again tempted by a berth as ship's doctor. It was not in the Arctic regions this time, quite the contrary: he shipped on a cargo-boat bound for West Africa.

It seemed to Conan Doyle that a certain number of voyages of this sort, with salaries that could be counted on in advance and all expenses paid while on board, might enable him to save enough in a year or two to set up in practice on his own account. For after several fruitless attempts during the summer, he had had to give up his first idea of getting a hospital appointment. Alas, his second voyage brought him nothing but misfortune. The *Mayumba* was uncomfortable in every way, rather like one of the old hulks a young man called Joseph Conrad had shipped aboard as mate at about the same time. Conan Doyle took his revenge on the *Mayumba* and her owners afterwards in a somewhat neglected adventure story called *The Firm of Girdlestone*. The African climate disagreed with him and he fell seriously ill at Lagos. The voyage itself was almost as bad: it began with a violent storm and ended with a fire on board, which was luckily got under control when they were in sight of the English coast.

Back in Edinburgh, Conan Doyle found himself in an extremely precarious position. He had given up the idea of going to sea again and his efforts to get a hospital job had come to nothing, yet as he was obliged to support his family he must at all cost solve the problem of his career without delay. 'Could there be anything more dreadful in

[1] Letter to Mary Doyle, n.d. (C.D.B.A.).

life than to have those whom you love looking to you for help and to be unable to give it?'[1]

His Doyle uncles and his aunt Annette were probably responsible for the situation in which he found himself. A sort of family council met at 17 Cambridge Terrace to consider what could be done for the heir of the Doyles—for these four unmarried relatives thought of Arthur practically as their son. They had not seen him often in the last few years, nor indeed since he was a child, when they used to take him to Madame Tussaud's or the museum of armour in the Tower in the holidays.

Perhaps they were sorry that he had not followed their own example and their father's by choosing to be an artist; but of course everything that advice, knowledge and connections could do for him should be done. He wanted to be a doctor, he was already a doctor— that was a come-down in their view; no matter, they might still be able to help give him a start. They invited him to London to discuss ways and means, and Conan Doyle accepted, probably feeling very nervous. After the first friendly exchanges they got down to business. What were his plans? As we know they were all too vague. Uncle Richard and Uncle James then put forward a plan that was both concrete and acceptable. It was unfortunately impossible for them to assist him financially, but perhaps something better could be done: almost all the Catholic families they knew would feel it a pleasure, if not a duty, to help Arthur start a practice, if he would merely say what district or town he preferred. A recommendation from them or any of their influential friends was all that was needed. Exactly in what term the suggestion was made we do not know, but at the mere mention of the word 'Catholic' Arthur reacted vigorously, and, perhaps even before hearing his uncle out, his mind was made up.

He told them that he had lost his faith, or at least that 'Catholicism' was now a word without religious meaning for him, which came to the same thing. Of course this had no effect on his respect for his family and his pride in his Doyle ancestry. It was in fact these very feelings which obliged him to speak out now. To accept his uncles' proposal would be nothing but a moral fraud. He probably spoke arrogantly and a little tactlessly: the effect was dramatic. They listened uncomprehendingly—it was a tragic, almost Shakespearian misunderstanding. Arthur's uncles were wounded to the quick, not

[1] *The Stark Munro Letters*, p. 89.

only in their affection for him, but even more in their sense of honour and their Catholic faith. Their nephew's career was indeed a problem! What he had just said amounted to sacrilege. There was a long silence. The breach was to be final. Only Richard, who was always a remarkably gentle character, intervened on behalf of his nephew a few months before his death, and sent him recommendations to the Catholic bishop of Portsmouth and the Duke of Norfolk. The young doctor destroyed his letters of introduction. His other two uncles lived until 1892 and therefore witnessed their nephew's literary success. But they made no sign: he had become a stranger to them. Conan Doyle was the chief sufferer from this crisis, but he had brought it on his own head. It undoubtedly originated in spiritual developments of which more remains to be said. All the same, the violence and passion of his outburst is surprising, and makes one wonder whether it was not some latent hostility to Charles Doyle that exploded on the heads of his paternal uncles. Such psychoanalytic hypotheses are always fragile, but it is at least clear that far the strongest bonds in Arthur's emotional relationship with his parents were those between mother and son. Also that his father's lack of warmth and strength of character accelerated the son's maturity.

Having burned his boats, Conan Doyle had to rely on providence or his own efforts to get him out of his difficulties. Did providence appear in the form of young Dr. Budd, who had qualified a little earlier and set up in Plymouth? Conan Doyle had known him slightly at Edinburgh, but mainly by hearsay. Budd had acquired a reputation for brilliance and eccentricity, and as a man who could be arrogant and vindictive on occasion. His career had begun eventfully, but at the moment he appeared to be well-established. How he heard of Conan Doyle's difficulties is not known, but one morning he sent him a long telegram inviting him to come and help him at Plymouth. Later on, in *The Stark Munro Letters*, Conan Doyle told the story of this strange collaboration. Budd, who figures as Cullingworth in the book, was an ingenious and inspired impostor, a sort of precursor of Dr. Knock who, by unscrupulously disregarding professional etiquette at the expense of his patients, quickly made an immense reputation. Several waiting-rooms were not enough to contain the crowds who came to consult him, and he thought that his old fellow-student Conan Doyle might help him deal with his ever-increasing clientele.

For the first few weeks Conan Doyle was hoodwinked, but then he began to be more and more disturbed by Budd's curious methods, however financially profitable they might be. He confided in Mary Doyle. His mother had avoided taking any part in the differences between her son and her husband's family, but this time she spoke her mind freely. In her view Budd was simply a shady adventurer, his friendship could only be compromising and his influence harmful; it was vital for Arthur to stop being involved in this man's dishonourable activities. For some weeks Conan Doyle hesitated, but events moved swiftly to get him out of his predicament. Whether by carelessness on his part or indiscretion on Budd's, a letter from Mary Doyle full of her usual admonitions was read by Budd. Furiously angry at her criticisms of himself, he secretly resolved to be revenged. He said nothing about his discovery and waited several days until he found a pretext to part with Conan Doyle. Their collaboration had not been as much of a success as he had hoped; and he even suggested that his new partner had lost him some patients.

' "Well," said I, "that's easily set right." I marched out of the room and downstairs, with both Cullingworth and his new wife behind me. Into the yard I went, and, picking up a big hammer, I started for the front door, with the pair still at my heels. I got the forked end of the hammer under my plate, and with a good wrench I brought the whole thing clattering on to the pavement.

' "That won't interfere with you any more," said I.'[1]

Feeling that he now knew something about the conditions of practice in the South of England, Conan Doyle decided to go by sea to Portsmouth and try his luck there.

In September 1882 he put up his plate in Southsea, and decided to get his young brother Innes to come and stay with him, both to keep him company and as a way of helping his mother and sisters. He was counting on Budd's help to pay for the house he had rented, but no sooner was he installed than his late partner let fly his carefully prepared shaft: he wrote that he had just discovered a letter from Mary Doyle full of extremely abusive remarks about him, and that he was immediately cancelling his offer of financial help as a result. His treachery was a severe blow to Conan Doyle's plans. Like Robinson Crusoe on his island, he made a list of his resources and then wrote to ask his mother whether she thought Innes had better join him or not. With characteristic high-mindedness and sense of responsibility,

[1] *The Stark Munro Letters.*

Mary Doyle decided not to keep the brothers apart, but to draw on her own savings for the monthly sum Dr. Budd had promised.

Conan Doyle's career had begun with difficulties—just as Dickens's did. And, like Dickens, his confidence in his luck helped him triumph over them, until success came to reinforce his optimism. His natural cheerfulness is well-illustrated by an incident over his tax declaration a few months later. As he had entered no taxable income on the form, the Inspector of Taxes returned it with the words 'most unsatisfactory' written in the margin. The young doctor sent it back again with 'I entirely agree' written beneath. During his first year at Southsea his earnings amounted to £154; by the following year this had increased to £250 and then subsequently remained in the neighbourhood of £300. It was not wealth by a long way, but it was quite enough for a bachelor and his young brother to live on in those days. And independence was what he most eagerly longed for. The impression we get from *The Stark Munro Letters* and his autobiography is that his eight years at Southsea were happy, untroubled and calm.

In 1885, after a brief engagement, he married Louise Hawkins, whom he had met in rather unusual circumstances. One day Dr. Pike, a colleague of Conan Doyle's, came to see him. He had been called in by a Mrs. Hawkins, a widow recently arrived in Southsea, to see her son Jack who was suffering from an attack of cerebral meningitis. The Hawkins family were staying in a boarding-house where it was very difficult to nurse the boy; on the other hand Mrs. Hawkins could not afford to send him to a nursing-home. It occurred to Dr. Pike that his colleague might take the patient into his house and look after him there. In spite of all Conan Doyle's care the little boy died a few days later. This was how he got to know Jack's elder sister Louise. Perhaps the feeling that sprang up between the two young people cannot be described as passionate love; they seem to have been drawn together largely by grief on one side and a strong impulse to bring comfort on the other. They were married on 6 August 1885, a few weeks after the University of Edinburgh had made Conan Doyle a doctor of medicine.

Some of his letters to 'The Ma'am', and perhaps the rather temperate atmosphere of *A Duet*, a story published in 1899, give us an idea of the domestic happiness of the young couple during the years they lived in Southsea. Louise was a tender and devoted companion, but her presence hardly made any change in Dr. Conan Doyle's existence—an active one, which his professional functions could not adequately fill. Portsmouth society knew him as a dilettante, a sportsman and lecturer, who was either to be found on the football or cricket ground or assiduously frequenting the Portsmouth Literary and Scientific Society, and (not long afterwards) spiritualistic seances.

Conan Doyle's first contact with the paranormal dates back to 1880, when he was at Birmingham attending a lecture called 'Does death end all?' by a spiritualist from Boston. At this time one of his friends, an architect called Ball, took him to some meetings devoted to psychic phenomena, but these aroused more curiosity than real interest in him at the time.

Literature was now his foremost preoccupation. In 1883 *The Cornhill Magazine* published one of his stories called *Habakuk Jephson's Statement*. This was particularly encouraging to the young writer. As a child at Edinburgh he had known Thackeray, the first editor of the magazine, and now he found that another contributor was his fellow-townsman Stevenson. Moreover the anonymous appearance of a story even as full of shortcomings as *Habakuk Jephson* had led to a flattering misunderstanding. James Payn, the editor of *The Cornhill*, had already written to ask Conan Doyle if the story was wholly fictitious, and on 6 January *The Illustrated London News* compared it to the work of Edgar Allan Poe, while actually attributing it to Stevenson. In fact Conan Doyle's story made quite a stir, for Solly Flood, Advocate General at Gibraltar and the Queen's representative at the Supreme Court of the Admiralty, involuntarily contradicted the incredulous editor of *The Illustrated London News* by telling the newspapers that Dr. J. Habakuk Jephson's statement was a complete fabrication!

In April 1886 Conan Doyle finished the book which really marks the start of his literary career: *A Study in Scarlet*. As a matter of course he sent it to James Payn, but the editor of *The Cornhill Magazine* could not make up his mind to publish it; he wrote to Conan Doyle that the story seemed either too short or too long for 'C.M.'

If this had been anything but a clumsy excuse, Payn would surely have asked for it either to be developed to full novel length or else reduced to the scale of a short story, such as Conan Doyle was to write for *The Strand Magazine* later on. As it was, the novelist sent his work first to Arrowsmith, then to Fred Warne & Co. and Ward,

Lock & Co., the last of whom offered him the meagre sum of £25 for the sole copyright on 30 October. Conan Doyle must very soon have regretted accepting this bad bargain. However the book had a tepid reception from the public—not at all what one would expect in view of Sherlock Holmes's subsequent fate, and justifying the publisher's hesitancy. Partly because of this, but even more because his real objectives lay in the realm of the historical novel, Conan Doyle now turned in this direction, and in 1888 he finished *Micah Clarke*, which was published by Longmans the following year. He felt confident that it would be a success. 'We must try and retain the copyright of *Micah Clarke*,' he wrote Mary Doyle. 'It should be an income in itself.'[1] Events proved him right. Critics found the title uninviting and the sub-title much too long; otherwise the book was favourably received on all sides. It was easy to see that a day would soon come when Conan Doyle must choose between a literary and a medical career. However he postponed the decision for some time longer, and even thought of specialising in some branch of medicine. He began studying ophthalmology while still planning new novels. His daughter, Mary Louise Conan Doyle, was born early in 1889. Her father obviously preferred the company of Commines and Jean de Troyes to hers, and that spring he rented a hunting-box in the New Forest where he could retreat to read, think and lay the foundations of a new book in which he was deeply absorbed—*The White Company*.

A few weeks later he went to London, at the invitation of Stoddart, agent of the American periodical *Lippincott's Magazine*. Here it was that he met Oscar Wilde, also a guest of Stoddart's. He agreed to let them have a detective story with Sherlock Holmes as hero. This was *The Sign of Four*. Meanwhile James Payn at last overcame his doubts and agreed to publish *The White Company* as a serial in *The Cornhill Magazine*. 1890 was therefore a decisive year. Out of professional loyalty and the need to carry out what he had undertaken, Conan Doyle stuck to his medical career. In October he joined some dozens of English and continental doctors in Berlin, to investigate Koch's claim that he had perfected a cure for pulmonary tuberculosis. As a result of a friendship struck up on the journey with a dermatologist called Malcolm Morris, who encouraged him warmly to go on studying ophthalmology, he decided to take a specialised course in Vienna before setting up in London. Little Mary Louise was entrusted to the

---

[1] Letter to Mary Doyle, n.d. (C.D.B.A.).

loving care of her maternal grandmother while Louise and Arthur Conan Doyle set off for Austria. They arrived in Vienna on 5 January 1891 and took rooms in a pension. On the journey an idea for a story had occurred to the novelist, and before going to the medical school he spent a fortnight writing *The Doings of Raffles Haw*. Afterwards when he found he was getting less out of his course of lectures than he had hoped, he made the best of a bad job and turned his professional journey into a holiday.

By the end of March the Conan Doyles were back in England and had rented a small flat in Montague Place, in Bloomsbury. Dr. Conan Doyle put up his plate as a consulting oculist in Devonshire Place a few hundred yards away, but this new enterprise was unpleasantly reminiscent of his early days at Southsea ten years earlier: 'Every morning,' he wrote philosophically enough afterwards, 'I walked from the lodgings at Montague Place, reached my consulting-room at ten and sat there until three or four, with never a ring to disturb my serenity. Could better conditions for reflection and work be found? It was ideal, and so long as I was thoroughly unsuccessful in my professional venture there was every chance of improvement in my literary prospects.'[1]

An unexpected crisis put a forcible end to this period of uncertainty. A violent attack of influenza kept him in bed for several weeks, and it was during his convalescence that Conan Doyle finally decided to give up the struggle to earn his living as a doctor and devote himself entirely to writing. He left the Harley Street area for the more rustic one of South Norwood, where the Conan Doyles rented a good-sized house at 12 Tennison Road, and invited Arthur's younger sisters, Connie and Lottie, to join them.

The July number of *The Strand Magazine* for 1891 contained the first of *The Adventures of Sherlock Holmes*. Meanwhile *The White Company* was still coming out as a serial in *The Cornhill*. Conan Doyle had for the first time left his transactions with the editors of *The Strand Magazine* in the hands of a literary agent, A. P. Watt. The first six Sherlock Holmes stories had hardly seen the light when he began on a short 'realistic' novel inspired by the suburban life he now had a chance to observe. The book was given the unpretentious title of *Beyond the City*; it never attracted much notice. But while the first Sherlock Holmes stories were having more and more success,

[1] AUT., p. 113.

their author embarked on a third long historical novel, about the Huguenots this time, called *The Refugees*. His work on this was interrupted by the triumph of Sherlock Holmes. The editors of *The Strand Magazine* now offered him a new contract. Watt had obtained £200 for the first six *Adventures*, the copyright to remain with his client. This time the *Strand* offered £300 for six new *Adventures*. Conan Doyle accepted, but as his heart was set on finishing *The Refugees* and reserving the right to exploit his other literary resources as he wished, he already began to contemplate the 'death' of Sherlock Holmes. One thing was obvious, Conan Doyle had no need to regret having given up medicine. By 1891 he estimated that he was earning £1,600 a year—about four times as much as his Southsea fees had amounted to. 1892 saw him deeply engaged in the same activities and even extending them. He finished *The Refugees*, and, keeping to French history, embarked on the epic events of the Napoleonic period in *The Great Shadow*, a novel with a distinct flavour of detection. There followed seventeen stories, eight of them *Adventures* of Holmes, and finally an operetta called *Jane Annie* in collaboration with James Barrie, which nobody, not even its authors, took quite seriously.

Barrie and Conan Doyle had met at the dinners of *The Idler Magazine*, and their friendship was to be a lasting one, always free from the slightest jealousy. In March 1892 the novelist visited Kirriemuir, and it must have been during his stay there that the somewhat absurd project of *Jane Annie* was hatched. A few months later the Conan Doyles took another holiday in Norway, with Jerome K. Jerome. Their stay seems to have been tinged with some of the flavour of *Three Men in a Boat*, if Jerome K. Jerome's account of the following incident is to be believed:

> Doyle was always full of superfluous energy. He started to learn Norwegian on the boat. He got on so well that he became conceited; and one day, at a little rest house up among the mountains he lost his head. We had come there in stoljas—a tiny carriage only just big enough for one person, drawn by a pony about the size of a Newfoundland dog, but marvellously sturdy. They will stride their 50 miles in the day, and be frisky in the evening. While we were lunching, with some 20 miles still in front of us, a young officer came into the room, and said something in Norwegian. Of course, we turned him on to Doyle; and Doyle rose and bowed, and answered him. We all watched the conversation. The young Norwegian officer was evidently charmed with

Doyle, who stood ladling out Norwegian as though it had been his mother tongue. After the officer had gone, we asked Doyle what it was all about. 'Oh, just about the weather, and the state of the roads, and how some relation of his had hurt his leg', answered Doyle carelessly. 'Of course, I didn't understand all of it.' He turned the conversation. When we had finished lunch, and the stoljas were brought out, Doyle's pony was missing. It appeared Doyle had 'lent' it to the young officer, whose own pony had gone lame. The ostler, who was also the waiter, had overheard the conversation. Doyle had said 'certainly, with pleasure'. He had said it once or twice. Also the Norwegian equivalent of: 'Don't mention it.' There wasn't another pony within ten miles. One of the party, who had taken a fancy to the view, and thought he would like to spend a day or two in the neighbourhood, let Doyle have his stolja. But for the rest of that trip Doyle talked less Norwegian.[1]

Though the year 1892 ended happily with the birth of a son, Alleyne Kingsley, sadder times were soon to follow. However 1893 began auspiciously, with two trips to Switzerland, one at the end of the winter and the second during the summer, when Conan Doyle gave a lecture at Lucerne on *Fiction as Part of Literature*. He planned a series of further lectures after his return to England but two events intervened. The first was the death of Charles Doyle, who had spent the last fifteen years in a nursing-home. The second was the illness of Louise who developed tuberculosis of the lungs and was given only a few months to live. But Conan Doyle refused to accept the opinion of his two colleagues, Dr. Dalton and Sir Douglas Powell. He decided to take his wife out of England at once and try the open-air cure at Davos. The month of December 1893 was thus the start of a long period of peregrination, thanks to which Louise's illness was kept in check for many years. But though her husband was both her doctor and her companion, he never relaxed his literary activity. Quite the contrary. During the two and a half years they spent abroad, he wrote dozens of short stories, *The Stark Munro Letters* (an auto-biographical novel) and *Rodney Stone* (a historical novel); he also gave nearly a hundred lectures and ended up as correspondent for the *Westminster Gazette* in Egypt.

In *The Stark Munro Letters* Conan Doyle for the first time showed a desire to take his spiritual bearings in the light of his recent traumatic experiences, and put into shape some reflections jotted down early in 1891, while he was convalescing in London. The manuscript

---

[1] Jerome K. Jerome, *My Life and Times*, 1926, p. 164.

had been in a drawer ever since. He set about making it suitable for publication by adding some 'action', taken—like Cullingworth's doings—from his own recollections. This led to a certain lack of unity, as John Dickson Carr has very fairly pointed out: 'This book contains some of the best scenes of broad comedy he ever wrote . . . Yet gloom is woven into the texture of the book; and at the end, which appears in some editions and not in others, Stark Munro and his wife die in a railway accident.'[1]

The seriousness of its aim and tone gave this book a special place in its author's affections: 'I am nearing the end of my book', he wrote to his mother in January 1894—'could end it this week easily. I cannot imagine what its value is. It will make a religious sensation if not a literary—possibly both.'[2]

Towards the end of that winter Conan Doyle took a short holiday, devoted to an activity which was none the less memorable for having nothing to do with literature—he introduced Norwegian skis into Switzerland. His first reference to a little event which was to have large international consequences occurs in a letter to Mary Doyle written in March, 1894, before his published account of it:

> . . . Yesterday I performed a small feat by crossing a chain of mountains on snowshoes (Norwegian Ski) and coming down to Arosa. Two Swiss accompanied me. I am the first Englishman who has ever crossed an Alpine pass in winter on showshoes—at least I think so. We left this at four in the morning and were in Arosa at 11.30. It has created quite a little excitement. I shall write an account of it for *The Speaker*. On Tuesday I shall (if the weather holds), ascend the mountain overlooking Davos—also on snowshoes . . .[3]

That spring various plans took shape. *Round the Red Lamp*, a collection of fifteen short stories based on the common theme of a doctor's life, was followed by the author's first approach to spiritualism in a little book called *The Parasite*, published by Constable; next he prepared a course of lectures for the United States, and finally his short play *Waterloo*, still associated with the famous name of Henry Irving, was put on the London stage and brought Conan Doyle to England for a brief time early in the summer of 1894. He was responsible for all the details of this production, which was first performed at Prince's Theatre, Bristol on 21 September. It was only a

---

[1] J. D. Carr, *The Life of Sir Arthur Conan Doyle*, p. 105.
[2] (C.D.B.A.)   [3] Unpublished (C.D.B.A.)

curtain-raiser lasting half an hour, but none of his later plays made such a hit, and Irving scored one of his most memorable successes in it. In May 1895 it was put on at the Lyceum Theatre in London, with *The Bells*: 'The play met with a success extraordinary even for Irving. The audience followed it with rapt attention and manifest emotion, swaying with the varying sentiments of the scenes. The brief aid to memory in my diary of that day runs: "New play enormous success. H.I. fine and great. All laughed and wept. Marvellous study of senility. Eight calls at end." '[1]

A few weeks after the Bristol first night, Conan Doyle was so carried away by an excess of optimism that he dashed off another play for Irving, called *The House of Temperley*. His first idea had been to write it in collaboration with Hornung, but the plan was abandoned after a few days. This play had a curious fate. It remained in a drawer until 1899, when it was assumed by public and critics to be an adaptation of the novel *Rodney Stone*, published in 1896. Yet, to judge from one of Conan Doyle's letters, just the opposite was the truth. 'I am getting a lot of my Regency business (which I shall afterwards use in a novel) into it,' he wrote to Mary Doyle on 14 September 1894. *The House of Temperley* was performed with some success, mainly due to the novelty of the subject; it was in fact one of the first sporting comedies, whose popularity lasted until about 1930, when they were taken over by the cinema, with its special facilities and techniques.

Early in October, Conan Doyle, accompanied by Innes, embarked for New York to give a series of lectures organised by Major Pond. He found himself suddenly swept away in a wild frenzy of receptions, lectures, interviews and journeys, and with a considerable post to answer. He was as exhausted by it all as Dickens had been twenty-seven years earlier. However he liked the Americans and their vast country. 'I expected to find much to like here and much to learn, but it is far finer than I expected,' he wrote to his mother on 19 October.

There was no doubt about his success, and his spontaneity, charm, modesty and eloquence were all loudly praised in the press. An extract from *The New York Recorder* for 11 October is typical:

... Upon the general subject of 'Readings and Reminiscences', Dr. A. Conan Doyle addressed his first American audience in the Calvary Baptist Church last night. His lecture was interesting, exceedingly so,

[1] Bram Stoker, *Personal Reminiscences of Henry Irving*, 1907, p. 162.

for while it lasted his audience listened intently to every word, followed carefully his explanations and digressions, and enjoyed not only the subject of his discourse but also the very sound of his voice. There are few physical gifts that are so delightful as a hearty, cheery, sympathetic voice, and such a voice is one of Dr. Doyle's most charming powers. Dr. Doyle read extracts from several of his stories, and all of them, particularly that from *The Lord of Château Noir* were received with enthusiasm.

Conan Doyle was surprised at the warmth of his welcome and the magnitude of his triumph. Modestly and seriously, he interpreted American friendliness in patriotic terms, tried to give it a more than literary reference and saw himself as the artificer of a rapprochement between two races speaking the same language and springing from the same stock. 'Such good people too!' he wrote to Mary Doyle. 'When I think of how far they have been allowed to be estranged, I would hang a few cabinet ministers and editors.'

At the end of November Conan Doyle met Kipling at the Thanksgiving Day celebrations in Vermont. The two men had a common interest in sport as well as literature; when he got back to England Conan Doyle sent his new friend a pair of skis like those he had worn himself on his historic visit to Davos. He summed up his impressions of Kipling a week after he got back: . . . 'I have been staying two days with Kipling and we had a great time and golf and much high converse. He is a wonderful chap. Have you read his poem, Mc Andrews Hymn, in Scribner's Xmas number. It's grand! He will never do a great long book . . .'[1]

Arthur and Innes left New York for Liverpool on 8 December. The novelist was pleased with his trip, both on literary grounds and because his public spirit and patriotism responded to the welcome the Americans gave him. He had been made to feel how solid were the cultural links between the two nations, and he believed them inseparable from the political links which he never ceased to value.

After his return from the United States he spent a short while in London and then hurried back to Davos. He found the weather there atrocious, and fearing for Louise's health began to think of wintering in Egypt next year. During his second winter in Switzerland he was writing the short stories published in *The Strand Magazine* as *The Exploits of Brigadier Gerard*. Next he set about revising *The Stark Munro Letters* with a view to publication in book form in

[1] Letter to Mary Doyle, n.d. (C.D.B.A.).

April (it had just come out serially in *The Idler*), and travelled to London to arrange about it. It was there that he met Grant Allen, who personally recommended the therapeutic qualities of the Surrey air, and told him that he believed Louise Conan Doyle would recover her health as quickly there as in a foreign climate. Won over by Grant Allen's view, Conan Doyle decided to look about for a piece of land; he found what he wanted on the hills of Hindhead, and asked his architect friend Ball to build him a house there.

Afterwards he rejoined his family at Davos and took them for a three months visit to the Upper Engadine, spent mostly at Maloja. Here it was that he used some of the notes on the Regency he had made for *The House of Temperley* to write the first chapters of *Rodney Stone*. The Conan Doyles spent the month of October at Caux and reached Brindisi in November, where they took the boat for Egypt. They put up in a hotel a few miles from Cairo and spent six months of open-air existence. The climate seemed to suit them both marvellously: '. . . Touie seems much better for the change', he wrote to his mother, 'and we are settling down to our new life very comfortably. It is a charming hotel and the air is splendid. I go for a ride every morning—of all things on this earth the last I should ever have prophesied is that I should ride on the Sahara desert upon an Arab stallion. Yet so it is. There is plenty to do—golf, tennis, riding, billiards . . .'[1]

The most memorable event of this long holiday was an excursion up the valley of the Nile to the Sudan. It was on this journey, accompanied by Louise and his sister Lottie (Caroline Doyle) that he hit upon the subject of his novel *The Tragedy of the Korosko*, a book which describes the dangers luckily escaped by the Conan Doyles, but none the less real in that treacherous region. He noted in his diary:

> . . . Jan. 16th. This day we had an interesting experience in the morning when we stopped at the village which was raided about a month ago by the Dervishes. It is an ordinary little mud village with castor oil plantations in front and a belt of palm trees. The survivors seem quiet and cheerful enough, but 17 of them were killed by their assailants who got away in safety. They are said to have been Dongolese. There were ninety of them, on camels and wearing red turbans. They came over the low hills to eastward about 4 in the afternoon. They were armed with Remingtons and had buglers with them. I saw

[1] Letter to Mary Doyle, 27 November 1895, unpublished (C.D.B.A.).

one poor old man with a Remington bullet through his neck. They had
a watchman on the hills, but I really cannot see what there is to prevent
incursions upon any of these riverside places. If I were a Dervish
general, I would undertake to carry off a Cook's excursion party with
the greatest ease.[1]

Conan Doyle becomes a Dervish general in *The Tragedy of the
Korosko*, which relates the misfortunes of a group of tourists travelling under the auspices of a well-known travel agency, when captured
by the Mahdi's men.

Meanwhile Kitchener had received orders to attack the Mahdi
and retake the Sudan. On the eve of this crisis Conan Doyle was fifty
miles from Cairo visiting a Coptic monastery with a Colonel Lewis
of the Egyptian army. Here it was he heard of the resumption of
hostilities, and telegraphed to *The Westminster Gazette* on the spur
of the moment, asking for the job of war-correspondent. It was the
only way for a civilian to get to the front line. As soon as the paper
had wired back agreement Conan Doyle was off to Assouan by
railway and boat, and from there he took a camel across the desert,
accompanied by three other pressmen and a guide:

> There are five of us including myself and my travelling companion.
> The three others being nothing less august than the Times, the Daily
> News and the Standard—the Times fresh from Madagascar, the Daily
> News fresh from the Armenian atrocities, and the Standard from Con-
> stantinople. Now these storm-petrels are all flying south. What men
> they are, these body servants of the press! Here is the Times, tall,
> straight and muscular, famous yachtsman and treasure seeker,
> traveller, fighter and scholar. Here, too, is the Daily News, small,
> compact, mercurial: full of life, fire and pluck; a man of many cam-
> paigns and singular adventures, with that strange combination of ruddy
> hair and black eye which is the outward sign of the splendid neuro-
> sanguine blend. And lastly the Standard, thin but wiry, with the slightly
> blasé pince-nez look of a man who has seen much life; cool, alert, a
> useful man to have by your side in a tight place.[2]

The nervous tension of that journey (these five men were at the
mercy of an encounter with the enemy) was followed by the disappointment of their arrival at Wadi Halfa, where they were told that
military operations had not yet begun and the preparations would
probably last several weeks. There was no question of waiting; it was
not that Conan Doyle would have disliked spending a little time in

[1] Egyptian Journal, unpublished (C.D.B.A.).   [2] Egyptian Journal.

the desert, but how would Louise stand the often torrid heat of an Egyptian summer? It would be better to go back to London. The novelist's last recollection of this 'funny war' was of dining with Kitchener at headquarters.

When they arrived in England the Conan Doyles had to put up first in a furnished house, then in an hotel, until their new house was finished. At last, in October 1896, they moved into Undershaw, their large comfortable house at Hindhead. There Louise was to spend the last ten years of a life dimmed by disease, in comparative peace, while her husband devoted his energy and his epic vision to literature.

Chapter 3

THE PATRIOT: THE BOER WAR

October 1899: as the result of her rejection of the ultimatum issued by President Kruger's government, Great Britain was in a state of war with the African republics of Orange Free State and the Transvaal. War had not been embarked on light-heartedly, but no one guessed how serious an affair it was to become. Who could have imagined, too, that Conan Doyle was to play a part in the national drama? He was by now one of the most popular English writers and at the height of his creative powers; but he was to add politics to his numerous other occupations and preoccupations.

Since the move to Hindhead he had seemed anxious to devote himself to writing for the theatre. In 1897 *Waterloo*—with Irving—was chosen to be performed in honour of the Queen's Jubilee, before a delegation of 2,000 soldiers representing the different countries of the Empire. The New York public were the first to see Sherlock Holmes on the stage, brilliantly performed by William Gillette; and the first night of a third play called *Halves*, adapted from a novel by James Payn, was fast approaching. Conan Doyle had also just published a collection of poems, called *Songs of Action*, and two novels. The first of these, *The Tragedy of the Korosko* was an adventure story, as we have seen; the second, *A Duet*, was in an entirely different vein. This was a literary experiment, both elegiac and realistic, and its author always had a special fondness for it. But none of these works could compare in quality with those published seven or eight years earlier. What had been happening to him?

About the middle of the year 1897, probably at one of the fashionable parties he now often went to, Conan Doyle met a young lady called Jean Leckie. This was the beginning of an episode which reveals him in his true colours, better than anything else that we know of him. His letters to his mother—who was not only his confidante but Jean's also—allow us to follow the development of the affair. An attachment but never a liaison, the relationship between Jean and the novelist remained platonic until Louise's death. Why was this? Certainly not out of fear of public opinion, but rather from some desire to put himself to the test, and an idealistic and chivalrous moral standard which set these two people apart from others at the height of the Edwardian epoch. Conan Doyle's chief concern for the next ten years was to respect his wife's dignity. Her bad health made the ordeal more severe. Imprisoned within the walls formed by his compassion, his medical knowledge, his duties as a husband, his love for Jean and his own chivalrous mysticism, Conan Doyle went through a time of nervous tension and inner conflict which may have been partly relieved by the active part he had a chance to take in public affairs.

When war was declared he was away in the country giving a course of lectures about his life and work, based on the pattern of those he had given in the United States. Returning to Hindhead he began a second novel about medieval times, in which we find the same characters as had appeared in *The White Company*. But this book was not finished and published until 1906. It was *Sir Nigel*.

In December, the reverses suffered by the British Army, particularly during 'black week', made a deep impression on the public. Under the influence of the general stupefaction, the newspapers probably exaggerated the gravity of the situation. Conan Doyle's attention was brought forcibly in contact with reality, and he again saw himself as war-correspondent of *The Westminister Gazette*.

It was as a patriot, a realist, and above all a deeply sincere man, that Conan Doyle decided on Christmas Eve, 1899, to volunteer for service in South Africa. No political attitude, no ulterior motive was involved in the slightest degree. The chief argument invoked by his family, especially his mother, to combat this decision, was the very same that had led him to make it—his being a man of letters—although in her eloquent and touching distress Mary Doyle left nothing untried that might dissuade her eldest son from his purpose:

> My own dearest and very naughty son,
> How dare you, what do you mean by it? Why, your very height and breadth would make you a simple and sure target, and is not your life, to say the least, of more value, even to your country—at home? Think of the pleasure and solace your writings afford to thousands, many sick and suffering among them. . . . Would you have the Boers who with infinite pain and toil made a home for themselves up there in the wilderness, hand it over to Rhodes and Co.? . . . *Mind*, you are not to go unless already bound in honour. Your first duty is to your own

family, of which you are the one staff, prop, support, pride and glory.
. . . It is *your duty not* to go—as much as it is Innes's most clear duty
to go *if sent*. Why, even Roberts or Kitchener did not go till they were
told to . . . There are hundreds of thousands who can fight for *one* who
can make a Sherlock Holmes or a Waterloo! You owe it to us all to care
for your life as a *great* treasure. But it is just a fever you have, dear one
—the old fighting blood—Percy and Pack, Doyle and Conan, all
struggling to push you on, to what, noble as it looks, would be, if
stripped to the core, a real crime, and a great and most useless folly.
For God's sake listen to me; even at your age, I am God's representative to you. . . . One son I have given—but not you—your duty is at
home, and with good pure leaven to raise the tone of the popular
taste and feeling! I am coming down if you leave me in uncertainty.
This is altogether too dreadful . . .[1]

Conan Doyle recognised the influence he had over his fellow
countrymen and was ready to assume it in this hour of danger and
critical responsibility. And since Mary Doyle would only listen to the
voice of honour, he wrote to her that he was now irrevocably involved:

I was afraid that you would be angry with me for volunteering.
But I rather felt it was my duty. I wrote a letter to *The Times* advising
the government to call upon the riding shooting men. They did so, and
of course I was honour-bound as I had suggested it, to be the first to
volunteer. I learned patriotism from my mother, so you must not
blame me. What I feel is that I have perhaps the strongest influence over
young men, especially young athletic sporting men, of any one in
England, (bar Kipling). That being so, it is really important that I
should give them a lead. It is not merely my 40 year-old self—though
I am as fit as ever I was, but it is the influence I have over these
youngsters.[2]

A completely objective observer is forced to admit that love of
adventure ('the old fighting blood') played its part in Conan Doyle's
decision, as 'the Ma'am' did not fail to realise. We must remember how
regretfully he had left Egypt before the end of the campaign he had
so much longed to take part in; and that when he heard that Khar-
toum had fallen, while watching the great summer manœuvres on
Salisbury Plain with Lord Wolseley in 1898, he showed intense
regret at not having been present. Now he had a chance to get his
own back on fate. To be an eye-witness of some great historical
event, to see for himself what he had so often described—the clash
of two armies—this was a prospect that inflamed his imagination.

[1] Extracts from Mary Doyle's letters, December 1899 (C.D.B.A.).
[2] December 1899 (C.D.B.A.).

He sent in his enlistment application to the War Office, then to Lord Chesham, commanding officer of the Imperial Yeomanry in South Africa, and lastly to the Middlesex Yeomanry. All to no purpose: he had not got the necessary qualifications. He therefore gave up trying to surmount the obstacles put in his way by an admirable bureaucratic system, and applied to John Langman the philanthropist (he became Sir John Langman in 1906) who was fitting out a field hospital for the South African army. Having offered his services as medical officer he found himself almost at once in charge of the hospital—a harder task than he had bargained for. Active service as a soldier was one thing, but to organise and control a hospital in time of war was a prospect that might well make him pause. He accepted and embarked on 28 February accompanied by John Langman's son, who was thirteen years younger than he was. Jean Leckie came to see him off and filled his cabin with flowers.

On 2 April, Conan Doyle was at Bloemfontein, capital of the Orange Free State. Lord Roberts's troops had been there for three weeks, trying to make headway to the north. Hardly had Conan Doyle arrived when news came of a battle having started some seven miles away; without hesitation he set off and covered the distance there and back on foot, but it was a disappointing journey and that same evening he began work with his orderlies. A few hours later the improvised hospital had been erected on an abandoned cricket-field where forty tons of equipment had been dumped. If his description of himself is accurate, Conan Doyle must have presented a curious spectacle:

> ... You would have smiled if you could have seen me in my pink undershirt, breeches and helmet, burned red and covered with dirt. Ah, if you could have seen the men! I mean the troops. A whole brigade passed us today, such splendid chaps, bearded and fierce, picturesque brigands, my word!—they look like fighting. How I would love to march them down the Strand just as they are. London would go mad. The Gordons passed me. 'Good old Gordons,' I yelled. 'What cheer, mate!', they cried back, seeing in the dirty man a brother tommy. They are splendid. We are not depressed by the recent cavalry reverse. Last night it was rumoured that the Boers would raise the town, but we saw nothing except our own ...[1]

He was not allowed any time for rest: the hospital had been installed at a providential moment, for an epidemic of typhoid broke

[1] Letter to Louise Conan Doyle, 3 April 1900 (C.D.B.A.).

out immediately. Conan Doyle had to triple the capacity of his hospital, without the help of any more doctors or orderlies. For three months his two young colleagues, Gibbs and Scharlieb, were his only assistants with the sick and wounded. Because of his very robust health, but also by extreme good luck, he never caught the infection, though overwork made the danger greater. However, at the beginning of May he decided to take five days leave. For a rest? Nothing of the sort. With John Langman's son, he went up to the front line to receive his baptism of fire. This escapade won him a touching tribute from a wounded man he met on the way '. . . I saw a man with a stretcher over his shoulder canter far ahead of the guns and I gathered that some wounded lay there. He went on north with great gallantry and disappeared in the direction of the original kopje. Soon I saw two men come back with the stretcher; so I rode out and met them a quarter of a mile out. It was a New Zealander shot in arm and stomach. The latter bullet lay under the skin, and I could assure the poor fellow that his hurts were not mortal. He opened his eyes. "I have read your books", said he, and was carried off.'[1]

Langman and Conan Doyle were present when Lord Roberts's troops crossed the river Vet in their advance on Pretoria. A melancholy duty awaited them on the return journey; they found the dead body of a young soldier lying on the veldt: '. . . We could not leave him, so we put him over my saddle—my hands were red with his blood—and so we walked him back to the road, his head and heels hanging over. There we laid him by a telegraph post and covered him with his overcoat. One still arm and clenched fist was raised in the air as if he were shaking it at the Boers.'[2]

A month later, Lord Roberts reviewed the British and Canadian troops under his command on the chief square in Pretoria. All the military observers, most of the diplomats, and even Cecil Rhodes himself, thought that the fall of Kruger's capital meant that the end of the war was imminent. So that Conan Doyle left Bloemfontein on 6 July to return to England and his family, with every reason to feel he had done his duty: 'I believe that between my history and my work there are few men in South Africa who have worked harder,' he wrote to his mother, '. . . but I have been cheered by loving words from home—yours as valued as any—and, thank God, I am the better, not the worse for the experience. What adventures I have had

---

[1] MS. entitled *Adventures from May 2 to 7*, unpublished (C.D.B.A.).   [2] *Ibid.*

too! The typhoid epidemic, which has been far the most important thing in the campaign, the Vet river battle, Pretoria, Johannesburg, I have dined in Steyn's house, and smoked in Kruger's chair, and seen many wondrous things.'[1]

What was his 'history'? The fact was that Conan Doyle was not content to take part in the drama, he now wanted to testify to what he had seen. He had collected information, whether from commanding officers or the humblest private soldiers, English or Boers, on a great number of subjects, and put it together in the form of a summing-up of more than 500 pages which he modestly baptised *An Interim History of the War*. It was 'interim' in comparison with the seven volumes to be published by Amery in 1909 on behalf of *The Times*, which gave a much more complete and authoritative account, particularly of the second phase of the war; but it was both a definitive and lucid narrative and an extremely valuable work of reference.

In this difficult genre of military history (which is neither journalism, novel nor treatise) Conan Doyle instinctively followed a tradition which lay close to the source of his literary education—a tradition handed on by Macaulay and ending with Winston Churchill, in which the general picture has a somewhat academic eighteenth-century nobility, while colour is reserved for the anecdotes, and a nostalgic poetry for the great battle scenes:

> It was the supreme instant of the Natal campaign, as, wave after wave, the long lines of infantry went shimmering up the hill. On the left the Lancasters, the Lancashire Fusiliers, the South Lancashires, the York and Lancasters, with a burr of north country oaths went racing for the summit. Spion Kop and a thousand comrades were calling for vengeance. 'Remember, men, the eyes of Lancashire are watching you,' cried the gallant MacCarthy O'Leary. The old 40th swept on, but his dead body marked the way which they had taken. On the right the East Surrey, the Cameronians, the 3rd Rifles, the 1st Rifle Brigade, the Durhams, and the gallant Irishmen, so sorely stricken and yet so eager, were all pressing upwards and onwards. The Boer fire lulls, it ceases—they are running! Wild hatwaving men upon the Hlangwane uplands see the silhouette of the active figures of the stormers along the skyline and know that the position is theirs. Exultant soldiers dance and cheer upon the ridge. The sun is setting in glory over the great Drakensberg mountains, and so also that night set for ever on the hopes of the Boer invaders of Natal. Out of doubt and chaos, blood and labour, had come at last the judgment that the lower should not

[1] 6 July 1900 (C.D.B.A.).

swallow the higher, that the world is for the man of the twentieth and not of the seventeenth century.[1]

In this passage Conan Doyle is on guard against his own facility as a narrator. He certainly possessed the war-correspondent's gift of vividness and of making a scene come to life. Moreover, his sense of contrast suggested very clearly the difference of scale between the Egyptian episode he had lived through four years ago and the present drama, where the honour of the British nation and perhaps the fate of the Empire were at stake. This point deserves a little more consideration.

Conan Doyle believed, rightly or wrongly, that he had a special part to play in this first campaign of the twentieth century; if not, why did he claim for himself and for Kipling the responsibility of influencing the rising generation? This claim implied obligations. His *History of the War* held for him a significance as vital, as normative, as his attempt to enlist or his devotion to his medical duties in Langman's hospital. Doctor and man of letters—neither role was enough by itself; as he possessed both qualifications he wanted to undertake a double task.

The *History* could not just be a simple chronicle of events. At this hour of national crisis, when consciences were troubled, it must make clear the origins of the conflict, discuss them thoroughly, take one side or the other. But it was also necessary to examine the way operations had been conducted from a purely military point of view, and draw a useful lesson from any failures. These aims controlled the plan of the book. The first eighty pages are devoted to the remote and immediate antecedents of the war, and the phase of diplomatic negotiations which heralded it. The clarity of this exposition is particularly striking: the author brings out two features of the situation often found together in English military history—on one hand, the justice of the cause defended, and the inadequacy of preparations for war on the other. Skilful rhetoric is at the service of the austerity of a memorandum. The rhythm and firmness of style play an important part in the general disposition of the book, and we reach the descriptions of the first battles with almost a feeling of relief. Behind his account of the facts we detect his anxiety to make himself understood, not only by the English public but by all readers of the language, in particular in America. Here as so often in his other works

[1] *The Great Boer War*, p. 290.

(whether novels, short stories or controversial articles) he takes trouble to make himself specially clear to the American reader. Thus when he describes the incident at Slagter's Nek, he is not content with noting the deterioration it caused in the relations between the English and Dutch in South Africa; he also compares it with the situation in the United States just before the Civil War. In both cases difficulties arose from divergent attitudes towards coloured people: 'Both branches of the Anglo-Celtic race have grappled with the question, and in each it has led to trouble.'[1]

These premises lead to reassuring conclusions about the post-war problems dealt with in his preliminary reflections. England should take American history as an example, and Conan Doyle firmly advocates a policy of amnesty: 'A brave race can forget the victims of the field of battle, but never those of the scaffold. The making of political martyrs is the last insanity of statesmanship.'[2]

Let us remember these words 'the last insanity of statesmanship', for they throw light on Conan Doyle's intervention in favour of Roger Casement, for whom he tried in vain to extract a pardon from the British government sixteen years later. The suggested analogy between English and American political problems led him to hope, more or less explicitly, that the two 'Anglo-Celtic' nations would consolidate their common racial, linguistic and historical interests.

The Cornhill Magazine published the last chapter of *The Great Boer War* under the title of 'Some Military Lessons of the War', a month before the book appeared. This article aroused immediate and widespread interest, and an indignant outcry from a small section of the army. At the risk of shocking his readers, Conan Doyle affirmed that there was not a moment to be lost. In the 6,000 words of his article, he explained with lucidity the chief reforms he hoped to see introduced as a result of his South African experiences, which had confirmed the unfavourable impression made on him two years earlier at the great manœuvres. The methods in force had then seemed to him hopelessly antiquated: 'In the Salisbury Plain manœuvres of 1898 I saw with my own eyes lines of infantry *standing* and firing upon each other at short ranges without rebuke either from their officers or from the umpires.'[3]

The war had brought home the need to revise not only military methods and traditional dispositions, but also tactical theory and

[1] *The Great Boer War*, p. 7.   [2] *Ibid.*, p. 7.   [3] *Ibid.*, p. 515.

even the role of the army under modern conditions. It might easily find itself simultaneously faced by two very distinct tasks—to defend the British Isles and also some remote territory overseas. For the defence of their native islands Conan Doyle stressed the importance of two lessons learned from the Boer War: the character of the terrain must be made use of, and all civilians capable of bearing arms must be mobilised. And he goes on to remark, thinking now not of the veldt but of green England, that 'a country of hedgerows would with modern weapons be the most terrible entanglement into which an army could wander'.[1]

It is easy for us after the lapse of half a century to applaud Conan Doyle's perspicacity: in 1940 it was precisely on these two factors of exploiting the terrain and mobilising all means of defence that Churchill and his associates counted for their victorious resistance against invasion. Though Conan Doyle was not advocating compulsory military service in 1900 (he was too English to want to deprive military service of the sporting element involved in its being voluntary) he did believe in the creation of a civil reserve force. He declared that 'every brave man with a rifle is a formidable soldier', and 'with his pen, with his voice, with his rifle, every man who has the privilege of a vote must do what he can to strengthen the fighting force of his country'.[2]

This national militia envisaged by him would have taken over almost the whole responsibility for home defence. What he had seen of the Boers' fighting methods and, by contrast, of the gaps in British military organisation, reinforced his spontaneous confidence in the resources of patriotism as opposed to the technique of the professional soldier. His books (*Rodney Stone*, *The White Company* and of course the Sherlock Holmes stories) all show this preference for the amateur rather than the professional: 'Our professional soldiers have not shown that they were endowed with clear vision. In the face of their manifest blunders and miscalculations, a civilian need not hesitate to express his own opinion.'[3]

If, adequately trained and equipped with modern arms, a citizen army could protect English soil, did this mean that the days of the regular army were numbered? Conan Doyle thought not; the professional army would be a small but highly trained force kept in a

[1] *The Great Boer War*, p. 516.   [2] *Ibid.*, p. 515.
[3] *Ibid.*, p. 516.

constant state of readiness to intervene in any theatre of operations however distant. In other words, Conan Doyle was here defining the modern 'commando' and its functions, without using the term. It is interesting to think that we have had to wait for a second world war for the theories he expounded in 1900 to be applied—and for the first time by an enemy nation: 'The lesson of the war, as I read it, is that it is better and cheaper for the country to have fewer soldiers which shall be very highly trained than many of a mixed quality. In the wars of the future, where a soldier has to be conveyed to the centre of Africa, the interior of China, or the frontier of Afghanistan, it is most necessary that the army so conveyed should be of the highest quality. It costs as much to convey and feed a worthless man as a good one.'[1]

What military theoretician had ever before so clearly conceived of two forces entirely different in function, numbers, formation and armaments acting together simultaneously? Thus the lessons learnt from the Boer War were translated into a strategical hypothesis valid for one or more world powers in the twentieth century.

Conan Doyle ended with some interesting remarks about the use of different arms, and here again his historical sense enabled him to grasp clearly the developments produced by the war. The use of cavalry had declined and artillery had come to the fore. Conan Doyle suggested that it might be a good thing to do away with the cavalry altogether. At least it was necessary to relegate to the museums all side-arms and revolvers, lightening the equipment of cavalrymen and arming them with carbines only, so that they would be capable of swift and prolonged pursuit. Then again the artillery must be better protected by camouflage, and batteries must be divided and scattered as much as possible. Conan Doyle saw that the increased power of firearms was one of the most characteristic tactical developments: 'In the wars of the future it is certain that very much heavier guns will be employed than in the past. The bullock guns of the Boers are the fore-runners of an artillery which in a country of good roads with steam traction available may assume the most monstruous proportions.'[2]

The Great Boer War was enthusiastically received even in military circles. For a work of this sort to sell 30,000 copies in two months was an outstanding success. The author declined to profit financially, and

[1] *The Great Boer War*, p. 517.   [2] *Ibid.*, p. 527.

distributed his royalties among different social organisations for the army. George Meredith wrote him the following letter:

> Dear Dr. Conan Doyle,
>
> Your thought of me in sending your book revives my feeling for you when I heard of your intention to take service in South Africa. I was restrained from writing you my send-off only by the monitory counsel to forbear from troubling you at such a time with a letter of no practical use. I followed your name while you were away. The book is the most luminous narrative I have read on this matter, fair to both sides. As to your conclusions, you are in the ring with Lonsdale Hall, well matched both, and I should like it to be fought out. At any rate, better pay for a more intelligent order of men, and officers bent seriously to their work —that cannot be contested. I had many a talk in old days with Charles Brackenbury on the subject. He was a loss to our army . . .
>
> Very truly yours,
George Meredith.[1]

The fairness of the book was remarked on in an article in *The Cornhill Magazine* for July 1901 describing its success with Boer prisoners, among others General Roux, who praised the author's disinterestedness: 'One seems to read a tale of knightly time of old and not an episode of our modern century of crass materialism. Surely such books are not written in vain, and will be read by generations to come on both sides.'[2] As for the figures Conan Doyle had quoted, the only man who seems to have questioned their accuracy was Major Runck, chief of the German Expeditionary Force in South Africa, who thought the Boer losses had been rated too high. Conan Doyle's criticisms of army organisation agreed with the general drift of opinion. Only one officer, Lieutenant-Colonel Maude, dared publicly defend the use of side-arms—without great success.

On the other hand quite a number of influential army officers approved Conan Doyle's views about the urgent need for reform of strategy. Among the most representative were Lord Dundonald, former commanding officer of the Third Cavalry Brigade in Natal; Baden-Powell, who had been a national hero ever since Mafeking; Ian Hamilton, who became Kitchener's Chief-of-Staff in 1901 and was to direct operations at Gallipoli in the First World War; and finally Lord Roberts, who backed Conan Doyle's idea of forming clubs for rifle practice all over the country. Conan Doyle seems in

---

[1] 12 November 1900, unpublished (C.D.B.A.).
[2] W. G. H. Koenneker, *The Cornhill Magazine*, July 1901, p. 295.

fact to have organised the first of these at Hindhead, on his own land at Undershaw, and he paid for the cost of rifles and targets out of his own pocket. This venture was the direct result of the plans outlined in his book, and the first attempt at creating a national militia of the type made famous by the Home Guard of 1940.

But though the end of the war had seemed imminent at the beginning of the summer of 1900, it now entered into a new phase, characterised by guerilla warfare, raids on communications and surprise attacks on base depots, with the help or complicity of the population. We know what sort of defensive measures and reprisals this kind of thing habitually stimulates in a regular army. Kitchener took the responsibility of evacuating large numbers of civilians and 'regrouping' them in improvised camps.

The conscience of Europe was already prepared to be indignant about such things, and its voice was heard from Paris, Brussels and the Hague, but particularly from Germany. One of the chief spokesmen of this movement in England was William Stead, whom Conan Doyle had known since 1890.

In 1898, after a visit to the Tsar, Stead had tried to found a pacifist league, with the support of Bernard Shaw and the Fabians. Conan Doyle was invited to a meeting on 28 January 1899 to consider what part they were all prepared to play. A letter to Conan Doyle from Shaw, who also lived at Hindhead, reminds us of this occasion:

Dear Conan Doyle,

Hadn't we better come to some agreement about the resolutions to be moved on Saturday? If we don't, we shall find ourselves landed with a string of rubbish about disarmament, truces of God, and the like, devised by Stead, and profoundly disbelieved in by all of us. I will move an amendment sooner than have all that stuff of the Tzar's (which he now repudiates, by the way—so Massingham tells me), rammed down our throats. I strongly object to making Queensberry rules for war: what I *do* believe in is a combination of the leading powers to police the world and put down international war just as private war is put down. The only thing that is not ridiculous in the Tzar's proposals is the international tribunal part. It is no use having the meeting at all unless it is sensible and unanimous. The speakers ought to meet and settle what they mean to support. Yours sincerely,

G. Bernard Shaw.[1]

Founder of the weekly *War against War*, and correspondent at the

[1] 24 January 1899, unpublished (C.D.B.A.).

Hague conference, Stead tried to stiffen opinion against the Boer War by a pamphlet called *Shall I Slay my Brother Boer?*, published that same year. Next year he published a second pamphlet, *Methods of Barbarism*, denouncing the rape and extortion of which the English had been guilty in the Transvaal, according to him.

Stead certainly wrote in good faith, but founded his remarks on hearsay; Conan Doyle had the advantage over him of having been in South Africa and talked to hundreds of soldiers. He believed that Stead's accusations were baseless and that it was his duty to refute them. This was how he came to write his pamphlet on the origins and conduct of the war, *The War in South Africa: its Cause and Conduct*. He wrote to his mother:

> I don't think you will resent my pamphlet 'The Cause and Conduct of the War' for it attacks no one else but only defends ourselves and our own methods and especially the soldiers who have behaved beautifully and been most cruelly slandered. There is no word too harsh to apply to such a man as Stead who safe at home concocts the most outrageous and false charges against them. I collect all the evidence in one small book which shall be sold at 6*d*. and translated and circulated in every European country.

On 7 January 1902 Conan Doyle was invited to one of Sir Henry Thompson's famous 'octave' dinners,[1] and while in London he read accounts in the newspapers of protestation-meetings in Germany against British 'atrocities' in South Africa. A few hours later he was calling on the man best suited to help him realise his plan: Eric Barrington, private secretary to the Marquis of Lansdowne, recently appointed Foreign Secretary and later one of the chief creators of the Entente Cordiale. He had formerly been Secretary of State for War. Next day Barrington informed Conan Doyle that the War Office archives were at his disposal, and introduced him to Colonel Altham, head of Military Intelligence. John Reginald Smith undertook the publication and distribution of the pamphlet in England and Europe. Conan Doyle set to work on it at once, and got *The Times* to print an appeal to the public to contribute towards the expenses of translating it into various languages. By the time he had finished writing it on 17 January about a £1,000 had come in—to an appreciable extent from Englishmen living abroad, or foreigners living in England, particularly Norwegians. Conan Doyle cherished

[1] The eminent surgeon gave dinners of eight courses to eight people at eight o'clock.

for many years the feeling that on this occasion he had acted in accordance with the inexpressed wishes of the majority. In 1906 he wrote: '. . . . Among all the great ground landlords of London, drawing their huge unearned increments, I cannot trace one who supported an attempt to state his country's case, while my desk was filled with the postal orders of humble citizens.'[1]

The proofs were issued by Smith, Elder and Co. on 21 January and a copy was sent to Barrington. On the 25th, Edward VII discreetly sent him a personal contribution of £500.

Conan Doyle had been presented to him the year before, in March 1901, a few weeks after the death of Queen Victoria. He described the occasion in a letter to his mother: 'He asked that I should be placed next to him. He proved an able, clearheaded, positive man, rather inclined to be noisy, very alert, and energetic. He won't be a dummy king. He will live to be 70, I should say'.[2]

This 'pamphlet' of about 60,000 words begins with theories already set out in *The Great Boer War*, about the origins of the war and the responsibilities for the outbreak; but Conan Doyle soon came to the question of accusations brought against the army and the British government for their treatment of civilians. He made no attempt to deny that this was cruel, total war, nor that a considerable number of farms had been burned. However this was not a case of systematic destruction but of measures decided upon and carried out according to article 21 of the Hague Convention, for purely military reasons, as Field-Marshal Roberts had pointed out in his message of 2 September to General Louis Botha: 'The orders I had at present issued, to give effect to these views, are that the farm nearest the scene of any attempt to injure the line or wreck the train is to be burnt, and that all farms within a radius of ten miles are to be completely cleared of all their stock, supplies, etc.'[3]

But Conan Doyle recognised that, as a result of the desperate character of the conflict, about 250 farms or dwelling-houses had been destroyed for reasons which were open to dispute.

Coming to the question of concentration camps, the pamphlet explained the difficulties for the British authorities of dealing with an influx of refugees which had mounted in the course of less than a

---

[1] 'An Incursion into Diplomacy', *The Cornhill Magazine*, June 1906, p. 8.
[2] Unpublished (C.D.B.A.).
[3] *The War in South Africa*, p. 101.

year from 20,000 to more than 100,000. Conditions of supply and hygiene admittedly were far from satisfactory. But this was still a long way from supporting Stead's accusations. In any case, Conan Doyle suggested, it was better to give shelter to thousands of women and children, even under such precarious conditions, than to leave them to die of starvation or disease in the veldt. He did not make light of the tragic news that hundreds of children had died when an epidemic of measles swept the camps. 'But whatever the immediate cause, the death of these numerous children lies heavy, not upon the conscience, but upon the heart of our nation.'[1]

Next he drew his readers' attention to the plight of English refugees who had also in some cases been received into the camps. The fate of those in the camps at East London and Port Elizabeth, for instance, had been no more enviable than that of the Boers. Conan Doyle quoted more than a dozen eye-witness accounts *in extenso*, from members of the church, civilians and soldiers, English as well as Boers. He took into account a statement signed by about a hundred Boers from the Kroonstad camp and concluded: 'But I cannot believe that any impartial mind can read the evidence without seeing that the British Government was doing its best under difficult circumstances to carry out the most humane plan possible, and that any other must involve consequences from which a civilised nation must shrink.'[2]

On the other hand Conan Doyle protested against the widespread accusations of looting, rape, brutality and using 'dum-dum' bullets made against British troops, and quoted a considerable body of detailed evidence. He also maintained that the Boers had over and over again taken advantage, not only of their recognised position as combatants although not in uniform, but sometimes also of the white flag, and that they had neglected their prisoners of war, murdered an officer, executed and sometimes tortured numerous Kaffirs.

His conclusions confirmed those of *The Great Boer War*, in so far as the political and diplomatic aspects of the post-war period were concerned. Conan Doyle believed in firmness: neither weakness, nor calumnies, nor above all fear of irreconcilable hostility between English and Boers should lead to premature concessions. Thinking of the American Civil War, he wrote: 'It is argued that the bitterness

---

[1] *The War in South Africa*, p. 110.   [2] *Ibid.*, p. 118.

of this struggle will never die out, but history has shown that it is the fights that are fought to an absolute finish which leave the least rancour.'[1]

The most interesting part of the conclusion is given over to a subtle appraisal of international opinion. With the same sort of intuitive understanding of the politics of alliances as was to be shown by Edward VII, he compared the disappointing attitude of Germany with that of France and Russia. Obviously England stood in isolation and without friends in Europe, he declared. But, bearing in mind the historical vicissitudes of Anglo-French relations, how could one hope that France would approve of Great Britain's policy in South Africa? Had not England herself criticised France hastily, excessively and inappropriately at the time of the Dreyfus affair? As for Russia, did such a thing as public opinion exist there? How did her press get its information?

The situation was very different in Germany. Her press was well-informed, her public opinion articulate, and above all she was bound to England by a tradition of mutual understanding; yet it was from this quarter that the most persistent calumnies had been heard. It seemed as though, in spite of formal disavowals, wrote Conan Doyle, the admirable discipline of the German people had been skilfully exploited by the authorities, with some long-term political object in view. And he warned the Germans: 'Very many years must pass before it would be possible for the public to forget and forgive the action of Germany.'[2] Adding, a little further on, the pregnant remarks:

It is not too much to say that five years ago complete defeat by Germany in a European war would have certainly caused British intervention. Public sentiment and racial affinity would never have allowed us to see her really go to the wall. And now it is certain that in our life time no British guinea and no soldier's life would under any circumstances be spent for such an end. That is one strange result of the Boer War, and in the long run it is possible that it may prove not the least important.[3]

One has every right to ask whether Conan Doyle's pamphlet had an influence only on the general public whom he set out to enlighten, or whether official quarters were also affected by it to the extent of

---

[1] *The War in South Africa*, p. 173.
[2] *Ibid.*, p. 175.　　　　　　　　[3] *Ibid.*, p. 177.

entertaining some of its recommendations. Here, as in his History, he advocated a future policy of appeasement rather than vengeance towards Britain's recent enemy.

It is interesting that Conan Doyle had several contacts at this time with Joseph Chamberlain, who invited him to dinner on the very day after the proofs of his pamphlet appeared, 22 January 1902. There were various economic considerations to do with South Africa, which had a bearing upon the policy of appeasement entertained by the Colonial Secretary now that the war was over: 'Already the Orange River Colony pays its own way and the Transvaal is within measurable distance of doing the same. Industries are waking up, and on the Rand the roar of the stamps has replaced that of the cannon. Fifteen hundred of them will soon be at work, and the refugees are returning at the rate of four hundred a week.'[1]

Although it is impossible to determine exactly how much effect Conan Doyle's pamphlet had in diplomatic circles, it is worth noting the coincidence between his views and the policy that was adopted. It is easier to measure the effect it had abroad. For reasons that are easily understood but unnecessary to repeat, Germany was the country that put up most resistance to the circulation of the pamphlet. In Austria, long extracts were published by the *Wiener Tagblatt*, after which a Berlin publisher agreed to distribute it. 20,000 copies of the German translation were distributed, the same number in France and Belgium, 5,000 in Holland, 8,000 in Hungary, 5,000 in Scandinavian countries, 3,000 in Portugal, 10,000 in Spain, 5,000 in Italy and 5,000 in Russia. Sir Frederick St. John, Minister Plenipotentiary at Berne, noted later that Conan Doyle's pamphlet rallied together all England's friends in Europe.[2]

In April 1902 Conan Doyle was notified that he would receive a knighthood in the forthcoming Honours List. This was officially confirmed in a letter from Lord Salisbury dated 20 June. No great lover of decorations, Conan Doyle at first thought of refusing the title, and explained his reasons to his mother with his usual freedom of expression. But in the end 'The Ma'am' overcame her son's obstinacy, though his reluctance found a belated expression in 1925 when Sherlock Holmes 'shortly after the conclusion of the South

---

[1] *The War in South Africa*, p. 173.
[2] Cf. Sir Frederick St. John, *Reminiscences of a Retired Diplomat*, 1906, p. 292.

African War', at 'the latter end of June, 1902', 'refused a knighthood for services which may perhaps some day be described'.[1]

However his interest in public affairs was not in any way affected by his acceptance of a title and his appointment as Deputy Lieutenant of Surrey, and in the period between the wars we find him offering his services to the most varied public causes.

[1] *The Three Garridebs*, HOL. II, p. 1196–7.

Chapter 4

THE PATRIOT: NOBLESSE OBLIGE

The year 1906 was a turning-point in this period of Conan Doyle's life, for it was then that he failed to get into parliament for the second time, and decided once and for all to renounce the temptations of a political career. But we must go back to his first attempt to gain the votes of his fellow-countrymen at the General Election of 1900. Three questions dominated this election: Home Rule, the problems of the Empire and Free Trade; and the figure that eclipsed all others on the political scene was Joseph Chamberlain's. He had never been, nor would he ever be, Prime Minister, but he was the leader of a parliamentary group whose influence had historic importance. In favour of Ireland remaining a part of the United Kingdom and hostile to Home Rule, he was the leader of the Unionists and, in fact, of a great Conservative coalition. There was no appeal against his arbitration. Conan Doyle might be said to be a Unionist by vocation, although his Irish birth and the Doyle family traditions helped him to understand the emotional strength of Irish nationalism. But he had been educated in England and was a peacemaker by nature as well as on rational grounds. Like Chamberlain, he was in favour of Anglo-American union (or as it was called at the time Anglo-Celtic union) on a world scale, and therefore not the man to encourage England and Ireland to separate! With his liking for historical explanations, in about 1896 he began searching Irish history for arguments favouring reconciliation between the two countries. In August 1894, Alfred Perceval Graves asked him to give a few lectures to the Irish Literary Society.[1] It was not until three years later, in March 1897, that Conan Doyle in fact carried out the project and read a very long paper to the members of the society about the 'Wild Geese', or the Irish mercenaries who enlisted with the French army in the eighteenth century.[2] Study of the past should not lead to a breach but to reasonable com-

---

[1] Letter from A. P. Graves to Conan Doyle (C.D.B.A.).
[2] *A History of the Irish Brigades in the Service of France*, MS. published for the first time in *The Irish Times* in 1954.

promise, and an attempt to save everything that could be saved. This, as we know, was Balfour's policy in 1903. Imperial policy and economic problems are of course closely linked. Formerly without a rival as an economic and industrial power, Great Britain was now hoping to find a new equilibrium through tariff reform. Faced with America, Japan and Germany as rivals, she was trying to build the Commonwealth into a political system of world importance. Here again Conan Doyle wholeheartedly approved the projects brilliantly outlined by Chamberlain. The first contact between the two men was, so far as we know, that mentioned in a letter from Chamberlain to Conan Doyle, dated 16 August 1900:

> Dear Doctor Conan Doyle,
>
> You need not fear that any letter from you would be considered an intrusion by me. I am only too glad to have intelligent suggestions and information on which I can depend. In regard to the point you now bring forward, I am quite prepared to agree with you in principle. I do not believe in underpaid men in the highest positions, and I am constantly struggling against the false economy which in many of our colonies would reduce the salaries until the appointments are not possible to men of the character and qualifications required. On the other hand I am very anxious in regard to all permanent officials in South Africa that the salaries shall not be set at an excessive rate, and that our officers shall not consider themselves bound in any way to imitate or to compete with the millionaires and capitalists by whom they are surrounded. The holder of a Government office has thereby a position which many men, I am glad to say, still value more than money. The Permanent Under-Secretary of the Colonial Office, for instance, has only £2,000 a year, which is not half what many bank managers and other important officials in great industrial undertakings can easily obtain. We can never hope to equal the payments made by private firms, and I hope our officials will maintain the traditions of simple as well as of dignified living. This is, of course, not an argument against your suggestion. They ought to be well paid, but at the same time they must be prepared to sacrifice something for the honour of serving the country. At present all appointments in the two Republics are being temporarily made by the military authorities, but the time is, I hope near at hand when a civil administration will be established.
>
> . . . Believe me, yours very faithfully,
> J. Chamberlain.

A few weeks later Conan Doyle was asked by the Unionists to represent them at the October election. On 27 August 1900 he noted in his Journal: 'I am 41. If I miss this election the chances are that it will be seven years before another. That would make me 48. Rather late to begin. So it is now or never.'[1]

Having refused Dundee, he claimed the honour of standing at Stirling against Campbell-Bannerman, the Leader of the Opposition; however Central Edinburgh was finally assigned to him. He was pleased to be standing in his native town, but it was anything but a safe seat! His opponent, George Mackenzie Brown, son of the ex-leader of the Canadian Liberal party, the Hon. George Brown, was a radical who had had a majority of 2,000 votes (or 50% more than the Conservative candidate) at the last election. Brown was ten years younger than Conan Doyle and a member of Nelson's publishing firm; he had powerful local backing. Conan Doyle opened his campaign on 21 September with the energy one would expect of him, and with the impressive oratory that came so easily to him. Wrongly, perhaps, he avoided dealing with purely local matters, thus disappointing some of the miners in the constituency, and took a rather neutral attitude towards fiscal questions, such as land tax, and social or current problems, like control of the sale of alcohol or women's suffrage. He strained every nerve to interest his audience in the problems set out in *The Great Boer War* and his *Cornhill* article: military reform, national defence, the Empire; and he asked his fellow-citizens to show their confidence in the party which had led the nation to victory. To withdraw that confidence, he suggested audaciously, would be to encourage the Boers.

Edinburgh can hardly have felt itself near the front line; none-the-less Conan Doyle succeeded in communicating some of his patriotic ardour to his hearers. A week before polling-day he began against all probabilities to hope he would win a good proportion of the votes, perhaps even a decisive one. On September 27 he wrote to his mother:

Dearest,
   Fighting famously. Six meetings and six long speeches yesterday. I speak in the streets and the people are wonderfully good and nice. All agree that I am making great progress but no one can say if it is enough to wipe out the huge balance against us. If we don't win, we will go very near to it. Thursday is the election. We have a letter which would damn our opponent utterly but I won't let them use it. It is below the belt. Adieu, dearest. I loved your letter to-day (though indeed I have hardly had time to digest it). It is sweet to me to think of J. with your sweet motherly arms round her. The dear soul gets these fits of depression

[1] Unpublished (C.D.B.A.).

(it is her artistic nature), and then her remorse is terrible and she writes, poor soul, as if she had done some awful thing. I never love her more than at such moments. Dearest, I don't know how to thank you for all your goodness to us. I hope my cold did not ever make me an irritable or bad companion. I recognise all your sweetness and goodness.

Your own A.

My hand is *black* with the hands I have shaken. The Porter's description of my meeting yesterday was 'Mun, the perspiration was just runnin down the stair.' It is only 12 o'clock but I have already made two speeches. Everyone says if I win it will be the greatest political thing done in Scotland in our time.

Two days later he was echoing the reactions of the Scottish press, talking of his wildly enthusiastic reception, and soon afterwards of his probable success—unless . . . !

Dearest,
They say this is the fight in Edinburgh which is exciting the people most since the days of Lord Macaulay—it is tremendous. I had the Operetta house packed, they followed me in crowds to the Hotel, Princes Street was blocked, and I had to speak from the steps of the Hotel, I did 14 speeches in 3 days—pretty good! . . .

On 1 October he wrote again: '. . . if things go on I shall not only carry the Central Division but all Edinburgh for the other candidates . . . It looks as if I were sweeping all before me—but there are still three days—May there be no contretemps. It is religion, I fear. But if it rises I shall be as straight as a die. I don't believe in the "vaut une messe" principle.'[1]

The attack came from the quarter he had foreseen. A man called Prenimer, whom he described in his letters and his autobiography as a semi-irresponsible fanatic, placarded the district on polling-day with notices apparently issued by an organisation for the defence of protestantism. Conan Doyle was described on the walls of the polling-booth as a Jesuit agent in disguise, a sort of reincarnation of Guy Fawkes. This last-minute manœuvre produced sufficient confusion in some people's minds to reverse the position. The count did in fact show a gain of 1,500 votes for the Unionists on the last election's figures. But Conan Doyle needed 600 more to be elected. Should he appeal against the result and sue Prenimer or Brown? The question was under discussion for forty-eight hours, after which the party

[1] Unpublished (C.D.B.A.).

decided to give in for tactical reasons. It was worse than a disappointment for Conan Doyle, it was a source of deep discouragement, and
it took all Joseph Chamberlain's powers of persuasion to get him to
stand again in January 1906. But his heart was no longer in it. Faithful to Scotland, the novelist stood this time as candidate for the small
town of Hawick in the Lowlands. The 1900 election had been to some
extent connected in his mind with the Boer War, and if successful he
would have worked hard to secure the acceptance of the ideas put
forward in his writings. But by 1906 patriotic fever had subsided; he
could no longer escape from the purely political aspects of a peace-
time election. He was not a party man by nature nor could he ever
succeed in flattering the electors in words. The 1906 election hinged
on the question of tariff reform. Conan Doyle's feelings about economic problems were like those of many other people, contradictory
to say the least of it. He was far from uninterested in finance and
business, but economic theory inspired him with the same mistrust
and uneasiness that he once felt for mathematics and the exact
sciences, although his gambler's instinct and optimism had led him to
speculate with varying degrees of caution and success. In 1902 he was
on the board of Raphael Tuck and Co., the leading producers of
Christmas cards; it is in this capacity that we find him corresponding
with Bernard Shaw and defending tariff reform as a means to full
employment, against the planned liberalism of the distinguished
Fabian.

In 1903 and 1904 Conan Doyle was preparing a dossier on tariff
reform, and he lectured on the subject several times. He offered his
speeches to Joseph Chamberlain, who thanked him but said that
he could only make limited use of them now that the election was
approaching. He presented himself to the electors of Hawick in
January 1906 in a very different style from that he had adopted in
1900 at Edinburgh. Instead of improvising he spoke from a carefully
composed brief based on local conditions. If there was any incon-
sistence in his arguments it was in the department of social problems.
He returned to some of the doctrines of orthodox liberalism, but refused to accept the concept of the class war, declaring: 'I do not
believe that there is any real antagonism of interests. The prosperity
of one class reflects upon the others.'

Fifteen years later, at the time of the crises which followed the
First World War, Conan Doyle's conservatism was to become more

enlightened, even in some respects revolutionary. Though he never went so far as to wish for a complete revision of Great Britain's economic structure, and always supported tariff reform, which was to triumph at the Ottawa Economic Conference, he admitted the possibility of limited agrarian reform in favour of the small-holder. However his hostility to organised socialism in its more militant forms and his dislike of professional agitators, whether political or revolutionary, always kept him at a safe distance from the Labour Party.

Sir Arthur accepted his second electoral defeat with supreme indifference and never stood for parliament again. From now on he was to take no part in public life—with a single exception! One of Conan Doyle's arguments against revolutionary action in England was its absurdity. Universal suffrage seemed to him an excellent scheme, allowing the millions of electors to express their agreement or discontent constitutionally. One might therefore have supposed that he would be in favour of any enlargement of the electorate, but he never wavered in his antagonism to women's suffrage, He explained his views on the subject during his electoral campaign at Edinburgh in 1900; he was only ready to make an exception in favour of women who were tax-payers. When the suffragette movement entered on its violent phase in 1911, he reacted with comparable violence—although only in words. In an interview published in *The New York American* for 28 May 1914 he declared: 'I can say that if I were a millionaire and strongly opposed to woman suffrage, the simplest way to work against their cause would be to support the militant movement. People are getting tired of all this window smashing, house burning and picture mutilating, and our Government, which is a pretty fair expression of public opinion, has come to the end of its patience.' No wonder the suffragettes several times poured vitriol into his letter-box at Crowborough.

His attitude to the question of votes for women was in contrast to his efforts for their social emancipation. In 1906 a certain number of prominent men, including E. S. P. Haynes, Sir John Cockburn, Sir Clifford Cory, Sir Frederick Pollock, Gilbert Murray and Thomas Hardy, founded a society for the reform of the divorce law—particularly aimed at its systematic unfairness to women. No legislation for divorce had been in existence until 1857, and before that date divorce could only be the result of a parliamentary decision, and procedure so complicated and expensive that it was a very rare occurrence. As a result of social, moral and political developments, the law of 1857 was passed, making divorce legally possible, but on different terms according to whether the plaintiff were husband or wife. A husband could get a divorce simply on the adultery of his wife. But it was not enough for the wife to prove her husband's adultery; she must also show either that her husband had deserted her for an uninterrupted period of two years or else that he had treated her with brutality. The first thing the reformers aimed at was equality before the law. Sir Arthur Conan Doyle was made president of the society, and his tract, *Divorce Law Reform*, was its third publication, appearing in 1909. It resulted in the creation of a Royal Commission of Inquiry under the presidency of Lord Gorell, who had recently acquired nation-wide authority by unravelling the complex case of the Great Eastern Railway Company. The report of Gorell's Commission was signed on 30 January 1912 and published on 2 November. Its chief recommendation, that 'the cause for divorce should be the same between the sexes', had been suggested by Conan Doyle, but it had to wait until 1923 to overcome the opposition of the Church.

As for the other recommendations of the Divorce Law Reform Union,[1] they could not be considered by the Gorell Commission, for reasons connected with the legal status of marriage. But the Commission did retain another of Conan Doyle's suggestions, namely the extension of the right to divorce where either party had been deserted for an uninterrupted period of at least three years. The Gorell Commission's recommendations on this point became law in 1937, after having been set aside in 1923, and rejected by the House of Commons in 1933, 1935 and 1936 successively. But Conan Doyle's pamphlet went much further, and upon less sure ground. He denounced judicial separation as a product of casuistical hypocrisy promoting illegitimate births, and 'a wretched attempt to compromise between the crying

[1] '. . . Any obstinate and incurable form of mania—including dipsomania—should be good cause for divorce . . . Where the doctors certify that lunacy is permanent, or that the drunken habit is ineradicable, a divorce should be granted to the sane and innocent partner. Let it always be remembered in these and other cases that the divorce is only granted upon application. The sufferer need not have it unless he or she wishes. But if it be desired it should be granted . . . Then there is the case of the man or woman whose partner is condemned to a long term of penal servitude. If the spouse be innocent, there is no reason why an invisible felon should for ever dominate his or her life. . . . There remains the question of desertion where the deserter should be heavily punished, but the deserted should not be compelled, as at present, to wait on, year in and year out, for the one who has passed out of sight and may never return.' *Divorce Law Reform*, p. 6.

needs of human life and the objection of the theologians.'[1] Knowing
very well that the stubbornest opposition to any reform of the law
came from the Church, he turned to polemic: 'Every church has a
right which none can deny to prescribe conduct for its own members.
None has the right to enforce views upon the general public. If it
pleases the ecclesiastical mind to consider that our present ethical
customs should be regulated by its own particular interpretation
of certain words uttered two thousand years ago, under absolutely
different social conditions, then that is its own affair.'[2]

It was during the campaign for divorce reform that Conan Doyle
first came into direct conflict with religious doctrine, thus preparing
the way for his choice of spiritualism. As we shall see later, this
seemed to him a hopeful approach to a new morality to take the place
of a formal system that had lost all its original vitality. However that
may be, this new attitude marks a stage in the development of current
ideas on divorce. It may seem old-fashioned to us today. It is certainly strange that, as a doctor, he could not go so far as to see *de facto*
separation as a motive for divorce, that he should not have gone beyond the strictly legal view and realised that this physical breach was
a pathological symptom in a marriage. This view seems to be gaining ground today.

*   *   *   *   *

But in 1909 Conan Doyle became involved in a much more sensational scandal—the situation in the Congo, which had already been
agitating international opinion for several years. This region of Africa
had been explored by Stanley a little before 1880, and afterwards
by Savorgnan de Brazza. While the latter was organising the territory
on the right bank under French control, King Leopold II of the
Belgians founded the International Association of the Congo in the
valley of the lower Congo. The administration of this country five
times as large as France was soon afterwards entrusted by the Congress of Berlin to the King of the Belgians, and in 1885 it became the
Congo Free State under his personal protection. In principle, Leopold
had agreed to allow free navigation of the river, free circulation of
persons and goods, and freedom of work and trade to all without
distinction of nationality, and to refuse monopolies to any individual

---

[1] *Divorce Law Reform*, p. 6.   [2] *Ibid.*, p. 7.

or country whatsoever. However the signatories of the Treaty of
Berlin soon afterwards authorised him to impose a fixed duty of 10%
on imports; Leopold then launched a series of loans in favour of the
Congo, so that first virtually and then legally Belgium became Leopold's successor in the Congo. At the same time a twenty-five years
régime began which was destined to victimise more inhabitants of the
Congo by terror and forced labour than slavery had done throughout
the whole of the nineteenth century in the rest of Africa. In the name
of this legal fiction of a Free State, Leopold II and his government
became in fact sole owners of the land and monopolised the entire
trade. In the name of the Free State the natives were suddenly deprived of all right to trade or cultivate the soil, except under compulsion and for the exclusive profit of the State. Arbitrary standards of
yield for the rubber harvest were imposed on them, and a wave of
brutal ill-treatment and mutilation spread throughout the whole region. The 'astute founder' of the State was all this time pretending to
champion the anti-slavery cause and organising military expeditions
against his rivals the slave-traders in the interior. Little by little,
rumours began to circulate about the state of things in the Congo
under Leopold's administration. But unimpeachable evidence was
hard to come by, public opinion was slow to consolidate, and the European conscience was already loaded with guilt concerning Africa. In
1896, Chamberlain admitted in the House of Commons that there had
been ill treatment of the Negroes from the British colony of Sierra
Leone employed to make a railway in the Congo. Instructions were
given that no more workers should be recruited on British territory.
A few months earlier an Englishman from German East Africa called
Stokes was arrested on Congolese territory on the orders of a
Belgian agent, Captain Lothaire. Stokes was accused, unjustly as it
seems, of being engaged in contraband traffic in arms with the slave-
trading tribes. After an extremely summary trial, Stokes was hanged
and his merchandise seized. The British authorities protested and insisted on an inquiry. Proceedings were brought against Lothaire, but
he was acquitted and even promoted—for in the following year he
was made head of the Antwerp Society for Trade with the Congo.

The Stokes affair was remembered when Roger Casement was
appointed British Consul at Kinchassa, near Leopoldville, in 1900.
Was he given special and detailed instructions or did he act from his
own initiative? In any case, he began to take an interest in the condi-

tions of the Negroes employed in the rubber harvest, and his presence certainly made itself felt, for two months after his nomination he was received by Leopold II in Brussels. It has been said that in the course of an interview lasting nearly two hours the King tried to minimise the abuses committed in the Free State or even to buy Casement's silence. In Liverpool at about the same time, Edmund Morel, the agent of a shipping line with connections in Central Africa, launched a humanitarian movement in favour of the Congolese with the support of *The West African Mail*. Returning to the Congo, Casement travelled up and down the river valley sending back voluminous reports to London; he met Morel and founded the Congo Reform Association, and in November 1903 he came to London, having sent forty-three reports to the Foreign Office since the beginning of his investigation. These reports recorded tortures, summary executions and particularly mutilations, and described the terrorisation of the Congolese by the whites under conditions of forced labour. Often working chained together, men, women and children died of starvation or misery. Casement thought it best to take action simultaneously through the official route and the Congo Reform Association, on behalf of which he made contact with several writers—Gilbert Parker, Anthony Hope, Joseph Conrad (who entertained him at Hythe on 3 January 1904) and Conan Doyle.

On 15 February the British government published a report on the Congo, mainly founded on Casement's account of his journey from Boma to Matadi between June and September 1903. The report was widely circulated, and was sent to Brussels and the governments of a dozen European nations: it was the first diplomatic step towards the abolition of Leopold II's régime. From an understandable desire to justify himself, the King of the Belgians appointed a Commission of Inquiry to investigate Casement's evidence. The British Secretary of State for Foreign Affairs, Lord Lansdowne, who had called for the Commission, wanted it to be truly international; but Leopold decided otherwise, and chose the three members himself. They were Jannsens, a Belgian lawyer; Dr. Schumacher, a Swiss, and Baron Nisco, an Italian member of the administration of the Congo Free State. The British government asked Leopold to appoint a British member, but by the time the King agreed, the other members of the Commission had already been on the spot for several months and their task was nearly finished. After hearing the evidence of missionaries and village chiefs, they were received in audience by Costermans, the Governor-General at Boma, the capital of the Free State. Was there any connection between this meeting and the fact that the Governor committed suicide next day? Why was the Commission's report not published until a year later, and why did it set so little store by the evidence collected? Of course it was favourable to the King, but it failed to assuage international mistrust, nor did it silence the voices beginning to be raised in Belgium, such as that of the Socialist deputy Vandervelde, against a régime that was becoming more and more cynical and cruel.

In 1908 Leopold II made a show of satisfying his critics by putting the administration of the Congo Free State in the hands of the Belgian government. This change did not lead to any immediate or genuine reforms; in fact it kept the scandalous state of affairs going for a while. The hand-over of power had taken place without any international agreement, as if it were a private matter between the King and Belgium. Sir Edward Grey, who had discreetly but firmly encouraged the Belgian government to assume responsibility for Congolese affairs, was disappointed not to see the hoped-for reforms enforced, and sent a despatch to Belgium asking for immediate measures to be taken. Not only did his action fail to do any good, but it displeased the Belgians and weakened Great Britain's position in Europe on the eve of the Bosnian-Herzegovinian crisis.

This was the state of affairs when the ever-vigilant Congo Reform Association set about redoubling its efforts, and when Conan Doyle met Edmund Morel in London, in the summer of 1909. Sir Arthur asked how he could help the cause of reform, offered to write upon the subject, and agreed to speak on behalf of the Association. Morel described this meeting in a letter to St. John Adcock:

> ... I came away deeply stirred by the magnetism of his personality, touched and grateful. Here was a friend, indeed! And right well did he prove it in the days that were to come. I pitched all my voluminous scribblings at his head and he set himself to master every detail of a most complicated and protracted struggle. For a couple of weeks hardly a day passed without a letter from him. Then, when he had probed the whole thing to the bottom, he shut himself up in his study and worked like a demon, hardly giving himself time to shave, as he put it. He wrote the book right off in a week. "I finished my book today: 45,000 words in eight days, one of which I spent in London. I think it is about a record."

Thus *The Crime of the Congo* came to be written.

Nothing remains of the correspondence between Conan Doyle and Kipling at this time, except a somewhat prophetic letter from Kipling showing that there was widespread anxiety lest Germany should take up the cudgels against Great Britain, if she adopted too firm an attitude towards Belgium:

> Bateman's, Burwash, Sussex.
> Aug. 29, '09.

Dear Doyle,

I knew you were keen on the state of affairs in the Congo, which is pretty bad and I am sure that what you write will wake people up. But the way I see it is that we haven't anything resembling an efficient army *or* a navy to back up our representations with; and if England goes into the Congo business, isn't she liable to lay herself open to the humiliation of having her bluff called? Neither France nor Russia are able to help us and if Belgium chooses to tell us to mind our own affairs (with a few nasty remarks about India thrown in), what can we do? It seems to me we are then opening a very awkward European situation with neither the means, nor (if I know the Radical party), the intention of doing anything. Then, isn't it possible that Germany might fold her protective wings round Belgium—same as the Austrian game a few months ago—and pose, not without advantage to herself, as Protector of oppressed nationalities? Belgium mightn't like it—we certainly shouldn't, but the rest would be a simple sum in arithmetic of men, guns and efficient boats. International guarantees aren't worth the paper they're written on when Germany edits the text.

Your book will rouse up the public to what is being done in the Congo, and then, let us hope they will realize that they must have armed power to make their justice effective. And *you* can make that clear to them—more power to your elbow.

> Yours sincerely as always,
> Rudyard Kipling.[1]

After some hesitation, Kipling declined to follow Conan Doyle, in spite of receiving from him a copy of Morel's *The Future of the Congo*:

> Bateman's, Burwash, Sussex.
> Sep. 5, 1909.

Dear Doyle,

I sent Morel's book back. It's a fairly black record and from what I've heard elsewhere, one that it would be difficult to disprove and not easy to deny. (. . .) doesn't seem to be as 'handy' a man as our friend Leopold. *Per contra*, if it comes to doing anything, the whole crux of

[1] Unpublished (C.D.B.A.).

the business is our Navy. The more one examines it and goes into things, the more is one convinced that even now (and I believe our Government knows it), we are in no shape to stand up to Germany on the sea. On land, of course, if it comes to fighting over Belgium (for the fifth time), we haven't an earthly. Where we should be by the time this row became ripe, I don't like to think. That's why I am frightened at possibilities; but I wish you'd look into this Navy business and reassure me.[1]

While writing his book for the Congo Reform Association, Conan Doyle took several other steps. On 13 August he wrote to President Roosevelt and received a reply from the Secretary of State, Robert Bacon:

> Department of State, Washington, File N° 1806/613,
> August 31, 1909.
>
> Sir,
> I have to acknowledge the receipt of your letter of the 13th instant, addressed to the President in regard to the condition of affairs in the Congo and the coming trial of Mr. Morrison, an American missionary in that country. In reply I have to say that your communication is appreciated and that Consul General Handley had already been instructed in the suggested lines and authorized to employ counsel to advise him in watching the proceedings.
> I am, Sir,
>
> Your obedient servant,
> [signature, A.A.A.]
> acting Secretary of State.[2]

He also wrote to the Kaiser and to various newspapers, and sent a circular letter to sixty American papers:

> Aug. 27, 1909.
>
> Sir,
> There are many of us in England who consider the crime which has been wrought in the Congo lands by King Leopold of Belgium and his followers to be the greatest which has ever been known in human annals. Personally I am strongly of that opinion. There have been great expropriations like that of the Normans in England or of the English in Ireland. There have been massacres of populations like that of the South Americans by the Spaniards, or of subject nations by the Turks. But never before has there been such a mixture of wholesale expropriation and wholesale massacre, all done under an odious guise of philanthropy, and with the lowest commercial motives as a reason. It is this sordid cause, and the unctuous hypocrisy which make the crime unparalleled in its horror.

[1] Unpublished (C.D.B.A.).   [2] *Ibid.*

The witnesses of the crime are of all nations and there is no possibility of error concerning the facts. There are British Consuls like Casement, Thesiger, Mitchell and Armstrong, all writing in their official capacity with every detail of fact and date. There are Frenchmen like Pierre Mille and Félicien Challaye, both of whom have written books upon the subject. There are Missionaries of many races, Harris, Weeks and Shannard (British), Morrison, Clark, Shepherd (American), Sjoblom (Swedish), Father Veermersch, the Jesuit. There is the eloquent action of the Italian government who refused to allow Italian officers to be employed any longer in such hangman's work, and there is the report of the Belgian Commission, the evidence before which was suppressed because it was too dreadful for publication. Finally there is the incorruptible evidence of the Kodak. Any American Citizen who will glance at Mark Twain's 'King Leopold's Soliloquy' will see some samples of that. A perusal of all these sources of information will show that there is not a grotesque, obscene or ferocious torture which diseased human ingenuity could invent which has not been used against these harmless and helpless people.

This would, to my mind, warrant an intervention in any case.

Turkey has several times been intervened with simply on the general ground of humanity. But there is in this instance a very special reason why America and England should not stand by and see these people done to death. They are in a sense their wards. America was the first to give official recognition to King Leopold's enterprise in 1884, and so has the responsibility of having actually put him into that position which he has since so dreadfully abused. She has been the indirect and innocent cause of the whole tragedy. Surely some reparation is due. On the other hand England has, with the other European powers, signed the treaty of 1885, by which each and all of them makes itself responsible for the condition of the native races. The other powers have so far shown no desire to live up to this pledge. But the conscience of England is uneasy and she is slowly rousing herself to act. Will America be behind? At this moment two American citizens, Shepherd and that noble Virginian Morrison, are about to be tried at Boma for telling the truth about these scoundrels. Morrison in the dock makes a finer Statue of liberty than Bartholdi's in New York Harbour. Attempts will be made in America (for the Congo has its paid apologists everywhere), to pretend that England wants to oust Belgium from her Colony and take it herself. Such accusations are folly. To run a tropical colony honestly without enslaving the natives is an expensive process. For example Nigeria, the nearest English colony, has to be subsidised to the extent of 2,000,000 dollars a year. Who ever takes over the Congo will, considering its present demoralised condition, have a certain expense of ten million dollars a year for twenty years. Belgium has not run the Colony. It has simply sacked it, forcing the inhabitants without pay to ship off everything of value to Antwerp.

No decent European power could do this. For many years to come the Congo will be a heavy expense and it will truly be a Philanthropic call upon the next owner. I trust it will not fall to England.

Attempts have been made too (for there is considerable ingenuity and unlimited money on the other side) to pretend that it is a question of Protestant missions against Catholic. Anyone who thinks this should read the book (*La Question congolaise*) of the eloquent and holy Jesuit Father Vermeersch. He lived in the Country and, as he says, it was the sight of the 'immeasurable misery' which drove him to write.

We English who are earnest over this matter look eagerly to the Westward to see some sign of moral support or material leading. It would be a grand sight to see the banner of humanity and Civilisation carried forward in such a cause by the two great English-speaking nations.

Yours faithfully,
Arthur Conan Doyle.[1]

When his book was published, he personally sent copies to influential people in England or America. Among the more interesting replies, Winston Churchill's may be quoted:

Board of Trade, Whitehall Gardens
5 Oct.

Dear Sir Arthur Conan Doyle,
    I am very glad you have turned your attention to the Congo. I will certainly do what I can to help you as opportunity offers. There are rumours in the newspapers today. I hope they are well founded—that we are to have a British Consul General at Berlin! In any case a change is being made.

Yours truly,
Winston S. Churchill.[2]

Conan Doyle had hardly had time to arrange for German and French translations when he started preparing the lectures on the Congo he had promised Morel. He gave nine of these: in London, on 29 October and 19 November, at Newcastle and Plymouth on 8 and 18, then at Hull, Liverpool, Edinburgh and Manchester. His last lecture was at Brighton on 12 December. His greatest successes were at Newcastle and Liverpool. At Liverpool, where the movement had begun, he spoke to an audience of 5,000. His second London lecture was at the Albert Hall and presided over by the Archbishop of Canterbury. Wanting to include all religions, he invited the Archbishop of Westminster, Cardinal Bourne, to join the Committee. But

---

[1] Unpublished (C.D.B.A.).   [2] *Ibid.*

the Cardinal had been educated at the University of Louvain and was above all anxious to avoid any trouble with the Belgian clergy, so after a long period of hesitation he told Conan Doyle that he disapproved of the Association's activities.[1] Conan Doyle was often criticised for the violence of his language about the Congo. 'There are times when violence is a duty' he replied.[2] It must be admitted that there are passages in *The Crime of the Congo* which partly explain the Cardinal's hostile attitude. Reproaching the Catholic Church for failing in its secular duties by its silence about the Congolese atrocities, he invoked the example of Bartolomé de Las Casas. He did however succeed in getting the support of the Duke of Norfolk, who had infinitely more influence both in England and abroad than the Cardinal.

Up till the middle of 1910 he was hard at work for the Association: we find him in July trying to get support from the Privy Council through the intermediacy of Lord Cromer, and he approached the press through his friend Blumenfeld, Editor of the *Daily Express*. There can be no doubt that his various activities had a considerable effect in hastening reforms.

> Conan Doyle's intervention at that time exercised a decisive influence on the course of events [wrote Morel]. It provided the best antidote possible to the reactionary influences at work against us. It effectually prevented the most fatal of all diseases to a movement of this sort, public lassitude. Yet it was not his book—excellent as it was, nor his manly eloquence on the platform, nor the influence he wielded in rallying influential men to our cause, which helped us most. It was just the fact that he was—Conan Doyle; and that he was with us. I do not think any other man but Conan Doyle could have done for the cause

[1] Cf. the correspondence between Conan Doyle and Francis Bourne, published both in *The Tablet* and *The Times*. On 30 October 1909 the Archbishop wrote:
'My dear Sir,—I have delayed acknowledging your letter of the 15th, and thanking you for your book which accompanied it in order to be able to find time to read what you have written. Now that I have done so, though naturally in somewhat hurried moments, you must pardon me if I say that the perusal has strengthened me in my distrust of the methods of the Congo Reform Association, and in my reluctance to see Catholics identified with it in any way. I have sufficient knowledge of, and confidence in, the Bishops and other authorised leaders of public opinion in Belgium to feel assured that they have taken, and will continue to take, all legitimate means to bring about such reforms as have been shown to be necessary. The fact that men in their responsible position are disinclined to hold public meetings and refrain from proclaiming their opinions or their actions in loud and exaggerated tones on the housetops is, in my judgment, no proof that they fail to perceive or neglect to perform their duty. I am not prepared to play the impertinent part of being their critic. The meeting which it is proposed to hold in the Albert Hall seems to me most inopportune, and very unfair both to our own Government and to that of Belgium.'
[2] Quoted by W. S. Adams in *Edwardian Portraits*, 1957, p. 198.

just what Conan Doyle did at that time. Now that we are nearing the end of a long fight, he shares in our satisfaction and makes light of his own efforts in those critical years, 1909–10. Of his generous friendship to myself, I can only say that the memory of it will never fade.[1]

[1] Letter to A. St. John Adcock, *The Bookman*, November 1912, p. 97.

Chapter 5

THE PATRIOT: THE GREAT WAR

Whether it was a question of the Boer War in 1900, or the Congolese atrocities in 1909, Conan Doyle was always careful to keep the American public informed, and eager that they should understand his motives. This was an instinctive reaction: he knew, without any trace of vanity, that he was one of the English writers best known and most popular in America. He made use of this fact in his civic and political activities, objectively and with some adroitness. A fortunate combination of circumstances had linked him with two countries that were to become closer to England in the course of the twentieth century: the United States and France. He was destined to play a part in this rapprochement. As we shall see when we come to his literary career, Conan Doyle was one of the first British writers to be inspired and enriched by American literary traditions. Bret Harte and Poe were his models, and for Poe in particular he felt unqualified admiration. Early in 1909 he presided at the celebration of the centenary of Edgar Allan Poe's birth. What was perhaps most striking and important about his attitude to the United States when he first went there in 1894, was his implicit or expressed admiration of their ancient and specifically American culture and traditions. There is no trace of cultural superiority in his comments, although this was a common tendency among Europeans at the time, especially in literary circles. On the contrary, speaking at the Lotos Club in November, he said:

> . . . It is only when a great American or Englishman dies, when a mighty voice is hushed for ever, a Tennyson, a Lowell, or a Holmes, that a thrill through both countries tells of that deep-lying race feeling in the development of which lies, I believe, the future history of the world . . . And the proudest thought of a literary man is that he, too, in his infinitesimal way, is one of the forces which make for unity of feeling amongst the English-speaking races, and for that 'peace and good-will to all men' which such a unity of feeling would entail . . .[1]

[1] Quoted by J. B. Pond in *Eccentricities of Genius*, 1901, p. 503.

His letters to his mother show us what genuine sympathy he felt for the Americans, and that he found two virtues in them that he particularly appreciated: tolerance and optimism. His books also testify to this sympathy, as well as to his hopes for a political and cultural fusion of the two races. As for the Americans, they saw him as an Englishman after their own hearts, and adopted not only his books (after all it was an American, William Gillette, who brilliantly launched Sherlock Holmes on the stage in 1899), but also his personality, his love of sport and fair play. Conan Doyle enjoyed the company of a group of men of American birth or descent who were serving the cause of Anglo-American friendship round about 1900 —men such as William Waldorf Astor, Winston Churchill and Arthur Lee. Like them he was one of the founders of the Pilgrims' Club, and did honour to the fellowship between the English-speaking races in glowing terms:

> It is a wonderful work in which we and others are engaged; and if one ventures to cast one's thought on the future of the English people, one is lost, not only in pride, but, most of all, in the sense of responsibility. For it is so obvious that the future of the world lies in our hands. If you take the two flags—the flag of St. George, with all the multitudes who dwell beneath its folds, and take the flag of that other George— George Washington, it is not too much to say that now almost one half of the human race is to be found under one or the other; nearly 500,000,000 is the gigantic total of those who live under those two flags; and when one thinks of such a fact as that, it is not, surely, an exaggeration to say that the future of the world lies especially in the hands of those who, realising their responsibilities, attempt to do away with every jealousy, with every cause of friction, and to cause those vast forces to work on towards one end, as the bodyguard of civilization, and as the guarantee of the future peace of the earth.[1]

His writings and thoughts aroused a response in bolder and more farsighted American minds. In 1909, a young officer in the American Army, who foresaw the coming conflict with Japan for dominance of the Pacific from his garrison in North Dakota, wrote to Conan Doyle to tell him of his enthusiasm for *The History of the Boer War*, and also of his belief in British Military virtues:

> . . . I have only just finished reading the final complete edition of your splendid *History of the Great Boer War* and my enthusiasm for the work and its purpose is so great that I cannot refrain from attempting

[1] Speech at the Pilgrims' Club banquet, 24 June 1912.

to express it personally to you (. . .) I have read that in certain German Army messes there is a toast drunk to 'the Great Day', the day when English military and naval supremacy shall have been supplanted by the triumphs of the Teutonic arms. If your generals, subalterns, and troopers still retain the wonderful courage and patriotism which they showed on the veldt in 1901–1902, then this day is, indeed, far distant, or, indeed, a dream which will be long in realisation. Let us hope that when our Great Day arrives, the terrible day of which we speak as yet only in whispers, the Day when we measure our arms with the victors of Mukden and Tsushima for the supremacy of the Pacific, we prove ourselves as worthy of our cause as did the men who died in South Africa for the Empire . . .[1]

Nothing could possibly have given Conan Doyle more pleasure than such a tribute. Ever since 1903, when there had been talk of his revisiting America, Theodore Roosevelt had expressed a desire to see him. The opportunity came in 1910, after Edward VII's funeral, when Arthur Lee invited him to meet the President and a party of journalists. Conan Doyle notes in his diary that Roosevelt felt encouraged by him to preach the advantages of a 'big stick' policy in Egypt at an official reception:

> . . . In May 1910 I met Theodore Roosevelt at lunch just after the King's funeral. There were present Arthur Lee (our host), Mrs. Lee, Mr., Mrs., Miss, and Kermit Roosevelt, Buckle of The Times, Maxse of the National Review, Seaman of Punch, and Sidney Brooke, a journalist (. . .) He asked me whether I thought Britishers would resent it if he gave them a lecture on their conduct in Egypt when he got his reception in a few days at the Guildhall. I said 'no'. Sure enough he gave a fine address, the point being 'you must either govern or clear out'. As he passed me in leaving the Mansion House (Guildhall), he said, 'What did you think of that?'[2]

Conan Doyle's second visit to the United States took place on the eve of the Great War, and he was accompanied by his second wife, Jean, whom he had married in September 1907, a little more than a year after the death of Louise. On their way to Canada the Conan Doyles received an enthusiastic ovation in New York, the national anthem was played in their honour, and Conan Doyle's old acquaintance Joseph Hodges Choate, former United States ambassador in London, introduced him as 'the best known living Britisher'.[3] At

[1] Letter from 2nd Lieut. C. W. Elliott, unpublished (C.D.B.A.).

[2] Unpublished (C.D.B.A.).

[3] Letter from Conan Doyle to Lily Loder-Symonds, 5 June 1914, unpublished (C.D.B.A.).

the moment when these words were being uttered, the mission of goodwill that Conan Doyle had been carrying out for more than twenty years was taking on a political significance whose importance has been, and still is underestimated. In Canada he was the official guest of the government, and had a chance to see the scenery that he had dreamt about ever since reading the works of Parkman, the historian. He went to stay at the national reserve of Jasper Park, made a trip to the Great Lakes and journeyed from one end of the country to the other in the special train placed at his disposal. There was one moment however when he may have disappointed some of the journalists who set upon him wherever he went: losing his usual presence of mind when asked what he thought of the suffragettes, he announced without hesitation that in this exceptional case he was in favour of lynching!

Conan Doyle's frequently reaffirmed sympathy with the United States can be considered as one aspect of his battle against prejudice and accepted ideas. From whatever side one approaches his personality and his work, it is clear that this Conservative traditionalist was above all a free and independent thinker and an idealist. Where divorce was concerned he stood for the individual and for personal dignity; in the Congo affair he wanted to infuse moral ideals into the colonial imperialism of Europe; and, as we shall see later, a miscarriage of justice was worse than crime in his eyes.

The same principle that dictated his feelings for America controlled his attitude to France, a country sometimes roughly treated by English public opinion. At first sight it seems as if this insular Celt might find it hard to make contact with France: was he not constantly saying that language and race were the only true links between men and nations? Yes indeed he was, and rather than betray his theory, he translated the ties of language and race in a very personal and somewhat mystical way in all his dealings with France. We have already seen that there was a traditional admiration for the French language and art on both sides of the family, that Mary Doyle had been educated in France and Michael Conan had spent more than half his life there. But although Froissart and Jules Verne were among the first books Conan Doyle read, and although he read a great many French books all his life, he only paid very brief visits to France, except during the Great War, and his contacts with the French language and people were few and far between. We do not know how well he spoke French, but it seems probable that, like his contemporary and friend Winston Churchill, it was with more enthusiasm than grammatical correctness. However the language was no real barrier between Conan Doyle and France. It was during the Franco-Prussian War that he first heard current affairs in France discussed. The war concerned the Doyle family closely. At the time of the invasion of France, Conan Doyle's sister Lottie was spending her holidays with the Conans, and she escaped from the siege of Paris with them to take refuge at Dieppe. Letters describing the ordeal of the French people were sent on by the Doyles to Arthur at school at Stonyhurst. It is not therefore surprising to find in Conan Doyle's writings a flattering and idealised image of France, which reached an immense public through the Sherlock Holmes cycle, the historical novels or the short stories:

> The land of France!—the very words sounded as the call of a bugle in the ears of the youth of England. The land where their fathers had bled, the home of chivalry and of knightly deeds, the country of gallant men, of courtly women, of princely buildings, of the wise, the polished and the sainted. There it lay, so still and grey beneath the drifting wrack— the home of things noble and of things shameful—the theatre where a new name might be made or an old one marred.[1]

As might have been expected, Conan Doyle passed this attitude on to his family and took steps to see that his children went to France as soon as possible. Mary Louise visited Paris in the spring of 1905 and her reaction to the museums and the Château of Versailles was expressed in the identical words used by her great-uncle, Richard Doyle, at the same age: 'What is there more fascinating than French history?'[2]

It goes without saying that the Doyles did not share the wave of francophobia which shook England for several months after the Fashoda affair. Mary Doyle wrote indignantly to her son about the anti-French propaganda she found in her *Daily Mail*:

> . . . Quite by mistake I subscribed—for only three months happily— to a dismal paper, dear, at a halfpenny, called the *Daily Mail*; its vulgar attitude to other countries, especially France, is simply odious; they now say 'Every one, particularly of the working class, in France, detests the English'. This is not true, no nation should be so judged by the scum or froth that rises to the surface in the baser parts of the daily

[1] *The White Company*, HIS., p. 192.
[2] Letter from Mary Louise Conan Doyle to her father, unpublished (C.D.B.A.).

press, but certainly if the *Daily Mail* is read in France, they must think us a very vulgar, boastful and swaggering sort of idiots, quite the extreme reverse of what we really are . . .[1]

This was the moment Conan Doyle chose to propose that what seemed to him a permanent insult to France should be brought to an end, and Nelson's anniversary be celebrated not on 21 October, the date of the battle of Trafalgar, but on the national hero's birthday. Admirable though this suggestion was, it might have been a little absurd had not Anglo-French relations been at the time rather strained; and it was in fact a way of protesting against a state of things for which Conan Doyle held his compatriots partly responsible. The proposal was not greeted with a chorus of approval, nor had he expected it. In spite of the sometimes heated protests it aroused, Conan Doyle went on inviting his fellow-countrymen to return to the objective attitude without which the alliance of Edward VII's reign would have been impossible.

Conan Doyle was of course in the front rank of those who were trying to interpret the Entente Cordiale in deeds, and his chance came in the summer of 1905. After a courtesy visit to the naval base at Spithead, Admiral Caillard and his officers were officially received in London. They told the Admiralty that they would like to meet Conan Doyle. Why? Because Sherlock Holmes and imitations of him (the most popular of which were by Maurice Leblanc) had created an image of Conan Doyle as a sort of British Alexandre Dumas. One might go so far as to say that the personality that emerged from his books has been ever since for most Frenchmen a part of their picture of England. The Admiralty probably understood his value as a friendly ambassador, and Sir Charles Thomas asked him if he would receive the French officers. Conan Doyle asked nothing better! Music, flags, flowers, but above all the beaming face of their host gave the Frenchmen the sort of cordial welcome that no official occasion could have provided so happily.[2]

There can be no question that during the first twenty years of the century his influence behind the scenes of politics was greater than is

---

[1] N.d. (C.D.B.A.).

[2] '. . . The big bluff man struck them as "un vrai Anglais", and a welcome from a "vrai Anglais" was dear to their hearts. He, too, struck the right chord. Nothing impressed the French officers so much as the Hindhead trip. It outshone Westminster Hall. "The best has been the last", they said, and undoubtedly Hindhead was cumulative.' *The Daily Chronicle*, 22 August 1905.

generally known, as his notes and correspondence with Chamberlain, Balfour, Churchill and Lloyd George all go to show. We have seen too, that the Boer War did not so much awaken his interest in military matters as increase and give scope to it. His military history and his articles in the press had helped promote reforms, even if they did not originate them.

In 1904 Balfour instituted the Army Council, an advisory body which in practice replaced the office of Commander-in-Chief and allowed a more flexible functioning of military administration. The Command was from now on divided among several generals. These measures were the prelude to the creation of the Committee of Imperial Defence, generally considered as Balfour's most important and original achievement. This was the exact moment when Conan Doyle was introduced to Balfour at the house of Lord Burnham, owner of *The Daily Telegraph*. The introduction was an unconventional one. Opening the door of one of the bath-rooms by mistake, the Prime Minister saw before him the gigantic frame of the novelist, impressively swathed in bath-towels:

> Lord Burnham's hobby was Turkish baths, and he had an excellent one in the front of the house, the drying-room being the first door on the right as one entered, and being a simple sitting-room as far as appearance went. With his usual kind hospitality Lord Burnham had urged me to try his bath, and having done so I was placed, arrayed in a long towel, and with another towel screwed round my head, in the drying-room. Presently the door opened, and entered Arthur Balfour, Prime Minister of England. He knew nothing of the house and its ways, and I can remember the amazement with which he gazed at me. Lord Burnham following at his heels introduced me, and I raised the towel on my head. There were no explanations, and I felt that he went away with the impression that this was my usual costume.[1]

In September 1906 Balfour invited Conan Doyle to spend a week-end at Wittingham, with Lord Roberts as fellow-guest. The military reforms under consideration by Campbell-Bannerman's government must have been the main topic of conversation. Conan Doyle's efforts to start rifle clubs all over the country in 1900 had borne fruit, and they were now a federation with Lord Roberts as president. 1906 was also a turning-point in British military politics; after conversations with the French the nation was now resolutely rearming. Two distinct forces came into being, following the principles laid

[1] AUT., pp. 285-6.

down by Conan Doyle in the last chapters of his military history. On
one hand Haldane raised a mobile active force, which by 1912 was
100,000 strong (the 'contemptible' little army). On the other, the
volunteer members of the rifle clubs were organised and trained so as
to form an effective secondary reserve force or territorial army.
Conan Doyle saw these as the descendents of the yeomen, or free
archers of medieval warfare. There is no doubt that Lord Roberts
considered Conan Doyle as something of a military expert, and was
as anxious to get him to contribute to a magazine he had founded as
to support the cause of compulsory military service:

> January 8th, 1913.
> Dear Sir Arthur—We are making a special effort to bring the question
> of National Service to the front, and I am glad to say that we are
> making real headway at last. We are organising a series of meetings,
> and I have promised to speak at several of them. I need hardly say
> how pleased I should be to have you as an ally in my campaign; and
> I should like to send one of my organisers to you, to give you a
> sketch of our plans, and proposed activities. Will you please let me
> know when and where it may be convenient for you to receive my
> organiser?
>
> Yours very truly,
> Roberts, F.M.[1]

But Sir Arthur remained faithful to the voluntary system, and it
took two wars before compulsory service won the day—too late
and probably in vain. Rearmament was not the only, nor the most
significant issue in Conan Doyle's view; a new weapon had appeared
which seemed likely to alter everything and whose eventual importance he understood very well: the submarine. How could there be
any urgent need to arrange military manœuvres between Calais and
Valenciennes if a flotilla of German submarines were to block the
passage of the English Channel to British troops as soon as war was
declared? We know how crucial the question of communications was
to become in both world wars, and that victory went twice to the side
which succeeded in keeping its communications intact. But Conan
Doyle was in advance of his time when, aware of this vital fact, he
clamoured for a Channel tunnel.

Just as his own Sherlock Holmes might have done, he was quick
to spot the signs of an approaching war with Germany. During the
summer of 1911 he took part in a rally of motor-cars organised by

[1] (C.D.B.A.)

Prince Henry of Prussia, and so happened to be in the Rhineland at the time of the Agadir incident.

> On the morning of the 8th July 1911, the inward bound *Norddeutscher* Lloyd boat *Der Grosse Kurfürst* steamed slowly up Spithead . . . Two passengers were leaning against the rail of the boat-deck, deep in conversation, when a voice broke in: 'Have you heard the news: The *Panther* is at Agadir!' Turning to me, Conan Doyle—for he and I were the passengers in question—said: 'Yes, it does look fishy, I admit there may after all be something in what you say, but personally I don't think you're right.' The subject of our conversation had been Anglo-German relations, and it had arisen from the fact that we were both taking part in the *Prinz Heinrich Automobilfahrt*, an Anglo-German motor tour . . .[1]

Without realising the imminence of war, he felt certain that it was inevitable, and that England must be on the alert. Other signs were: two books by the German general von Bernhardi, *On War of To-day* and *Our Future*, in which his famous theories of 'living-space' and 'lightning war' were set forth. Meanwhile it seemed to Conan Doyle that English eyes were focused on the suffragettes, or the struggle between the Commons and the Lords. He tried to shock public opinion into awareness of the German menace by an article for the February number of *The Fortnightly Review* entitled 'Great Britain and the Next War':

> The element of danger, which is serious in either form of war, but more serious in the latter, is the existence of new forms of naval warfare which have never been tested in the hands of competent men, and which may completely revolutionize the conditions. These new factors are the submarine and the airship. The latter, save as a means of acquiring information, does not seem to be formidable—or not sufficiently formidable to alter the whole conditions of the campaign. But it is different with the submarines. No blockade, so far as I can see, can hold these vessels in harbour, and no skill or bravery can counteract their attack when once they are within striking distance. One could imagine a state of things when it might be found impossible for the greater ships on either side to keep the seas on account of these poisonous craft. No one can say beyond question that such a contingency is impossible.

Taking the most optimistic view, he went on, and allowing that the English fleet could transport our expeditionary force across the

[1] General Swinton, *Eyewitness, Being Personal Reminiscences of Certain Phases of the Great War, including the Genesis of the Tank*, 1932.

Channel without irreparable losses, how could the army be kept supplied for months or years at a time? Until some means of defence against submarines had been devised the only remedy was obviously a Channel tunnel. And if England were threatened with blockade in her turn, the population would thus be saved from famine by supplies coming through France: 'The Germans have made great works like the Kiel Canal in anticipation of war. Our answer must be the Channel Tunnel, linking us closer to our ally.'

Conan Doyle went on to discuss the details of the plan, and dealt with the technical objections raised in the past. He estimated that, with modern materials and techniques, an impregnable tunnel could be constructed within three years at a depth of about a hundred yards. This challenging article led to the appointment of a parliamentary commission to consider the tunnel project, with Arthur Fell as president. But matters moved too slowly for Conan Doyle's taste. In order to speed things up by creating a wave of public interest sufficient to exert the necessary pressure, he started a controversy in the correspondence columns of *The Times*, and replied to fears lest the tunnel be used by the enemy:

> The idea of the invasion of a great country through a hole in the ground 26 miles long and as many feet broad seems to me to be a most fantastic one. An enemy to use the tunnel has to hold both ends of it. In the unlikely event of a quarrel with France it is surely not difficult to seal up our end. I cannot imagine the circumstances under which any other power could gain both ends. If such circumstances did arise, it would surely mean that tunnel or no tunnel we were beaten to the ground.[1]

Then he tried to ram home his point by writing a short story combining suspense and propaganda, called *Danger*. The plot was as follows: Great Britian is at war with Norland, a small imaginary country owning a modest fleet of ships of conventional type and a squadron of eight submarines commanded by a certain Captain Sirius. As soon as war is declared the surface fleet takes refuge in the Norland port of Blankenberg, hoping thus to escape from the English navy, but Blankenberg is blockaded by our ships and the Norland fleet annihilated. Meanwhile Captain Sirius has sent his submarines to a secret base, where they remain at a safe depth by day, only surfacing at night for air and provisions. While the English fleet is

[1] *The Times*, 12 August 1913.

approaching Blankenberg, Sirius carries out several reconnaissances, even getting through a barrage of British torpedo-boats into the mouth of the Thames. The submarines make no attack on units of the enemy navy, and choose for their first victim a New Zealand cargo-boat of high tonnage carrying supplies, in preference to smaller merchant vessels. This is the beginning of a campaign against all merchant ships heading for England, whether British or neutral, including American. They are attacked even in the territorial waters of neutral countries, even in the port of Boulogne. Soon there is famine in England, economic equilibrium is destroyed, and while the English press is acclaiming the victory at Blankenberg, fresh destruction by Captain Sirius's torpedoes forces the government to ask the Norlanders for peace. As Conan Doyle's French translator remarked, Conan Doyle had 'foreseen everything, the sinking of merchant ships, great liners sent to the bottom with thousands of passengers on board, infringement of neutrality'.[1]

The story was published in *The Strand Magazine* just before the opening of a parliamentary session in which the report of the Commission on the Channel tunnel was to be read. The Chairman, Lord Sydenham of Combe, announced that his colleagues were in favour of the project and of the opinion that the tunnel should be constructed with as little delay as possible. He received a sympathetic hearing and, in the course of the debate, a Conservative member, Sir John Rolleston, referred to a certain 'Sir Conan Doyle', whose 'very interesting article' had appeared in this month's *Strand Magazine*.

Having no wish to set himself up as an expert on naval matters, Sir Arthur sent copies of his story to various authorities on the subject, inviting them to give their views in *The Strand Magazine* on the hypothetical situation in the story *Danger*. Twelve responses were published, including seven from admirals. Only two agreed with Conan Doyle: a civilian, Sir Douglas Owen, Professor at the London School of Economics, and an admiral, Sir Percy Scott. The former said that Conan Doyle had carried out his mission as a writer by this warning to the public.

But what did Sir Percy's colleagues say? Admiral Sir Compton Domville treated Conan Doyle's story as stuff and nonsense in true English style, and compared it to Jules Verne. Admiral Fitzgerald declared his confidence in the enemy's sense of 'fair play'. So did

---

[1] Louise Labat, Preface to *La Brèche au Monstre*, 1932, p. 6.

Admiral Henderson, who also counted on the powers of resistance of British warships. As for Admiral Sir William Kennedy, he declared: 'Having already expressed my opinion in *The Times*, I can only repeat what I then said, that as "God made us an island, by all means let us remain so." '

On 29 June the debate on the Channel tunnel opened in the House of Commons. The Archduke Francis Ferdinand of Austria had been dead for twenty-four hours. It was already too late to build a tunnel which would have shortened the war by two years, as Foch was to say later.

* * * * *

Hostilities began a few weeks after Conan Doyle's return from Canada and the United States. He was just fifty-five, but his first idea was to enlist, as it had been fourteen years earlier. When he offered his services to the War Office he referred to his experience as drill-master and his physical toughness:

> I have been told that there may be some difficulty in finding Officers for the New Army. I think I may say that my name is well known to the younger men of this country and that if I were to take a commission at my age it would set an example which might be of help.
>
> I can drill a company—I do so every evening. I have seen something of campaigning, having served as a surgeon in South Africa. I am fifty five but I am very strong and hardy, and can make my voice audible at great distances, which is useful at drill.
>
> Should you entertain my application, I should prefer a regiment which was drawn from the South of England—Sussex for choice. I am, Sir, yours faithfully,
>
> Arthur Conan Doyle
>
> P.S.—Should there be no difficulty in getting Officers, then there is no occasion for my volunteering.

His application was rejected at the end of August. He wrote about his desire to join the army to his brother Innes, who was waiting in England to be sent to one or other theatre of war: ' . . . I have only one life to live and here is this grand chance of a wonderful experience which might at the same time have a good effect upon some others.'[1] After this he had to contribute to the war effort as best he could as a civilian.

[1] 25 August 1914 (C.D.B.A.).

His most important and lasting contribution was his history of the Great War, but before this he undertook various propagandist, military and patriotic tasks. While Lady Conan Doyle was installing a reception centre for Belgian refugees, he was busy founding a militia for national defence (the Civilian National Reserve). All the young men of the family had joined the colours: Jean's brother Malcolm Leckie; Sir Arthur's nephews Oscar Hornung and Alec Forbes; his brother-in-law Leslie Oldham; his brother Innes Doyle, and his eldest son Kingsley Conan Doyle. The war was to mow down every one of them. Oscar Hornung and Captain Oldham were killed at the front in 1915; Captain Leckie in the retreat from Mons under circumstances which brought a recommendation for the Victoria Cross and resulted in a posthumous D.S.O.; Kingsley and Innes both died of Spanish flu, Kingsley a fortnight after the signing of the armistice, weakened by a wound in the throat.

During the first month of the war, Sir Arthur wrote a pamphlet called *To Arms* which was published by Hodder and Stoughton with a preface by F. E. Smith, the future Lord Birkenhead. In a style that reminds one of his writings about the Boer War, he expounded the justice of the British cause both for the benefit of neutral readers (the pamphlet was immediately published in Denmark, Holland, the Argentine, and above all the United States) and for the English themselves. *To Arms* had a definite success among the writer's countrymen, and he received nearly 1,000 letters during August 1914. He was also busy on a pamphlet to be distributed to the German army: he sent a copy to the authorities, who thought the project impossible to carry out, for obvious reasons. He also raised the question of safety measures for combatants. In September he started a campaign with the Admiralty and press (*The Times* and the *Daily Mail*) to equip all troops embarking for France with inflatable rubber collars, and this plan was adopted soon afterwards. Then, after the sinking of the *Formidable* off Plymouth on 1 January 1915, Conan Doyle laid a similar project before the *Daily Mail* and the *Daily Chronicle*—all warships should be provided with inflatable life-boats. These were the precursors of the rubber dinghies of the Second World War. He had another suggestion for the protection of the infantry. During the first phase of the war, before the front line had been stabilised, they had suffered extremely cruel casualties for lack of adequate protection, and the problem that had first arisen and been stressed by Conan Doyle at the time of the Boer War was occupying the authorities more urgently than ever. Conan Doyle studied the question of plated armour, and had several different models made and tested with bullets. The idea was never adopted in the form he had envisaged, but these were among the earliest experiments in protective armour made during the war, and led first to the tin hat of the English infantry and later to the caterpillar armoured cars and tanks, first conceived of as methods of defence.

But it was as witness of events and historian that Conan Doyle had most effect. He gave lectures with commentaries about the first battles of the war in several provincial towns, and began to write his *History*. At this moment he received news of two deaths almost simultaneously: after the deaths of Malcolm Leckie and Oscar Hornung, Conan Doyle's *History* took on a more directly patriotic note. While trying to analyse and describe to his countrymen the vast conflict he was witnessing, he wanted also to pay homage to the fighting men and the memory of the dead. This precise intention gave life to his efforts and inspiration to his pen. Just as he had in the past sung the praises of England's military virtues, he now, with even more fervour, set about collecting all the information that was available. He had no hesitation in writing to commanders-in-chief. In 1915, Bulfin (a fellow-pupil at Stonyhurst), Haig and Smith-Dorrien all agreed to send him regularly all the information he needed. 'My hand is fairly cramped with writing history,' he writes to Innes. 'I have had great luck. *Between ourselves* I have Smith-Dorrien's diaries and am promised Haig's, so on the top of Bulfin's, I am pretty well informed. I shall now do a worthy book and it may well be my Magnum Opus for the subject will make it illustrious. I should be proud to do *the* record of this war. It can never be precise, but it will be true and, I hope, interesting. I have already done as far as Sept. 13th, the crossing of the Aisne.'[1] He was now in a position to write the narrative which can be found in the first five chapters of the definitive edition of 1928—the edition which will be referred to here.

In his preface, Conan Doyle alludes to his documentary sources, whether written (in the form of letters and diaries) or oral (reports from eye-witnesses or military authorities). Part of his correspondence with Smith-Dorrien still exists—the letters exchanged between them in June 1915, when the General was in London at his house in

[1] N.d. (C.D.B.A.).

Eaton Terrace. As for Haig, on 3 December 1914 he wrote to Conan Doyle asking him to apply to Lady Haig for the notes she had in safe-keeping at Farnborough, as they might be useful to him. Conan Doyle met Lady Haig, not at Farnborough but at General Gough's house at Farnham; General Doran, commanding the Eighth brigade, was with her. 'Perhaps some other chap is hunting down evidence, as I am,' he wrote, 'but I doubt it—unless it be Belloc. I have wonderfully good inside knowledge.' the *Daily Chronicle* gave Conan Doyle exclusive access to confidential information coming from a wide network of sources. In October it published a long article by him called 'The Outlook on the War', and arranged for it to be translated into German and Spanish at his request. C. F. Masterman, Director of the Propaganda department of the Home Office, approved this article and took responsibility for circulating it in Switzerland, Spain and South America. In November he charged Robert Donald, Editor of the *Daily Chronicle*, with thanking Conan Doyle for his services to national propaganda.

The correspondence of June 1915 with General Smith-Dorrien mainly concerns the battles of 26 to 29 August 1914, when the British army was retreating on orders from Marshal French. We know that Joffre expressly disapproved of this retreat, and that having been unable to agree upon a joint strategy with his English homologue, he wrote: 'I had now no hope of keeping our allies on the prearranged line of battle; they were preparing to retreat on a level with Compiègne and Soissons, thus creating an extremely dangerous hiatus between our 6th and 5th armies.'[1]

It is clear from Smith-Dorrien's letters to Conan Doyle that French's tactics were not entirely approved of by the English generals: 'Sir John French was certainly not at his best in the days of Mons and Le Cateau. I think he was overwhelmed by the prospect of certain disaster, and I am not surprised for none of us generals had learned then what marvellous fighters our soldiers are.'[2]

When on 26 August Smith-Dorrien decided on delaying action, French no longer had exact information as to the tactical strength of the various units under his command. His order to retreat on 25 August took so little account of their various situations, wrote Smith-Dorrien, that 'Lord Roberts and many others wrote to me

[1] Joffre, *Mémoires*, Vol. I, p. 346.
[2] Smith-Dorrien to Conan Doyle, 1 June 1915 (C.D.B.A.).

afterwards complimenting me on having appreciated that there are times when a general is justified in disobeying orders.'[1]

Finally, when Sir John French deliberately attacked the behaviour of the French army, his subordinate officer gave Conan Doyle a quite different version:

> ... I don't know why he is so unjust to General Sordet, for on the morning of the 27th I sent Sir J. a special message in my own handwriting telling him how General Sordet with his cavalry had fought well the day before between my west flank and Cambrai, and had prevented the Germans from getting round my west flank, and I particularly asked him to thank him. I afterwards asked Sir. J. to correct his dispatch, but it is one of his peculiarities that he will never admit he can be wrong and he tried to make out I had mistaken the date—hardly likely since in that anxious afternoon I actually galloped out to that flank and saw the French cavalry fighting splendidly.[2]

Conan Doyle had the great merit of knowing how to make use of divergent or sometimes contradictory facts in the official communiqués in the discreetest possible manner, not in order to start ill-timed controversy but in the interests of historical objectivity: 'I have had to modify my judgement of certain people, and have done so—to the extent at least of ceasing to give praise where none was due. An historian, in my judgement is not bound to say all he knows, but is bound not to say what he knows to be untrue.'[3]

The following judgement on French, published in the *Daily Chronicle* for 20 December, shows Conan Doyle's deliberate and characteristic restraint: 'It can be said with absolute certainty that John French's name will go down in history as having been the general of our European armies during the sixteen months of greatest national pressure. We have much yet to do, but nothing in the future can be charged with the same possibilities of danger and even disaster as those operations of the past through which the returning General has successfully brought us.'

Conan Doyle's judgements concerning military history were always moderate, and certainly influenced other war historians. Thus, after publishing *The World Crisis* in 1929, Churchill rectified one of his own statements in a letter to Conan Doyle: 'No doubt you are right

---

[1] Smith-Dorrien to Conan Doyle, 4 June 1915 (C.D.B.A.).
[2] *Ibid.*, 12 June 1915 (C.D.B.A.).
[3] Conan Doyle to Smith-Dorrien, 4 June 1915 (C.D.B.A.).

about Mons and Le Cateau, and my phrase about Haig was too sweeping.'

In April 1915 Conan Doyle began a correspondence with Colonel Edmonds of the General Staff in France. Edmonds had begun to collect together documents and archives to be used from 1919 onwards in writing the Official History of the War, and he kept Conan Doyle posted with divisional reports and journals. But Sir Arthur did not always get such amiable treatment from the War Office; for instance Sir Reginald Brade, head of the censorship department, not only refused him access to the official archives but took the trouble to warn General Macdonough, Chief of Military Intelligence, against his attempts to extract confidential information from different generals. But Conan Doyle refused to be discouraged by such obstacles. Beside the names already quoted, at least fifteen generals and a great many officers provided him with detailed information, and odd scraps of evidence were legion.[1]

When Conan Doyle began bringing out his history of the war in 1916, he received letters spontaneously offering supplementary pieces of information or correcting his version of a battle. Sometimes these letters came by devious routes: a colonel, interned in Holland, wrote to him through the British Legation at the Hague, and sent details of the circumstances which led to his regiment's taking refuge in a neutral country. A captain who had escaped from Germany, and was the only survivor of a battalion destroyed in the first battle of Ypres, came to see Conan Doyle in 1917 and offered to enlighten him about hitherto unknown episodes. Is it necessary to say that Colonel Innes Doyle made effective contributions to his brother's system of private intelligence? During the last months of the Great War, Conan Doyle was constantly kept supplied with information and received at least five letters from generals by every post.

In 1916 the Secretary for Foreign Affairs proposed that he should make a report from the Italian front. He accepted the offer and got permission to spend a few days at the French front on the way. He

---

[1] The Biographical Archives contain letters from the following generals: Allenby, Bainbridge, Babington, Birdwood, Bols, Byng, Braithwaite, Capper, Cavan, Campbell, Cameron, Daly, De Lisle, Deverell, Fergusson, Gough, Gorringe, Higginson, Haldane, Heath, Hickie, Harrington, Haig, Hunter-Weston, Jeffreys, Jacob, Lawford, Landon, Lawrence, Maxse, MacCracken, Ponsonby, Pinney, Pulteney, Plumer, Robertson, Reed, Ross, Ritchie, Rawlinson, Shea, Shute, Scott, Smith, Smith-Dorrien, Strickland, Watts, White.

embarked on General Robertson's destroyer: 'As I had the right to wear several medals, including the South African, the general effect was all right, but I always felt a mighty imposter, though it was certainly very comfortable and convenient. I was still a rare specimen, and quite a number of officers of three nations made inquiry about my silver roses. A Deputy-Lieutenant may not be much in England, but when translated into French—my French anyhow—it has an awe-inspiring effect, and I was looked upon by them as an inscrutable but very big person with a uniform all of his own.'[1]

This mission gave him a chance to combine personal with public affairs and see Innes and Kingsley, as well as several generals, Haig among others, who granted him long interviews. On his return he went to see Clemenceau, accompanied by the Editor of the *Daily Chronicle* who had arranged the meeting. He describes the picturesque and at the same time disappointing impression made on him by Clemenceau, whose voice had the resonance of a powerful phonograph with a bad needle. He criticised everyone: 'I was not impressed by the judgement he showed in our conversation,' Conan Doyle wrote in his autobiography, 'if a squirt on one side and Niagara on the other can be called conversation.'[2]

Before getting back to work on his book he became involved in the Casement affair, which will be dealt with later. He also approached Lloyd George and Winston Churchill with further suggestions about the protection of the troops. Lloyd George wrote in reply:

> I may tell you that we are giving very special attention to this question of body shields, but, strange to say, our great difficulty is to get the soldiers at the Front to take them into use. Even with the steel helmet there was a considerable amount of grumbling when they were called upon to wear it, and it is only experience which has taught them the very great value and safety given by it, and now, as you know, they will not do without the steel helmet. I am taking a very early opportunity of discussing this matter personally with Sir Douglas Haig and others at the Front, and I can assure you that we shall not lose sight of the matter.
>
> I may say that the Ministry of Munitions has already been in communication with Mr. Grist with regard to his specially treated steel, and this and other natures of steel are all engaging our attention. Our real great difficulty is to provide a shield of sufficient size that is completely bullet-proof without throwing an impossible weight on the soldier. We have already got a light shield which is merely splinter-

[1] AUT., p. 380.   [2] *Ibid.*, p. 408.

proof. This has been tried at the Front with such success that a large number of them have been asked for and are in course of supply.[1]

A letter from Winston Churchill to Conan Doyle, dated 1 October 1916, reads:

> I am much obliged to you for your kindness in writing to me about the caterpillars. There are plenty of good ideas if only they can be backed with power and brought into relief. But think what a time it took—from February 1915 when I gave the original orders—to Sept. 1916 when the first use was made of these machines! And even then I think it would have been better to wait and act on a much larger scale—having waited so long. The caterpillars are the land sisters of the monitors. Both were intended to restore to the stronger power an effective means of offensive. The Monitor was the beginning of the torpedo-proof fleet. The caterpillar of the bullet-proof army. But *surprise* was the true setting for both.[2]

When Lloyd George left the War Office for Downing Street he invited Conan Doyle to come and see him. Conan Doyle briefly describes this interview in his autobiography, but gives Lloyd George's remarks in a much more condensed form than do his notes taken at the time. For instance in the published account Lloyd George quotes a remark of Miss Violet Asquith's about Kitchener's death in the following form: 'If he is not a great man he is a great poster'; but the notes give a more peremptory version:

> K (Kitchener) grew very arrogant. He had flashes of genius but was usually stupid. He could not see any use in Munitions. He was against Tanks. He was against Welsh and Irish Divisions. He refused the flags which the ladies worked. He obstructed in all things and ruined the Dardanelles. But he was a great force in recruiting. Miss Asquith said of him, 'He is not a great man. He is a great poster.' L.G. had a row with him in the Cabinet and said to him 'Please remember that you are only one of 19.' I told L.G. of my experience with K. He was shocked. L.G. had sent a Welsh painter to do Mametz Wood. Listened with interest to my account of the action. Said it was a beautiful story. Was interested to hear how I did the History and said it was probably better done from human documents. Asked me whether I had picked out any particular man among the Generals. I said I had seen no genius but that they were all capable. He agreed. Wanted to know if I had met Bridges. Seemed to think most of him. Got onto Armour and found him very keen. He said he had no doubt about it. Said the soldiers always obstructed. He had sent many devices but they were all shelved.

[1] 4 September 1916 (C.D.B.A.).   [2] (C.D.B.A.)

I mentioned Watts of the 7th Division as open to armour. He said 'Yes' and seemed to know all about Watts and admired him.[1]

The last really essential event in Conan Doyle's development must also be placed about the middle of 1916: his intellectual and mystical acceptance of spiritualism. However, before joining this new crusade, he had to finish off the job on hand. Among the most useful documents he received were letters from Haldane of the 6th Army Corps, from Allenby of the 3rd Army, from White and Gough. Haldane's letters (September 1916) concern the battles around Ypres. Conan Doyle was thus in a position to understand the campaign of October 1917, better known as the battle of Passchendaele. Allenby had let him see plans and aerial photographs of the operations affecting the Arras sector during April 1917, and from White he had received documents on which he based his very exact account of the second battle of the Somme in March 1918. As for Sir Hubert Gough, who was to be 'sacrificed' by Lloyd George on the altar of Anglo-French co-operation[2] after his defeat at Passchendaele, he was one of Conan Doyle's oldest friends. The information he had provided had been mainly oral, and it was only at the time of the retreat of the 5th Army (under his command) in April and May 1918 that he entrusted to paper information of interest to a modern reader. In February 1918 he gave Conan Doyle his opinion of Lloyd George in no uncertain terms: '. . . The chief cause of anxiety now is our Prime Minister, his methods and his men. The Bosch himself is quite a secondary danger.'[3]

After the end of the war, Gough complained to Conan Doyle of the 'politicians' who had clamoured for his resignation: 'The war is over—won by the British Army under its "stupid" Generals and "ignorant" Staff!—so said Lloyd George, Churchill and F. E. Smith, and their host of London Gossips.'[4]

Sir Arthur played a part in his being rehabilitated after a fashion; in 1919 Gough was put at the head of a mission to the Baltic, and when he resigned in 1922 he was appointed Army Commander. He recognised what Sir Arthur had done for him in his preface to *The True Conan Doyle*: 'He was convinced that I had been unjustly condemned, and he was determined, as far as lay in his power, to remove that injustice.'[5]

---

[1] Unpublished MS. (C.D.B.A.).   [2] Obituary note in *Le Monde*, 21 March 1963.
[3] Letter from Sir Hubert Gough, 20 February 1918 (C.D.B.A.).
[4] *Ibid.*, 7 November 1918 (C.D.B.A.).
[5] Sir Hubert Gough, Preface to *The True Conan Doyle*, 1946, p. 4.

In 1918 Innes Doyle was promoted to the rank of brigadier-general, and was therefore in a better position to give his brother news of the spring offensive, particularly the battles of Lys, Mont Kemmel and the Chemin des Dames. Conan Doyle was corresponding at this time with Generals Bainbridge, Hunter-Weston, Beauvoir de Lisle, Lawford and Birdwood. In October 1918 the Australian High Command invited him to visit the sector of the front held by the famous Anzacs at Péronne, and he witnessed the first phase of the Allied offensive against the Hindenburg line. Then came the Armistice, and double tragedy for Conan Doyle: the loss of his brother, and then of his son Kingsley at the age of twenty-six. His *History* became a tribute to their memory and it was for this reason that he never got over his disappointment at its reception by the public. He wrote of 'literary disappointment', but it was really the indifference, the fickleness of the public that he minded: 'For the moment war literature is out of fashion and my war history, which reflects all the passion and pain of those hard days, has never come into its own. I would reckon it the greatest and most undeserved literary disappointment of my life if I did not know that the end is not yet and that it may mirror those great times to those who are to come.'[1]

The book is in fact a memorial to the fighting-men, in the form of a narrative which he tried to make as plain and unadorned as possible. 'I hate fine writing about the war,' he wrote, 'it needs no gloss.'[2]

It is perhaps this very restraint which betrays Conan Doyle's true purpose. The *History*'s most ardent admirers were to be found among those who had fought in the war. George V was one of the first to applaud Conan Doyle's work and send him a message of encouragement. A week after the Armistice had been signed, Haig wrote to him: '. . . You have followed our doings with close attention all these four years and are well able to judge of how well these splendid troops have lived up to the finest traditions of their race.'[3] But it was the book's historical accuracy which impressed an attentive reader more than anything else. Who was better fitted to recognise it than General Edmonds? After receiving a copy of the definitive edition he wrote thanking Conan Doyle: 'I have now reread *The British Campaigns* and am more than ever amazed at its accuracy . . . I am much inter-

[1] AUT., p. 368.
[2] Letter quoted in G. S. Hutchinson's *Footslogger, An Autobiography*, 1931, p. 248.
[3] Letter from Sir Douglas Haig to Conan Doyle, 19 November 1918.

ested in your account of Mont Sorel—May 1916. You obviously quote from a report of Byng's missing from the Canadian Corps diaries, but of which Lord Haig had a copy which he gave me! You might get Sherlock Holmes to investigate.'[1]

Whereas in his history of the Boer War the narrative was set against a discussion of the rights of the British cause and the lessons to be learned from the war, in the present work there was only a brief introduction, and the final chapter put forward no theories about the best way of making a lasting peace. Nor were there any general conclusions about the global strategy of the Great War, nor the aims of the various belligerent nations. These problems were too complex to be dealt with after the elapse of so short a time. *The British Campaigns in Europe* is thus less a military history than a chronicle of operations. Here and there a certain number of sources, documents and other evidence are quoted in the definitive edition, but not very systematically. These are chiefly from Germany, such as figures given by archives of the Reich or in the memoirs of Von Kuhl. The value and profundity of the account as well as its lyrical qualities come rather from exactness of detail than power to evoke the scene. The book gives the effect of an immense tapestry. For instance, how does Conan Doyle recreate the physical conditions in which the battle of Passchendaele took place in October 1917? How does he translate Haig's dry official communiqué?[2] By emphasising wherever possible the rain, the mud, the cold, the difficulties and miseries endured by the troops:

> For four days and nights the men were in shell-holes without shelter from the rain and the biting cold winds, and without protection from the German Fire. At 6 p.m. on the evening of October 13th, the 66th and also the 49th fell in to move up the line and make the attack at dawn. So dark was the night and so heavy the rain that it took them eleven hours of groping and wading to reach the tapes which marked the lines of assembly. Then worn out with fatigue, wet to the skin, terribly cold, hungry, and with weapons that were often choked with mud, they went with hardly a pause into the open to face infantry who were supposed to be second to none in Europe, with every form of defence to help them, which their capable sappers could devise . . . They reached their utmost limit, and then, half buried in the mud and stiff with cold, their blue and cramped fingers still held steady to their triggers and blew back every counter-attack which the Germans

---

[1] 9 November 1928 (C.D.B.A.).
[2] 'This offensive, maintained for three and a half months under the most adverse conditions of weather.' *The British Campaigns in Europe*, p. 588.

could launch ... On both sides the making of trenches had entirely ceased, as it had been found that a few shell-holes united by a small cutting were sufficient for every purpose as long as the head of the soldier could be kept out of the water ... On October 26, the rain still pouring down as heavily as ever, and the earth about as liquid as the heavens, the advance was once again renewed upon a narrow front which was mostly on the slope of the hill and therefore offered some foothold for the struggling infantry.[1]

His treatment of some very controversial incidents—and this was one of them—could hardly go uncriticised. But we see Conan Doyle's moderation in his treatment of Passchendaele and the advisability of the offensive. After summing up the various elements on which the controversy hinges, he concludes:

If the troops were weary, there was good evidence that the Germans were not less so, and their minds and morale could not be unaffected by the fact that every British attack had been attended by loss of ground and of prisoners. Then again, it was known that the French meditated a fresh attack in the Malmaison quarter, and good team-play called for a sustained effort upon the left wing to help the success of the right centre. Again, the rainfall had already been abnormally high, so that on a balance of averages, there was reason to hope for better weather, though at the best it would hardly be hoped that the watery October sunshine would ever dry the fearsome bogs which lay between the armies. Of two courses, it has always been Sir Douglas Haig's custom to choose the more spirited, as his whole career would show, and therefore his decision was now given for the continuance of the advance. In the result the weather failed him badly, and his losses were heavy. Looking back with the wisdom that comes after the event, one can clearly see that had the whole operation stopped when the rain fell after the first day, it would have been the wisest course, but when once such a movement is well under way it is difficult to compromise.[2]

Given the difference in scale between the two wars, this *History* lent itself less easily to a continuous strategic commentary than that of the Boer War, and his study of practical tactics is more fluid and discursive. However it is not absent, as is shown by his comments on the German retreat after the Marne: 'The Germans were retreating fast, but rather on account of their generally faulty strategical position than from tactical compulsion, and they covered themselves with continual rearguard actions, especially along the line of the Petit Morin. It is one of the noticeable results, however, of the use of aircraft, that the bluff of a rearguard has disappeared and that it is no

[1] *The British Campaigns in Europe*, p. 581.   [2] *Ibid.*, p. 578.

longer possible to make such a retreat as Massena from Torres
Vedras, where the pursuer never knew if he were striking at a
substance or at a shadow.'[1] Or another on the enemy's manœuvres
in the St. Omer sector on 14 October: 'Such an attack in modern
warfare can only hope for success when carried out by greatly
superior numbers whereas the Germans were now stronger than their
assailants.'[2]

Nevertheless strategical comments are fairly numerous if scattered.
They bear for instance on the disposition of lines of defence, the role
of forts (which Conan Doyle thought obsolete) and of the new forms
of body armour: 'Students of armour in the future may be interested
to note that this was the first engagement in which British infantry
reverted after a hiatus of more than two centuries to the use of
helmets.'[3]

Conan Doyle often discusses the significance of different Staff
decisions. Thus he studies the defence of the Ypres salient in spite of
inevitable difficulties, and shows the importance this sector of the
British front was to have at the time of Haig's offensive in July 1917.
In another passage he explains how various strategical theories came
into being, such as that of small attacks with limited objectives, which
prevailed during the last year of the War.

The style and inspiration of this history and its many reflections
about the art of war, give it epic dimensions that are lacking in the
History of the Boer War:

> The sky had clouded, the days were mirk, the hanging Madonna had
> fallen from the cathedral of Albert, the troops were worn to shadow.
> The twilight of the gods seemed to have come.[4]

Conan Doyle sets his scene with an artistry suitable to the austere
grandeur of his subject, nor does he forget the part played by the
Empire:

> It is a remarkable illustration, if one were needed, of the unity of the
> British empire that, as the weary men from Montreal or Manitoba
> moved from the field, their place was filled by eager soldiers from the
> Punjab and the slopes of the Himalayas.[5]

The first echoes of mysticism can be heard in his description of the
regenerative force of the baptism of blood and fire. With the Mani-

[1] *The British Campaigns in Europe*, p. 75.   [2] *Ibid.*, p. 107.
[3] *Ibid.*, p. 300.   [4] *Ibid.*, p. 661.   [5] *Ibid.*, p. 205.

chaean viewpoint suitable to an epic, Conan Doyle denounces the Germans for having degraded the essential nobility of war by using chemical weapons:

> It is with a feeling of loathing that the chronicler turns from such knightly deeds as these to narrate the next episode of the war, in which the Germans, foiled in fair fighting, stole away a few miles of ground by the arts of the murderer. So long as military history is written, the poisoning of Langemarck will be recorded as an incident by which warfare was degraded, and a great army, which had long been honoured as the finest fighting force in the world, became in a single day an object of horror and contempt.[1]

It is also in the epic manner that Conan Doyle occasionally praises some isolated deeds of heroism: 'It was in this action that Colonel Forbes-Robertson, one of the heroes of Cambrai, earned the coveted Cross by fighting on horseback at the head of his men like some knight of old, and repeatedly restoring the line when it was broken.'[2]

Whereas his account of the Boer War ended with military and political considerations, *The British Campaigns* concludes with a moral and puritanical exhortation. The strain this war had imposed on so many sons of Britain had created a debt of gratitude which must be paid by the entire nation in terms of their rehabilitation: 'So great was the pressure that the reason not infrequently gave way, and a general officer has described how he saw men dancing and singing in the road from pure insanity. They had given their all, almost their humanity to save Britain. May the day never come when Britain will refuse to save them.'[3] And this leads to one of the mystical and spiritualistic themes to which Conan Doyle devoted his energies when peace was restored:

> War is not all careless slang and jokes and secrets, though such superficial sides of it may amuse the public and catch the eye of the descriptive writer. It is the most desperately earnest thing to which man ever sets his hand or his mind. Many a hot oath and many a frenzied prayer go up from the battle line. Strong men are shaken to the soul with the hysteria of weaklings, and balanced brains are dulled into vacancy or worse by the dreadful sustained shock of it. The more honour then to those who, broken and wearied, still hold fast in the face of all that human flesh abhors, bracing their spirits by a sense of soldierly duty and personal honour which is strong enough to prevail over death itself.[4]

[1] *The British Campaigns in Europe*, p. 194. [2] *Ibid.*, p. 761. [3] *Ibid.*, p. 157.
[4] *Ibid.*, p. 317.

Chapter 6

THE LOVER OF JUSTICE:
ROGER CASEMENT

In 1916 Conan Doyle tried to obtain a pardon for Sir Roger Casement: how are we to understand an action which seems in such flagrant contradiction to his opinions and principles? Sir Arthur had twice stood at general elections as a candidate for the Unionist party, who were pledged to keep Ireland within the United Kingdom. In siding with them, he was showing his loyalty to that enlightened Conservatism which had been typical of English intellectuals towards the end of Queen Victoria's reign. As G. M. Trevelyan tells us: 'Unionism prevailed among the leaders of literature and thought, men like Robert Browning, Leslie Stephen, Lecky and many more, as also in that part of the professional and scientific world which had not previously become Conservative.'[1]

Sir Arthur's particular dream was that his country should become a great community founded on economic interests, as well as linguistic, cultural and racial links—a community which should some day include the United States, where Conan Doyle saw the Anglo-Saxon inheritance coming into its own. The Boer War had taught him the dangers of a small country becoming too jealously nationalistic; and since Ireland had been given greater autonomy as to local government at the beginning of the twentieth century, he hoped that the causes of her misunderstandings with England were disappearing. The flexibility of the present relationship between the two countries should show Ireland the danger, as well as the uselessness, of complete independence. This, he believed, would lead to economic asphyxia and a rupture between the two cultures. However the constitutional crisis of 1911 brought to light certain aspects of the Irish question which had hitherto been ignored. Profiting by the limitation of the power of the Lords, the Irish members in the Commons started a systematic war of aggression, which nearly caused an even more serious governmental crisis than that of the previous year. They had in fact managed

[1] *British History in the Nineteenth Century and After*, p. 397.

to make it seem as if Home Rule would solve all the difficulties in the United Kingdom, quite apart from the Irish Question; and a certain number of people, including Sir Arthur Conan Doyle, revised their views of Home Rule. Of course he made some reservations, but from now on he accepted it in principle. The example of the Union of South Africa, independent since 1909, provided a new argument in favour of granting Ireland autonomy. The turning-point came in 1912, at a pro-Home Rule meeting in London. Bernard Shaw, Sir Alfred Turner, James Douglas and Clement Shorter were among the speakers, and Conan Doyle found himself in agreement with them. He justified his change of view by the fact that religious dissension in Ireland had died down; from now on it was possible to imagine an independent Ireland with a federal constitution. But already the violently separatist and anti-British 'Sinn Feiners' were making the moderate Home Rulers look like old-fashioned Tories. In a letter probably destined for an Irish paper Conan Doyle explained his position:

> I am an Imperialist because I believe the whole to be greater than the part, and I would always willingly sacrifice any part if I thought it to the advantage of the whole. It was the apparent enmity of Ireland to the Empire which held me from Home Rule for many years, and it is still that view which is the hardest to overcome. But I came to understand that these cheers for the enemies of the Empire were symptoms and not the disease . . . I hope the Nationalists will soon cease to allow their opponents the use of the Union Jack as a symbol. More Irishmen have died for that flag than men of any other race in proportion to numbers. It is the sign of the Empire which Ireland has helped to build and which, be the local exception what it may, has stood for freedom and progress all the world over . . .
>
> It may be objected that it is putting the cart before the horse, but I am convinced that if the flag was honoured in Ireland as elsewhere, it would weaken British resistance to Home Rule more than any other cause . . .[1]

Two years later, at the outbreak of the Great War, the 'Sinn Feiners' became Germany's natural allies; Conan Doyle could not forgive them this, and he felt the same scorn for enemies at home, among whom he classed pacifists and socialists: ' . . . In our battle for freedom, we have continually been *hampered by* all sorts of socialist Cranks who, according to their views should have been the champions

[1] Letter or draft of letter, 2 April 1912 (C.D.B.A.).

of extra-democracy and yet by some queer twist have made themselves the chief ally in actual fact of the most autocratic tyranny ever seen.'[1]

Like Churchhill, he became the advocate of the 'die-hards'. During the war he publicly called for reprisal air-raids against German cities, and on 26 February 1916 he defended this project in *The Saturday Review*. Towards the end of the war he was afraid of German atrocities being committed on prisoners of war, and suggested that the government should announce that they held high German authorities including the Kaiser personally responsible for them, and threatening possible reprisals.[2] Of the Russian Revolution he wrote that: 'The phenomenon of that great fermenting, putrefying country was more like some huge cataclysm of nature, some monstrous convulsion of the elements, than any ordinary political movement . . . It was as though a robust man had suddenly softened into liquid putrescence before one's eyes.'

How are such views to be reconciled with his apparent indulgence towards Casement, who had not only deserted to the Germans but was also said to have used pressure or even brutality on Irish prisoners wearing British uniform in the prison camps of Germany? The fate of prisoners had been one of Conan Doyle's main concerns throughout the war. In 1915 he described the Germans as 'the European Red Indians who torture their prisoners',[3] and called for the distribution of pamphlets about German atrocities to prisoners, hoping that once broadcast the scandal would be brought to an end, and also that the pamphlets would stir up anger among the armed forces: ' . . . We should use the weapons which the enemy has put into our hands . . . If our enemy is unchivalrous, he at least is intensely practical, and if he realised that we are gaining any military advantage from his misdeeds, he may, perhaps, reconsider, not their morality but their wisdom.'[4]

Two years later Conan Doyle was sounded about accepting the directorship of an official propaganda department, to be supplied with information by the War Office. He preferred to be free to act according to his conscience, but he went on denouncing the behaviour of the

[1] Letter to Upton Sinclair, 29 March 1918, published in Upton Sinclair's *My Lifetime in Letters*, 1960, pp. 163–4.
[2] Letter to *The Times*, 14 October 1918.
[3] *Ibid.*, 13 April 1915.   [4] *Ibid.*

Germans to British prisoners. After the publication of a letter from him in *The Times* of 26 December 1917, his post-bag showed his influence with the public. We also learn from his correspondence with Colonel Arthur Peebles, in January 1918, that Conan Doyle tried to conduct an enquiry into the treatment of British prisoners by certain members of the Kaiser's immediate circle, particularly Prince Münster. His letters make it clear that 'psychological' warfare was already being practised in prison camps during the First World War, and such notions as the British 'plot' against Belgian neutrality in 1914, and the negligence and cowardice of military leaders were being made use of. During the years after the signing of the Treaty of Versailles, Conan Doyle was always opposed to the revisionists, such as Bernard Shaw and Israel Zangwill.

It is against this background that Conan Doyle's curious intervention in favour of Casement must be seen. An Irishman but a British diplomat, Sir Roger was a public hero in the years before the war. In 1903 his reports on the Congo under Leopold's régime set going an agitation for reform, with Morel and Conan Doyle as prime movers, as we have seen. A few years later, while consul in Brazil, he denounced the atrocities at Putamayo, which had their origin in the greed of the planters, as in the Congo.

But this chivalrous defender of the unfortunate and the oppressed had other sides to his character, and the World War brought these suddenly to light. Casement had been clandestinely in touch with the Irish Nationalists for several years. For several months, in all probability, his diplomatic uniform and immunity had been abused in characteristic fashion. A few days after the declaration of war, Casement met some of the leading Sinn Feiners in New York and issued a manifesto calling upon all Irishmen to fight against England and therefore on the side of Germany. Claiming the right to speak for his country to the German authorities, he next travelled to Berlin to see what were the possibilities of collaborating with the Wilhelmstrasse. His first attempts were directly concerned with English prisoners of war. Among those of Irish nationality, he tried to recruit a 'free brigade' to take arms against their old comrades. Casement visited several of the camps, made a great many speeches on behalf of a more or less imaginary Nationalist government, and when he could not persuade, did not hesitate to threaten. His efforts won over about fifty prisoners—a pitiful result which lost him the respect of the

Germans. Moreover, Casement's homosexuality, all too obvious since he had taken under his protection in Berlin a young Norwegian sailor called Adler Christensen, made the Irish rebel an inconvenient if not undesirable ally. So that the Germans were not sorry to hear of the plan for a rising in Dublin on Easter Sunday 1916, and shipped Casement off to Ireland a few days beforehand. He embarked on a submarine with two other Nationalist leaders, and landed secretly on the west coast. When challenged a few hours later by a policeman, Casement behaved suspiciously, was arrested, recognised and taken under safe escort to London. The Dublin rising was a bloody affair; several of the Nationalists were seized with rifles in their hands and shot. This did nothing to lessen Casement's guilt. He was tried at the end of June, condemned to death, and executed on 3 August.

After his efforts on behalf of prisoners of war it would seem as though Conan Doyle might be the last man to take a lenient view of Roger Casement; furthermore he had often denounced the Sinn Feiners, and their sectarianism had no appeal whatever to his sympathies. But suppressing his usual feelings, and braving the disapproval of a nation that was clamouring all the more eagerly for Casement's death because he had betrayed his legend, Conan Doyle himself framed a petition asking for a pardon for the condemned man. When the case was being heard Sir Arthur happened to be at the French front; immediately on his return he got in touch with Clement Shorter, whose influence was a good backing for this hasty and unpopular venture. Shorter agreed to collect signatures; the petition was addressed to Asquith and entirely written by Sir Arthur. Its text was as follows:

> We the undersigned, while entirely admitting the guilt of the prisoner Roger Casement, and the justice of his sentence, would desire to lay before you some reasons why *the extreme sentence of the law* should not be inflicted:
>
> (1) We would call attention to the violent change which appears to have taken place in the prisoner's previous sentiment towards Great Britain (as shown, for example, in his letter to the King at the time of his Knighthood[1]) from those that he has exhibited during the war.

[1] This letter, addressed to Sir Edward Grey on 11 June 1911, figured in the charge, and ran as follows: 'I find it very hard to choose the words in which to make acknowledgement of the honour done me by the King. I am much moved at the proof of confidence and appreciation of my services on the Putamayo, conveyed to me by your letter, wherein you tell me that the King has been graciously pleased upon your recommendation to confer upon me the honour of Knighthood. I am indeed grateful to you for this signal assurance of your personal esteem and support, and very deeply sensible of the honour done to me by His Majesty. I would beg that my humble duty

Without going so far as to urge complete mental irresponsibility, we should desire to point out that the prisoner had for many years been exposed to severe strain during his honourable career of public service, that he had endured several tropical fevers, and that he had experienced the worry of two investigations which were of a peculiarly nerve-trying character. For these reasons it appears to us that some allowance may be made in his case for an abnormal physical and mental state.

(2) We could urge that his execution would be helpful to German policy, by accentuating the differences between us and some of our fellow subjects in Ireland. It would be used, however unjustly, as a weapon against us in the United States and other neutral countries. On the other hand, magnanimity upon the part of the British Government would soothe the bitter feelings in Ireland and make a favourable impression throughout the Empire and abroad.

(3) We would respectfully remind you of the object lesson afforded by the United States at the conclusion of their Civil War. The leaders of the South were entirely in the power of the North. Many of them were officers and officials who had sworn allegiance to the laws of the United States and had afterwards taken arms and inflicted enormous losses upon her. None the less not one of these men was executed, and this policy of mercy was attended by such happy results that a breach which seemed to be irreparable has now been happily healed over.

(4) Being ourselves deeply convinced of the wisdom of such a policy, we feel constrained to approach you with this petition, hoping that you may find yourself in agreement with the considerations which we advance.

On 14 July, Conan Doyle wrote to Shorter from Manchester where he had been making a speech about his recent experiences to the Anglo-French Association. He had had an audience with the Under-Secretaries of State at the Foreign Office before leaving London the previous evening, and they tried to get him to give up his project by revealing Casement's character in the light of the 'black books' discovered by the police when they searched his house in Dublin. 'They told me that his record for sexual offences was bad,' he told Shorter, 'and had a diary of his in proof of it. I had, of course, heard this before, but as no possible sexual offence could be as bad as suborning soldiers from their duty, I was not diverted from my purpose.'[1] At the time of the trial these diaries were discreetly shown to various people suspected of being in favour of lenience to Casement. For instance, the

---

might be presented to His Majesty, when you may do me the honour to convey to him my deep appreciation of the honour he has been so graciously pleased to confer upon me.' Quoted by R. MacColl in *Roger Casement, A New Judgment*, 1956, p. 97.

[1] Letter from Conan Doyle to Clement Shorter, 14 July 1916, unpublished (C.D.B.A.).

Pope and President Wilson were both informed about the diaries. But to Conan Doyle, Casement's homosexual obsessions were merely additional proof of his unbalanced mental state, on the basis of which he claimed extenuating circumstances. Towards the end of 1914, when Casement arrived in Berlin, Conan Doyle had written to the editor of the *Daily Chronicle*:

> I am sure that you are wise to use no stronger term than 'infatuation' for Sir Roger Casement's journey to Berlin. He was a man of fine character, and that he should in the full possession of his senses act as a traitor to the country which had employed and honoured him is inconceivable to anyone who knew him. He had, it is true, a strong prepossession in favour of Germany before the war, but this was due to his belief that she was destined to challenge the Monroe doctrine, which Casement bitterly resented as being the ultimate cause of that Putamayo barbarism which he had officially to investigate. I may say that I disagreed with him upon this subject, but in all our discussions I have never heard him say a word which was disloyal to Great Britain. He was a sick man, however, worn by tropical hardships, and he complained of pains in his head. Last May I had letters from him from Ireland which seemed to me so wild that I expressed fears at the time as to the state of his nerves. I have no doubt that he is not in a normal state of mind, and that this unhappy escapade at Berlin is only an evidence of it.[1]

Bernard Shaw had also drawn up a petition in favour of a pardon for Casement; it was longer than Conan Doyle's but used the same arguments.

Among the eminent persons approached by Shorter who refused to sign Conan Doyle's petition we may mention Lord Sydenham, Sir Alfred Turner, Sir George Trevelyan, Mrs. Humphrey Ward, H. G. Wells, Eden Phillpotts, Sir Frederick Pollock, Lady Ritchie, John Burns, Laurence Binyon, Sidney Colvin, Kipling and Sidney Lee. The forty signatories included prominent scientists such as Sir Clifford Allbutt, Sir Thomas Barlow, Sir Francis Darwin and Sir James Frazer; and politicians like Sir Sidney Olivier, Beatrice and Sidney Webb. The press was represented by Robert Blatchford, Muirhead Bone, Gardiner, Massingham, Sir William Robertson Nicoll, Louis Vincent and C. P. Scott; and literature by Hall Caine, Harold Begbie, William Archer, Arnold Bennett, G. K. Chesterton, John Drinkwater, Galsworthy, Maurice Hewlett, Israel Zangwill, Jerome K. Jerome and John Masefield. Delivered in Whitehall on

[1] N.d., unpublished (C.D.B.A.).

20 July, the petition was never published for the reasons explained to Sir Arthur by Herbert Samuel, the Home Secretary:

> A formal acknowledgment was sent yesterday of the recipt of the Petition on behalf of Casement, which you sent to the Prime Minister. As you are good enough to say that the petitioners desire to leave it to the discretion of the Government whether the Petition should be made public, I am writing to inform you that the Government prefer that it should not be published. All the circumstances relating to the case of Casement are receiving the earnest consideration of the Government.[1]

As usual, Conan Doyle took full responsibility for his venture and thought it his duty to contribute to Casement's legal expenses. Except for William Cadbury, he was the only man among those who helped Roger Casement financially who had not been one of his intimate friends. It is also noticeable that Conan Doyle gave far more liberally than anyone: he put up £700, nearly half the whole amount and £500 more than the next largest contribution. Such munificence is a proof of Conan Doyle's generosity of heart, and it also makes it clear that his interest in Casement had nothing to do with politics. In this he differed from the other signatories, and it is in a sense surprising. The two men had got to know each other over the campaign for reform in the Congo, but this hardly led to real friendship. Conan Doyle did not really understand Casement, and preferred to take the line that he was insane at the time of his trial; while for his part Casement never hesitated to express his indifference and scorn for Sir Arthur. Conan Doyle's generosity to someone he took for a madman is certainly something of a psychological enigma. There is one possibly too speculative hypothesis which might explain his feeling of personal responsibility for Casement at the time of that tragic hero's trial. Sir Arthur had been spokesman for the Congo Association, whose treasurer was Count Blücher, a German diplomat living in London and a descendant of the famous general. Count Blücher had married an Englishwoman. In 1912, at the time of the Putamayo affair, he was again co-operating with Casement and agreed to be treasurer of the Putamayo Mission Fund. On the declaration of war in August 1914 the Blüchers of course had to leave London and go back to Germany. They went to live in Berlin, and when Casement went there it was natural for him to think of looking up his friends the Blüchers. This was exactly what happened—as Conan Doyle must have known.

[1] Letter to Conan Doyle, 27 July 1916, unpublished (Photocopy, C.D.B.A.).

Casement went to see the Blüchers at the Esplanade Hotel, where they were staying soon after his arrival in Berlin in January 1915. Conan Doyle had been distressed by the news of Casement's treachery and knew very well that Blücher would have conscientious scruples about the Irishman. Considering Blücher's past career, his links with England, his friendship with Morel (now one of the scapegoats of the British press) how could anyone think he would be in favour of Roger Casement's plan? In fact he did his best to persuade him that he was 'to put it mildly, in a dreadfully false position and that the only possible thing for him to do was to get out of Germany without delay. But Casement would not listen.'[1]

Blücher had for excellent reasons been enrolled in the Medical Corps and worked in an organisation affiliated to the International Red Cross—the Order of the Knights of Malta. He was also a member of the Kaiser's circle, and when his work did not take him abroad or into prisoners' camps, he was in constant contact with the official set in Berlin. It was through Blücher's intervention that Casement was received by them also, although he continued to make his disapproval plain. Thanks to Blücher, some of Casement's correspondence was sent to England. This was a detail which Conan Doyle could not have known, nor yet that all the letters sent by Blücher's agency were intercepted by English counter-espionage. Finally, he did not know that when Casement was arrested in 1916, Princess Blücher (Blücher had become a Prince of the Empire during the war) had tried to do something to help their unfortunate friend. 'I have written to a friend in England,' she wrote in her memoirs. 'But have little real hope that it will save him from his fate.'[2] Whom did the Princess approach? It was probably Sir William Tyrrell who—was it a complete coincidence? —was the first person Roger Casement asked to see the day after his arrest. The request, however, was rejected. On the other hand, Conan Doyle knew that ever since the beginning of the war, English counter-espionage was in touch with the Kaiser's circle through a man mentioned by William Le Queux in a letter dated 15 February 1915:

> . . . Now as regards the Kaiser's speech, the source from which I obtained it was a most reliable one—a personage *very* high in the German diplomatic service, and whose wife is English. I only wish I

[1] MacColl, *Roger Casement, A New Judgement*, p. 152.
[2] *An English Wife in Berlin*, 1920, p. 138.

could give you his name in confidence, but it would be unpatriotic of me to do so, for he has furnished us with much important—even vital—information, and I am, on my honour, not to divulge . . .[1]

It is difficult to imagine that this description did not immediately call Blücher's name to Conan Doyle's mind. And perhaps his conscience told him that there was reason to see Casement in the pitiable role of a traitor betrayed by those he wanted to make his allies. We must not exceed the limits of speculation, for we do not know exactly what part Blücher played in this affair. It does however seem certain that the German authorities more or less openly hoped for Casement's failure and even death. Alive, he was only a compromising and ignoble collaborator; dead, the halo of martyrdom with which Ireland would surround his memory would be much more effective. Conan Doyle was not the only one to realise this. At the time of the trial, Sir Cecil Spring Rice, British Ambassador at Washington, wrote to Sir Edward Grey that in view of the activities of Irish Nationalists in the United States 'all here are agreed that it will be dangerous to make Casement a martyr'. He went on:

> The great bulk of American public opinion, while it might excuse executions in hot blood, would very greatly regret an execution sometime after the event. This is the view of impartial friends of ours here, who have nothing to do with the Irish movement. It is far better to make Casement ridiculous than a martyr. The universal impression here seems to be that he acted like a madman. There is no doubt whatever that the Germans here look forward with great interest to his execution, of which they will take full advantage.[2]

In spite of everything, Conan Doyle expected Casement's execution to take place, and it had little effect on his opinions about the Irish question or his feelings towards the Nationalists. He appealed to the common sense and honour of the Irish when he made a last attempt to wean them from separation. Praising the contribution Ireland had made to the war, he invited her to go on supporting it without reserve, in a letter to *The Freeman's Journal*, on 31 October 1916:

> I do not think that Irishmen in Ireland appreciate the consternation and shame which is felt by men of Irish blood throughout the Empire at the present shocking state of affairs, where, on account of politics

---

[1] Unpublished (C.D.B.A.).
[2] Quoted by R. MacColl, *op. cit.*, p. 276.

gone mad, the Irish Division are left without recruits in the face of the enemy. Politics can wait, but war cannot wait, and the events of the next few months will determine the position which Ireland will hold in the future, both in the Empire and in the estimation of civilised Europe. . . . If Irishmen do indeed desire Home Rule, then is it not clear that it is madness to turn their friends over here into enemies, and to bitterly affront so many who have worked for their cause in the past? Ireland is in imminent danger of losing not only the fruits of the last thirty years of political work, but her honour as well.

Conan Doyle's intervention in favour of Casement was in line with the principles of independence and free speech which governed his public life, but though future events justified him, government circles were surprised. They pretended not to understand; this episode may even have lost him a peerage. From now on, Conan Doyle took a less direct interest in politics. The cause of spiritualism was soon to absorb his interests, without involving a total retreat from public life. He believed that Casement's execution had been a political error, but an even earlier case, the Slater affair, gave him a worldwide reputation as a passionate lover of Justice.

Chapter 7

THE LOVER OF JUSTICE: GEORGE EDALJI

The Slater affair was to give Conan Doyle the chance to play a similar part in England to Zola's intervention in the Dreyfus affair in France; but the creator of Sherlock Holmes had already crossed the barrier separating fiction from fact in 1907.

For several years criminologists had been trying to give the legend the stamp of authenticity, and were taking very seriously a character who had become almost an encumbrance to his creator. Having made Sherlock Holmes disappear for a time, Conan Doyle was preparing the way for his return in *The Hound of the Baskervilles* with three studies in the history of crime, published by *The Strand Magazine* in March, April and May 1901 under the collective title of *Strange Studies from Life*.

These three articles are marginal to the 'detective story' proper, for they are straightforward accounts of three episodes gleaned by the author from the annals of crime. As literature, their only value is that they stress Conan Doyle's new attitude to crime. Otherwise they do not contain as much information for the criminologist as the volumes of *The Notable British Trials*, for instance, edited by Harry Lodge from 1905 onwards. But they do show that, as Conan Doyle's historical interests developed, he was as much attracted to these news items as to military events. We also see that his curiosity about criminal investigations was growing, and that he was beginning to use on his own account the intellectual methods that were characteristic of Sherlock Holmes. There seems no doubt that this happened almost against his will; the reading public had always believed that Sherlock Holmes's marvellous gifts were really possessed by his creator. He was subjected to a sort of tacit but permanent challenge, occasionally expressed in the form of questions about some mysterious crime. Consulted by his friend Blumenfeld of the *Daily Express* about a case of disappearance, we see Conan Doyle suggesting the very same trick as Sherlock Holmes uses in the story *Black Peter* in *The Strand Magazine* for March 1904:

Dear Blumenfeld, I find it hard to think that the letter is in any hand but that which wrote the telegram. Could not a trap be laid in this way? The man naturally wants to get out of the country. He is a chauffeur. Suppose you put an advertisement in the *Express* and other papers 'Skilled chauffeur. A gentleman starting on an extended tour in Spain needs services of chauffeur. Steady man over 25 years—for four months. Apply by letter.' The replies would be very likely to contain one from him. All which are like his writing could be interviewed. He could fill up paper for passport. Then you could see scratches, etc., on hands. Don't you think this a possible line?[1]

Not only was Conan Doyle called upon for his help and advice as a 'consulting detective', but the problems brought to his notice had a strange similarity with those Sherlock Holmes had solved in the course of his legendary career. Very often they concerned disappearances. In 1909, a girl, who was not however Miss Mary Sutherland,[2] asked him to help her find her fiancé who had vanished without a trace. Sir Arthur solved the problem, as we see from the girl's letter to her 'benefactor' as she called him:

> Torquay, 7th August 1909.
> I don't know how to thank you sufficiently for all your kindness. Please accept my most grateful thanks for all you have done for me. As you say, I have had an extraordinary escape, and I dread to think what might have happened.[3]

And also from his autobiography: 'In another case, where a girl had become engaged to a young foreigner who suddenly disappeared, I was able, by a similar process of deduction, to show her very clearly both whither he had gone and how unworthy he was of her affections.'[4]

In the same way the correspondence between Conan Doyle and Sir Arthur Vickers, Ulster King of Arms, shows us that he had successfully investigated the theft of jewels from the royal crown of Ireland. An American journalist quotes unnamed witnesses as evidence that in 1900 Conan Doyle put the police on the track which led Inspector Neill of Scotland Yard to arrest the murderer George Joseph Smith a few years later.

This *de facto* identification of Conan Doyle with Sherlock Holmes, combined with a fantastic tendency to give the fictitious hero the prestige of a myth, even spread outside England. In 1913, a reader who does not seem to have been a hoaxer wrote to ask Conan Doyle

---

[1] N.d. (C.D.B.A.).   [2] In *A Case of Identity*.

[3] (C.D.B.A.)   [4] AUT., p. 132.

to come at once to Warsaw to prevent a miscarriage of justice.[1] We see from incidents such as this that Sherlock Holmes imposed responsibilities on Conan Doyle—one might almost say obligations. It is interesting that he did not shirk them. But the only scandals he felt impelled to combat were moral ones, such as judicial errors rather than the intellectual problems of criminology. His interest in the Slater and Edalji affairs was not that of a dilettante; he was measuring his strength against the prosaic but real difficulties of the legal world. The identity and motives of the criminal were of secondary importance; what he cared about was that an innocent man should not be condemned. It is true that the man who espoused the causes of Edalji and Slater was the creator of Sherlock Holmes, but he was above all a redresser of wrongs, a lover of justice, a just man in fact, who, as we saw in the Congo affair, instinctively sided against cruelty, prejudice and oppression.

The village of Great Wyrley, where the Edaljis lived, lies in the mining district to the north-west of Birmingham. The Reverend Edalji, father of George, had gone to live there after marrying the niece of a local clergyman. He was a Parsee, that is to say a Hindu, and the darkness of his skin probably did not make it easier for him to function as Anglican priest of a parish in the heart of England. However he carried out his duties at Great Wyrley for fourteen years without incident until 1888; then, when his son George was twelve, he received several anonymous and threatening letters. There was an investigation, and a servant confessed to having written them. But between 1892 and 1895 a new series of anonymous letters began to arrive, addressed not only to the Edaljis but to other families in the district as well. The writer—who could not have been responsible for the first letters—poured insults and hatred on the Edaljis, particularly George. There were even threats of death. The mysterious correspondent appeared to know several of the villagers intimately, and either was, or pretended to be, to some extent insane. The police were unable to make an arrest, and while the anonymous letters continued to pour in, the Edaljis were also the victims of several practical jokes, mostly taking the form of bogus advertisements in the newspapers, or miscellaneous objects left in the parson's garden, or in the doorways or on the window-sills of his house.

One day the key of the Walsall Grammar School was found lying

---

[1] Letter from Felix de Halpert to Conan Doyle, 19 October 1913 (C.D.B.A.).

on the doorstep. This was reported to the Chief Constable of the
county who quickly came to the conclusion that the culprit was none
other than George Edalji, the parson's son. The Chief Constable,
Captain the Hon. George Anson, himself wrote to the Reverend
Edalji and told him of his suspicions, adding that he would not
believe the young man even if he protested his innocence. George was
only seventeen when the police, in the person of their Chief Constable,
first accused him, without any justification or giving him a hearing.
Two years later Captain Anson again wrote to the Reverend Edalji
to tell him that his investigation of the anonymous letters was going
well, that his suspicions were becoming more definite every day, and
that once the culprit was arrested he hoped he would receive a
severe prison sentence. This letter covertly hinted that George
Edalji was the culprit. The young man was now a law student, and
apart from the improbability of his having written the letters, why,
since he was to all appearances perfectly sane, should he have
threatened himself with death? And why should he have risked
ruining his career if his crimes were eventually unmasked? But no
charge was made against him in 1895, and at the end of the year the
practical jokes and anonymous letters suddenly stopped. For several
years everything seemed to have returned to normal at Great Wyrley,
but then in 1903 there was a serious outbreak of murderous attacks
on animals. Between February 1903 and March 1904, sixteen animals—sheep, cattle and especially horses—had their stomachs ripped
open at night in spite of the watchfulness of a large number of police.
George Edalji was arrested in August 1903 and imprisoned on the
charge of having disembowelled a pony in a field a few hundred yards
from his house. At the same time a new series of anonymous letters
written in different hands were sent to various people in the village
and to the local police. Some of them had the forged signature
'Greatorex', the name of a schoolboy living nearby who had nothing
whatever to do with the affair. They denounced George Edalji as
one of an organised gang of cattle murderers, and implied that the
writer of the letters, himself a member of the gang, was none the
less ready to collaborate with the police on certain conditions. George
Edalji was arrested at Birmingham, where he had been in practice as
a solicitor since finishing his studies. But he still lived with his
parents at Great Wyrley, and that morning soon after he had left
for the office the house was ransacked from top to bottom, on no

better excuse than that the police hoped to find the evidence they
needed. The only weapons they found were the parson's razors, some
of which had suspicious stains: however, chemical analysis proved
that they were rustspots. Twelve men looked in vain for buried
weapons in the garden. But the searchers did discover a jacket which
was damp according to police evidence (it had rained in the night)
and stained. Conan Doyle objected to the insinuations made by the
prosecution and also to some horse-hairs, said to come from the
jacket, being produced in evidence:

> Now, the police try to make two points here: That the coat was damp,
> and that there were stains which might have been the traces of the
> crime upon it. Each point is good in itself; but, unfortunately, they are
> incompatible and mutually destructive. If the coat were damp, and if
> those marks were blood-stains contracted during the night, then those
> stains were damp also, and the inspector had only to touch them and
> then to raise his crimson finger in the air to silence all criticism. But
> since he could not do so it is clear that the stains were not fresh. They
> fell twelve hours later into the capable hands of the police surgeon, and
> the sanguinary smears conjured up by the evidence of the constable
> diminished with absurd swiftness until they became 'two stains in the
> centre of the right cuff, each about the size of a threepenny bit'. This
> was declared by Dr. Butter to be mammalian blood. He found no more
> blood at all. How these small stains came there it is difficult to trace—
> as difficult as to trace a stain which I see now upon the sleeve of my own
> house-jacket as I look down. A splash from the gravy or underdone
> meat might well produce it. At any rate, it may most safely be said that
> the most adept operator who ever lived would not rip up a horse with
> a razor upon a dark night and have only two threepenny-bit spots of
> blood to show for it. The idea is beyond argument.[1]

The mother and sister of the accused man had all along denied the
truth of the police allegations. But, rather than call on the impartial
evidence of a doctor or vet, who should see the hairs removed and
placed in a sealed envelope, the police smuggled the jacket into a
sack where there was already a piece of horse's hide. Twelve hours
later, Dr. Butter, police surgeon, testified that there were horse-
hairs on the coat. How could evidence obtained under such conditions
be taken as conclusive? Conan Doyle did not fail to point out its
weakness:

> There is one test which occurs to one's mind. Did the hairs all corre-
> spond with the type, colour and texture of the hairs on the sample of
> hide? . . . The cut was down the belly, and the portion taken off was

[1] *The Story of Mr. George Edalji*, H.M. Stationery Office, 1907, p. 17.

from the side of the cut. The under-hair of a horse differs greatly from the longer, darker, harsher hair of the sides. A miscreant leaning against a horse would get the side hairs. If all the hairs on the coat were short, belly hairs, then there is a suggestive fact for the enquiry. Dr. Butter must have compared their appearance . . . I have been able to get the words of Dr. Butter's evidence. They are quoted: 'Numerous hairs on the jacket, which were similar in colour, length, and structure, to those on the piece of skin cut from the horse.' In that case I say, confidently,—and all reflection must confirm it—that these hairs could not possibly be from the general body of the pony, but must have been transferred, no doubt unconsciously, from that particular piece of skin. With all desire to be charitable, the incident leaves a most unpleasant impression upon the mind.

If one could for a moment conceive oneself performing this barbarity, one would not expect to find hairs upon one's coat. There is no necessary connection at all. Anxious to avoid the gush of blood, one would imagine that one would hold off the animal with the flat of one hand and attack it with the other. To lean one's coat against its side would be to bring one's trousers and boots in danger of being soaked in blood.[1]

Finally the police took possession of a pair of wet boots, covered in blackish mud, and some trousers, stained at the bottom with mud of the same colour. Now, for one thing, the earth where the pony had been found was a mixture of clay and sand of a reddish ochre colour; for another, on the evening before his arrest Edalji had gone to see a bootmaker at Bridgtown, a village not far from Great Wyrley. It had been raining all day and the road he had taken was covered with blackish mud. The bootmaker declared that Edalji had been wearing the blue serge suit on whose trousers stains had been found. Nevertheless, when the accused came up for trial at Cannock in October, the prosecution produced the boots, trousers, some razors and the famous jacket as evidence. Besides which, a handwriting expert called Gurrin (who had on his own admission given incorrect evidence in the case of Adolf Beck) testified that Edalji had written the letters accusing himself of the crime for which he was being tried. So Edalji was sentenced to seven years' penal servitude, just as Captain Anson had prophesied ten years before.

But his imprisonment did not put an end to the attacks on animals. The police took this as proof that Edalji had accomplices, who were trying to establish his innocence. This did not deter a young man from admitting in writing, after a brief inquiry, that he had disem-

[1] *The Story of Mr. George Edalji*, H.M. Stationery Office, 1907, p. 20.

bowelled his own horse on the night of 21 September 1903, and then, a few weeks later, emigrating to South Africa, where he declared that his confession had been extorted from him by the police. These events, coming on top of the inexcusable way George Edalji had been treated, led to a protest from a certain number of lawyers, colleagues and friends of Edalji's. A well-known judge, R. D. Yelverton, sent a petition to the Home Office, with 10,000 signatures, including those of several hundred solicitors and barristers—a very effective testimony to George Edalji's character. Among the signatories was the head-master of his school, the solicitor with whom he had kept his terms and the president of the Law Department at Birmingham. This petition had no effect. Naturally Yelverton and his friends tried to get per-mission to see Edalji's dossier at the Home Office, but this was re-fused them. When Yelverton first began to make efforts on Edalji's behalf he received a letter from Captain Anson trying to discourage him, and again stating, without the smallest proof, that Edalji had been a writer of anonymous letters for a long time. After three years in prison, with four years of his sentence still to go, Edalji was sud-denly released without any explanation. He was in good health; this mysterious release, without his character being cleared, was in a sense a fresh injustice. True, Edalji was no longer a prisoner, but in the eyes of the world he was still guilty and his career was shattered. He set out his own case in the pages of *Truth*. The affair was once more taken up by the press and attracted the attention of Sir Arthur Conan Doyle: 'It was late in 1906 that I chanced to pick up an obscure paper called *The Umpire* and my eye caught an article which was a state-ment of his case, made by himself (Edalji). As I read, the unmis-takable accent of truth forced itself upon my attention, and I rea-lized that I was in the presence of an appalling tragedy, and that I was called upon to do what I could to set it right.'[1]

This affair seemed to him to be an English version of the Dreyfus case. Like the unjustly condemned French officer, Edalji had become the victim of racial prejudice at the outset of an honourable career. In both cases there had been public protests immediately after the trial. In both cases there was a question of forged handwriting, Esterhazy in the Dreyfus case corresponding to the writer of the anonymous letters in the Edalji affair. Finally, if the conduct of certain French officials over the Dreyfus affair had been far from

[1] AUT., p. 256.

irreproachable, what was to be said about the Staffordshire police, who, acting no doubt on instructions from their chief, set aside all evidence, hypotheses or reasoning which might possibly prove Edalji's innocence?

Conan Doyle set himself to study the details, first in the press, afterwards by going in person to visit the scene of the events. He met Edalji of course, questioned his family and friends and dozens of witnesses, and ended his investigation by publishing a series of articles in *The Daily Telegraph* at the beginning of January 1907. They were at once reprinted in other newspapers and in booklet form, and soon most of the public was aware of the victimisation of George Edalji. The public view no longer thought of Conan Doyle as a flesh and blood Sherlock Holmes. He was their champion, their Emile Zola. Perfect strangers wrote to him, and George Meredith expressed a widely held view:

> You have done a great public service. I had my suspicion at the time of the trial, though I did not conceive of a deadly conspiracy. I shall not mention the name which must have become wearisome to your ears, but the creator of the marvellous Amateur Detective has shown what he can do in the life of breath; and I confess to the hope that besides vindicating the innocent, he may strike the guilty; not only for vengeance—and certainly this is a case to make us thirst for it—, but that the country may feel assured of there being no impunity for temporarily successful villainy. It concerns the country to see this; and as you have said, opinion will move the Government. H. Gladstone is easily moved by a decided expression of it. In fact, we are all guilty until justice is done. The tone of your articles is good throughout. I am one of the many in your debt for them.[1]

A remarkable letter. A spontaneous response to Conan Doyle's generosity and clearsightedness, it shows the moral ascendency Sir Arthur exercised over his contemporaries: 'we are all guilty until justice is done'. Who could deny that Conan Doyle was the incarnation of the English conscience? James Barrie also praised his friend's courage:

> I read your statements with care, and could not doubt that at all events Edalji had been convicted without any evidence worthy of the name. The conduct of the police still seems to me the worst part of the affair. If you can bring the real criminal to justice it will be a fine thing, but you have done a fine thing already, and so courageous.[2]

[1] Letter to Conan Doyle, 14 January 1907 (C.D.B.A.).
[2] *Ibid.*, 2 February 1907, unpublished (C.D.B.A.).

As Meredith had foreseen, the Home Secretary, Herbert Gladstone, submitted to the pressure of events: as there was no Court of Appeal competent to deal with the affair, he appointed a commission of three to make a report on the first trial. The members were Sir Arthur Wilson, judge of the High Court and Privy Councillor, Sir Albert de Rutzen, a judge, and John Lloyd Wharton, Conservative member of Parliament and legal expert. The commission published its report in May 1907 and the conclusions it came to were very strange. On one hand it disagreed with the jury which had condemned George Edalji in 1903 for disembowelling a pony, and declared the verdict unfounded; on the other hand it stated that Edalji was the writer of the anonymous letters incriminating himself. Having deliberately tried to make the police suspect him, he could hope for no further redress than he had already had, namely to be released. There was no question of granting him damages for his three years in prison nor an official vindication. These conclusions were published by the commission, in May 1907. But a few days after his plea on Edalji's behalf had appeared, and before receiving Barrie's encouraging letter, Conan Doyle had begun to grapple with the mystery surrounding the whole affair, in an attempt to uncover the real criminal or criminals. He made enquiries at Great Wyrley, and in Sherlock Holmes's own manner constructed a working hypothesis completely exonerating Edalji. Before examining this hypothesis and describing the discoveries it led to, we must explain why Conan Doyle was so convinced of Edalji's innocence before he had ever begun to investigate the matter. On his first visit to Great Wyrley he walked across the field where the disembowelled animal had been found. According to the police theory, the crime had been committed between two and three a.m. on a rainy, moonless night, thus escaping the vigilance of the police who were watching the Edalji's house. Conan Doyle noticed that George Edalji would have had to walk about a mile there and back again, and twice cross a main railway line, protected by a double fence, or else avoid this obstacle by taking roundabout paths, wading through sodden fields, crossing ditches and climbing over hedges and banks. This was why Conan Doyle so confidently declared his belief in Edalji's innocence:

> The first sight which I ever had of Mr. George Edalji was enough in itself to convince me both of the extreme improbability of his being guilty of the crime for which he was condemned, and to suggest

some, at least, of the reasons which had led to his being suspected. He had come to my hotel by appointment, but I had been delayed, and he was passing the time by reading the paper. I recognised my man by his dark face, so I stood and observed him. He held the paper close to his eyes and rather sideways, proving not only a high degree of myopia but marked astigmatism. The idea of such a man scouring fields at night and assaulting cattle while avoiding the watching police was ludicrous to anyone who can imagine what the world looks like to eyes with myopia of eight dioptres . . . But such a condition, so hopelessly bad that no glasses availed in the open air, gave the sufferer a vacant, bulge-eyed, staring appearance, which, when taken with his dark skin, must assuredly have made him seem a very queer man to the eyes of an English village, and therefore, to be naturally associated with any queer event. There, in a single physical defect, lay the moral certainty of his innocence, and the reason why he should become the scapegoat.[1]

There were two phases to Conan Doyle's investigation, one before and one after the publication of the report of Gladstone's commission. During the second, he called upon Dr. Lindsay Johnson, a hand-writing expert of some notoriety (he had been consulted by Maître Labori, counsel for Dreyfus, about the famous *bordereau*). As Conan Doyle wrote in *The Daily Telegraph* of 11 June 1907:

> Dr. Lindsay Johnson's methods have been to procure photographic positives of the writings in question, and to project them immensely enlarged (20–50 diameters) on a screen by means of two lanterns. By having one of the lanterns on a stand provided with all azimuth motions, one can bring any word or line underneath or above the line of comparison. By these elaborate methods even the pulse beat can in many cases be detected and a minuteness of comparison be effected unknown by any previous method.

Sir Arthur's point of departure was the series of incidents (anonymous letters, threats and hoaxes) to which the Edalji family had been subjected before the young solicitor's arrest. Most of the anonymous letters written in 1892 had been posted in Walsall, not far from Great Wyrley. In 1903 a fresh series of letters purporting to be written by a friend of the police described Edalji as the leader of a gang: these also came from Walsall. It will be remembered that the Edaljis had found the key of Walsall Grammar School on their doorstep, and that Greatorex, the name used by the anonymous correspondent, was the real name of a pupil in the school, though he could not be guilty

[1] *The Story of Mr. George Edalji*, p. 1.

as he had been many miles away from the place where the letters had been posted. It therefore seemed to Conan Doyle that the enquiry should begin at Walsall. As for the criminal, might he not be a pupil or an old boy of the Grammar School who knew both Edalji and Greatorex? His suspicions soon became more precise: ' . . . All my energies have gone towards the capture and exposure of the real offenders,' he wrote to his mother. 'These are three youths (one already dead), brothers of the name of Sharp. The case I have against them is already very strong but I have five separate lines of enquiry on foot, by which I hope to make it overwhelming. They are decently educated men, as is evident from the letters.'[1]

Now it was the novelist's turn to receive anonymous threatening letters, though this new development had no effect on the official view of Edalji's guilt. Comparing these new documents with other specimens of handwriting, Dr. Lindsay Johnson ascribed them to one of the Sharp brothers. Conan Doyle had in fact got hold of some samples of the handwriting of this boy, Royden Sharp, one of which was a letter from him to the father of Greatorex. He now got in touch with an ex-headmaster of Walsall Grammar School, who gave him some information as to Sharp's academic career. The school records made him out a thoroughly bad lot. However, as if to facilitate his enquiries, Conan Doyle's anonymous correspondent wrote him an insulting letter abusing the headmaster: 'You blind fool,' it ran, 'don't you know he was at school with that blasted Greatorex lads Will and Antony and he hated them like poison. There was no education to be got at Walsall when that. . . Aldis was high school bos [sic].'[2]

Starting from these facts, Conan Doyle began on a report of the evidence against Royden Sharp, entitled: 'The Case against Royden Sharp for the committing of those outrages upon cattle from February to August, 1903, for which George Edalji was condemned to seven years' penal servitude at Stafford Assizes, November 1903.' The points tending to establish his guilt were: that the interval between the two series of anonymous letters (1895 to 1903) corresponded to the period when Sharp had left the neighbourhood of Great Wyrley. After being apprenticed to a butcher he had joined the merchant marine, and in 1902 was serving on a cattle-boat. Conan Doyle realised that this gave Sharp a chance to learn how to manage

[1] 29 January 1907 (C.D.B.A.).   [2] (C.D.B.A.)

cattle and perhaps also an opportunity to concoct the criminal scheme which he carried out after returning to Great Wyrley in July 1903. At this point he referred to the evidence of Mrs. Greatorex: when she went to the house where Sharp lived, he had waved a veterinary lancet at her, saying that the mysterious criminal had used something of the kind. Sir Arthur managed to get possession of this object and added a sketch of it to his report.

This document did not probably constitute incontestable evidence of Royden Sharp's guilt, but in so far as it brought to light the weakness of the charge against Edalji it made it clear that he was the victim of a definite miscarriage of justice. The conclusion is striking:

> This seems to me in itself to be a complete case, and if I—a stranger in the district—have been able to collect it, I cannot doubt that fresh evidence would come out after his arrest. He appears to have taken very little pains to hide his proceedings, and how there could at any time have been any difficulty in pointing him out as the criminal is to me an extraordinary thing.

While Conan Doyle's report was in the hands of the Home Secretary, the Gladstone Commission gave its verdict.

Meanwhile the Law Society, with Sir George Lewis at its head, decided to vindicate George Edalji, and *The Daily Telegraph* opened a subscription-list to pay for a retrial. In official quarters, Conan Doyle's report was almost entirely ignored. The Home Secretary announced in the Commons that nothing new had come up, and Mr. Ernley Blackwell (who became Under-Secretary of State six years later) said he considered Sharp to be entirely innocent. The passage in Conan Doyle's autobiography referring to the case has an unaccustomed flavour of bitterness:

> The sad fact is that officialdom in England stands solid together, and that when you are forced to attack it, you need not expect justice, but rather that you are up against an avowed Trade Union, the members of which are not going to act the blackleg to each other, and which subordinates the public interest to a false idea of loyalty. What confronts you is a determination to admit nothing which inculpates another official, and as to the idea of punishing another official for offences which have caused misery to helpless victims, it never comes within their horizon. Even now, after the lapse of so many years, I can hardly think with patience of the handling of this case.[1]

[1] AUT., p. 256.

Were his recriminations justified? Certainly. Conan Doyle knew what he was talking about. The official solidarity he alludes to had indeed figured at George Edalji's trial. Sir Arthur knew, for example, that the Attorney-General, Sir John Lawson Walton, was privately convinced of the innocence of the accused. Above all, he knew why the Gladstone Commission of 1907 had been unable to give an impartial verdict. There can be no doubt that the official whose offences had 'caused misery to helpless victims' was Captain Anson, Chief of the Staffordshire police. He had gone so far as to write to George's father, the Reverend Edalji, to try and influence him; he had personally approached Mr. Yelverton in order to postpone a revision of the verdict, and finally he had done his best to thwart Conan Doyle's investigation.

The Gladstone Commission consisted of only three members, and one of these, Sir Albert de Rutzen, was a second cousin of Anson's. The Commission confined itself to docilely repeating Anson's theories about the anonymous letters. Instead of shedding new light on the Edalji affair, its practical result was to shield Anson.

But Conan Doyle did not give up his attempt to clear George Edalji. In 1911 he thought the political situation more favourable and tried to get the dossier re-examined. 'I have written to the new Home Secretary about Edalji,' he wrote to his mother. 'I'll win that fight yet.'[1]

His efforts did not result in a spectacular retrial, as in the case of Oscar Slater. But by proving that there were gaps in the national system of justice, he paved the way for the creation of the Court of Criminal Appeal, a new organisation within the High Court, whose function was precisely to avoid such abuses as had appeared in the prosecution of Edalji and the report of the Gladstone Commission.

[1] 2 November 1911 (C.D.B.A.).

Chapter 8

THE LOVER OF JUSTICE: OSCAR SLATER

At the root of Conan Doyle's activities on behalf of George Edalji, and (to a lesser degree) of Roger Casement, we find an impulsive sympathy called out by the personalities of both men. Perhaps sympathy is rather too strong a word for his attitude to Casement, but whereas homosexuality was an aggravating circumstance to most people, Conan Doyle saw him as the victim of a trauma. His view of the Edalji case was even more definitely opposed to that of the man in the street. His intervention sprang from his desire for justice, but it was also a personal protest against racial prejudice. When we come to Slater we find a similar impulse and the same tolerant response, but considerably weakened by the character of the man in question. Edalji was a Parsee, Slater was a German Jew. But the fact that both men belonged to a racial minority could not disguise their wide differences in other respects. George Edalji was a young lawyer, whose morals were vouched for by everyone. Things were very different with Slater. He was born Joseph Leschziner, in Silesia, about 1870. At the age of fifteen he left his native village, where his father was the baker, and after working in a bank at Hamburg for a short while he decided to try his luck in Great Britain. First in London, then in Scotland, he led a very erratic existence. He went twice to the United States. For the sake of euphony he took the name of Slater. What money he had came from shady transactions: he earned his living, if it can be so described, on race-courses and in gambling-halls. About 1902 he got married, but abandoned his wife, and at the time of his arrest was living with a Frenchwoman whose avowed profession of night-club singer may have concealed less artistic activities. This well-matched couple arrived in Glasgow in November 1908, that is to say—and this point is important evidence in favour of Slater's innocence—only six weeks before the assassination of Miss Gilchrist. Slater, who was going under the name of Anderson at this time, passed himself off as a diamond-cutter, but still went on frequenting gambling-halls as usual. Such was the individual whom Sir Arthur Conan Doyle was to rehabilitate after long years of struggle. This success, even more than what he did for Edalji, gained him a generally accepted reputation as a criminologist and champion of the oppressed.[1]

Of what crime was Slater accused? On 21 December 1908, at seven o'clock in the evening, an old spinster called Marion Gilchrist was found murdered in the dining-room of her Glasgow flat. Miss Gilchrist's servant, Helen Lambie, had gone out for ten minutes on an errand, and the murder took place during that time. Miss Gilchrist appears to have been a mistrustful character: her front door had more than one lock. Hidden in a wardrobe among her clothes she kept several thousand pounds' worth of jewellery. Below the victim's flat lived the Adams family who said, when questioned, that they had heard the noise of a fall and three separate blows. Mr. Adams ran upstairs and rang Miss Gilchrist's bell, but got no reply, though he continued to hear suspicious noises which he described as being like someone chopping sticks. He had just gone back to his own flat when Helen Lambie, the servant, returned home. As she went towards the kitchen, the bedroom door opened and a man passed behind her and in full view of Mr. Adams who had come back for news. Then this mysterious individual slipped discreetly away. Since Helen Lambie paid no attention to him, Adams saw no reason to stop him. However he did ask the servant where her mistress was. When Helen Lambie went into the dining-room, she found Miss Gilchrist's body stretched in front of the fireplace. A wooden box in which she kept her private papers lay broken on the ground, its contents scattered everywhere. On a table Helen Lambie caught sight of her mistress's jewels, and she knew them well enough to realise that a diamond brooch in the form of a crescent was missing. The police were summoned, and circulated a rather vague description of the man they were looking for, based on the evidence of the two witnesses: about five foot six, dark, well-shaved, light grey overcoat, dark cap. Next day a third witness came forward: a fourteen-year-old girl called Mary Barrowman, who had been walking past Miss Gilchrist's house at the fatal moment, when a man suddenly emerged and bumped into her slightly

---

[1] Cf. the following comment on the part he played in the Thorne case: '. . . Conan Doyle entered the lists, with the honours of Oscar Slater upon him. He was not quite easy about the case; there seemed to him a faint doubt existing. *Doyle was always on the side of the underdog.*' Browne D. G. and Tullett E. V., *Bernard Spilsbury, His Life and Cases*, 1955, p. 173.

in his haste. She gave a quite different description. Mary Barrowman had seen a tall young man, wearing a fawn cloak or macintosh, a round hat and brown boots. Four days later the police found out that a man called Slater had tried to sell a pawn-ticket for a crescent-shaped diamond brooch. Slater and his mistress had already left Glasgow for Liverpool and embarked on the *Lusitania* for New York. The police believed he was the criminal. Unfortunately, further information disclosed that Slater's brooch had been pawned more than a month before Miss Gilchrist's death, and that it was in fact a totally different one. But the Glasgow police went ahead, regardless of this, and asked the American police to arrest Slater on arrival in New York. For an extradition order to be obtained the three witnesses had to identify Slater. To this end they were subjected to various tendencious manœuvres. They were shown photographs of Slater, and the police made sure they would give the evidence they wanted. In New York, before the extradition proceedings began, a Scottish inspector, who had come over with the witnesses, stage-managed the proceedings, and arranged that the witnesses should see Slater as he was escorted along the corridor to the court-room by two American policemen. The evidence, especially that of the two females, was entirely satisfactory to the Scottish police. Adams would say no more than that there was a certain resemblance between Slater and the man he had seen in Miss Gilchrist's flat, and that without great conviction.

Slater's American Counsel advised his client to resist extradition on the grounds that the Scottish police had confused two different pieces of jewellery. Slater refused to take his advice, thinking to get off more lightly by offering of his own accord to go and prove his innocence before a Scottish jury. Seals had been put on his luggage, but it was opened and searched as soon as they reached Glasgow, as the police wanted at all costs to find the murder weapon. For lack of anything better, they chose a small upholsterer's hammer from a card of assorted tools which Slater had bought from a cheap shop, as anyone else might have done. 'But what man in his senses, planning a deliberate murder, would take with him a weapon which was light, frail, and so long that it must project from any pocket? The nearest lump of stone upon the road would serve his purpose better than that.'[1]

[1] Conan Doyle, *The Case of Oscar Slater*, 1912, p. 44.

The first hearing of the Slater case took place at Edinburgh on 3 May 1909, under Lord Guthrie. The Lord Advocate was Alexander Ure, and Slater was defended by MacClure. The prosecution produced as many as twelve witnesses ready to swear that they had seen Slater wandering round Miss Gilchrist's house just before she died. But not one of these witnesses knew by sight the man he was supposed to have seen, not one of them knew Slater by sight, not one of them had spoken to either of the two men whom the prosecution declared were one and the same. These twelve witnesses, like the previous three, had photographs of Slater in front of them and were subjected to the same sort of pressure. Slater's very un-Scottish features were a help to the police. Technically speaking he was fit to stand his trial—a scapegoat would have been nearer the mark. One of the witnesses had heard the voice of the mysterious prowler, but had not noticed that he had a foreign accent, whereas Slater spoke with a very strong German accent indeed. The formality of identifying Slater was also stage-managed to a ludicrous extent. The accused was placed among a group of Scotsmen, as different from him as possible, and nine of them were policemen in plain clothes. This enormously facilitated the witnesses' task. Counsel for Slater denounced the proceedings as tendencious: the prosecution countered with 'normal practice'. And little trouble was taken to establish any connection between the mysterious prowler and the seemingly unpremeditated character of the crime. The servant, Helen Lambie, had an afternoon off every week; why not choose this time rather than the few moments when no one could have known she would be absent?

The prosecution also took no trouble to construct any hypothesis as to how Slater—a stranger in Glasgow—could have found out about the old spinster's wealth. He had never even heard of Miss Gilchrist, Slater declared. Unfortunately for him, his alibi was of the most banal description. When Miss Gilchrist was killed he was dining at home with his mistress and the servant. Both witnesses confirmed this, but the prosecution of course refused to accept it; they also rejected a witness whose importance was realised later on, when it helped Slater prove his innocence at the rehabilitation proceedings. Finally, in an eloquent and fiery indictment, the Lord Advocate uttered a number of untruths which influenced the jury. In particular he suggested that when Slater realised that his name and description were being circulated, he hurriedly left Glasgow on the evening of Christmas Day, which was completely false, and incredible into the bargain. The evidence of the doctor who had first examined the corpse was set aside: his opinion might have weakened the police theories about the weapon. The police doctor declared that about forty blows from the weapon produced in court could cause death. Finally, no trace of blood was found either on the toy-sized hammer or on the accused's clothing. As the analysis of the crime itself seemed unlikely to ensure conviction, Slater's morals were put forward as evidence, and they tried to make use of the evidence of his servant to convict him of procuring. Slater hardly tried to defend himself against this new accusation, and made a highly unfavourable impression on the jury. The prisoner's shady morals did duty for actual proof.

In the extremely emotional atmosphere invoked by the prosecution, Counsel for Slater was at a loss how to defend his client. His professional conscience prevented him counteracting the effect of the Lord Advocate's brilliant lies. Nine out of the fourteen jurymen declared Slater guilty, only one voted him innocent and the rest abstained. He was condemned to death. And then a revulsion of feelings set in. During the trial Glasgow had been living through an atmosphere like that of Salem. With the verdict, the fever subsided; a vague shame felt by some, and a conviction that Slater was innocent on the part of fewer still, combined to create a wave not exactly of sympathy but of tolerance towards the prisoner. The margin of doubt as to his guilt was sufficient to enable his Counsel to draw up a petition based on his own report on the case, asking for the sentence to be commuted, for which he collected 20,000 signatures. It was addressed to the Secretary of State for Scotland and pleaded insufficient evidence as well as improper pressure exercised on the jury by the Lord Advocate. Counsel's memorandum alluded among other things to an extremely prejudicial suppression by the prosecution of evidence which would have completely invalidated the Barrowman girl's testimony. As a result, Slater's execution, fixed for 27 May, was cancelled two days before that date, and the prisoner's sentence commuted to hard labour for life.

Nor did the movement in favour of Slater end here. In England and Scotland alike the press went into the affair in detail, usually concluding that the sentence was incorrect. In April 1910 a complete account of the case appeared in the *Notable British Trials* series, and the theory of a miscarriage of justice was put forward unambiguously. But since there were no legal means of re-opening the case without pressure from public opinion, Slater's champions appealed to Sir Arthur Conan Doyle, and it was his influence that set going the slow—desperately slow—movement for a retrial. 'That Paladin of lost causes,' wrote William Roughead, 'found in the dubious circumstances of the case matter after his own heart. *The Times* and *The Spectator* opened their columns to a discussion of the verdict, and many distinguished authorities, including Sir Herbert Stephen, supported Sir Arthur's contention that there had been a gross miscarriage of justice.'[1]

Conan Doyle's first action was to write a report of eighty pages, *The Case of Oscar Slater*, in which he viewed the different aspects of the affair from a fresh angle. He noted the gaps in the prosecution's case, the way witnesses contradicted each other and the triviality of the explanations suggested by the prosecution. He also questioned the motives for the crime. Theft did not seem to him sufficient, and he was the first to put forward the hypothesis that the criminal was less concerned to steal Miss Gilchrist's jewels than to get hold of some private document, such as a will. Perhaps the disappearance of the diamond brooch was a false trail, by which the criminal hoped to remove suspicion from himself. However, aware of the fragility of such a hypothesis and the necessity of proceeding with the utmost caution, he did not pretend to have solved the problem, and called for a fresh trial:

> I leave the matter now with the hope that, even after many days, some sudden flash may be sent which will throw a light upon as brutal and callous a crime as has ever been recorded in those black annals in which the criminologist finds the materials for his study. Meanwhile it is on the conscience of the authorities, and in the last resort on that of the community that this verdict obtained under the circumstances which I have indicated shall now be reconsidered.[2]

Meanwhile in December 1912, Edward Marshall Hall, the barrister, a personal friend of Conan Doyle's and a Conservative member of Parliament, asked a question in the House about the improper conduct of the prosecution. The reply was that as no new evidence had come up the affair was now closed. Not until March 1914 did

[1] *Famous Trials*, 1941, p. 70.   [2] *The Case of Oscar Slater*, p. 79.

a Glasgow solicitor called David Cook make public some remarks made by one of the detectives employed by the prosecution in the Slater case. Cook revealed that one of the witnesses had indicated a different suspect; also that a second witness had given false evidence; lastly that information had come in, proving that Slater had made no attempt whatever to conceal his departure from Glasgow, which the Public Prosecutor had presented in the light of a flight. These were all circumstances in Slater's favour, and at last the authorities were forced to act. A Commission of Inquiry was appointed, presided over by the Sheriff of Lanarkshire. But what conclusions could it possibly reach when Slater had no means of being represented at it and the authorities had no desire to have their verdict reversed? The composition and methods of the commission showed that same solidarity which had made Conan Doyle so very indignant with the commission appointed to enquire into the Edalji affair. It was easy to foresee what would happen.

The Commission of Inquiry met *in camera* and the witnesses did not have to give evidence on oath. The writing of the report was left to the direction of the president, an assize barrister called Gardner Millar, formerly secretary to the magistrate who was then Lord Justice General. In spite of the cautiousness of the Commission's conclusion, new aspects of the case were revealed in their report. Published on 27 June 1914 it produced a *tertium quid* described by the initials 'A.B.', although it never revealed exactly what the different witnesses, particularly Helen Lambie, had testified about him. What David Cook had said was confirmed, and the evidence of a new witness, Agnes Brown, was set against that of Mary Barrowman. Finally, Slater's alibi gained additional support from a grocer called MacBrayne, who declared that he had seen Slater standing on his own doorstep at about 8 o'clock on the evening of the crime. Mac-Brayne said that he had gone to the police before the case came on, been confronted with Slater and made a statement. The defence had never been informed of this important piece of evidence and it had quite simply been removed from the record. In spite of this accumulation of fresh evidence, the Secretary of State for Scotland refused to order a retrial, and Slater remained in prison. Meanwhile a sordid settlement of accounts had changed the course of events. Detective Trench had been the source of the revelations made by Cook, which had led to the appointment of the Commission of Inquiry. In 1915

Trench was subjected to a series of acts of persecution by his colleagues and superiors, and was finally wrongfully charged with con-
cealment, along with the solicitor David Cook. The new Lord Justice
Clerk, appointed in 1915, put an end to this ignominious action.

By the time the war was over the affair was forgotten; so was
Oscar Slater, in prison at Peterhead, though he still hoped someone
would turn up to rescue him from darkness. Towards the end of
1924, through the instrumentality of a discharged fellow-prisoner,
Gordan, Slater sent a pathetic appeal to Conan Doyle. Gordan's
letter to Sir Arthur was published in the *Sunday Mail* of 15 February 1925:

> I have been an unfortunate inmate of Peterhead Prison where I met
> Slater (. . .) I made a promise that I would see you and deliver a verbal
> message on his behalf. The enclosed is a written message he gave me
> a few hours before my discharge. I secreted it in my mouth and got it
> out safely . . .

Slater's message ran as follows: 'Gordan, my boy, I wish you in
every way the best of luck. Please do what you can for me. Give to the
English public your opinion regarding me. Please don't forget to
write or see Conan D.'

What could Conan Doyle do? Despairing of being able to get a
belated revision of the verdict, he consulted Sir Herbert Stephen and
Craigie Aitchison. The two lawyers encouraged him to ask for a
pardon for Slater, and he wrote to Sir John Gilmour, Secretary of
State for Scotland, to this effect. Once again nothing happened.
Abandoning a frontal attack, Conan Doyle again decided to stir up
public opinion, wrote letters to the press and won over a Glasgow
journalist called William Park to his side. In July 1927 Park published
a manifesto entitled *The Truth about Oscar Slater*, maintaining that
Helen Lambie had been responsible for a judicial error and an accomplice in it. A few weeks later Edgar Wallace took up this hypothesis
in an article in the *Morning Post*. According to the new theory,
the servant's brief absence just when the murder was committed
showed her complicity. Needless to say this new campaign was not
welcomed by the authorities. In the House of Commons on 29 July,
the Lord Advocate contradicted the rumours being circulated in the
press that a new enquiry was to be set on foot. However, four newspapers—the *Solicitors' Journal*, the *Daily News*, the *Empire News*
and the *Morning Post*—went on with the campaign on behalf of

Slater. The *Daily News* took the initiative and sent a special correspondent to Scotland, whose articles, signed 'The Pilgrim', appeared in September and October. On 23 October the *Empire News*
exploded a fresh bombshell: their special representative had succeeded in finding Helen Lambie in the United States, and she had
told him that when first interrogated by the Glasgow police she had
given them a description and a name which they had suppressed. She
had afterwards been dissuaded from standing by her first statement.
She also revealed that Miss Gilchrist sometimes received mysterious
visitors, and that on these occasions she used to send her servant on
an errand to be out of the way. And, again according to Helen
Lambie, the man she had mentioned in her first statement had been
to see Miss Gilchrist several times before, and knew his way about
the house. She added: 'I am convinced that the man I saw was better
dressed and of a better station in life than Slater. The only thing
they had in common was that, when standing sideways, the outlines
of the faces from the left were much the same.'

Four days after the appearance of this article, the *Empire News*
published a personal appeal to Helen Lambie, asking her to come
forward and make a statement on oath to the authorities. For obvious
reasons Helen Lambie remained deaf to this appeal, but she did not
deny the statement attributed to her. Encouraged by this partial
success, the *Daily News* instituted a search for Mary Barrowman and
found her near Glasgow. She also confessed to the journalist who
questioned her the circumstances in which she had made her de-
position nineteen years ago. The police, she said, had practically
dictated her statement. She was quite ready to sign this new account
of the affair and it was published in the issue for 5 November. Five
days later, by some strange coincidence, it was announced that Oscar
Slater was to be discharged as a reward for good conduct during his
eighteen years of incarceration. This so-called act of mercy aroused
Conan Doyle's indignation: 'I should have sent you Lambie's confession in the *Empire News*, but I guess you saw it. That should be
final. What a story! What a scandal! She says that the police *made* her
say it was Slater. Third degree! What a cesspool it all is! But we have
no words of hope from those wooden-headed officials. I shall put on
the political screw and I know how to do it. I'll win in the end but it
has been a long fight.'[1]

[1] Postcard to J. Cuming Walters (C.D.B.A.).

Oscar Slater was set free on 14 November and Conan Doyle circulated a letter to members of Parliament giving the reasons for retrial and asking them to insist upon one. A special act of Parliament would have to be passed. On 15 November the government did in fact announce its intention of applying to Slater's case an act of 1926 according to which the Scottish Court of Criminal Appeal (who would normally hear the appeal) was not competent to deal with a verdict given before this act had come into force; whence the necessity of a special act to authorise the Court of Appeal to deal with Slater.

The bill had its first reading on 16 November, passed the second reading on the 19th and was ratified by the House of Lords on the 30th. It was now possible for the retrial to take place. Preparations lasted for about six months. Slater had already written to Conan Doyle the day after his discharge, expressing his gratitude in moving terms: 'Sir Conan Doyle, you breaker of my shackles, you lover of truth for justice sake, I thank you from the bottom of my heart for the goodness you have shown towards me.'[1]

As may be imagined, the expenses of the case were extremely high; Conan Doyle advanced Slater the necessary sum, and engaged three barristers, one of them Craigie Aitchison who had just got John Merrett acquitted of parricide. Incidentally it may be noted that Slater never repaid the £1,000 lent to him.

The first hearing took place on 8 June at Edinburgh, and was the occasion of Conan Doyle's visiting his native town for the last time. Aitchison had no difficulty in destroying the supposed proofs of guilt advanced at the first trial and Sir Bernard Spilsbury was called to give evidence about the weapon. The Court adjourned on 9 July and gave its verdict on the 20th. Four questions had been asked: Was the verdict of the first trial without foundation? Had decisive new evidence appeared to throw fresh light on the affair? Had the retention of certain evidence by the Public Prosecutor been to the detriment of the appellant? Had the attitude of the presiding judge contributed to falsify the verdict? If the court answered only one of these questions in the affirmative the judgement of 1909 would be quashed. It chose the last of the four. Slater was thus cleared of all possible suspicion. The criminal was never known, though in his study of the affair published in 1927 Park attributed the crime to the victim's nephew.

[1] Letter from Oscar Slater, 17 November 1927 (C.D.B.A.).

Thus, while the shadow of death was already hovering over him, Conan Doyle won his last and surely his most glorious victory for a just and humane cause. Thirty years after his death his compatriot Compton Mackenzie reminded us that 'not many men in this century have shown as much consistent moral courage as the creator of Sherlock Holmes and Dr. Watson showed right through the seventy years of his valuable life.'[1]

On this final note of appraisal we will pause for a moment. Despite the complexity of the issues involved and the diversity of his activities, we see Conan Doyle tirelessly ready to support the rights of the individual, thus defending an ideal which transcended all categories of mankind and all beliefs.

[1] *On Moral Courage*, 1962, p. 164.

Chapter 9

THE PROPHET: IN THE CAUSE OF
SPIRITUALISM

My one aim in life is that this great truth, the return and
communion of the dead, shall be brought home to a
material world which needs it so badly.[1]

We have now reached the most delicate part of this biographical
study: Sir Arthur Conan Doyle's career as a spiritualist. In the
second edition of his *Memories and Adventures*—a book which is not,
nor set out to be, a confession or introspective autobiography, but
more of a running commentary on his own life—Sir Arthur briefly
describes his spiritualistic activities as the most important adventure
in his life and one which gave it real meaning. The author died soon
after the publication of this second edition, whereupon a spiritualist
friend, the Rev. Dr. John Lamond, paid a tribute to him in a biographical study giving primary importance to his mystical phase. He
treated the first sixty years of Conan Doyle's life as a sort of prelude to
his conversion, after which came the glorious years when he was the
inspiration of the spiritualist crusade to which Lamond himself
belonged. Although this biography, with its postscript by Lady Conan
Doyle, might have been approved by Sir Arthur himself, it suggests in
an extremely inexplicit manner that he had experienced some form of
revelation, without going into the psychological factors which prepared the way for it.

On the other hand Conan Doyle's second biographer, Mr. John
Dickson Carr, was much too reticent about the spiritualistic phase,
which is all the more to be regretted because he was a great deal
better informed than his predecessor as to the reasons for Sir Arthur
Conan Doyle's adherence to spiritualism. While Lamond devotes
two thirds of his book to the question, Mr. Dickson Carr uses his own
incredulous attitude to spiritualism as a pretext for declining to give
an opinion, and gives barely a twentieth of his book to it.

[1] Private papers, 2 July 1926.

On whatever level one may undertake to examine or expose the doctrines of spiritualism, problems and contradictions will be discovered in them which may well baffle and perhaps discourage a biographer. Nevertheless, whatever our own philosophical or religious beliefs, can we possibly deny the importance of spiritualism to Sir Arthur Conan Doyle himself? Indifferent to his religious message, Conan Doyle's friends were for the most part resigned to the fact that they did not understand his faith, nor his vehement loyalty to the spiritualistic movement. Assuming that spiritualism was completely futile, and adopting an attitude of mocking and impertinent compassion, some of them tried to explain his position in a way that deprived it of all nobility, by alleging every kind of fraud and assuming the existence of unconvincing sentimental motives. Was the orator who continued his speech after hearing the unexpected news of his son's death the sort of man who would be driven to believe purely from the desire for consolation? Nor does the image of a man constantly taken in by the tricks of bogus mediums stand up to examination. To account for Sir Arthur Conan Doyle's conversion we must first reject every over-simple *a priori* argument and try to see this long and complicated process of development, not in the light of what parapsychology has taught us today, but in that by which his contemporaries tried to understand the occult phenomena upon which spiritualism is founded, especially Anglo-Saxon spiritualism.

The English form of spiritualism to which Sir Arthur Conan Doyle sacrificed his talent and his wealth at the end of his life, and for which he risked part of his reputation, is a neo-Christian cult with tens of thousands of devotees. It is connected with similar cults all over the world, especially in Europe and North America, and also in the Far East, where caodaism is its most recent manifestation. The English terms 'spiritualist' and 'spiritualism' are unfortunate—Conan Doyle repeatedly wrote that he detested them—and, what is more important, they tend to introduce confusion whenever we remember their meanings in the history of Western philosophy. In this sense 'spiritualism' is neither a cult nor a religion; and every philosophical doctrine or theory of knowledge opposed to materialism, like those of Berkeley, Reid or Kant can be called 'spiritualist', though it is more convenient to speak of idealism, as opposed to realism. The word 'spiritualism' should really be reserved for doctrines affirming the natural priority and superiority of mind over matter, and this makes the terminology of English spiritualists regrettable. We may wonder if a certain incoherence and inability to justify itself may not be found in the doctrines and practice of a religion with such a name. For the sake of clarity we must continue to speak of Anglo-Saxon 'spiritualism', adding that the word '*spiritisme*' does not necessarily imply the existence of any religious cult in other countries such as France.

The remarkable thing about Anglo-Saxon spiritualism is that it sets up to be both a form of empirical knowledge, in the scientific sense, and a practical religion; and that it attempts to link the physical with the metaphysical in an Aristotelian synthesis. It is the same with the adjective 'psychic': we must ignore its exact significance, and accept the spiritualists' conventional use of the word when speaking of the phenomena connected with their belief. These phenomena may be physical (such as raps, movements of objects with no apparent cause, appearances of lights or ectoplasm) or mental (cryptaesthesia or telepathy, 'supra-normal' knowledge or clairvoyance). These manifestations are seldom thought to be spontaneous, and in most cases depend upon the presence of a more or less active agent known as a medium. One must admit that the history of psychic phenomena goes back to such remote times that it is difficult to distinguish it from primeval magic. Many spiritualists speak with great respect of the sibyls of antiquity and the biblical prophets, and believe that they were the precursors of modern mediums. Spiritualism proper is however a comparatively recent movement, and we can trace its history.

At the beginning of the nineteenth century two ideas that are not always clearly distinguished—magnetism and hypnotism—spread far and wide. In 1847 it seems that cases of haunting were recorded in the United States, at a farm-house in Hydesville, near New York. Mr. Fox, his wife and their two daughters aged fifteen and twelve, declared that they had been visited by an obstinate 'spirit', who manifested his presence by knocking on the walls (the 'raps' of the spiritualists) and moving furniture about. They believed that this 'spirit' was that of a man who had been murdered in their house many years before, by a previous tenant. Digging under the cellar brought to light pieces of crockery and bones. The Fox family saw no reason to inform the police, so there was no official enquiry, but the affair created a sensation in the United States and the Fox sisters set up in New York as professional mediums, thus starting a fashion followed by thousands of others who had hitherto been unaware of their powers.

By 1854 there were about 3,000,000 devotees of spiritualism in the United States, making use of 10,000 mediums. In 1852 a spiritualistic mission gave a series of public demonstrations in England. In the following year another mission travelled all over Germany and France, where in spite of—or perhaps because of—the ban laid on spiritualism by the Académie des Sciences, there were some scientists who took an interest in psychic phenomena. During the next fifty years or so, the activities of the spiritualists were the cause of a great many investigations, experiments, meetings and debates, and aroused the interest of intellectuals all over Europe. The formation of groups to study occultism provoked a great deal of incredulity. Nor is it possible at the present day, in spite of progress in the methods used and the nature of the results obtained, to say that scientific opinion has cast off its habitual reserve on the subject.

The two fundamental problems concern the reality of phenomena and their interpretation. In 1869 the Royal Society of London, with Sir John Lubbock as vice-president, appointed a committee to study supra-normal physical phenomena. It came to the conclusion that table-turning and rapping were genuine manifestations, and the messages communicated through the spiritualistic code intelligible. The committee's report was not, however, accepted by the whole Society, since it had failed to bring to light any one convincing and rigorous experiment inexplicable by preconceived ideas, to which scientists are as prone as other men. Is it necessary to say that no such experiment has yet been carried out? Have the spiritualists then achieved nothing remarkable during nearly a century? Probably science today, becoming less and less dogmatic, is able to approach the study of psychic phenomena more calmly than was possible at a time when its attitude was more totalitarian.

The example of Sir William Crookes was to have considerable repercussions in England. Crookes carried out experiments with the medium Dunglas Home over a period of three years, with results which challenged the laws of weight, or more generally of classical physics and mechanics, though he could not bring himself to form a hypothesis as to the existence of intelligent 'spirits'. He contented himself with suggesting that the phenomena might be caused by some form of energy inherent in the human organism. Later on, after experiments with another medium, Florence Cook, and the spirit guide known as Katie King, Crookes accepted the spiritualistic hypothesis. He went on with his experiments, but with such a changed orientation that, in spite of the authority and respect his earlier work had earned him, their scientific value was more and more frequently questioned. Both Crookes's detractors and his partisans must have been prejudiced; probably also the experimenters were trying to convince the sceptics of something which was not susceptible of strict geometric proof, because it depended finally on the evidence of the senses. Lastly, the very conditions in which the most conclusive experiments were carried out unfortunately did not admit the absolute exclusion of fraud by careful control. The scientists who were attracted to the domain of speculation were the first to deplore the absence of a suitable method for making a decisive experiment— one that could be repeated at will and in perfectly familiar conditions.

At the time when Crookes was carrying out his experiments, Frederic Myers was founding the Society for Psychical Research at Cambridge. The aims of this society were mainly ideological. Its learned members wanted to combat the dangers of what they denounced as materialism, namely the atmosphere of total moral indifference in which biological or psychological research was carried out. Thus 'psychical research' offered Myers and his friends a chance to prove the existence of a 'spirit' world and define its laws, as well as to investigate accepted phenomena like hypnotism, and others that were more problematical derived from the literature of spiritualism.

Successively presided over by Henry Sidgwick, Balfour Stewart, William Crookes, William James and A. J. Balfour, the Society could boast the patronage of Gladstone, Ruskin, Lord Tennyson and Alfred Russell Wallace. Their activities aroused a great deal of interest abroad, especially in France; and scientists and thinkers such as Janet, Théodule Ribot, Taine and Charles Richet were corresponding members. After a few years the investigators had collected an impressive amount of material bearing particularly on telepathy. The cause of psychical research was also furthered by Edmund Gurney, the Wingfield sisters, Malcolm Guthrie and Sir Oliver Lodge, who was the first to approach the public through the newspapers in order to collect evidence of the pathological phenomena of telepathic hallucination. But no theory, no truly scientific hypothesis was found to explain the mechanism of these phenomena. They could be recorded objectively and critically, but this led to no laboratory experiments or new methods, and left the door open to the traditional metaphysical hypothesis of the duality of human personality.

Thus the inability of science to explain certain para-normal phenomena whose existence it could not categorically deny, led to a new spiritualistic philosophy, which, combined with the religious philanthropy of the English Liberal tradition, became the doctrine known as 'spiritualism'. The fact that Frederic Myers was a believer impressed scientific circles and led to more conversions. Myers based his spiritualistic metaphysic on the psychology of the unconscious and a study of mental functioning during sleep. He treated supranormal phenomena as intrusions from a disembodied or immaterial mode of existence into the heart of our world, and assumed that the task of scientific research into this domain was necessarily a theological one: to demonstrate the truth of the essential religious dogma of the immortality of the soul, and of its most vital manifestations for Christians—the resurrection of Christ and the communion of the Saints.

Sir Arthur Conan Doyle announced his conversion to spiritualism before the publication of *The New Revelation* in 1918. People like to say that Sir Arthur became a spiritualist as a result of the Great War. Nothing could be further from the truth; his conversion took place nearly three years before the Armistice and was closer to the beginning than to the end of the war. This chronological error follows from a more plausible one relating his conversion to the death of his eldest son, Kingsley. This falsehood is all the less pardonable because it suggests that he was an impressionable and morbid man.

Perhaps because everything to do with the creator of Sherlock Holmes had to be in some way spectacular, his conversion to spiritualism seemed an unexpected volte-face. It is easy to oppose a mystical or mystified Conan Doyle to the sceptical logician of the Holmesian mythology. But this constrast is purely imaginary as we shall show. The ground was prepared for this last phase of his life by a long period when, finding scepticism intolerable, he had pondered deeply about the nature and significance of spiritualistic phenomena. It is necessary to go back to his childhood in order to understand this development. It will be remembered that the intolerance of the

Jesuits at Stonyhurst had a profound effect on him, and led to his final breach with his Doyle uncles during his memorable visit to them at the outset of his medical career. There was only one person who could have kept him an orthodox Catholic during his adolescence —'The Ma'am'. But although she had been brought up in the faith and was not in the least a weak character, Mary Doyle was not a devout Catholic: towards the end of her life she became an Anglican. In *The Stark Munro Letters* Conan Doyle tells the following anecdote to illustrate his mother's religious feelings: 'I can recollect her coming to see me at a junction through which my train passed, with a six month's absence on either side of the incident. We had five minutes conversation, my head out of the carriage window. "Wear flannel next your skin, my dear boy, and never believe in eternal punishment," was her last item of advice as we rode out of the station.'[1]

There seems no doubt therefore that his mother's example made it easier for Conan Doyle to drift away from Catholicism during his adolescence. At the time of the definite breach with his father's family, Mary's neutrality was in contrast with her usual outspokenness and can be interpreted as silent acquiescence, while the influence of his stalwart godfather, his great-uncle Michael Conan, tended in the same direction as 'The Ma'am's'. Before little Arthur went to Hodder preparatory school, he had continually warned the parents of the danger of putting their son into the hands of Jesuits. He always took a great interest in his godson's education and never missed a chance of advising the greatest possible watchfulness, in a sarcastic tone which only emphasised the seriousness of his fears: ' . . . When you write next to Master Arthur Conan (not Ignatius) Doyle, tell him to write to me, a long letter description of all that he is doing . . .'[2]

Knowing very well that the boy would easily divine his motive, Michael Conan carefully mutilated the copy of Macaulay's *Lays* he sent him at Stonyhurst, explaining his reasons in a letter to his niece:

> We have had Henry here for a week and I take advantage of his return to England to send you this billet and its enclosure. The latter comprises three leaves of my little present to Arthur—the Macaulay Lays—I was obliged to cut them out, because, they contain, as you will perceive, a Huguenot outburst. Which would not have been at all

[1] *The Stark Munro Letters*, p. 56.
[2] Letter from Michael Conan to Mary Doyle, 30 May 1871 (C.D.B.A.).

relished at Stonyhurst and might have thrown some difficulty in the way of the book reaching him.[1]

These innocent ruses were probably more effective than lengthy sermons. Uncle Conan was trying to counter-balance an influence whose harmfulness he exaggerated, but at his age it was impossible for him ever to be the keeper of his godson's conscience. Later on, Conan Doyle's mother played this part to some extent. But during his adolescence, when he needed some masculine influence to take the place of his father's, Conan Doyle turned to Dr. Waller, who encouraged him to take up medicine and helped prepare him for the university entrance examination. Soaked in neo-Kantian idealism, Dr. Waller tried to get his young friend to read Carlyle and Emerson and practice their theories. He it was who sowed the seeds of that agnostic idealism whose echoes reverberated in Conan Doyle's mind for a very long time. He was a vigorous supporter of a vitalistic philosophy, and an ethics showing alarming anticipations of Nietzsche. Extracts from a letter written to Conan Doyle in 1876, give some idea of the nature of his influence:

> Absolve you to yourself and you shall have the suffrage of the whole world. If any one imagines that this law is lax, let him keep its commandment one day. Thus far, Emerson, in his never sufficiently to be extolled essay on Self Reliance. And here we put our finger on the weakness of all blind vicarious and fiducial trust in a hypothetical Providence which forsooth is to help those who cannot or will not help themselves . . . This manful and true inward life is what theology would fain kill by making us hold ourselves vile and sinful and degraded, which is a pestilent lie, and cuts at the root of all that is best in our nature . . . No truly self-reliant man can descend to the meanness of petty vanity: he knows himself far too truly to deem that he needs to have recourse to officious display: and in the end, he will make others know him too. Men of this mould die not with death: some of them write their names in the world's album: others influence an age or a generation: others but a smaller circle of personal friends. Yet when they pass away their place remains empty . . . Thus 'Do' is a far finer word than 'Believe'; and 'Action' a far surer watchword than 'Faith'.[2]

For a while his philosophy of action brought an almost physical release to the young, energetic giant that Conan Doyle was at the time. His voyage to the Artic on board the *Hope* strengthened his scorn for the ritual side of religion, as we have seen. He had not yet

[1] 16 August 1874 (C.D.B.A.).
[2] Letter from Dr. Waller to Conan Doyle, 1876 (C.D.B.A.).

broken with his father's family, but new prospects were already opening before him: he had attended a lecture on spiritualism at Birmingham a few weeks before leaving for the Arctic, and listened—sceptic-
ally but with interest, as he told his mother: ' . . . My only amusement
lately has been a couple of lectures. One was on Wale and Enracht—
a soft affair. The other was capital: "Does Death end all?" by Cooke,
the Boston Monday lecturer: A very clever thing, indeed. Though
not convincing to me . . .'[1]

After 1880 Conan Doyle's letters and private diaries, as well as some
of his published works, give us very complete information about his
religious development. Although he afterwards spoke with violent
hostility of a certain sort of Catholicism as 'obscurantism', at the
time of his quarrel with his uncles it only inspired him with a rather
condescending indifference. It was the same in 1900; he foresaw the
difficulties his Catholic upbringing might create over his candidature at
Edinburgh, but he does not seem to have shown the smallest animosity
towards the Church itself. It is however astonishing that Charles
Doyle, who did not die until 1893, made no attempt to prevent his
son rejecting Catholicism. He remained an ardent Catholic himself
till the end of his life, but his only means of self-expression was
through his art.

Even if definite personal influences, not rated at their true importance by Conan Doyle himself, may have involved him in a crisis of
scepticism or religious doubt at adolescence, one cannot attribute his
final development to them. We must not forget that at the time when
he was starting his medical studies, Darwin, Spencer and Huxley
were the thinkers who dominated his generation. He himself compared the theory of evolution to a doctrine of progress within a moral
and religious order. Biology and psychology had taken over from the
older sciences in revising traditional Bible teaching. Atheism was no
longer suspect on logical grounds, and could make a stronger and more
lucid case for itself. A coherent and acceptable ethical system could
be founded on recent archaeological and anthropological discoveries.
Having refused to accept literally a religion that seemed to him narrow and inflexible (a very Darwinian point of view), Conan Doyle tried
to defend the sense and significance of agnosticism against atheism:

> It was, then, all Christianity, and not Roman Catholicism alone,
> which had alienated my mind and driven me to an agnosticism which

[1] Letter to Mary Doyle, 30 January 1880 (C.D.B.A.).

never for an instant degenerated into atheism, for I had a very keen
perception of the wonderful poise of the Universe and the tremendous
power of conception and sustenance which it implied. I was reverent in
all my doubts and never ceased to think upon the matter, but the more
I thought, the more confirmed became my nonconformity. In a broad
sense I was a unitarian, save that I regarded the Bible with more
criticism than Unitarians usually show.[1]

This statement is confirmed by our knowledge of the facts, and
we shall see that it is fully corroborated also by Conan Doyle's private notes. It was not only that he had become absorbed in the most
crucial theological problems of the day. He was never again to lose
his interest in them. Beside Conan Doyle the writer and Conan Doyle
the deeply involved observer of his own time, there was another
Conan Doyle, whom one is tempted to call a mystic, except that he
so often observed facts that had nothing to do with philosophy. Let
us rather call him a sage, whose speculations led in 1915 to a conversion which left no room for any other vocation. He had studied the
subject of spiritualism for a long time, but this is not to say that his
conversion was merely the endorsement of a long present and clandestine spiritualism, as it were. This was not the case: he was a man who
had been for over thirty years deeply interested in the evidence for
spiritualistic phenomena. He declared his belief in them when some
unexpected event, whose nature he never explained, forced him to
depart from his usual prudent reserve. Then, it is true, he could offer
his new faith the fruits of thirty years of research and thought, which
had had hardly any effect on his attitude to religion before 1915. At
most, his agnosticism had become tinged with a vaguely Unitarian
deism, without his feeling the need to join any non-conformist sect—
which is hardly surprising. His feelings towards the Unitarians were
very friendly, as this letter written in 1896 to Coulson Kernahan
shows:

> My dear Kernahan,—It is a charming little exposition of the view
> which one would wish to believe, and I do not wonder that it has won
> such praise on all hands. As you say my own belief is otherwise, but by
> many roads one may attain the same end. I would only put forward
> as a mitigation of your severe view of the prospects of a Christless
> world that there exists now in England and America a considerable
> sect of Unitarians who hold very much the views which you fear may
> be universally adopted, and that they are generally accounted good

[1] AUT., p. 40.

citizens, with a high standard, and a sensitive conscience. As you are aware, the early Abolitionists were mainly Unitarians and some of them died for their belief. Again, when you describe the Christian idea of this life as being the 'anti-chamber of heaven' you must also allow that its teaching has always been that to half the race it is the ante-chamber of hell. But this is ungracious carping and I thank you very much for your present and the pleasure I have had in reading it . . .[1]

His four Southsea notebooks, and the one written at Norwood, plot Conan Doyle's spiritual course for us and particularly his religious and ethical development between 1885 and 1925. These five unpublished notebooks are the most essential items in his private papers, except for his letters.[2] We find in them stray thoughts, and notes of what was occupying his mind or of books he had read during his long enquiry into spiritualism, as well as descriptions of experiments he had witnessed. In 1880 and for the next five years he was observing psychic phenomena with sceptical curiosity, and hardly seems to have thought of making any investigations on his own account. And how could he find the time? He had only just set up in medical practice, and was also getting his name known by London publishers with his first stories. But in 1885 or 1886 he met a General Drayson at Southsea, who persuaded him that spiritualistic experiments could be interesting. It is significant that, instead of rushing straight into table-turning seances, Conan Doyle first made a methodical study of a number of books which might justify direct and thorough investigation of the subject. His essential seriousness is to be seen in this extremely exhaustive preliminary investigation, for the list of books he consulted over a period of about two years contains more than seventy titles.

It is interesting also that a great number of books on the history of occult religions were among the young doctor's reading: with the exception of Kardec and Swedenborg the list of books in the first Southsea Notebooks might be part of a syllabus for the study of comparative religions. So that Conan Doyle's later reflections on the significance and value of spiritualism must be seen against a background of theological and sociological erudition; and this tells us a great deal about his approach to metapsychological research. First

---

[1] (C.D.B.A.)

[2] Southsea Notebook No. 1, 1885; Southsea Notebook, No. 2, 1886–7; Southsea Notebook, No. 3, 1889–90; Norwood Notebook, No. 1, 1891–4; Southsea Notebook, No. 4, begun in 1890 and continued from 1894 to about 1925.

we find a scrupulous search for information resulting in almost encyc-
lopedic erudition, without which no study of metapsychology could
be fruitful; secondly a moral purpose kept steadily in view—that the
results of his enquiry should if possible contribute to a religious revival based on universal tolerance. Here Conan Doyle's position is
very close to that of Myers and his Cambridge friends, and it is not
surprising to find that the two men corresponded, the initiative having
come from Myers. On 2 July 1887 the magazine *Light* published a
letter from Conan Doyle describing results obtained through a medium; Myers at once wrote asking him to help the researches of his
society: 'Your profession has doubtless accustomed you to weighing
evidence, and you will recognise that inquiries like the above are dictated by no idle curiosity . . . '[1]

A few weeks later they had got down to details:

> I am very glad that you can now get some phenomena without a
> paid medium. What you say as to *raps* deeply interests me as raps are
> such *extremely rare* things, though spoken of by some spiritualists
> as if so common. Did the raps answer questions? did they come 3 at
> a time, 5 at a time, etc., as you ordered? did they spell out a word?
> These are questions of great importance in making sure that *raps* are
> not *creaks* . . .[2]

Myers certainly had an influence on Conan Doyle's theory of the
universe. Instead of keeping the critical examination of psychical
phenomena entirely separate from the hypotheses that might explain
them, he followed Myers in adopting an attitude closer to the historical than to the classic scientific method. Instead of trying to isolate
a single incontrovertible case, he examined an enormous mass of
evidence and tried to decide whether the spiritualistic hypothesis was
valid or not by the light of his own judgement. He brought to this
task the utmost caution and all the watchfulness of an infinitely serious mind. However he was behaving less as a research-worker than
an arbiter, rejecting or accepting the authority and veracity of the
various sources on entirely subjective grounds, rather than starting
from a scientific *tabula rasa:* 'The end and aim of spiritual intercourse,' he wrote in his second Southsea Notebook, 'is to give man
the strongest of all reasons to believe in spiritual immortality of the
soul, to break down the barrier of death, to found the grand religion
of the future'.[3]

[1] 7 March 1887 (C.D.B.A.).   [2] 10 December 1887 (C.D.B.A.).   [3] p. 125.

But he cannot be blamed for failing to invent a method or experiments which would verify the reality of psychic phenomena, No such experiments were actually made until about 1930, and the mere possibility of metapsychological research was hardly accepted before 1920. In 1888 an unpublished essay in which Conan Doyle tries to take his bearings among intellectual phenomena, cryptaesthesia and supra-normal knowledge, shows that he was at that time already well acquainted with everything essential that had been written on the subject.

Like Gurney and Myers, Conan Doyle made a close study of Tchermak, and the Nancy school (including Durand de Gros and Liébault) and was keeping a watchful eye on the work done by the followers of Charcot, Pitres and Pierre Marie. He had read Binet's important work on *Animal Magnetism*, published the year before, as well as Charles Richet's observations, whose ultimate relevance for metapsychological research we know. His philosophic comments on all this reading are interesting:

> These results have evidently an important bearing upon the problem of free will. A man is impelled to do some act by the irresistible action of a hypnotic suggestion which may have been made some months before. Yet to him the action appears to emanate from himself and however *outré* it may be he will always invent some plausible reason why he has done it. He would scout the idea that the impulse came from without, and yet we know that it is so. How can we tell that all our actions are not of this nature? What appears to us to be our own choice may prove really to have been as unalterable and inexorable as fate—the unavoidable result of the sum total of suggestions which are acting upon us. As Spinoza remarks, 'the consciousness of free will is only ignorance of the causes of our acts.'[1]

Thus the young Southsea doctor's mind kept moving to and fro between the scientific and ethical planes, in an effort to make a personal synthesis of the rational and religious elements that he had been unable to get from Catholicism. His Southsea Notebook No. 2 reveals his ambitious yet hesitant advance even more clearly; in it we find lists of books read, quotations and private thoughts.

In fact a comparison of Conan Doyle's Southsea notes with the account of the conflict between religion and rationalism described in *The Stark Munro Letters*, published in 1895, naturally leads the reader

[1] Unpublished essay on animal magnetism (C.D.B.A.).

to see the spiritualistic writings of the last years as the outcome of a genuine spiritual conflict that had long remained unresolved.

This work was written in Switzerland soon after Louise Conan Doyle first became ill, and it is the author's first attempt at autobiography. It is more interesting as such, than as a narrative of the early career of Dr. Stark Munro, alias Conan Doyle. Under transparent disguises we recognise 'The Ma'am', little Innes, the Doyle uncles, Louise Conan Doyle, and above all the picturesque Dr. Budd (Cullingworth in the book), who holds the front of the stage throughout most of the story and introduces an element of comedy to the otherwise serious theme. But it would be wrong to take *The Stark Munro Letters* as a humorous book because of Cullingworth's part in it. On the contrary, the author's primary aim was to externalize his religious doubts, the better to exorcise them. Afterwards autobiography took over; then, with characteristic modesty, he began to see the humourous possibilities of his adventure with Budd at Plymouth, and so, by tempering his gravity with comedy, combined a confession with deliberately exaggerated burlesque.

The idea dominating all his ethical and religious reflections was tolerance. We see this in his literary work of this period (*Micah Clarke*, 1889; *The Refugees*, 1893), and his political activities were animated by the same principle, whether it was a question of furthering Anglo-American understanding, trying to pacify the Irish, or putting an end to religious discrimination.

It is evident from *Memories and Adventures* that Conan Doyle had already begun to react against religious intolerance even in his Stonyhurst days: 'I remember that when, as a grown lad, I heard Father Murphy, a great fierce Irish priest, declare that there was sure damnation for everyone outside the Church, I looked upon him with horror, and to that moment I trace the first rift which has grown into such a chasm between me and those who were my guides.'[1]

In September 1913 he wrote to his faithful Edinburgh friend, James Ryan:

> Faith however is a very dangerous thing, for if I may have faith one way, my neighbour may have faith another, and if both our faiths are real and earnest, then we have as an unavoidable result inquisitions, persecutions, religious wars, family feuds and all the other fearful results which have so long plagued humanity—and still in less bloody

[1] AUT., p. 27.

forms continue to plague it. I do not admit that any faith—but only pure reason—is needed to get the idea of God and also to evolve a sufficient moral law for our needs. Had faith never been we should, as I read history, have been far more united and happier, so it seems to me.[1]

He attacks intolerance in practice as well as theory, because of the suffering it causes. He uses this same method of empirical reasoning elsewhere to subordinate the idea of God to an ethical system adapted 'for our needs'; and, in order to preserve the integrity of the pragmatic edifice he is constructing, Conan Doyle goes so far as to disassociate this practical idea of God from all subjectivity or revelation. In 1923, dominated more than ever by the principle of tolerance, he wrote between two notes on the part played by Christianity in the development of civilisation: 'In Spain the Inquisition killed thirty-two thousand.'[2]

But already in *The Stark Munro Letters* the second notion on which Conan Doyle rested his critique of religion was taking shape—his belief in progress. As with the eighteenth- and nineteenth-century thinkers who had influenced him, like Auguste Comte, whose system had somewhat vaguely impressed him, two aspects of progress were combined and confused in his mind—the scientific and the ethical. Emphasising the part all religions must play in the service of moral progress, Conan Doyle criticised the completely obsolete interpretation of history and view of the universe on which they were founded: 'I have mastered the principles of several religions. They have all shocked me by the violence which I should have to do to my reason to accept the dogmas of any one of them. Their ethics are usually excellent. So are the ethics of the common law of England. But the scheme of creation upon which those ethics are built!'[3] And further on: 'Is religion the only domain of thought which is non-progressive, and to be referred for ever to a standard set two thousand years ago?'[4]

It was not a question of doubting the existence of God, for Conan Doyle's vision, like that of the deists of the age of reason, was so solidly realistic and anthropomorphic that atheism seemed to him an absurd proposition:

I confess that I have never been able to understand the position of the atheist. In fact, I have come to disbelieve in his existence, and to look

---

[1] (C.D.B.A.)   [2] Southsea Notebook, No. 4 (C.D.B.A.).
[3] *The Stark Munro Letters*, p. 16.   [4] *Ibid.*, p. 21.

upon the word as a mere term of theological reproach. It may represent a temporary condition, a passing mental phase, a defiant reaction against an anthropomorphic ideal; but I cannot conceive that any man can continue to survey Nature, and to deny that there are laws at work which display intelligence and power. The very existence of the world carries with it the proof of a world maker, as the table guarantees the pre-existence of the carpenter. Granting this, one may form what conceptions one will of that Maker, but one cannot be an atheist.[1]

We notice that he sees Nature as ordered, coherent, harmonious.

In this, the critical part of the book, we see the influence of Renan, Winwood Reade and, above all, Carlyle.

Carlyle's systematic pessimism and discontent must have been unacceptable to a mind disposed to believe in the inevitable advance of spiritual progress. Probably also, the intolerant, cantankerous and unsociable temperament of the hermit of Chelsea was incompatible with what we know of Conan Doyle's character. In the Southsea Notebook No. 4 there is a note dated 22 March 1894, in which Conan Doyle waxes indignant over Carlyle's recriminations and their practical uselessness:

> . . . What was it that this great man was striving for so strenuously during his long life? I confess that I don't know. He proclaims war against shams and yet has never a word against the Christian explanation of the Universe. What has he ever suggested that was practical? I can only remember two things: Queen's Members in Parliament who should be permanent under-secretaries of the various departments and (2) Organised labour regiments. The first is largely met by permanent officials, as at present. The second must either be employed on unprofitable labour, or else must compete with existing labour. Instead of looking forward Carlyle always looked back. He wished to refurbish dictators, aristocracy, rule of force. As the times change Providence employs new tools, not the old ones with a fresh edge. He says 'let us choose our best man'. But who is to choose? The people? That is the system we have and the method which gives us our prime-ministers. He cries against wealth and in the same breath against anarchy. What would he have? If we work our coal and iron some must be wealthy. He never advocates socialism, the only alternative. Or would he have us relapse into the stone age. He will neither take one line or another. He appears to have wished everything to be done in a thunder-clap. Providence is more deliberate. What does he mean by England rushing towards a Niagara. Education has spread. The franchise has extended. A period of long commercial depression has passed without riots.

[1] *The Stark Munro Letters*, p. 46.

Crime has decreased. Libraries have increased. What then is this trouble which is so pressing . . .

Very true—but we are left feeling that Conan Doyle's reading of Carlyle was affected by his own spiritual crisis during his approach to maturity, and even more by what we must call his 'prophetism', the first echoes of which are to be heard in *The White Company.* In a letter to his mother written at the beginning of 1886 he declared: 'Carlyle has started a fermentation in my soul and made me ambitious.'[1]

But even in *The Stark Munro Letters* he pays unequivocal homage to Carlyle as an influence on his own spiritual development. Did he not say, immediately after his renunciation of Catholicism, 'Good old Carlyle came to the rescue'?[2] Did he not admire his vague but sturdy confidence in the ways of Providence, and did he not rate him, with Emerson, among the great prophets of modern times? 'The Almighty has not said his last say to the human race,' exclaims Stark Munro. 'And he can speak through a Scotchman or a New Englander as easily as through a Jew.'

It was in this context then, in the middle of his most productive phase as a novelist, and (as his first visit to the United States showed) while preparing to take that part in public affairs which we have already outlined, that Conan Doyle started collecting data about spiritualistic phenomena. His attitude to religion changed hardly at all during the twenty years that followed the publication of *The Stark Munro Letters*, and it was for this reason that the book always kept a special significance for its author. As he clearly stated in a letter to Captain Stanbury on 10 July 1913:

> About twenty years ago I wrote a book called *The Stark Munro Letters* . . . I there give the reasons which brought me to a broad Theism. I find myself still practically in the same position, though for those twenty years I have kept my mind very open, and have read much and thought much on the subject . . .

And, turning to spiritualism, he added:

> I, too, have studied Spiritualism for many years, and cannot easily dismiss it, in spite of the presence of frauds. It is hard to put aside the experiences of trained observers like Crookes, Russell Wallace, etc. and say that it was a delusion. I believe that there was objective truth in their observations . . .

[1] Unpublished (C.D.B.A.).   [2] *The Stark Munro Letters*, p. 45.

The tone of this letter is much less uncertain than that of his writings of 1890. It is that of a man long accustomed to base his opinions on tangible proof. In this respect his adherence to spiritualism was more definite than that of Carlyle, Tennyson or Longfellow, all of whom spoke of it in a language full of vague images such as 'vibration' or 'atmosphere':

> The spirit world around this world of sense
> Floats like an atmosphere, and everywhere
> Wafts through these earthly mists and vapors dense
> A vital breath of more ethereal air.[1]

The exact date of his religious conversion, as John Dickson Carr pointed out, must have been somewhere between the beginning of September 1915 and the end of January 1916. But by May 1915, although he had not yet received the intimate, decisive proof he was hoping for, he had already rid himself of his more serious doubts about the immortality of the soul, and could write to Lily Loder-Symonds: '. . . You know what I think of death. It is a most glorious improvement upon life, a shedding of all that is troublous and painful and a gaining of grand new powers which are a supreme happiness to the individual . . .'

We have come a long way from the 'Come what may after death' of young Dr. Stark Munro, and it is clear that conversion is not far off. The final stimulus may have been a 'message' a few months later from his brother-in-law Malcolm Leckie, killed at the front in 1914. Other 'messages' followed during the next few years, among them one which made a particularly lasting impression on Conan Doyle, as he tells us in his autobiography: this was a dream he had on 4 April 1917 which is first described in a letter to Innes:

> About six months ago I had a dream which I felt was of great importance but could only record the word Piave which rung in my head. I looked it up in the atlas index and found it was a river near Venice. I had never heard of it. I was so impressed that I at once made Pat and Jean my witnesses and said the crisis of the war would come there. It seemed most unlikely as they had taken Gorizia. But now![2]

During the autumn of 1917 Conan Doyle gave his first series of lectures on the problem of survival. At Bradford on 7 October and in

[1] Longfellow, *Haunted Houses*.
[2] Unpublished (C.D.B.A.). Though undated, it must have been written during the first battle of the Piave, in October 1917.

London on the 25th he proclaimed what he called 'the new revelation'. The following years strengthened his belief in spiritualism; the nature of the messages he received, and the confidence with which he accepted them as proofs while controversy on the subject raged more bitterly and violently, give us a foretaste of the line he was to take during the crusading years: 'Either the observers are liars or lunatics —or their observations are true. When one considers that among these observers are many of the first scientific brains in the world, Crookes, and Wallace, Lombroso and Richet, Zollner, Morselli, and hundreds more, it will be clear how formidable is the dilemma which Mr. Wells' complete denial must entail . . .'[1]

During the last twelve months of the war he was working on two books, *The New Revelation* and *The Vital Message* published respectively in June 1918 and August 1919. He undertook more and more lecturing: the south of England in the summer of 1918, the Midlands, Leeds and Nottingham in October. When he was giving his second lecture at Nottingham his daughter Mary brought him a telegram with the news that his son Kingsley, who had been wounded in the throat, was now dying of Spanish influenza. But he did not interrupt his lecture, nor did Kingsley's death lead to any change in his arranged programme; he gave forty lectures during the next twelve months in Scotland and the north of England, twenty more during the winter of 1919, all organised entirely for the benefit of spiritualistic societies. They aroused a great deal of interest. Conan Doyle's personality produced a wide range of different reactions, and he may have impressed the great public more than did Oliver Lodge or Russell Wallace.

After 1920 there was no question of confining his crusade to the British Isles, and the voyage to Australia was the first of a series which took Conan Doyle and his family to the four corners of the world. Between the end of September 1920 and February 1921, he went in turn to Perth, Adelaide, Melbourne and Sydney, preaching tirelessly on the two main themes—the scientific character of spiritualistic dogma and its religious value—and reinforcing them with new arguments. As soon as he was back from Australia he began a new series of lectures, and the next year he made his first visit to the United States as a preacher, from April to July 1922, followed by hard work on his great *History of Spiritualism* in two volumes. He

[1] 'Why H. G. Wells is peeved', *Sunday Express*, 8 January 1928.

made a second trip to the United States and Canada in 1923. The figures given by John Dickson Carr may suggest the scope of his activity: 'By the end of 1923 he had traversed fifty thousand miles and addressed nearly a quarter of a million people . . . His correspond- ence . . . in America had reached the figure of three hundred letters a day.'[1]

In 1924 he undertook more written propaganda, and returned to his *History of Spiritualism*, which was published at his own expense. But he was author-bookseller as well as author-publisher, for in 1925 he opened a spiritualistic bookshop. When his friend John Lamond went to see him one day he found him 'with his coat off and a great bundle of books between his arms. That a man whose time was so precious should be engaged in that manual task of carrying about bundles of books seemed to me to be the decisive proof of his interest in the enterprise.'[2]

Then came more lectures in England, Belgium and France. He presided over delegates from thirty-seven countries at the Inter- national Spiritualistic Congress of 1925 in Paris. In 1928 he went to South Africa, Rhodesia and Kenya, and in 1929 to Holland and Scandinavia. He returned from Sweden so exhausted that he had an attack of angina pectoris and was carried home on a stretcher. But a few days later he was speaking again at a meeting in commemora- tion of the Armistice, against the advice of his doctors. Another heart attack. He was confined to his room all that winter. In the spring he was convalescing and learning to paint. '. . . He clung to the great Victorian tradition that taking exercise was a duty and getting fat a sin! To the last that huge frame retained its steel and whalebone characteristic, with no hint of flabbiness.'[3]

But during the night of 6 July 1930, a new attack struck him, and Sir Arthur breathed his last sitting in his arm-chair, perfectly lucid, at half-past eight next morning.

*   *   *   *   *

Sir Arthur Conan Doyle's thesis was based on two principles. The first was the failure of religion, or rather of the churches, to stem what

---

[1] *The Life of Sir Arthur Conan Doyle*, p. 329.
[2] John Lamond, *Arthur Conan Doyle*, 1931, p. 216.
[3] Letter from Mary Conan Doyle to Pierre Nordon.

he called the mounting tide of materialism. 'Religions are mostly petrified and decayed, overgrown with thorns and choked with mysteries,' he wrote in *The New Revelation*.[1] The second principle was that a positive religion (the 'science of religion' as he called it) was possible, and need not be incompatible with traditional religious teaching.

Although Conan Doyle made every effort to persuade the public of the truth of the scientific facts and experimental data on which he based his doctrine, the religious aspect was much more important to him. It even seems, paradoxically enough, that although he had for a long time felt sure of the scientific basis of spiritualism and made use of it in argument, he had some difficulty in fitting it into his philosophic system. We notice his dislike of the word 'spiritualism' and his comment in *The New Revelation* that 'psychic religion' would be better. His purpose was entirely different from that of Lodge or Russell Wallace, whose efforts were directed essentially towards what might be called the substructure of spiritualism. Though he was drawn into endless discussions in the press about the reality of this substructure, it was with the greatest reluctance. He wanted to be, and was above all, the apostle of a new belief. Religious and moral themes were those he chose to discuss and was happiest with. His confidence in human progress, and his deep-seated optimism brought him back again and again to the reality of a semi-material or 'spiritualised' future life in which hell did not exist: 'Just as wild beasts in the early days of the world were controlled and tamed by fire, so the barbarous human soul was held in some check by the flames of hell waved before him. In this stage of the world a material devil and a material hell belong only to pantomime.'[2]

Now that humanity's belief (or 'faith' as he called it) in some remote and very problematic spiritual resurrection had been replaced by a fortifying certainty of a future in another world, it should advance with giant strides towards a moral order in conformity with the principles of Holy Writ:

Soak yourself with this grand truth. Make yourself familiar with the overpowering evidence . . . broaden and spiritualize your faults. Show the results in your lives. Unselfishness, that is the keynote to progress. Realize, not as a belief or a faith, but as a fact which is as tangible as the streets of London, that we are moving on soon to another life,

[1] p. 59.   [2] Southsea Notebook, No. 4, unpublished.

that we will all be very happy there, and that the only possible way in which that happiness can be marred or deferred is by folly and selfishness in these few fleeting years.[1]

As Conan Doyle was one of the greatest defenders of spiritualism, and his lectures aroused public interest all over the world, it is not surprising that he wrote hundreds of articles in reply to his adversaries' objections. A list of all the controversies in which he took a prominent part during those twelve or thirteen years of crusade would be very tedious, because the same arguments repeat themselves and each side was left unconvinced. It will be enough to mention the points Conan Doyle was continually combating. He was often asked about cases where mediums, sometimes on their own admission, had used conjuring tricks to create the illusion of supranormal phenomena, either by slight of hand or with the help of an accomplice. Conan Doyle made little attempt to deny the fact, but said that it proved nothing, and that if there were impostors and honest men among mediums (as there were among all mortals) one had no right to condemn the latter because of the dishonesty of the former.

Hearing that Bernard Shaw had boasted of having successfully taken in some of his friends during a spiritualistic seance, Conan Doyle replied: 'I have in the presence of witnesses unquestionably seen my mother since her death. But what I say must be false because Bernard Shaw cheated his friends. Was there ever a more absurd *non sequitur* than that?'[2]

Other opponents of spiritualism were amazed that the spirit 'messages' were so banal, and their descriptions of the next world so uninteresting, suggesting that the human spirit did not progress but suffered an intellectual decline in passing from this world to the next. Conan Doyle retorted that the transition did not entirely alter our personalities and that we should find the next world only a disembodied extension of this. To those who accused him of credulity, he never grew tired of saying that he had studied and sieved the evidence for thirty-five or forty years, that his convictions were not the fruit of a superficial examination, that other men with irreproachable scientific reputations had arrived at the same conclusions, that his entire past life denied the truth of such accusations, that events had often proved him right, and finally that the evidence of his own

[1] *The New Revelation*, p. 60.
[2] *Our African Winter*, 1929, p. 231.

senses had unquestionable validity for him. But the door was left open to discussion—a discussion which did not end with Conan Doyle's death.

Before 1915 Conan Doyle's writings show a double approach—one ethical and religious (mainly ethical) but without clear conclusion; the other scientific, and concerned with psychic data. Scientific, although he used no computers and described so few experiments? Certainly, for although Conan Doyle did not belong to a group of metapsychological researchers, his attitude to the phenomena was, for a time at least, scientific. Up to 1915 he observed them as Myers or Lodge might have done, and since he became a devotee of the spiritualist religion many years later than they did Conan Doyle seems to set an example of objectivity. But, above all, the circumstances of his conversion are so significant that we see in them one of his most secret characteristics, which set him apart from his age. This element of revolt in him was opposed both to the open, active side of his nature and to his confidence in man's steady progress. But there was a Carlylian element of deep seriousness in Conan Doyle's personality, which caused him to testify with increasing vehemence to what he had himself witnessed. This hermetic side of him was hidden by his various social activities and his popularity as a writer. It was in a sense the moral skeleton of the 'good giant', and his love of mankind was a mask concealing a man in revolt against the outrages and atrocities of his age. Differing in their object and their importance but identical from the moral point of view, the stands he took up on behalf of Edalji and Slater, for the Congo, or for divorce law reform, all sprang from the same sense of indignation, and defended the same cause—the cause of human dignity. He was enough of a Doyle and enough of a historian to see how badly it had suffered during the twentieth century. This was the supreme outrage, and if there is any passage that expresses better than the rest his refusal to go with his century, it is probably these reflections on the value and meaning of the bloody ordeal with which the twentieth century opened:

Why was this tremendous experience forced upon mankind? Surely it is a superficial thinker who imagines that the great Designer of all things has set the whole planet in a ferment, and strained every nation to exhaustion, in order that this or that frontier be moved, or some fresh combination be formed in the kaleidoscope of nations. No, the causes of the convulsion, and its objects, are more profound than that.

They are essentially religious, not political. They lie far deeper than the national squabbles of the day . . . The shock of the war was meant to rouse us to mental and moral earnestness, to give us the courage to tear away venerable shams, . . . to consider the awful condition of the world before this thunderbolt struck it. Could anyone, tracing back down the centuries and examining the records of the wickedness of man, find anything which would compare with the story of the nations during the last twenty years? Think of the condition of Russia during that time, with her brutal aristocracy and her drunken democracy, her murders on either side, her Siberian horrors, her jew-baiting and her corruption. Think of the figure of Leopold of Belgium, an incarnate devil who from motives of greed carried murder and torture through a large section of Africa, and yet was received in every court, and was eventually buried after a panegyric from a cardinal of the Roman church—a church which had never once raised her voice against his diabolical career. Consider the similar crimes in the Putamayo, where British capitalists, if not guilty of outrage, can at least not be acquitted of having condoned it by their lethargic trust in local agents, think of Turkey and the recurrent massacres of her subject races. Think of the heartless grind of the factories everywhere, where work assumed a very different and more unnatural shape than the ancient labour of the fields, think of the sensuality of many rich, the brutality of many poor, the shallowness of many fashionable, the coldness and deadness of religion, the absence anywhere of any deep, true spiritual impulse. Think, above all, of the organised materialism of Germany, the arrogance, the heartlessness, the negation of everything which one could possibly associate with the living spirit of Christ as evident in the utterances of Catholic Bishops, like Hartmann of Cologne, as in those Lutheran Pastors. Put all this together and say if the human race has ever presented a more unlovely aspect.[1]

Before the urgent need to transform the conscience of humanity—or arouse it from its spiritual torpor—practical problems must take precedence over logical scruples. The probability of the truth of the spiritualist postulates was so high, such eminent minds had rallied to them, the old religions were so powerless against materialism—'that great curse weighing on the world'—that the intervention of a new force was needed. And so a more coherent explanation of his belief in spiritualism than chance circumstances, signs and augurs, is forced on our minds, one that springs from his gloomy, rebellious and prophetic view of history and the spiritual state of the world on one hand, and on the other from that realism which made him so impatient of Carlylian impotence.

[1] *The Vital Message*, pp. 77–9.

Conan Doyle constantly used four quite different arguments to support his claims, the two first logical, the two second ethical. This chapter will conclude with a brief examination of them. The rational basis for his credo is established: 1. By reference to the evidence for the genuineness of spiritualistic phenomena and the reliability of witnesses. 2. By reference to his own experience. As to the first Conan Doyle contents himself with repeating what he had already written in *The Vital Message*, and calling upon the evidence of various biologists, astronomers, doctors or chemists. These men, he tells us, were neither fools nor credulous.

But this is clearly not the point. Every scientist has a right to his opinion, but when he backs it up by affirmation instead of demonstration one cannot treat his evidence as scientific. As doctor, historian and investigator, Conan Doyle had long been accustomed to rely on the accuracy of evidence, whether to confirm a diagnosis or for historical or legal documentation. But such methods can only lead to approximate certainty unless the evidence is corroborated by mathematical proof. In the experimental sciences the evidence is not always entirely conclusive. As for using authority as a criterion, no rationalist would appeal to it as such: 'The first step,' writes Descartes, 'was never to accept anything as true unless I had clear knowledge of its being so; that is to say carefully to avoid precipitancy and prejudice and to include nothing more in my judgement than what was presented to my mind so clearly and distinctly as to exclude all doubt of it.'[1]

Conan Doyle was aware that belief in the reality of spiritualistic phenomena was based on feeble arguments; he wrote that 'the phenomena are and have long been firmly established for every open mind'.[2]

This 'for every open mind' restricts what goes before to a remarkable degree. It was probably dictated by scrupulous intellectual honesty, but in another passage the author confuses the very distinct notions of 'good faith' and 'objectivity', which are methodologically speaking of unequal value. No one was more ready than he was to admit that there were numerous cases of fraud and imposture by mediums. This concession shows both good faith and intellectual honesty, but its value is purely rhetorical, and to state that there are cases of fraud cannot be taken as a premise in a syllogism proving

[1] *Discours de la Méthode.*   [2] *The New Revelation*, p. 57.

the reality of other phenomena by a simple process of subtraction. The argument from authority appears fairly often when Conan Doyle is dealing with some experience of his own. It takes two forms—he either refers, as we have already seen, to the body of knowledge about psychic matters studied by him in the period before his religious conversion; or, much more rarely—because of his natural modesty—he reminds us of the many occasions when his perspicacity has been confirmed by events. But when affirming his own certainty he invariably goes back to the evidence of his senses. Again, after his conversion he set no store by theories based on using psychological methods to investigate psychic phenomena. In a long letter to Upton Sinclair he alludes to this in terms which make one wonder whether he ever understood the methodological principle of the least costly hypothesis:

> ... As to the subconscious mind being an explanation of psychic phenomena, it does not seem to me to be a possible one. How can the subconscious mind produce a loud independent voice talking in the air or an ectoplasmic figure which walks and talks, or the mould of a materialised hand or a psychic photograph? The theory to which Charles Richet still clings has been riddled with criticism and seems to me to be quite impossible . . .[1]

We cannot blame Conan Doyle for being a spiritualist, nor for having felt the need to spread his faith abroad. But, having denounced theology for its lack of rationality in wishing to attribute greater value to science than to faith, he is caught in an irreducible fallacy. On one hand he is saying: 'There is something stronger than faith, and that is science', and on the other 'I affirm this, because I have experienced it. I do not believe, I know.'

Was there ever a more characteristic expression of faith?

Although he constantly uses affirmation instead of demonstration when trying to support the existence of phenomena by logical argument, Conan Doyle is on much firmer ground when he claims ethical value for spiritualism. We find here a strange transposition of the theory of evolution, or more precisely a historico-sociological extrapolation of the theory, which in some respect forestalls such interpretations of history as Arnold Toynbee's 'challenge and response' or Teilhardism.

Sir Arthur's first biographer, John Lamond, deserves the credit for

[1] Letter to Upton Sinclair, 21 December 1929.

pointing out this theory, but he does so rather summarily: 'He found
a system of evolution applied not only to the various phases of animal
life that function on this material globe, he found the evolutionary
process applied to the spiritual life of mankind . . .'[1]

The point of departure is a dynamic and dualistic view of history,
more clearly expressed in his private papers:

> Man is the offspring of Nature, it is true, but the rebel offspring. He
> is the only force that combats Nature. He makes the weak and the ill
> to live, prevents famine, irrigates deserts, moves fauna and flora from
> one Continent to another. Brings about great achievements and
> hideous disasters. So there are two forces in the world, Nature's more
> or less blind and yet purposive force, and man's more definite and
> limited purposive force.[2]

Progress is thus the result of human forces, analogous to evolution
among natural ones; both are in essence the same, and subject to the
laws of adaptation. In the history of human societies we see institutions, discovery amd research adapting themselves to the needs of
those societies according to their urgency. Any institution that does
not adapt becomes fossilised and dies, and according to Conan Doyle
this had happened to the old religions. We have seen him pronounce
judgement of failure to adapt on those religions which could not
satisfy the spiritual aspirations of humanity. It was spiritualism's task
to come to the rescue, and this is the theme of what he calls 'the
religious argument'.

The evolution of religion obeys the divine law as well as the laws of
history. God exists and possesses all the attributes of existence, among
others that of perseverance in his creative activity.

At the same time he deals with an objection often levelled at
spiritualists: that such undeniably trifling or childish phenomena can
have little interest or value. The religion of the future will develop
according to the laws of progress. Alluding to the distinction between
'physical' and 'mental' phenomena, Conan Doyle claims that the
latter have greater value and already reveal this development:

> But spiritualism is developing. It is undergoing a process of evolution,
> as our world itself did, according to Darwin. And just as we are
> told that man has descended from the monkey, so from the visible
> phenomena of early days, when spiritualists commenced table-

---

[1] *Arthur Conan Doyle*, p. 169.
[2] Southsea Notebook, No. 4, unpublished (C.D.B.A.). Probably written in 1924.

lifting and other like experiments, we are now changing to something
higher, something more intelligent. There is, for instance, clairvoyance.
That is spiritualism on a higher plane.[1]

As an apologist, Sir Arthur 'staked his all', if one may so express
it, on the value of scientific proof. This is perhaps to underestimate
the psychological importance of uncertainty. However that may be,
Conan Doyle tried to defend and illustrate the value of spiritualism
as a religion from an empirical standpoint which calls to mind
Pascal's famous paradox. Spiritualism, he says, is not a new entrant
in the lists of the dying theologies, but their ally in the struggle
against religious indifference. This, it would appear, is what is meant
by an unpublished statement, dated 1928:

> The complete denial of any life after death, which has become quite
> common in scientific circles, and has recently been supported by so
> high an authority as Sir Arthur Keith, cuts at the very root of revealed
> Religion. Therefore every creed, no matter which, has the most vital
> interest in supporting that psychic movement which undertakes to
> meet Science upon its own ground, and to *prove* that man survives and
> that a glorious future awaits him if he will but struggle from the
> material to the spiritual. Any religion which fights against modern
> psychic knowledge is really fighting its own best ally—the one thing
> which can avail it in argument with the unbeliever.

Spiritualism is not addressed only to those who already belong to
one church or another, but to the majority, including those whose
faith is dead or wavering. It brings them, Conan Doyle believed, a
promise which has the merit of being no illusion.

*   *   *   *   *

We have seen how he became a spiritualist and in what a militant
form; we must now ask ourselves what benefit he got from his new
faith. It probably satisfied two needs. Firstly, it gave him the spiritual
balance he had lost ever since his years at Stonyhurst, a balance that
agnosticism could not provide. It was spiritualism of a deeply
Christian, Emersonian colour. He notes at the end of his Southsea
Notebook No. 4:

> Speaking for myself I have infinite and unquestioning confidence in the
> goodness of God, and I have unstinted admiration for the Character of

[1] Interview with Sir Arthur published in the Buenos Ayres *Standard*, 4 August 1929.

Christ, whose example I would wish to follow as far as the conditions of our Western Civilisation permit. *But* I have no respect for the Old Testament, no conviction that Churches are necessary, and no desire at all either to be baptised, confirmed, receive the Eucharist or any such form. I do not wish extreme unction and I desire to die as I have lived without clerical interference, and with that peace which comes from acting honestly up to one's own best mental convictions.[1]

The controversies aroused by the subject of spiritualism must not make us forget that to Conan Doyle it was part of a crusade whose object was not so much to prove the reality of para-physical or para-psychological phenomena as to encourage all like-minded men to make an effort towards moral regeneration. The arguments he used led him into the arena, and his crusade became a battle. Did the aggressive character of his beliefs correspond to some inherent need of his personality? Conan Doyle was essentially a fighter, a man of action, stimulated and even enriched by opposition. And spiritualism gave him an adventurous view of the next world, as well as the feeling of fulfilment and pride in the face of death which prompted his very last words: 'The Lord is on my side. I will not fear what man doeth unto me.'[2]

[1] N.d., *circa* 1926.
[2] 'Envelope found in my father's wallet', Adrian Conan Doyle, (C.D.B.A.).

Chapter 10

THE PERSONALITY OF CONAN DOYLE

In the pages devoted to Sir Arthur Conan Doyle's extra-literary activities, we have accumulated evidence of the most obvious elements of his character. We shall now attempt a psychological exploration which will be completed by an analysis of his literary work. How is such an investigation possible? Every writer who cares about his posthumous reputation, or is merely interested in his own inner life, feels the need to orientate himself by means of memoirs or confessions —the special domain of introspection. In this respect Sir Arthur Conan Doyle's two autobiographical works, *The Stark Munro Letters* and *Memories and Adventures*, are equally deceptive. His indecision is apparent even in the earlier of the two. He hesitates to draw the reader into purely autobiographical regions. His only justification for analysing his spiritual problems is the belief that they might interest his young contemporaries. But he is not concerned with exposing his own personality or trying to interest his readers in it. He shuns the 'self' as plainly in his second volume, with its significant title. Although he takes himself as hero, he does so without the least egocentricity, never sacrificing adventure to character, the picturesque to the personal, or the story to the teller. This reluctance to occupy the centre of his own stage considerably reduces the psychological interest of the two books, and prejudices the reader's judgement. Perhaps Conan Doyle gives undue importance to some of the picturesque episodes in his life, while his laconic style may lead us to undervalue others. For instance, in *The Stark Munro Letters*, Dr. Budd of Plymouth, disguised as Cullingworth, becomes almost as important a figure as the hero, who represents the young Conan Doyle. Nor has he much to tell us about his wife or family.

The same selective process is seen in *Memories and Adventures*: men like Edalji or James Barrie are described with a wealth of detail denied to the author's intimates. He devotes several chapters to his travels in the Arctic, Egypt and South Africa, and these are of obvious interest; but we find almost nothing about his daily life at Hindhead or Crowborough, and he would rather write about his sporting than literary activities. It is no exaggeration therefore to say that Conan Doyle deliberately concealed the more intimate and important parts of his personality from posterity, and also from his contemporaries. We shall see how seriously he took his writing, what patience, study of detail and hard work he devoted to an historical novel. But in his autobiographical works he only lets us see the outer layers of his personality, and shows a modesty almost amounting to affectation in pretending to be only an amateur writer. Sometimes the pretence succeeded. In 1912 St. John Adcock wrote that 'no author could be farther from being "all author" than he is'.[1]

Conan Doyle surrounded himself and his writing with a tall screen of other activities. This screen is what most journalists have described, and even then only its most spectacular features. What is its psychological significance?

Physically, Conan Doyle was in every sense a giant, over six foot tall and weighing over seventeen stone. He was well-proportioned, held himself very erect, and his physical and nervous energy was prodigious. Having bought a motor-car at the beginning of the century, he was driving it near Hindhead one day, when he lost control of the steering and it climbed a very steep bank and turned over on top of him:

> The steering-wheel projected slightly from the rest, and thus broke the impact, and undoubtedly saved my life, but it gave way under the strain, and the weight of the car settled across my spine, just below the neck, pinning my face down on the gravel, and pressing with such terrific force as to make it impossible to utter a sound. I felt the weight getting heavier moment by moment, and wondered how long my vertebrae could stand it. However, they did so long enough to enable a crowd to collect and the car to be levered off me. I should think there are few who can say that they have held up a ton weight across their spine and lived unparalysed to talk about it. It is an acrobatic feat which I have no desire to repeat.[2]

Conan Doyle was proud of his physical energy and felt the need for exercise right up to his death. Refusing to die in his bed, he insisted on being helped to an arm-chair. His abounding vitality showed itself in his work as a writer and doctor, in his intellectual appetite and his appetite for sport. Jerome K. Jerome, who went with him to

[1] *The Bookman*, November 1912. [2] AUT., p. 333.

Norway talked of him as an indefatigable worker and Jean confirmed this:

> My husband had no fixed hours for work. Sometimes he would go early into the study to write before anyone was up, or he would come in from a round of golf and go straight to his desk and write. He had the remarkable power of being able to detach his thoughts from what was going on around him. I have known him write a Sherlock Holmes story in a room full of people talking. He would write in a train or anywhere . . .[1]

This picture of Conan Doyle absorbed in work with people talking all round him naturally suggests that he had great powers of concentration, but this does not mean that his working habits were regular. His youngest son, Mr. Adrian Conan Doyle tells us: 'My memories as a youth are mottled with sudden, silent periods when, following some agitated stranger, or missive, my father would disappear into his study for two or three days on end.'[2]

If we think of a writer as a sedentary man, always at his desk, Conan Doyle was not a typical one, for he spent a large part of his life on his feet. But one must not be misled by the diversity of his interests any more than by his physical need for action, into overlooking the equal enthusiasm with which, if the occasion arose, he concentrated all his energies on a single task and determined to do it well.

As a medical student he swotted hard. The lack of crossing-out in his manuscripts indicates his prodigious facility, but the even regular handwriting shows his unfaltering attention to detail, and a scrupulous desire to carry out the concept already elaborated in his mind. This mental elaboration of course depended on his excellent memory, and like Sherlock Holmes he depended mainly on mental images:

> Conan Doyle's memory was so extraordinary that it entered the realms of the freakish. For instance, if one examined him on any book that he had not read for as much as twenty years, he could give a fair outline of the plot and the name of every principal character. I have tested him on this on many occasions. Again, meeting any ex-serviceman years after the Great War, and having ascertained his regiment, he could, and would, immediately inform the astounded recipient not only of his former brigade and division but the principal actions in which he took part![3]

---

[1] Jean Conan Doyle, *Epilogue*, pp. 281–2.
[2] Adrian Conan Doyle, *The True Conan Doyle*, p. 16.　　　　[3] *Ibid.*, p. 18.

Superficially clumsy and sometimes absent-minded, he was extraordinarily methodical in the way he organised the numerous tasks he set himself. Having first surveyed them, he would always select one for priority, not because of its intrinsic merit or his own preference, but out of a very strong sense of duty. When he was writing an historical novel like *The White Company*, he shut himself up for several weeks, far away from his family in a lonely house in a wood. A few years later the Edalji affair monopolised all his attention for several months. And when he was converted to the spiritualist religion in 1916 he did not give up writing his history of the British army; he merely postponed the propagandist work which already occupied his mind although he knew better than anyone how important it would be to him. The reward of his diligence and persistence was a profound serenity, which makes us think of him less as a literary man than one of the many great public servants who figure in the history of England. The Boer War effectively engendered and fostered this mysterious yet definite feeling he had of being born to accomplish some important task, of having made himself worthy to be the instrument of fate by his confidence in his own efforts, as Dr. Waller had long ago taught him. Though his religious doubts had developed while he was a medical student they did not shatter his confidence in his own powers. About 1886 (the letter is not dated) he wrote to his mother describing his daily life at Southsea. He still had very few patients and was occasionally forced to borrow small sums to get him out of some financial difficulty. When 'The Ma'am' advanced him five pounds to settle the monthly bills, the young doctor wrote to thank her, promising to pay it back soon and telling her that he was hoping for fees from a consultation on behalf of an insurance company. Then he told her about his literary plans: 'I must hurry on and write something larger and more ambitious. I want some three figure cheques and shall have them too. Why should I not have a future before me in letters? . . . I am conscious too of a well marked style of my own which should single me out among the crowd for good or evil.'[1]

His success justified his confidence, and consolidated his special brand of optimistic but clear-headed fatalism. From South Africa he wrote: 'It is curious how in spite of rows, some privation and much hard work I feel so completely in the hands of fate in this matter and

[1] N.d. (C.D.B.A.).

so certain of the propriety of being here that the idea of being anywhere else never occurs to me.'

He sounded the same note months later, before standing for parliament at Joseph Chamberlain's request:

> I am of the opinion that our careers are marked out for us and that
> a Providence gets the greatest good out of a man at the right time. I am
> always on the alert to be ready to be such an instrument, but I like to
> see very clearly first that it really is the main path of my life and not
> a side track (. . .) There are many questions to be weighed, but in the
> main I feel with you that I possess qualities which have hitherto met
> with no field, and also that the first duty of a man is to get out all that
> is in him.[1]

It was completely in accord with his logical temperament that,
having taken a decision on his own responsibility alone, he should be
ready to shoulder that responsibility as dramatically as possible.
This was why, when he stood for parliament, he wanted to oppose
the leader of the other party; this was why he was to be found at the
head of so many different humanitarian causes; this was why, when
he became a spiritualist, it was not enough to join the movement, he
felt obliged to be its leader. No other writer of his time could claim
to be more committed than he was, and his moral prestige among
them all has never been questioned. His sense of responsibility and of
human solidarity was clearly the dominant note of his character, and
everything he undertook bore the impress of his exacting moral
standard. His family background probably had something to do with
this. When still very young he had to take his duties as an elder
brother seriously, and, as we have seen, the prospect of having to
support his family had a decisive effect on his choice of a career. But
even as a child his letters show his interest in his little sisters, and he
used to help them with their lessons during his school holidays. At
the age of fourteen he wrote to his mother from Stonyhurst, 'In three
days I expect to resume my duties as private school-master, teaching
Virgil to Lottie, junior Reader to Lottie, and step by step to Connie.'[2]

When he started practice in Southsea he sent for his young brother
Innes, and took over his education completely. Afterwards he encouraged him to become a regular soldier, and asked favours for him
which he would never have dreamed of asking for himself. In 1897 he

---

[1] Letter to Mary Doyle, n.d., unpublished (C.D.B.A.).
[2] *Ibid.*, December 1873, unpublished (C.D.B.A.).

approached Kitchener, reminding him of their meeting in Egypt and asking for a battery for his younger brother, so that he could have a chance to distinguish himself: 'There (in Egypt or the Indian frontier) lie the roads to honour and success.'[1] Later on he wrote to Sir Edward Ward, Secretary of State for War, to recommend Innes to him.

He took an almost paternal interest in his brother's matrimonial plans. In February 1897 we find him travelling to Exeter to meet the family of a certain Miss Dora Hamilton, whom Innes wanted to marry. During the Great War he treated Innes's family as if they were his own.

From his letters to Mary Doyle we see clearly that she set the greatest possible store by her eldest son's advice about her four daughters, particularly their marriage plans. In 1893 Constance, the eldest, married Hornung the writer, of whom Conan Doyle had written a year before: '. . . I like young Willie Hornung very much. He is one of the sweetest natured and most delicate-minded men I ever knew. He is 26, and an author standing certainly much higher than I did at his age . . .'[2]

Five years later, Jane the third daughter got engaged to Nelson Foley, of the Lismore family already connected with the Doyles. Here too Arthur had played an elder brother's part: Nelson Foley was often at the house of Lady Jeune, to whom Conan Doyle had introduced his sister Jane the year before. As for the youngest, Dodo, she was engaged to a young clergyman called Cyril Angel, a friend of both Louise and Arthur Conan Doyle. When they married, Conan Doyle made an allowance to his sister and later lent his brother-in-law the money to start a private school. Circumstances having made him head of the family, he unhesitatingly demanded complete loyalty, as we see from his behaviour to Constance and William Hornung over a quarrel which will be described later. Though he probably never quite realised the fact, there was only one member of the family whose authority it would never have occurred to him to question—his mother. Dr. Stark Munro says of his father and mother:

> You know how I admire him, and yet I fear there is little intellectual sympathy between us. He appears to think that those opinions of mine upon religion and politics which come hot from my inmost soul have

[1] Letter to Mary Doyle, 31 January 1897, unpublished (C.D.B.A.).
[2] *Ibid.*, 1892, unpublished (C.D.B.A.).

been assumed either out of indifference or bravado. So I have ceased to talk on vital subjects with him, and, though we affect to ignore it, we both know that there is a barrier there. Now, with my mother—ah, but my mother must have a paragraph to herself. You must remember her sweet face, her sensitive mouth, her peering, short-sighted eyes, the general suggestion of a plump little hen, who is still on the alert about her chickens. Ever since I can remember her she has been the quaintest mixture of the housewife and the woman of letters, with the high-bred spirited lady as the basis for either character. Always a lady, whether she was bargaining with the butcher, or breaking in a skittish charwoman, or stirring the porridge, which I can see her doing with the porridge stick in one hand, and the other holding her *Revue des Deux Mondes* within two inches of her dear nose. That was always her favourite reading, and I can never think of her without the association of its browny-yellow cover.[1]

No doubt Conan Doyle was always aware, however affectionately, of 'The Ma'am's' little eccentricities; he would have been less human if he had ignored them.[2] But he had developed his tougher characteristics in reaction to his father's apathy, which had caused him deep frustration ever since childhood. The violence of his quarrel with his Doyle uncles, and the irreparable breach it led to, were to a large extent the result of his father's day-dreaming and wine-bibbing, contrasting with the radiant strength of his mother's character: 'I have often heard her say (and I am quite convinced that she meant it) that she would far rather see any one of us in our graves than know that we had committed a dishonourable action. Yes: for all her softness and femininity, she could freeze iron hard at the suspicion of baseness; and I have seen the blood flush from her white cap to her lace collar when she has heard of an act of meanness.'[3]

It was from her more than anyone else that he got the rules of honourable behaviour to which he kept during his whole life, and which have left their mark as plainly on his writings as on his services to his country.[4] She was his confidante; she took a masculine in-

---

[1] *The Stark Munro Letters*, pp. 52–4.

[2] 'My study is heaped with ear-trumpets of every size and shape. I mentioned my mother's deafness to a London aurist firm, and I am buried under an avalanche of ear-trumpets. The one she is drawn towards looks more like a tea-pot.' Postscript to a letter to Lily Loder-Symonds, 19 May 1915.

[3] *The Stark Munro Letters*, p. 179.

[4] Mr. Adrian Conan Doyle and Miss Mary Conan Doyle both recall hearing their father declare: 'There are three tests and three tests only, of a gentleman and they have nothing to do with wealth, position or show. What alone counts is: Firstly, a man's chivalry towards women; Secondly: his rectitude in matters of finance; Thirdly, his courtesy towards those born in a lower social position, and therefore dependent.'

terest in everything he undertook. She was his collaborator; he often took her advice on financial matters; she corrected the proofs of many of his novels and stories, and also of his more serious books, particularly the history of the Boer War. Her tastes had inspired an important part of his work, for without 'The Ma'am' Conan Doyle might never have developed that interest in history, particularly in medieval history, which shines from the pages of *The White Company* or *Sir Nigel*. His love and respect for the past, his sense of the marvellous, his devotion to courtesy and chivalry, his discreet tenderness, all these are connected with his mother. And how surely, how justly she used the power whose limits she herself had set! Though he was sometimes a rebellious son, almost all his differences with his mother ended in a triumph for her. Two instances will be enough to show how Mary Doyle's authority sometimes came into conflict with her son's most fundamental moral principles. In 1889 his eldest daughter Mary Louise Conan Doyle was born, just when Conan Doyle was going through the phase of rather aggressive agnosticism already described, and he categorically set himself against the baby's being baptised. In February 1890 Mary Doyle came to see her grand-daughter and succeeded in persuading her son to have her given an Anglican christening.

Twelve years later, after Conan Doyle's treatise on the British army in South Africa was published, the new King decided to confer a knighthood on him. We know that his first impulse was to decline the honour, but once again Mary Doyle had her way; and after a long exchange of letters she extracted an acceptance from him by telling him that a refusal would be a personal insult to the King.

It is impossible to imagine two more different women than Mary Doyle and Conan Doyle's first wife, Louise Hawkins. As we know, the marriage was the result of a very peaceful idyll.[1] The young doctor had so far escaped the storms of passionate love, and he found with Louise the warm and glowing sweetness of home life, an almost forgotten sweetness from which he had been separated since he went to Stonyhurst. The somewhat facile pleasure he took in the early years of his married life may have been a sort of pilgrimage to the lost paradise of his childhood. And his wife's delicate health and gentle character aroused an ever watchful protective instinct, with

[1] Cf. *The Stark Munro Letters*, pp. 314 *sqq.*, where Louise Hawkins appears as Miss Winifred La Force.

something almost paternal about it, reminiscent of his behaviour to his young brother and sisters. So that the love he felt for her was mixed with a sort of grateful pity: 'I did not know how the love of a woman will tinge a man's whole life and every action with unselfishness. I did not know how easy it is to be noble when someone else takes it for granted that one will be so.'[1]

Her daughter, Mary Conan Doyle, has described her gentleness and resignation:

> My mother was a tiny little woman with dainty hands and feet, and lovely shadowy eyes that always seemed to see beyond what she was looking at. There was a gentle all-lovingness about her that drew the simple folk, children, and animals to her, as to a magnet. She had the quiet poise that comes rather from the wisdom of the spirit than from the knowledge of the world, and there ran through her a bright ripple of fun, that would glint in the eyes, and hover round her mouth. It was a sense of fun rather than the more sophisticated sense of humour, because Mother never smiled at a joke at anyone else's expense. At such moments a shadow passed over her face, and her silence would rebuke the joker. But she loved the comical aspects of life and the unconscious humour in people and things.[2]

This self-effacing and stoical woman has left very little trace in Conan Doyle's writings, or even in his private papers. Yet she was his companion for over twenty years. But thirteen years of their married life were darkened by the tuberculosis of the lungs which finally vanquished her in 1906. With that rare understanding that comes from the heart, Louise Conan Doyle did her best to safeguard the unity of the family after her death:

> Some two months before the end she called me in for a talk. She told me that some wives sought to hold their husbands to their memory after they had gone—that she considered this very wrong, as the consideration should be the loved one's happiness. To this end she wanted me not to be shocked or surprised if my Father married again, but to know that it was with her understanding and blessing.[3]

Did she know of the place Jean Leckie already occupied in her husband's heart? This passage makes it seem likely. Moreover, there was nothing clandestine in Conan Doyle's attitude to Jean. He had known her since 1897 and introduced her to his sisters and to his mother, who was well aware of the passionate love he felt for her.

---

[1] *The Stark Munro Letters*, p. 329.
[2] Letter from Mary Conan Doyle to Pierre Nordon, 31 January 1957.　　[3] *Ibid.*

Jean was entirely different from Louise: charming, dignified, sensitive and demonstrative, she had an ease of manner which came from the advantages she was born to. This woman who might have been the heroine of a novel by George Meredith aroused in the mature Conan Doyle an intensity of passion he had never before experienced. For ten years she was his mystical wife, and he her *cavaliere servente* and her hero; they were years of sometimes painful emotional tension for him, providing a test of his chivalry which he was better fitted to meet than any man of his generation, and which he may even have desired. Like a lamp under a parchment shade, this enduring passion lit up the unexpected paths of his public life during those ten years. When, on Jean's birthday in 1902, he wrote to his mother 'I fight hard against all the powers of darkness and I win,' we may take it as something more than an allusion to his book on the war in South Africa—a declaration of the manly honour of his feeling for Jean Leckie. We cannot understand this platonic relationship simply by recalling Conan Doyle's moral principles, and his strict attachment to a puritanism which was already out-of-date in Edwardian times. Here was a man nourished on Froissart and the ideals of chivalry. Circumstances, his character, his literary talent, his epoch had, whether he wished it or no, made him an essentially modern man, a doctor, the creator of the detective story, someone to be reckoned with in politics. In his private life—and his wife was very far from counting for nothing—he appears to have kept to standards of marriage of which millions of examples were to be found in England at the time. But his passion for Jean Leckie did more than involve him in an ordinary moral conflict. It offered him a marvellous chance to test himself by a code of chivalrous love which seemed to have been buried long ago in the past. A physical relationship would not only have been a betrayal of his wife but an irreparable personal degradation. It would have destroyed the mystical basis of his passion; it would have signified total failure in his own eyes; it would have transformed his life into a sordid adventure. The value of his passion was essentially connected with the exalting ideal it provided, and it is only with this in mind that we can appreciate the part played by each character in this family drama. Louise—ill and silent, but full of warm admiration for a husband whose secret could not be told although no shame at all attached to it. Mary Doyle—understanding everything also, but not content with mere forgiveness, for only her

guiding principles were able to fortify her son in moments of discouragement and impatience. And William and Constance Hornung
—too remote from their brother to understand the true nature of his
relations with Jean, but close enough for them to set themselves up as
strict censors of any breach of the conventional moral code whose
absurdity they failed to realise. In the middle of the summer of 1900
Conan Doyle was in London for the cricket season and had been
playing at Lords. Jean Leckie and William Hornung were both
watching the match. Conan Doyle described what followed in a
letter to his mother:

> William came down on Tuesday and found us together there, so in fear
> of his thinking evil I told Connie the facts that evening, and gave her
> leave to say what she liked to Willie about it, afterwards speaking a
> little to him myself, when I went downstairs and referring him to her
> for the details. She was very nice and promised to lunch with us at Lords
> next day. Willie also seemed nice and said 'that he was prepared to
> back my dealings with any woman at sight and without question'. Next
> day however I had a wire of excuse from Connie both for lunch and
> dinner (tooth-ache, dentist). I went down about 11, found she had
> gone to bed, and Willie highly critical and argumentative. I suppose
> their hearts spoke first and then they were foolish enough to allow their
> heads to intervene. Willie's tone was that of an attorney dissecting a
> case, instead of a brother standing by a brother in need. Among other
> remarks he said that I attached too much importance to whether the
> relations were platonic or not—he could not see that 'that made much
> difference'. I said 'the difference between guilt and innocence'. But
> could you conceive such nonsense. Of course when I saw this carping
> tone I refused to speak further upon so sacred a matter, and I left the
> house not angrily but in a serious frame of mind which is more
> formidable. When have I failed in loyalty to any member of my family?
> And when before have I appealed to them? . . .[1]

In July 1900 he wrote to his mother again:

> I have nothing but affection and respect for Touie. I have never in my
> whole married life had one cross word with her, nor will I ever cause
> her any pain. I cannot think how I came to give you the impression
> that her presence was painful to me. It is not so. William's argument re
> Connie, himself and you, is most unsound. He is not Touie's mother.
> If he were, I should have expected him to see it with a mother's
> eyes. I should be unreasonable if I expected sympathy from Mrs.
> Hawkins. But I expected the attitude of a friend, and a brother, from
> William and I got neither . . .[2]

---

[1] Unpublished (C.D.B.A.).　　　　[2] *Ibid.*

And in August: 'It is really ludicrous to think of you, and Lottie and above all her own dear mother condoning the thing, and then Connie jibbing at it . . .'[1]

As for Innes, Conan Doyle had confided in him in 1899, when the long idyll had already been going on for about two years: 'My last letter about my private affairs must have surprised you rather. You need not fear however that any harm will arise from it or that any pain will ever be given to Touie. She is as dear to me as ever, but, as I said, there is a large side of my life which was unoccupied but is no longer so.'[2]

Conan Doyle had shown sufficient firmness to keep to a line of conduct dictated by his own moral standards, and submit to a test his natural temper made necessary, but he would have been less than human if his private papers had not shown signs of emotional tension, which he dominated with difficulty. The state of his nerves sometimes revealed what a heavy constraint circumstances had imposed on him: ' . . . I have lived for six years in a sick room and, oh, how weary of it I am: Dear Touie: It has tried me more than her—and she never dreams of it and I am very glad.'[3]

For the first time thoughts of death began to obsess him to a dangerous extent, and he made his will. For several months the Boer War acted as a counter-irritant to his morbid thoughts, but after his return, particularly after his quarrel with the Hornungs, he was exasperated to find the prospect unchanged.

> . . . I am feeling the strain of a hard year's work last year, and also my soul is naturally and inevitably rather wrenched in two all the time. I am most careful at home and I am sure that at no time have I been anything but most considerate and attentive. But the position is difficult, is it not? Dear J is a model of good sense and propriety in the whole thing. There never was anyone with a sweeter and more unselfish nature.[4]

His feelings for Jean were a reserve of moral energy from which he drew endless strength, although his devotion took a romantic form and did not change his married life. The mystical vision of love ex-

[1] Unpublished (C.D.B.A.).
[2] Letter to Innes Doyle, 17 June 1899, unpublished (C.D.B.A.).
[3] Letter to Mary Doyle, 30 December 1899 (C.D.B.A.).
[4] *Ibid.*, March 1901 (C.D.B.A.).

pressed in his novel *Sir Nigel* corresponds to a reality he had lived through between 1901 and 1907. In 1902 he wrote to his mother:

> Letters from you and J reached me together this morning—a conjunction which I love. I enclose hers—which please burn, or tear up and scatter among the flowers. Only in those two ways would I ever have any note of hers disposed of. I send it that you may see how fresh still are our feelings after the searching trial of years encompassed with difficulty . . .[1]

Until his death Conan Doyle kept the aniversary of the day he first met and fell in love with Jean Leckie, on 15 March 1897:

> From the time of his marriage in 1907, he had the habit at the beginning of each early spring, to go into the garden to search for the first snowdrop in order to give it to my mother. Every year without fail he searched for and found the first snowdrop. In the early spring of 1930, the hand of death was already closing around him. He had suffered more than one heart attack and was under close medical supervision. On that cold February day, unseen by any of us, he left his bedroom for the garden. A few minutes later he was found by Rogers, the butler, collapsed in the passage with another heart attack. In his hand he held the first snowdrop.[2]

In April 1902 he took a few weeks holiday to join his sister and Nelson Foley on their little island in the Gulf of Gaeta. Afterwards he went to Sicily, Venice—where he wrote one of the adventures of Brigadier Gerard—the Italian lakes and Switzerland. Jean Leckie came to say goodbye to him at Southampton and decorated his cabin with flowers. He wrote a short novel, *A Duet*, which always remained one of his favourite works although its success did not come up to his hopes. He had the manuscript bound as a present for Jean—it was by gestures such as these that their mutual love proclaimed its unique and marvellous character. 'Was there ever such a love story since the world began?' wrote Conan Doyle; and again: 'How many folk in the world have ever had their love tested as ours has been. I should think that our case was about unique.'[3]

At the beginning of 1906, after her state of health had remained unchanged for several years, Louise Conan Doyle suddenly got worse, and this loving, patient, courageous woman died on 4 July:

> The illness was a painless one [wrote her husband in his private diary].

[1] Letter to Mary Doyle, 26 August 1902 (C.D.B.A.).
[2] Letter from Adrian Conan Doyle to Pierre Nordon, 2 November 1959.
[3] Letters to Mary Doyle, 1901 and 16 March 1904 (C.D.B.A.).

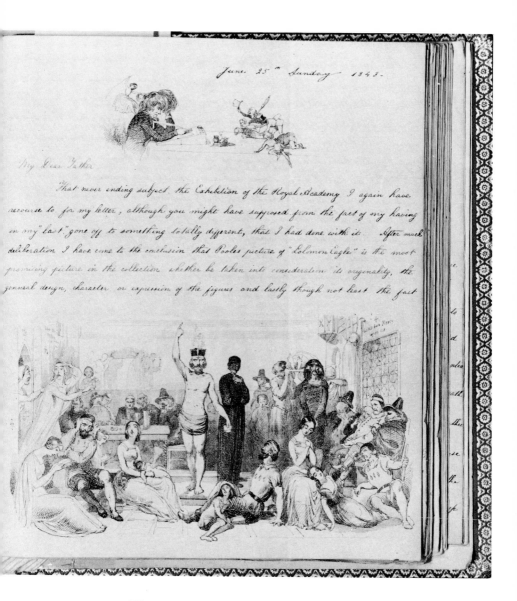

June 25th Sunday 1843.

My Dear Father

That never ending subject the Exhibition of the Royal Academy I again have recourse to for my letter, although you might have supposed from the fact of my having in my "last", gone off to something totally different, that I had done with it. After much deliberation I have come to the conclusion that Pooles picture of "Solomon Eagle" is the most promising picture in the collection whether be taken into consideration its originality, the general design, character or expression of the figures and lastly though not least the fact

Illustrated letter from Richard Doyle

Conan Doyle at Edinburgh University

Study in Scarlet

Ormond Sacker - from Soudan from Afghanistan
Lived at 221 B Upper Baker Street
with

I Sherrinford Holmes -

The Laws of Evidence

Reserved -

Sleepy eyed young man - philosopher - Collector of rare Violins.
An Amati -   Chemical laboratory

I have four hundred a year -

I am a Consulting detective -

What rot this is" I cried - throwing the volume
: petulantly aside " I must say that I have no
patience with people who build up fine theories in their
own armchairs which can never be reduced to
practice -
                    Lecoq was a bungler -

Dupin was better. Dupin was decidedly smart -
His trick of following a train of thought was more
sensational than clever   but still he had analytical genius.

A Study in Scarlet: the first manuscript conception of
Sherlock Holmes

Sir Arthur Conan Doyle at his desk in Southsea,
writing *A Study in Scarlet*

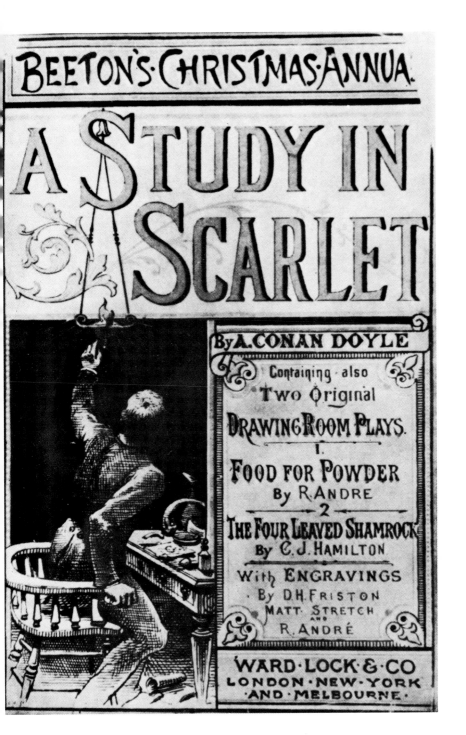

The first appearance of *A Study in Scarlet*

Sir Arthur Conan Doyle from a portrait by Sidney Paget, 1897

Jean Conan Doyle, 1910

Sir Arthur Conan Doyle towards the end of his life.
Photo: Paul Thomson. Copyright: Paul Popper

From first to last there was not the pain of a toothache. A tumour seems to have formed in the brain. There was partial paralysis of half the face and left side.

She always recognised me. She said 'Bless you'; also 'Thank you, dear' and once 'That's the ticket' when I raised her. She told me that she had no pain and was easy in her mind. I was much in her room after her death and standing by her body I felt that I had done my best . . .[1]

Conan Doyle's stoicism in the face of misfortune has already been mentioned in connection with the death of his eldest son Kingsley just after the First World War. But the death of Louise had visible repercussions on his mental life. After being under pressure for so many years, his emotions were now as it were suddenly released, and this man whose health had stood up to everything, even a typhus epidemic in South Africa, who had written to his mother in the middle of April 1906 that he had never been in better health in his life, now went through a period of depression accompanied by digestive and nervous disorders and insomnia, that forced him to take several weeks rest. More significant even than this is the fact that his normally very active temperament became devitalised to such an extent that he complained of boredom. This far from sentimental man began to brood about his past, and to distract his mind he began a dramatic adaptation of *The Tragedy of the Korosko*, which remained in a drawer until 1909, when Lewis Waller took the part of Colonel Egerton in *The Fires of Fate*. Of course he had been prepared for Louise's death for a very long while, and it at last made it possible for him and Jean to marry—a happiness they had in the past resolved to sacrifice if necessary. Although his mourning for Louise was not a period of heartbroken sorrow, and although his marriage to Jean (on 18 September 1907) fulfilled a longing he had not even dared to formulate ten years earlier, his desire for action remained in abeyance for several months after his second marriage. And we find this unexpected comment in his Journal for 16 August 1908:

> . . . We are very happy. Our wedded life has been a dream, which surely proves that God's blessing has been upon it. I have cleared up all my work for the time and will await a strong impulse before I do any more.[2]

This phlegmatic euphoria is in lively contrast with Conan Doyle's

[1] 15 July 1906.   [2] (C.D.B.A.)

normal emotional state, but it is clear that this man who was always struggling against his own expansiveness and always in command of his feelings did not often give himself away. His usual calm self-control gave no real clue to his personality except on the rare occasions when he abandoned it; these were picturesque and extremely suggestive, like an incident at Nairobi in 1928. The scene was the railway-station of this town, where he had given a lecture on spiritualism the day before; and that same morning a local journalist had stupidly and spitefully suggested that Conan Doyle was making capital out of his son Kingsley's death for propaganda purposes. From the window of his compartment in the train the lecturer caught sight of the sneerer among the crowd who had come to see him off. He seized his umbrella from the rack and rushed at the journalist, who only saved himself from the septuagenarian's righteous anger by taking to his heels. His son has confirmed the impression made on several of Conan Doyle's contemporaries, particularly Coulson Kernahan, who declared that he would rather look into a pistol barrel than into the steely gaze of Conan Doyle when he was angry. His apparent impassivity was the result of a constant and sometimes very visible effort at self-control. How otherwise can the interest and affection he lavished on his children be reconciled with the fact that he inspired them with holy terror? And surely we cannot fail to see a similarity between his character and the armour of imperturbability in which the hyper-sensitive Sherlock Holmes occasionally allows us to see a chink?

While a phlegmatic temperament often tends to melancholy, Conan Doyle's normal state was calm—because he knew how to control his emotions—but cheerful. Like Holmes he liked to act a part. Of course he could be boisterous on occasion, and like his own Challenger he often laughed at his own jokes. 'He had a tremendous sense of humour and such an infectious laugh!' Jean Conan Doyle tells us,[1] and he was good at imitating the gestures and speech of his friends. More significant and revealing was his habit of self-parody; this showed that he saw his own character with detachment and that there was normally an element of calculation in the control of his behaviour by his will. Nor did he scorn mystification: one day he greeted Hornung wearing a false beard. When he discerned the trick, his brother-in-law flew into a violent rage. Conan Doyle's roars of

[1] *Epilogue*, p. 282.

laughter did not mend matters, and the recollection of the incident always provoked him to noisy delight. But his sense of humour usually manifested itself in discreet smiles, more in keeping with his serenity and his secret timidity—his first public lectures were a terrible ordeal to him—than were outbursts of this sort. There is a vein of humour running through his books and giving the different characters a family likeness. In his private correspondence, his simplicity, liveliness, amusing self-revelations and brief exclamatory style do not reveal someone trying to shine, but spontaneous and natural good-humour about people and events. And as an extempore speaker his sense of humour was always particularly happy, his gift as a story-teller coming naturally to his aid.

Conan Doyle's serene gaiety came also from an optimism based, as we have seen, on unshakeable confidence in human progress and the final victory of good over evil; and he felt himself one of those directly responsible for the realisation of this epic vision—particularly during his crusading years, when we see a remarkable development in his character. Carr tells us truly that he was literally petrified with terror when he gave his first lectures. When he visited the United States in 1894 his impresario, Major Pond, noticed signs of nervousness in the young orator. Conan Doyle has himself described a memorable entrance into the lecture hall, when he stumbled at the door and burst onto the platform at a run, scattering books and papers as he went. But the calm lecturer of thirty years later, always careful to be objective and seldom giving way to anger, was a completely different person from the fiery but obviously impressionable speaker of the 1890s. As he matured, and later as he grew old, he felt an increasingly serene confidence in his own mental and spiritual resources. His children found this note after his death:

> As a man grows older there comes a time when he feels that the shadows thicken round him. He feels at last his mortal limits, his eyesight contracts, his hearing dulls, the strength which had seemed to be an inexhaustible well, has now to be collected before it is used. But when that time comes, I know, and I would have you know, that with a true knowledge of what is before us, the shadows all turn gold, and that there is much more of hope than of fear in the prospect.[1]

But because of a certain rigidity of temperament that might have led to lack of generosity or nobility in a less tolerant man, he

[1] Unpublished (C.D.B.A.).

sometimes expressed his opinion with trenchant vehemence. Mainly because he felt he had the right. When he was assistant to Dr. Elliot at Ruyton in 1879 he wrote to his mother: 'I said yesterday that I thought capital punishment should be abolished—a trite enough remark—but he went into a fury, said that he would not have such a thing said in his house. I said I would express my opinions, when and where I liked and we had a fine row. All right now.' It is important to realise that his liveliest outbursts of indignation were directed at two forms of the same moral perversion: impertinence and gratuitous cruelty. Like another generous man, whose example he followed, the novelist Fielding, Conan Doyle had very precise ideas as to the functions of critics, men of letters and journalists, and he was punctilious in matters of etiquette. His letters to the newspapers show this clearly, whether he is reproaching the *Daily Express* for its lack of courtesy to the Japanese during the war with Russia:

> Might I ask you as a matter both of courtesy and common sense what is the object of constantly alluding to the Japanese as the 'Japs'? It is well known that it is exceedingly offensive to them. What, then, is the exact reason for habitually doing it? It is little British *gaucheries* of this kind which have made us so unpopular in the world.[1]

Or protesting against the account of Casement's trial:

> No man with any heart or perception could read your description of Roger Casement's death sentence without shame and disgust. Such words in an English paper are likely to do more enduring harm than ever poor misguided Casement achieved. They will certainly be exploited by every enemy of England from Dublin to San Francisco.[2]

Or defending a colleague against an anonymous journalist:

> My dear Colles, I observed a very insolent paragraph in the 'Pall Mall', asking why Sir Walter Besant should have a title. Don't you think it would be a fair retort to say in the 'Author' that while 300 brother authors showed that they knew why he should have one, it is doubtful whether anyone in the wide world knows why Sir Edward Cust should. The reply should be anonymous, as the attack has been so.[3]

[1] *Daily Express*, 1 November 1904.
[2] *Ibid.*, 29 June 1916.
[3] Letter from Conan Doyle to William Morris Colles, 1 July 1895, unpublished. Communicated to Pierre Nordon by James Keddie Jr. Colles was founder and president of the Authors' Syndicate. Sir Edward Cust owned the *Pall Mall Gazette*.

From a personal point of view he hardly ever had grounds to complain of criticisms, or of critics in general, with the exception of Robertson Nicoll who published the same article attacking him in five or six papers simultaneously, under different pseudonyms! But this was a single case, and Conan Doyle was able to make fun of Nicoll instead of abusing him; it has nothing to do with the animosity he showed towards newspaper critics in general. He saw them as detractors rather than instructors; he reproached them for their partiality for too facile, sterile sarcasm and their uselessness to society. This may have been because the estimate of his books by the public was not the same as his own, because Holmes's popularity always eclipsed the real merit of the novels and historical stories. And what could be more irritating for a writer who believed that the end never justified the means than to owe his fame to writings he thought of secondary importance? Besides, he never in the whole course of his career found in newspapermen that sense of responsibility which he believed to be so vital in a writer. On the contrary he witnessed the spread of the modern press, beginning with the founding of the *Daily Mail* in 1896. And was it not Northcliffe's associate, Kennedy Jones, who declared that he had succeeded in transforming what used to be a profession into a business? Making a lot of fools laugh was too often the only thing journalists cared about, according to Conan Doyle. He was indignant too at finding real talent side by side with 'sneering commentators'.[1] and expressed his indignation loudly if he had to deal with someone like Bernard Shaw.

The tragedy of the *Titanic* was only the final pretext for the quarrel between the two men in the columns of the *Daily News* and *Leader* during May 1912. Even allowing for Shaw's verbal sentimentalism, he was too much of a professional journalist to be really indignant over the comments in the popular press and the perhaps too flattering portrait it painted of Captain Smith. The fact was that Shaw's surprising dishonesty and instinct for publicity seized upon an easy opportunity of stealing the limelight. It was his attitude of unjustified superiority, much more than his easily refuted sophisms, that provoked Conan Doyle to intervene. He decided that the dramatist's behaviour was unworthy of his talents: ' . . . But surely it is a pitiful sight to see a man of undoubted genius using his gifts in order to misrepresent and decry his own people, regardless of the fact that

[1] Letter to the *Sunday Express*, 8 January 1928.

his words must add to the grief of those who have already had more than enough to bear.'[1]

If Conan Doyle expressed his indignation in public over something that offended his high sense of honour, particularly when another writer was responsible, it goes without saying that he did the same in private. Without being brusque or unapproachable, he was not easy of access and anything but a flatterer. Very reserved, he hardly ever encouraged his friends to call him by his first name and certain liberties seemed to him physically intolerable: 'There were few things that could stir Conan Doyle more swiftly to a roar of Celtic rage than the clap on the back, the uninvited use of his Christian name, or the presumptuous observation.'[2]

On the other hand, because he was, as Jean Conan Doyle wrote, 'utterly devoid of conceit and false pride',[3] his attitude to servants and his social inferiors was always full of kindness, as well as generosity and compassion when the occasion arose. In 1921, for instance, he was actively engaged on behalf of the under-servants in the hotel industry, who had been threatened with reductions in their wages or being out of work.

No humanitarian cause seemed to him unworthy of his interest; another example was his propaganda in favour of the Indian Famine Fund in 1897. His tendency to take a broad view of social problems did not leave him by any means indifferent to isolated cases, but the intimate character of these transactions gives us no chance to find other witnesses beside the interested parties. For instance Samuel McClure tells in his autobiography how Conan Doyle helped him make a new start in 1894:

> On that day he was staying at the Aldine Club. I had been so weighed down by business cares that I had not seen him since his arrival in the

---

[1] Letter to the *Daily News* and *Leader* 20 May 1912. Cf. also Shaw's letters of 14 May 1912 and the following passage from Conan Doyle's autobiography, pp. 299–300, relating to Shaw: 'I can recall a smaller but even more unjustifiable example of his sour nature when he was staying at Hindhead. A garden-party had been got up for some charity, and it included the woodland scenes of "As You Like It", which were done by amateurs, and very well done, too. Shaw with no provocation wrote a whole column of abuse in the local paper, spattering all the actors and their performance with ridicule, and covering them with confusion, though, indeed, they had nothing to be ashamed of. One mentions these things as characteristic of one side of the man, and as a proof, I fear, that the adoption by the world of a vegetarian diet will not bring unkind thoughts and actions to an end.'

[2] Adrian Conan Doyle, *The True Conan Doyle*, p. 15.

[3] Jean Conan Doyle, *Epilogue*.

United States . . . In apologizing to him for my seeming indifference to his presence in America, I told him that I had been upset by business anxieties, remarking incidentally that I had to finance the magazine as well as edit it. Conan Doyle then said that he would like to put some money into the business himself if I needed it, that he believed in the magazine and in me. I lunched with him at the club, and after lunch he walked over to the office with me, and wrote out his check for $500, exactly the sum we were owing to English authors. When that check was written every one in the office felt a new vigour and a new hope.[1]

We also find, in the biographical archives, the story of the old soldier who said he owed him his life, as well as various letters showing what Conan Doyle had done for some family in difficulties. These different acts of generosity did not belong only to his prosperous years. In 1879 he was at Birmingham, earning £2 a week as assistant to Dr. Hoare, when a regular visitor to the house, a German professor who had been utterly ruined by unfortunate investments and was the father of three children, appealed to the pity of the young assistant. Having only the modest sum of 1s. 6d on him, Conan Doyle gave him his gold watch and chain.

The only part of Christian doctrine that Conan Doyle had preserved was its overt moral discipline, and he repudiated this whenever it encroached aggressively on liberty of opinion and conscience. In the same way, in politics he was a patriot but not a partisan; his imperialism may look a little old-fashioned today, but at least one cannot suspect its sincerity, nor smile at the motives inspiring it. He shared the anthropological view of international politics taken by nineteenth-century thinkers. Just as he believed that different races were connected by ethnic factors, so he thought other responsibilities, similar to those of parent to child and child to parent should be accepted by great and small nations.

It was for the reasons he had explained in his letter to Upton Sinclair,[2] and also because he felt the trades unions made too many claims on the Labour Party, that while theoretically accepting some parts of their programme, Conan Doyle condemned their demagogy in characteristically neo-Conservative style:

This I say with full sympathy for the Labour party, which I have often been tempted to join, but have always been repelled by their attempt to bully the rest of the State instead of using those means which could

[1] S. S. McClure, *My Autobiography*, 1941, p. 217.   [2] See pp. 105–6.

certainly ensure their legitimate success, even if it took some years to
accomplish. There are many anomalies and injustices, and it is only a
people's party which can set them right. Hereditary honours are an
injustice, lands owned by feudal or royal gift are an injustice. Increased
private wealth through the growth of towns is an injustice. Coal royalties are an injustice, the expense of the law is a glaring injustice, the
support of any single religion by the State is an injustice, our divorce
laws are an injustice—with such a list a real honest Labour party
would be a sure winner if it could persuade us all that it would not
commit injustices itself, and bolster up labour artificially at the expense
of everyone else. It is not organised labour which moves me, for it can
take care of itself, but it is the indigent governesses with £30 a year, the
broken people, the people with tiny pensions, the struggling widows
with children—when I think of all these and then of the man who owns
a county I feel that there is something deeply, deeply wrong which
nothing but some great strong new force can set right.[1]

This human, concrete nationalism, ignoring dogma or considerations of State, this inherited good-citizenship, is evidently inseparable
from the sense of history we see in his novels. When in 1892 Conan
Doyle declared that the fourteenth century was 'the most glorious
epoch in English history; the English alone were never so strong as
just then',[2] he was not thinking of the flag, or the prestige of the
monarchy, or military and naval power, or industrial output, or
Empire; he was thinking of course of the individual qualities of
homo anglicus, of his courage, his independence and initiative, his
efficiency, everything in short that distinguished him from other
products of Western civilization at that time.

Without going into Conan Doyle's aesthetic emotions in detail, it
is important to realise how much he appreciated order and coherence,
whenever they were the result of will, direction or dynamic activity.
The intellectual processes which led him to note on the same page
the two comments: 'The greatest liberty is to be guided or compelled
by some one wiser than yourself. We hear too much of the rights of
men and too little of their duties,' and: 'A dead body is a sad thing,
but a dead soul far more so,'[3] is characteristic of a man who deliberately associated ethics with aesthetics. He had already observed that
the perception of some natural harmony implying a mysterious de-

---

[1] *The Wanderings of a Spiritualist*, pp. 228–9.
[2] Interview between Conan Doyle and Raymond Blathwayt in *The Bookman* for May
1892.
[3] Southsea Notebook, No. 2.

sign supported his belief in a supreme intelligence, and that his great desire was to find a metaphysic in keeping with that supreme intelligence, whose fundamental principle should be a permanent attempt at synthesis: 'A religion to be true must include everything from the amoeba to the milky way.'[1]

As for the human mind, his aim was not to understand it completely, but to understand it better, and to this end he tried to look at it from a distance, or rather from above: 'As one rises one's horizon enlarges.'[2]

And Conan Doyle's aesthetic emotions were conditioned by the same purpose, giving his writing an epic quality and his personal vision a panoramic breadth: ' . . . If a man can look down from that point, upon the noble bridge, upon the two rivers crowded with shipping and upon the magnificent city with its thousand evidences of energy and prosperity, and can afterwards find nothing better than a sneer to carry back with him across the ocean, he ought to consult a doctor . . .'[3]

This reflection illustrates the strength and permanence of the impressions made on Conan Doyle's imagination, and also reveals another extremely important element of his character—his powerful faculty of mental control and systematisation.

This faculty is not immediately apparent to those who only consider the surface aspect of things. For instance, if we look at Conan Doyle's behaviour after losing someone he loved—his first wife, his brother, his eldest son, his mother—there is no evidence that he mourned for them for a long time. Louise Conan Doyle's death was the only one that slowed up his activity and crushed his mental energy for several weeks. With this exception, his control over the repercussion of his intimate grief on his activities was so great that we hardly notice any inflection, much less change of direction in them. In the same way, the private or public quarrels in which he was involved very seldom left any residue of active or vindictive hostility in him. He soon made it up with William and Constance Hornung, and also with various literary men he had violently attacked, such as Hall Caine, Stead or Robertson Nicoll. His fits of bad temper were sometimes violent but seldom lasted long, and they were never provoked by personal motives, but always when some idea or principle

[1] Southsea Notebook, No. 2.   [2] *Ibid.*
[3] Speech to the Lotos Club of New York, 17 November 1894 (C.D.B.A.).

was involved. Then, whether it was a question of Oscar Slater or of spiritualism, he would never give in.

We hardly ever find Conan Doyle giving special value to personal recollections of the past; his respect for history did not take this form. He was proud of his ancestors and their traditions in a collective way, but he never cared at all about personal honours and was genuinely indifferent to titles and decorations. The Doyle dining-table and John Doyle's Van Dyck were far more important relics to him. He was only interested in his own past in so far as he could extract some objective and general conclusion from it, and as has already been remarked, his autobiography shows him as a man of 'adventures' rather than 'memories'. His attentive interest in the world around him made him essentially a man of his day and concerned with new inventions. Wireless and motor-cars fascinated him; he liked to take part in current events. His remark in a letter to his mother: 'It seems a pity to have historical events going on so near and not to see anything of it'[1] is entirely typical. And what he saw was valuable in so far as he could draw a lesson from it. His love of action drove Conan Doyle to try all sorts of experiences, from whale-fishing at twenty to going round Brooklands racing track at 100 m.p.h. when he was seventy, with ballooning thrown in. In 1903 he confided to P. G. Wodehouse that he would like to learn to para-chute: 'I think the man who first tried coming down in a parachute was the pluckiest man on earth, he said . . . I should like to try it, just for the sake of the one great experience!'[2]

Yet this man who always considered the end in view, both in his private and public life, was uncommonly indifferent to money. Too acutely aware of his responsibilities, too serious to be a spendthrift, he did not of course deny its importance. He regularly kept an approximate check on his financial situation (at the end of each year, as his diaries show); and from time to time he raised the subject in his letters to 'The Ma'am', to prove to her—or perhaps to himself? —how well he looked after his income. But a time came when he had to admit that he was not always so good at weighing up the risks he took with his investments in industry or mines, as at reckoning the size of his losses. His speculations were only one aspect of his love of adventure. But he was aware that he valued money too little, and

---

[1] Letter from Cairo, 19 March 1896 (C.D.B.A.).
[2] *Victoria Club Magazine*, 2 July 1903.

remembering the example set by his father, feared that this might perhaps be harmful to his dependents; he always tried to reassure Mary Doyle on this point.

But would a self-seeking man have so frequently refused his rights as an author, paid a large part of the expenses of the Slater and Casement trials out of his own pocket and sacrificed about £250,000— earned by great talent but also by much hard work—to the cause of spiritualism? Would he have thought it sensible to kill the goose that laid the golden eggs by refusing to write any new Sherlock Holmes stories for many years? And did not his contempt for every form of remuneration (a trait he shared with Sherlock Holmes) colour his evaluation of his own creation, and make him see him as a new Midas rather than a reflection of his own personality?

Indifference to money is the only thing that can explain Conan Doyle's failure to exploit his manifest powers of invention and analysis. Seldom impulsive, in his political and public life he constantly showed a far-reaching vision and interest in long-term results, regardless of whether his suggestions would be welcomed or not— as was shown in the Casement affair. His influence, if not his authority, was strengthened by this, and towards the end of his life those who talked to him were impressed by the glow of mental or spiritual autonomy that as it were impregnated his features: 'I saw him in his study in the Victoria district. There seemed to be the light of another world on his distinguished face. Here was a man who gave you the impression that he really was in touch with forces unknown on this earth. Everything about Conan Doyle was big . . . here was a man whose depth of sincerity seemed to be immeasurable.'[1]

This radiance is in fact visible in some of the photographs of Conan Doyle in old age; it expresses the final triumph of his will over the ruggedness of temperament he attributed to his Celtic origins. This is a little-known aspect of Conan Doyle, and one which may have come from an element of puritanism—we must not forget that he was in some respects easily shocked—or from a desire for even greater efficiency, based on his animistic view of human nature. His puritanism was not merely a relic of Victorianism. It came from his allegiance to the masculine and social model of the 'gentleman', an ideal that is both aristocratic and bourgeois—aristocratic because it establishes a hierarchy of duties and rights amongst the different social categories,

[1] R. Stannard, *With the Dictators of Fleet Street*, 1934, p. 278.

and bourgeois because it rejects the dialectic of the class-war and treats society as a single organism. Conan Doyle's 'enlightened' conservatism coloured his writings just as it found characteristic expression in his personal reactions. His son Adrian has given an example:

> When I shot a crocodile in East Africa—an actual man-eater which had taken a negro the night before—a lad plunged into the water to see if he could reach with a pole the body which had submerged. We did not know if the monster was dead or not or whether it had a mate. The lad went in against my father's shouted orders, but once in, I had to go in too: Terrified, of course, but I knew that my father would take it as a natural necessity that I should *disobey* his orders rather than permit someone of lower status than his son to take a hideous risk from which I shrank. It was a code as clear as a flame before an altar and just about as comfortable as the periodic application of that flame to one's living flesh![1]

Conan Doyle's way of life was not particularly austere; he was far from preaching the renunciation of 'cakes and ale'. He sometimes abstained from alcohol for periods of several weeks or months—not without some difficulty, as the notes of his progress in his private Journal show. But usually he was no enemy to good wine, with a preference perhaps for burgundy. Worldliness was antipathetic to him, but his hospitality was lavish and he employed as many as eight servants in his house at Crowborough. He smoked cigars, and even more often a pipe, and judging from the numerous press photographs, he dressed with a certain elegance. All these characteristics were external signs of a solidarity with his own class of which he was probably barely aware. More revealing of the 'secondary characteristics' of Conan Doyle's ego was his delight in collections of every description. It is not surprising that he should have collected books on criminology; but the fact that he also collected military relics of the Napoleonic period, antique pottery and statuettes, coins and medals,

---

[1] Letter to Pierre Nordon, 7 December 1959. Compare also the conversation about prize-fighters of the Regency Period, in *Three of Them*, pp. 93–4: ' "If ever you have to fight a long fight, either with your mind or your body, and if you sicken and weary, as all of us do in our weaker moments, say to yourselves.' Well, if those poor ignorant chaps would fight to the last gasp for next to nothing, is it not for me, a gentleman, to fight till I am senseless too, or dead, if you like, before I give in over what I know to be right?" I don't mind telling you, my dears, that there have been times when it was not the words of good and pious men, but it was the memory and example of those old rascals, that helped me over a rough patch of the road.'

tells us more about him than that as a writer he needed to possess a library.

But why should a man with such a prodigious memory have to surround himself with such formidable piles of notebooks, if he had not had a fundamental need to preserve and reproduce what he had seen or read in the most orderly and exact way possible? This was one of the subjects about which he was sometimes dictatorial. He wrote to Jean telling her what to read, and to his friend Hemingsley on the subject of note-taking:

> . . . Read solid books, history, biography and travel—and above all take notes of what you read. Reading without note taking is as senseless as eating without digesting. It is easy to condense into a single page all that you really want to remember out of a big book, and there you have it for reference for ever. When you have done that systematically, for five years, you will be surprised at the extraordinary amount of available information which you can turn upon any subject, all at the cost of very little trouble.[1]

An assiduous reader and attentive listener, he was also a delightful talker. The style of the conversations in his books was that which came most naturally to him in life. Already as a schoolboy he could keep a whole dormitory awake and enthralled with some more or less imaginary story, and when he indulged the same instinct in later life among his intimate friends, they were quickly charmed by his tone of voice and the unforced and casual rhythm of his diction.[2]

However he mistrusted his own facility, and as Jerome K. Jerome observed, he would often choose to retire into a corner of the room with a manuscript, and listen to other people rather than talk himself. Like Holmes he attended to everything that other people said, and the day after a meeting or conversation he would sit down and make a note of it, just as he did of the books he had read. His son Adrian tells us that the social status of the person he was talking to made no difference to him, and this is confirmed by the fact that in *Memories and Adventures* he does not only report conversations with celebrities, but also with sailors, a sweetshop assistant, a policeman, an anonymous billiards player, an aged Boer and hecklers at political meetings.

The attraction that the human context of situations and events had

---

[1] Letter to Hemingsley, 1890 (C.D.B.A.).
[2] Cf. the recording *Conan Doyle Speaking*, made by the Gramophone Co. Ltd. (His Master's Voice) in 1929.

for Conan Doyle's mind explains the selective nature of his memory
and powers of observation. Like Sherlock Holmes he possessed to a
spectacular degree the ability to read a man's past or his occupation
from his physical appearance or clothing. On the other hand there
are sometimes inexactitudes in his letters—which were more often
than not undated—and in some details of only secondary importance
to their author which are the joy of Sherlock Holmes's interpreters.
Whether the houses in Baker Street had bay-windows or not, whether
such and such a place was served by one or two railway-lines, whether
Dr. Watson's first name was John or James, mattered very little to
him, as he admitted with genial good grace.

He showed the same indifference towards material objects as such.
Though enchanted by new gadgets, and good at various games (football, cricket, billiards) he seemed hardly aware of the surroundings
in which he worked.

In the same way, his personal modesty did not imply a sense of
inferiority, but merely the desire to respect as objectively as possible
the true hierarchy of values, to which he was very much alive. At times
his modesty seems to have been excessive, for instance when he refused to have his portrait included in the first edition of his *History of
the Boer War*; at others he even seems a little arrogant. He was only
just twenty-three and at the start of his medical career when he
wrote the following aggressive declaration of independence: ' . . .
I don't want a connection among *medical men* nor to appear as the
hanger on of any of them. I hope to have cut the lot of them out
before another year. When I have beaten them I don't mind knowing
them, but I can *not* stand patronage.'[1]

One of the most revealing passages about himself occurs in a letter
he wrote to his mother during the summer of 1900, wherein he weighs
up with detachment the advantages and eventual disadvantages of a
political career:

> . . . What is to be gained? A full and varied and perhaps useful life.
> The assurance that come what may I have at least tested my fate, and
> done my duty as a Citizen. The participation in many interesting scenes.
>   What is against it? I shall be bored by dinners, deputations, func-
> tions, etc. I shall have less freedom—(enjoy it all the more when I do
> get it)—less sport (could do with less as I grow older). Sometimes my
> duties will be irksome (not a bad thing in life).[2]

[1] Letter to Mary Doyle, n.d. (C.D.B.A.).
[2] *Ibid.*, 27 August 1900 (C.D.B.A.).

Ambition that was both realistic and disciplined by a very acute sense of duty, public spirit, and a constant unwearying desire for action—these were the dictating principles of his intelligence. Since he was incapable of lightening load by abandoning his moral outlook, he had no use for so-called intellectual games, or mathematics— to which he was almost hostile, witness the fact that Professor Moriarty, 'the Napoleon of crime', was a professor of mathematics. On the other hand he played a great many games with enormous concentration. He played football at Southsea as a young man, golf with varying success, and cricket for about thirty years. At fifteen he was already trying to join the Edinburgh Cricket Club on the fallacious excuse that 'it was a jolly game and does more to make a fellow strong and healthy than all the doctors' prescriptions in the world'.[1] The culminating point of his career as an amateur cricketer was the match when he bowled W. G. Grace. He played for the M.C.C. against Kent, Derbyshire and Warwickshire, and rather less seriously in James Barrie's eleven, with A. E. W. Mason and his old schoolfellow Bernard Partridge of *Punch*. He took an interest in exploration as well as in traditional games. In 1894, with the Branger brothers, he was the first to go on skis from Davos to Arosa by way of Furka, thus encouraging the sport of ski-ing in that part of the world. In his adventurous youth he was an enthusiastic bicyclist and later a balloonist. 'I made a balloon ascent on Thursday,' he wrote to his mother in 1902, '—great fun!—we went up from the Crystal Palace and fell at Sevenoaks, twenty five miles. We went one and a half miles high. It was a most extraordinary sensation and experience.'[2] Finally, at the age of fifty-two, he took part in the famous Anglo-German motor rally, taking the wheel himself for nearly 4,000 kilometres. But it was characteristic of Conan Doyle to stress the social and political importance of sport. Like Baden-Powell he soon realised that certain forms of physical training could be useful from a military point of view, and we know already that he encouraged clubs for rifle practice just before the Boer War. But whereas Baden-Powell regimented his groups of boys, Conan Doyle's attitude was that of a civilian who believed in the English tradition of a small regular army, and he was not interested in systematised sport. As Deputy Lord Lieutenant of Surrey he was expected to be in favour

---

[1] Letter to Mary Doyle from Stonyhurst, June 1874 (C.D.B.A.).
[2] Unpublished (C.D.B.A.).

of recruiting, but he found it an unpleasant necessity, and always preferred the idea of a nation of civilians ready to play their part when
the time came, to the apparent servitude of conscription. He was
content to encourage love and respect for sport by his influence and
example. Famous sportsmen sought his support more often than
military men. In 1901 Grace asked him to be president of a club he had
just founded, and the same year the great Sandow asked him to come
to the Albert Hall and choose the best English athlete from among
eighty competitors.

Conan Doyle did not in fact think of sport as a form of political or
national aggrandisement, but as a powerful force for international
understanding. Having been, like Kipling, one of the warmest friends
of America among English writers ever since 1894, he received in
1909 an unexpected proof of his popularity there: the Editor of the
New York *Morning Telegraph* asked him to judge the heavy-weight
championship of the world: 'Believe me among sporting men of the
best class in America you have many strong admirers,' he wrote,
'your splendid stories of the ring, and your avowed admiration for
the great sport of boxing have made you thousands of friends. It was
because of this extremely friendly feeling for you in America that I
took the liberty of cabling to you.'[1] Two years later he took part in
Prince Henry of Prussia's motor rally: and thus had a chance to
measure the deep enmity separating England and Germany; he was
very genuinely disappointed to find that although as a sporting event
the rally was a success it had taken place in an atmosphere of much
less friendliness and trust than he had hoped for. It seemed to him
that the German competitors were animated by ulterior motives, and
some of them behaved as if they had been told to collect information.
He took the first opportunity that offered to put things right, by
accepting Lord Northcliffe's invitation to preside over the committee
charged with preparing the British team for the Olympic Games,
planned to take place in Berlin in 1916. The diplomatic part of the
mission entrusted to him would have followed the same lines as his
reception of Admiral Caillard and his French naval officers.

The temperament and character-traits we have described went to
make up a personality whose complexity could not be grasped at a
first meeting; this would give fleeting glimpses, sometimes of a
dominantly emotional, sometimes of a dominantly phlegmatic nature.

[1] Letter from Irving Jefferson Lewis to Conan Doyle, 9 December 1909 (C.D.B.A.).

Among the character-groups, perhaps he falls into the passionate-methodical class. René Le Senne's necessarily synthetic picture of such a character confirms our analysis, and so finds a place here:

> These are deeply serious-minded men, loyal to whatever task they undertake, capable of the highest social virtues, devoted to the State, the Church and the other institutions they serve, having a lively sense of their own worth but dedicating that worth to the services they render. Their regular conduct, serious interests and the somewhat austere nobility of their actions, almost always gain them general esteem or even admiration. Among the constituents of their characters it is the secondary ones that give them their charm. They are hardly ever impulsive, work hard and regularly, and seem to be essentially meditative—but their meditations are intellectual rather than emotional, unlike those of parasentimental characters. The existence of God is revealed to such men, rather than intuitively known, their country and the community are indistinguishable from the State. But however intellectual they may be they are not phlegmatic as is often shown by the way their thoughts enter into some social institution, or by the place in their lives taken by military or political action. In short, they are like all men of strong emotions, extremely highly strung, but this quality tends to greater systematisation.[1]

Just as Sherlock Holmes has come to stand for something more than a mere hero of fiction in the public mind, so Conan Doyle's name cannot be kept within the frame of mere literature. It was not only that he developed to a remarkable degree those qualities of leadership which his godfather detected in him at an early age, but also that he made the same impression on millions of readers. For more than forty years he was in constant conversation with the public. His interlocutors belonged to every social class without exception, even including inmates of His Majesty's prisons. Their voices are preserved in the biographical archives. On the eve of his departure for South Africa in 1900 the master of a trawler wrote to wish him good luck, and summed up in a single phrase what Conan Doyle stood for to the man-in-the-street: 'You can fight, mend a broken leg or any other wound and write a true account of it all when it is all over.'[2]

A clergyman who had watched his electoral campaign at Hawick expressed his parishioners' admiration for his courage, sincerity and courtesy: 'Your name will always be honoured here by men of every shade of opinion for the manliness and sincerity and unfailing

[1] *Traité de Caractérologie*, p. 414.
[2] Letter from James Brown, 23 January 1900 (C.D.B.A.).

courtesy with which you fought your fight. The most strenuous of your opponents speak of you with warm admiration. And this is a victory in itself, and I fear it is not being often won in these days when partisanship runs so high, and men are eager to secure their place on any terms.'[1]

An influence greater than that of most writers has been attributed to him. The explorer Robert Scott held that his facilitation of the arrangements ensured the success of the voyage of the *Discovery*; Edward Spence, a barrister, begged him to defend Haldane against public criticism at the time of the ministerial re-shuffle of 1915; and when Theodore Roosevelt heard that the novelist was thinking of visiting the United States he took the initiative and sent him an invitation.

Man of letters? Man of action? He was both. We shall see the same duality—passion and method—in his writings that we found in his character. All his work bears the imprint of the need for action which quite literally possessed him; but this led to two contradictory results. There was an orientation towards the unknown. In a sense, all Conan Doyle's writings are dominated by the desire to investigate and explore. His detective stories come from an impulse to unveil the mysteries of daily life, his historical or prehistorical novels are voyages of exploration. Whether expressed in speech or print, his spiritualistic crusade drove him in search of the next world, and was for the uninitiated—as it was for Conan Doyle himself to some extent—an adventure in anticipation. But beneath his curiosity, beyond his voyages of discovery, we detect an insistence on certainty which plots out a system of ideal references in the past rather than in the future. We have seen that his spiritualism was neo-Christian, and his neo-Conservatism is clearly apparent in his literary output. The first question we need to ask about his work as a writer is this: to what extent was it purely creative and an original achievement?

[1] Letter from the Rev. D. Cathels, 22 January 1906 (C.D.B.A.).

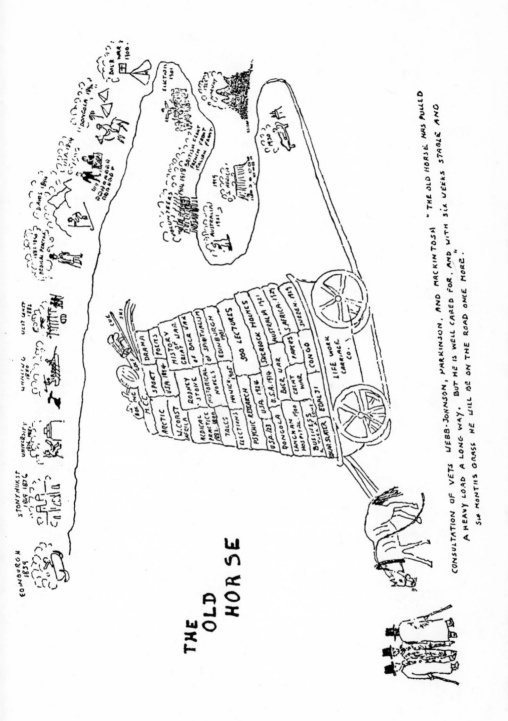

THE OLD HORSE

CONSULTATION OF VETS WEBB-JOHNSON, PARKINSON, AND MACKINTOSH "THE OLD HORSE HAS PULLED A HEAVY LOAD A LONG WAY, BUT HE IS WELL CARED FOR, AND WITH SIX WEEKS STABLE AND SIX MONTHS GRASS HE WILL BE ON THE ROAD ONCE MORE."

PART II
The Writer

Chapter 11

SHERLOCK HOLMES: THE MYTH

One day a woman of exceptional taste and sensibility,
who had been absorbed in reading *Grandison* said to a
friend who was leaving for London: 'Please go and see
Miss Emilie and Mr. Belford for me, and above all
Miss Howe, if she's still alive.'

DIDEROT *Praise of Richardson*

Sherlock Holmes figures in sixty narratives: fifty-six short stories and
four full-length novels. Nearly all of these were published in *The
Strand Magazine* before being collected into separate volumes
between 1891 and 1927. The first novel, *A Study in Scarlet*, appeared in 1887, and it is in this work we first meet the detective. We
are given a precise but undetailed description of his character, and the
qualities which distinguish Holmes from common mortals are barely
hinted at. According to Dr. Watson: 'In height he was rather over six
feet, and so excessively lean that he seemed to be considerably taller.
His eyes were sharp and piercing . . . his thin hawk-like nose gave
his whole expression an air of alertness and decision. His chin too,
had the prominence and squareness which mark the man of determination.'

The very stylisation of this portrait draws our attention to the essential qualities of the amateur detective: his energy and the acuteness
of his senses. We see why Conan Doyle never felt it necessary to fill
in this rough outline; it at least left something to the imagination of
his illustrators. Before publishing *The Adventures of Sherlock Holmes*,
the editor of the *The Strand Magazine*, Greenhough Smith, bethought
himself of an artist called Paget, whose sketches had appeared in *The
Illustrated London News*. From ignorance or absence of mind, Smith
wrote not to Walter Paget, the artist responsible for these drawings,
but to his younger brother Sidney. Nevertheless Sidney agreed to
illustrate the *Adventures*, and asked his brother Walter to sit for him.
As a result, thanks to Sidney the artist and Walter the model, a definite picture of Sherlock Holmes was quickly accepted by the public.

When he was in the country Sidney liked to wear a deer-stalker, and he thought it a good idea to give Sherlock Holmes the same now almost allegorical headgear. Between 1891 and 1893 (in *The Adventures* and *The Memoirs*) and 1901 and 1904 (in *The Hound of the Baskervilles* and *The Return*), tens of thousands of reproductions of Sidney Paget's illustrations spread abroad an image which was confirmed in so far as its vagueness would allow by the text. Between these two periods Conan Doyle, who had been too ready to believe he had got rid of Holmes in the falls of Reichenbach,[1] discovered to his cost that, like the Duc de Guise, his hero was more famous dead than alive. Young men wore mourning for Sherlock Holmes in Piccadilly, and his creator received letters of protest followed by entreaties.

At the same time Scotland Yard became a poste restante for letters addressed to Mr. Sherlock Holmes. As a result of ill-founded rumours, *The Cape Town Times* for 15 July 1896 announced the arrival of Sherlock Holmes and Dr. Watson in South Africa.

In 1899 the American actor William Gillette asked Conan Doyle's permission to put on a stage adaptation in the United States in which he intended to 'marry' Sherlock Holmes. Conan Doyle replied with lazy indifference that Gillette could do just as he liked with Holmes, marry him or finish him off for good and all. Gillette's adaptation was played with success over a period of more than thirty years, and the American actor imposed a certain image of Sherlock Holmes on his audiences, just as Sidney Paget's illustrations had done on the reading public. When Frederick Dorr Steele was commissioned to illustrate the American editions of the Sherlock Holmes stories, he followed his compatriot's interpretation rather than Conan Doyle or Sidney Paget. He would probably have got into trouble if he had done otherwise. The American version of Holmes is thus rather different from the British one. Perhaps with Oscar Wilde in mind, his dandyism and somewhat sinister charm are emphasised, also his 'disappointment with the Atlantic', thus combining homage to the two writers whose visits to America in the latter half of the nineteenth century had left the liveliest impression. Beside the stories themselves, theatrical adaptations, drawings, and—later on—the cinema and television, have contributed to build up a complete personality with an independent existence of his own.

The resumption of Sherlock Holmes's Adventures in 1901 might

---

[1] *The Final Problem.*

have been expected to compete with the apocryphal legend or even put an end to it. Nothing of the sort. As we shall see later, this legend fulfilled a need beyond the realms of literature. In the story called *The Second Stain*, Dr. Watson tells the reader that the detective 'has definitely retired from London and betaken himself to study and bee-farming on the Sussex Downs.' No sooner had this number of *The Strand Magazine* appeared in December 1904 than Sir Arthur received two offers from would-be employees of Sherlock Holmes. The first came from a house-keeper wanting a post in the country, the second from a bee-keeper who wanted to give Sherlock Holmes the benefit of his experience. Finally, as if to add the final touch of reality to Holmes's existence, a certain Stephen Sharp, who believed he actually was the detective, made several attempts to visit Conan Doyle from 1905 onwards. Shown the door more than once, he ended by writing a threatening letter.

This extreme case emphasises the extraordinary hold that Holmes's character quickly obtained on the imagination of the public. Every amateur posing as a detective, magnifying-glass in hand, tried to imitate him. As an article in *The Times Literary Supplement* for 29 July 1960 expressed it: 'A detective is the ideal adventurer for an intellectual to identify himself with. His triumphs are cerebral and even sedentary. Bishops and dons and schoolmasters have to stretch their imagination outrageously to see themselves as pirate chiefs or intrepid explorers: but they have no difficulty in being Sherlock Holmes or Nero Wolfe, shrewdly observing what others have missed, expounding the proper deductions from facts which their colleagues have doltishly misunderstood.' The fascination exercised by Holmes's personality over less active temperaments may to some extent account for the development of the myth, but it is not the whole story.

It is hardly necessary to repeat here what has already been written about the influence of Sherlock Holmes on the heroes of the twentieth-century detective-story. (The most recent and best-balanced account will be found in A. E. Murch's *The Development of the Detective Novel*, 1958.) He is generally accepted as the prototype of the detective, and if influence can be taken as the test of worth, Conan Doyle has certainly left an indelible mark on the detective-story. He also supplied Sherlock Holmes with a decor and orchestration that have helped make him as proverbial a character as Don Juan or Robinson Crusoe. His name has become almost a by-word. A railway-engine, two Dior models (in 1956), a London pub and innumerable clubs and magazines have been called after him. He has been treated like a national hero.

When it was first suggested that there should be a Sherlock Holmes Exhibition during the 1951 Festival of Britain, the Borough Council of St. Marylebone hesitated for some time before deciding to devote public funds to honouring the memory of a fictional character. Some members of the council thought it would be more respectable to organise an exhibition of town-planning since 1851. An argument followed. In any other country but Great Britain it would probably have ended in the triumph of realism, but here town-planning was sacrificed to Sherlock Holmes. As a result of the industrious efforts of the Holmesian clubs, all sorts of 'relics' began to arrive at Baker Street: fire-arms, violins, magnifying-glasses, deer-stalkers, meerschaum pipes, typewriters, etc. The Post Office provided a telegraph form dating from 1890. The editor of *Who's Who* compiled a biography of Holmes, the British Museum furnished portraits connected with the Vernet family from whom Holmes was descended through his maternal grandmother. Finally, Professor Williams of the University of Southampton offered the exhibition a study of the botanical and zoological problems raised in the stories of Sherlock's investigations. The key exhibit in this picturesque affair was a reconstruction of Sherlock Holmes's study. The exhibition stayed open for three months and was visited by over 65,000 people. Some idea of the atmosphere in which the plan was organised and received will be got from a letter sent to the organisers by the head of the Raleigh factory at Nottingham, along with a bicycle of the period:

Dear Lord Donegall,
　　Referring to your letter of the 20th April, in which you inform me of your present researches into the whereabouts of the cycle belonging to Miss Violet Smith of *The Solitary Cyclist*, Sherlock Holmes's case, I am pleased to be able to tell you that on looking back through our files for 1895 and 1896 we have been able to trace a Humber bicycle which we delivered to Miss Smith's father at Charlington Hall.
　　As you recall in your letter, Miss Smith married and having no further use for the vehicle sold it back to us.
　　Many years later when it became apparent that our earliest products would be of historical interest, it was placed among other examples of the firm's craftsmanship.
　　It was not, however, until your letter calling attention to the fact, that Raleigh Industries Limited realised the very special value of this

bicycle, in view of its association with the immortal detective, Mr. Sherlock Holmes.[1]

The spirit of the 1951 exhibition was also present in the celebrations of the centenary of Sherlock Holmes's 'birth' in 1954. On 8 January the B.B.C. devoted a special programme and several speakers to this event. One of these remembered his schooldays with the detective, another said he had been Holmes's violin master. All expressed the hope that their old friend was listening to them from his country retreat. And Holmes played a large part in the widespread celebrations in 1959 of the centenary of Conan Doyle's birth. In France, the illustrated papers and the radio saluted his memory as well as his creator's in a television programme lasting fifty minutes. In comprehensive studies of the detective-story we sometimes find Holmes taken as a pretext for articles on regional customs and folklore, centring round the districts where his investigations took place. One book is devoted mainly to the different settings of the stories, particularly in London.[2] These writers about Holmes and his world make use of some of the methods of literary or historical criticism, and their 'Holmesian studies' pretend to treat Holmes, Watson and other characters in the cycle as though they were historically real. Other writers beside Conan Doyle have had similar homage paid to the picturesque vitality of their characters, especially during the nineteenth century, but the peculiarity of Sherlock Holmes's case is that critics often ignore his creator altogether, or put him between brackets. Perhaps it is because of Holmes's frequent dogmatic utterances or—who knows?—his French blood, that Holmes has even been given independent life in a textbook of the French language: '*Sherlock Holmes (Conan Doyle's famous creation); quelques chapitres de sa vie, a few chapters of his life; avec questions et réponses, with questions and answers, présenté par* Roth, E. Philadelphie, 1902.'

While, year after year, more or less successful parodies of *The Adventures of Sherlock Holmes* have been published, Ronald Knox had already written an essay about him in 1911, while still an undergraduate, and it was published in a collection of his satires when he was Chaplain at the University of Oxford.[3] His great interest in detective-stories had blossomed under Sherlock Holmes's aegis. This essay is

[1] Letter from G. H. B. Wilson. Cf. Catalogue of the Exhibition, 1952, p. 26.
[2] M. Harrison, *In the Footsteps of Sherlock Holmes*, 1958.
[3] *Essays in Satire*, pp. 98–121.

not a critical study, however. The future Protonotary Apostolic had merely conceived the idea of denouncing the extremes to which theologians could go when criticising Holy Writ, by humorously applying their methods to a modern and profane text. His attempt to expose absurdity by absurdity resulted in coherent nonsense of the Lewis Carroll type, which set a fashion. Sydney Roberts, professor of English Literature at Cambridge, was interested by Knox's essay. He had just published his first book on Dr. Johnson and was working on a translation of André Maurois's *Études Anglaises*, so that his mind was full of biographical problems. By giving Conan Doyle's characters a sort of pseudo-reality, and by references to Dr. Watson's 'reminiscences' quite out of their dramatic context, Knox had accidentally brought out an anology between Holmes and Watson and another couple well known to Sydney Roberts—Johnson and Boswell. So the Cambridge professor decided to play the Oxford game, and set out to refute Knox's hypotheses. This was the beginning of a series of 'Holmesian studies' which has gone on ever since.

The controversy between the two universities mainly concerned the chronology of Sherlock Holmes's Adventures and of the episodes in his life and Dr. Watson's. Thus Conan Doyle's works were made the excuse for a literary game. Ronald Knox and Sydney Roberts were soon joined by other performers from both sides of the Atlantic. Between 1928 and 1932 at least eight Holmesian studies of this sort were published, perhaps the most learned and ingenious being by Blakeney and H. W. Bell.[1] Bell succeeded in establishing an exact and detailed chronology of the Adventures described by Watson, and even of others in which Holmes had been involved but which are never gone into. Two years later Bell produced a collection of articles by eight different authors, entitled *Baker Street Studies*. Dorothy Sayers and her detective Lord Peter had already shown their devotion to Sherlock Holmes; she now tried to prove that he had been an undergraduate at Cambridge, at Sidney Sussex to be exact. Ronald Knox, on his side, produced just as convincing arguments in favour of Christ Church, Oxford. It was at about this time that members of the two universities became rivals in the domain of the detective-story proper. Cambridge was represented by Professor Glyn Daniel, and Oxford by Ronald Knox, G. D. H. Cole, and—

---

[1] T. S. Blakeney, *Sherlock Holmes: Fact or Fiction?*, 1932; H. W. Bell, *Sherlock Holmes and Dr. Watson, the Chronology of their Adventures*, 1932.

more recently—J. C. Masterman (Vice-Chancellor from 1957 to 1958), J. I. M. Stewart, and finally by the poet Cecil Day Lewis, under the pseudonym of Nicholas Blake.

Up to the present moment, there have been four biographies of Sherlock Holmes, and Guy Warrack has written a book devoted to his knowledge of music. These works show a love of detail which would certainly have delighted the detective had he been able to read them. For instance, so as to fix the exact date of the adventure of *The Beryl Coronet*, in which footprints in the snow play an important part, the archives of The Royal Meteorological Society have been consulted.[1] Such detective methods remind one of the way *A Midsummer Night's Dream* has been dated by its allusions to the weather. Some writers have gone pretty far in this direction. The exact position of Sherlock Holmes's house in Baker Street has been one of the great problems, for no number 221 B ever existed. Of course such parlour games have led to a great many special clubs being founded, not only among English-speaking nations but in countries like Denmark, Holland and Japan. There are more than thirty in the United States, the best known of which is called The Baker Street Irregulars. President Roosevelt belonged to it, and during the Second World War he christened the Intelligence department of his headquarters 'Baker Street'.

The remarkable popularity of Sherlock Holmes's exploits in the United States is a literary fact which must be emphasised. Their being written in English is not enough to account for it and we must look for justifying circumstances both inside and outside the works themselves. As will be shown later, they make a strong appeal to American historical sense; two of the longer stories, *A Study in Scarlet* and *The Valley of Fear* are set partly in the United States, at the time of the conquest of the West, and belong to the American literary myth of the period. The sources for these books were largely American. Also Conan Doyle's works appeared at a time when the curiosity of the American public about Great Britain had taken a new lease of life, and when American literature often presented England and the English for the benefit of trans-Atlantic readers. The Adventures of Holmes give a condensed, accessible, coherent and intelligible picture of English life. Just as Conan Doyle's historical novels give the reader a sense of security with their coherent picture of English

[1] G. Brend, *My Dear Holmes, a Study in Sherlock*, 1951, p. 9.

history, so the picture of English society in the Holmes stories is for the American reader a mirror of the 'Old Country'. To these reasons relating to the internal structure of Conan Doyle's books we must add others, probably less obvious, which depend upon the social conditions in America between 1900 and 1940. During this period crime became an acute problem, and figured widely in literature, the drama and the cinema. It is significant that the detective-story proper, and novels with a detective element, are even more popular in the United States than in England. Sherlock Holmes's Adventures have therefore as much ideological value in the United States as in England. But one of the short novels, *The Valley of Fear*, has a special interest for Americans. In it Conan Doyle describes a mining settlement, the miners themselves and, by implication, their managers. We know from various historical works (such as Henry Fern's biography of Mackenzie King) that the miner's conditions of life in some of these settlements were deplorable. Yet in *The Valley of Fear* Conan Doyle gives us to understand that the management was good. In fact Sherlock Holmes intervenes on this side. We see here how the Adventures of Holmes gave ideological security to Americans as well as to English.

But we must return to Great Britain and its Holmesian societies, the most important of which is the Sherlock Holmes Society presided over by Sir Sydney Roberts. Founded in 1934, it ceased to exist two years later, but started again in 1951, and still publishes a magazine devoted exclusively to Sherlock Holmes. If the specialists we have mentioned find the Holmes stories an inexhaustible source of essays each more humorous and ingenious than the last, they have also attracted the interest of more practical minds. The fact that the publication of Conan Doyle's first books coincided with progress in the science of criminology raised the question as to whether these could be cause and effect and if so to what degree. Conan Doyle's first novel was not exclusively concerned with detection, but he prepared the way by insisting on the value of observation and scientific methods. When Dr. Watson first meets Holmes, he finds him in the middle of a chemical experiment. Afterwards he gives a proof of his skill by instantly recognising the origin of a mud-stain. Little by little the investigator becomes an expert criminologist. This is something that distinguishes Holmes from earlier fictional detectives and has aroused the interest of real criminologists, with Edmond Locard of

Lyons among the foremost.[1] It may be true, as Locard and after-wards Rendall[2] have said, that Sherlock Holmes knew nothing of the advances made in identification by finger-prints between 1880 and 1900. Sherlock Holmes makes only slight use of this science in the story called *The Norwood Builder*. It is also possible that although he pays homage to Bertillon, Conan Doyle had never studied his findings in anthropometry. This does not alter the fact that *The Adventures of Sherlock Holmes* has been actually used as a text-book for the instruction of detectives. Locard tells us that a medico-legal study of the book was made by the Faculty of Medicine at Lyons at the request of Bertillon himself, and probably its influence still goes on. The criminologist Ashton-Wolfe wrote:

> Many of the methods invented by Conan Doyle are today in use in the scientific laboratories. Sherlock Holmes made the study of tobacco-ashes his hobby. It was a new idea, but the police at once realised the importance of such specialised knowledge, and now every laboratory has a complete set of tables giving the appearance and composition of the various ashes, which every detective must be able to recognise. Mud and soil from various districts are also classified much after the manner that Holmes described . . . Conan Doyle made Holmes a complex personality: not only a tracker, but a logician and an analyst, and thus evolved and disseminated successfully the constructive method in use to-day in all Criminal Investigation Departments. Poisons, hand-writing, stains, dust, footprints, traces of wheels, the shape and position of wounds, and therefore the probable shape of the weapon which caused them; the theory of cryptograms, all these and many other excellent methods which germinated in Conan Doyle's fertile imagination are now part and parcel of every detective's scientific equipment.[3]

Nearer the present day, the German cipher expert Sittig gives Sherlock Holmes's creator the credit for describing the technique he himself used to decipher Cretan inscriptions.

Such indications as these go to show how wide an influence, even outside the literary context, Sherlock Holmes has had on the world of today.

[1] E. Locard, *Policiers de Roman et de Laboratoire*, 1924. The author proves the importance of Conan Doyle's influence on modern criminology and declares that his works are extremely interesting to specialists in that field.
[2] V. Rendall, *Baker Street Studies*, pp. 65 and sqq.
[3] *The Illustrated London News*, 27 February 1932.

Chapter 12

THE CHARACTER OF SHERLOCK HOLMES

The character of Sherlock Holmes did not emerge fully-fledged from
Conan Doyle's imagination. When questioned about the origins of
his detective, Sir Arthur claimed for him one literary ancestor, Edgar
Allan Poe's Chevalier Dupin, and another from real life, Dr. Joseph
Bell, professor of medicine at the University of Edinburgh. Dupin and
Holmes certainly have an extremely striking family resemblance, and
much has been written on the subject. They are both self-proclaimed
rationalists. Both have a habit of beginning to tackle their problems
with a period of often abstract preliminary reflection, and their
subtle methods of analysis lead to results which astonish their
listeners. Both enjoy giving displays of virtuosity disconnected with
the affair on hand. And we find in them both, though in Holmes more
than in Dupin, that casual dilettantism which coloured a whole current
of sensibility at the end of the last century in England. Was the
resemblance deliberate on Conan Doyle's part? Probably it was, because before he had even chosen his detective's final name (he was
still 'Sherrinford Holmes') he had already referred to him as Dupin's
successor: 'Lecoq was a bungler. Dupin was better. Dupin was
decidedly smart. His trick of following a train of thought was more
sensational than clever, but still . . .'[1]

Conan Doyle explained Poe's influence on his imagination by his
vivid memories of reading him in childhood. But if there is no need to
say more about a writer so well-known as Poe, what do we know
about Dr. Joseph Bell, Conan Doyle's Edinburgh acquaintance?

When Conan Doyle began to study medicine, Bell was already a
well-known character in Edinburgh medical circles. He was born
there in 1837 and his whole professional life had been spent in the
town, starting as a mere hospital attendant and ending as head of the
medical school and professor in surgery. He was also editor of the
Edinburgh Medical Journal and had a considerable reputation among
the students. He certainly made a deep impression on the young

[1] Draft of a monologue by Holmes for *A Study in Scarlet* (C.D.B.A.).

Conan Doyle. When the Sherlock Holmes myth took shape there were plenty of inquisitive people wanting to know if he had taken his model from life. He mentioned the name of the Scottish doctor, who was surprised and flattered to find himself the object of such unexpected publicity, but politely denied having had anything to do with the creation of Sherlock Holmes:

> Dr. Conan Doyle's education as a student of medicine taught him to observe, and his practise, both as a general practitioner and a specialist, has been a splendid training for a man such as he is, gifted with eyes, memory and imagination . . . If in addition the doctor is also a born story-teller, then it is a mere matter of choice whether he writes detective stories or keeps his strength for a great historical romance as in *The White Company.*[1]

However we know that Sherlock Holmes led to a rapprochement between Bell and Conan Doyle, also that Bell was interested in criminology and sent the novelist suggestions for plots. What were these suggestions? Conan Doyle tells us that they were not much use to him: 'Bell took a keen interest in these detective tales and even made suggestions which were not, I am bound to say, very practical. I kept in touch with him for many years and he used to come upon my platform to support me when I contested Edinburgh in 1901.'[2]

Since Bell and Conan Doyle had been on friendly terms for a great many years, it is a pity that Sir Arthur has not left us a detailed portrait of the Scottish surgeon. But we only find one well-known anecdote in his autobiography:

> In one of his best cases he said to a civilian patient: 'Well, my man, you've served in the army.' 'Aye, Sir.' 'Not long discharged?' 'No, Sir.' 'A Highland regiment?' 'Aye, Sir.' 'A non-com officer?' 'Aye, Sir.' 'Stationed at Barbados?' 'Aye, Sir.' 'You see, gentlemen,' he would explain, 'the man was a respectful man but did not remove his hat. They do not in the army, but he would have learned civilian ways had he been long discharged. He has an air of authority and he is obviously Scottish. As to Barbados, his complaint is Elephantiasis, which is West Indian, and not British.' To his audience of Watsons it all seemed very miraculous until it was explained, and then it became simple enough.[3]

This sketch of Joseph Bell takes us straight back to Sherlock

[1] J. Bell, *Mr. Sherlock Holmes*, Introduction to the 'Author's Edition', 1903, pp. xi and xii.
[2] AUT., p. 34.   [3] *Ibid.*, p. 33.

Holmes. It is too like Holmes to be true. Conan Doyle never describes Bell in a way that allows us to distinguish him from his fictitious character; it is as if Bell only existed for him as the function of a literary illusion. Nor is it possible to ignore the fact that there is only one passage in all the Holmes stories in which the detective is described as behaving like a surgeon in front of an audience of students: 'Holmes was turning the pipe about in his hand and staring at it in his peculiar pensive way. He held it up and tapped on it with his long, thin forefinger as a professor might who was lecturing on a bone.'[1]

Are we not then justified in suspecting that Conan Doyle's portrait of Bell was not entirely accurate? Or rather, can this portrait perhaps have been an artifice designed to strengthen the illusion that Holmes really existed, as a member of the Holmes-Watson partnership in the stories? How are we to discover whether Conan Doyle was aware of his own quasi-professional distortion of the old professor's portrait? It is certainly not impossible that Bell had some part in the birth of the Holmes cycle. Sir Arthur's anecdote about the surgeon bears the stamp of truth, and is a good example of what Sherlock liked to call his 'method'. But it tells us less about Dr. Bell's particular mental gifts than about his ingenuity in showing them off to the best advantage, just as Sherlock Holmes liked to do. Even admitting that his memories of Bell were crystallized in the character of the detective, this idea of a formal dialogue controlled by the questioner was not original. It is found in early scientific writing, and Poe's Chevalier Dupin also amuses himself by reading the secret thoughts of the person he is talking to.

The inductive method, too, works on the same principle: observations lead to reconstructing the events connected with them. This method is used by such widely different writers as Defoe, Beaumarchais, Voltaire, Fenimore Cooper, to mention just a few. In his autobiography Conan Doyle tells us how he tried to imagine Bell as a detective: 'If he were a detective he would surely reduce this fascinating but unorganised business to something nearer to an exact science. I would try if I could get this effect.'[2]

Thus scientific prestige on the one hand and poetic realism on the other made it essential that a model for Sherlock Holmes should be found *a posteriori*, and that that model should be a man of science.

---

[1] *The Yellow Face*, HOL. II, p. 335.   [2] AUT., p. 89.

We have very little idea what sort of man Joseph Bell really was, for Sherlock Holmes has blurred his outlines. While still a student, and before he had met Bell, the young Conan Doyle had probably begun inventing a rather vague imaginary character; then, when once he had fallen under the spell of his professor's personality, he found it intervening and filling out the details of his fictitious creation. To this extent perhaps it is true to say that Holmes reflects something of Dr. Bell's character.

The suggestion that Holmes was connected with another of Conan Doyle's acquaintances was first put forward by Klinefelter and taken up later by Pearson.[1] According to Klinefelter some of Holmes's habits were inspired by recollections of Dr. Budd, Conan Doyle's eccentric partner at Portsmouth. But since we only know Budd through Conan Doyle's book, and Klinefelter was unable to pursue his enquiry further, we are up against the same difficulty here as with Dr. Bell. Conan Doyle never even wrote of Budd under his real name, sometimes calling him Crabbe and sometimes Cullingworth. So that it is impossible to credit him with greater objective reality than any other character in his works. Such are the difficulties we meet when trying to find the 'original' Sherlock Holmes.

All the same, if he had not been linked with the collective consciousness and the sensibility of his readers, if he had not been in harmony with the ideological climate of the day, Sherlock Holmes would never have become an integral part of civilisation, as he is today. In so far as that climate impregnated Conan Doyle's ego, Sherlock represents that ego. And how could we identify ourselves with the hero if he did not emerge from the stories with sufficient consistency and a convincing enough individuality? Before making an inventory of the psychological contents of his character, we must first approach it from the periphery: contents is the appropriate word, because Sherlock Holmes was at first a mere outline, a type, a shape, an abstraction, before ever he developed a more complex interior and really began to exist. It seems as though Conan Doyle had always had two quite distinct images of Holmes in mind. Technically speaking, he is the 'detective'—that is part of the mechanism of the plot. Before being placed in 'a situation' he has to 'function'; but no aesthetic value necessarily attaches to this functional aspect. Hamlet would

---

[1] W. Klinefelter, *Ex-Libris A. Conan Doyle*, 1938, p. 26, and H. Pearson, *Conan Doyle*, 1943, *passim*.

not have been Hamlet if he were simply an avenger. It is probably because they have been unable to go further than Conan Doyle in giving their characters inner life, that subsequent detective-writers have so rarely succeeded in creating an original or convincing detective who is not a copy of Holmes. But Sherlock Holmes has another aspect, at first sight somewhat disconcerting and at odds with his essential function, but clearly important to his creator for it is already apparent in 'Sherrinford Holmes', the first sketch for Sherlock: 'a sleepy-eyed young man—philosopher—collector of rare violins. An Amati . . .'[1]

This psychological dualism is not found in Poe's Dupin; it harks back to a *fin de siècle* dandyism, first connected with a detective by Stevenson in *The Dynamiter*, a work written shortly before the appearance of Conan Doyle's hero:

> 'Do you then propose, dear boy, that we should turn detective?' enquired Challoner.
> 'Do you propose it? No, Sir,' cried Somerset. 'It is reason, destiny, the plain face of the world, that commands and imposes it. Here, all our merits tell; our manners, habits of the world, powers of conversation, vast stores of unconnected knowledge, all that we are and have builds up a character of a complete detective. It is, in short, the only profession for a gentleman.'

With perspicacious humour, Stevenson here clearly suggests a relationship between the detective as a social type and a middle-class ideology concerned with dignity, security and liberalism.

But in all the portraits of Holmes in the Adventures, this dualism is manifest—these two basic systems are always in opposition. Quite early on in the stories, we come across frequent comparisons of the detective to a fox-hound: 'I was irresistibly reminded of a pure-blooded, well-trained foxhound as it dashes backwards and forwards through the covert, whining in its eagerness, until it comes across the lost scent.'[2]

Why a fox-hound? Because it calls up an image of exactly that controlled alertness which should be second nature to a detective in Holmes's own view, and also the most traditional of English sports—for we must not forget that Holmes is a gentleman. The metaphor emphasises the functional side of his character, and, by its allusion

---

[1] Draft for *A Study in Scarlet* (C.D.B.A.).
[2] *A Study in Scarlet*, HOL. I, p. 29.

to hunting, that he belongs to the upper class. The fox-hound image seems so to have obsessed the narrator, that if he, or rather Watson, is to be believed, Holmes becomes almost literally metamorphosed, when he is in his own element, or his own field of action:

> Sherlock Holmes was transformed when he was hot upon such a scent as this. Men who had only known the quiet thinker and logician of Baker Street would have failed to recognize him. His face flushed and darkened. His brows were drawn into two hard, black lines, while his eyes shone out from beneath them with a steely glitter. His face was bent downwards, his shoulders bowed, his lips compressed, and the veins stood out like whip-cord in his long, sinewy neck. His nostrils seemed to dilate with a purely animal lust for the chase, and his mind was so absolutely concentrated upon the matter before him, that a question or remark fell unheeded upon his ears, or at the most only provoked a quick, impatient snarl in reply.[1]

Here we see a man transformed with all speed into a fox-hound before our very eyes, until he seems almost to have lost the power of speech and be reduced to expressing himself by sounds. But the fox-hound motif recurs insistently: 'Holmes hunted about among the grass and leaves like a retriever after a wounded bird.'[2] 'See the fox-hound with hanging ears and drooping tail as it lolls about the kennels and compare it with the same hound as, with gleaming eyes and straining muscles, it runs upon a breast-high scent!—such was the change in Holmes since the morning.'[3] 'In an instant he was tense and alert, his eyes shining, his face set, his limbs quivering with eager activity. He was out on the lawn, in through the window, round the room, and up into the bedroom, for all the world, like a dashing fox-hound drawing a cover. . . . Then he rushed down the stair, out through the open window, threw himself upon his face on the lawn, sprang up and ran into the room once more, all with the energy of the hunter who is at the very heels of his quarry.'[4]

In contrast to this imaginary and almost stereotyped vision of Holmes in action, or as a countryman, we have Holmes the Londoner. Here is a personality as entirely different as is Doctor Jekyll from Mr. Hyde—an absent-minded, taciturn, disturbing morphia-addict who is also a rather Bohemian, fastidious, sceptical music-lover. It is not so much a contrast between two aspects of the same person as

---

[1] *The Boscombe Valley Mystery*, HOL. II, p. 92.
[2] *The Dancing Men*, HOL. II, p. 628.
[3] *The Bruce-Partington Plans*, HOL. II, p. 980.
[4] *The Devil's Foot*, HOL. II, p. 45.

one between two ways of life and modes of consciousness, the first sensitive and impressionable, the second intellectual. And this very coexistence of two antithetical sides to Sherlock Holmes's character is essential to his status as a hero:

> My friend was an enthusiastic musician, being himself not only a very capable performer, but a composer of no ordinary merit. All the afternoon he sat in the stalls wrapped in the most perfect happiness, gently waving his long thin fingers in time to the music, while his gently smiling face and his languid, dreamy eyes were as unlike those of Holmes the sleuth-hound, Holmes the relentless, keen-witted, ready-handed criminal agent, as it was possible to conceive. In his singular character the dual nature alternately asserted itself, and his extreme exactness and astuteness represented, as I have often thought, the reaction against the poetic and contemplative mood which occasionally predominated in him.[1]

The picture of Holmes in his room in Baker Street, lying propped among a heap of cushions, with clouds of tobacco smoke rising through the dimness, evokes the characteristic pose of the 'decadents'. Cushions, tobacco—Holmes needs a special sort of environment and special stimulants in order to think; and he is a creative as well as an analytic thinker, as we shall have occasion to show. His addiction to morphine and cocaine (disapproved of by Watson) and to tobacco (which he tolerated) are the only links connecting him with the romantic idea of the artist, the decadent poet. It is easy for Watson, as a doctor, to trace the effects of narcotics in his friend's gaze—a gaze which clearly expresses Holmes's two modes of mental functioning, the extrovert and sensory, and the purely speculative. When he is under the influence of narcotics, Watson finds him even more mysterious than usual. As soon as he sees that dreamy look in Holmes's eyes, suspicions are aroused that were first hinted at in *A Study in Scarlet*:

> For days on end he would lie upon the sofa in the sitting-room, hardly uttering a word or moving a muscle from morning to night. On these occasions I have noticed such a dreamy, vacant expression in his eyes, that I might have suspected him of being addicted to the use of some narcotic, had not the temperance and cleanliness of his whole life forbidden such a notion.[2]

Holmes's gaze, so faithfully rendered by Sidney Paget, soon becomes one of his most striking characteristics, indispensable to our

---

[1] *The Red-Headed League*, HOL. II, p. 45.   [2] HOL. I, p. 10.

image of his personality: 'Holmes sat in his big arm-chair, with the weary, heavy-lidded expression which veiled his keen and eager nature.'[1]

As for the objects with which he surrounds himself in his Baker Street rooms, they tell us as much about him as clues do about a criminal, emphasising his interest in science and crime, and suggesting the intimate and endearing side of Watson's hero in terms that are sometimes not far from caricature:

> The rough-and-tumble work in Afghanistan, coming on top of a natural Bohemianism of disposition, has made me rather more lax than befits a medical man. But with me there is a limit, and when I find a man who keeps his cigars in the coal-scuttle, his tobacco in the toe-end of a Persian slipper, and his unanswered correspondence transfixed by a jack-knife into the very centre of his wooden mantelpiece, then I begin to give myself virtuous airs.[2]

Of all the objects associated with Holmes, the most familiar is of course his pipe. Is that because he prefers it to a cigar? No: it seems to mean more to him than a mere means of absorbing tobacco. It is, above all, the companion of his long, studious nights. The difficulties of some investigation on which Holmes has begged Watson to accompany him, have overcome the doctor's powers of resistance and he has fallen asleep in his chair:

> So he sat as I dropped off to sleep, and so he sat when a sudden ejaculation caused me to wake up, and I found the summer sun shining into the apartment. The pipe was still between his lips, the smoke still curled upwards, and the room was full of a dense tobacco haze, but nothing remained of the heap of shag which I had seen upon the previous night.[3]

The pipe is a necessary adjunct to his spells of thought, measuring their duration by the time taken to smoke a pipeful of tobacco.

> 'What are you going to do then?' I asked.
> 'To smoke,' he answered. 'It is quite a three-pipe problem, and I beg that you won't speak to me for fifty minutes.'[4]

Thus Holmes's simple outline developed a certain number of clear and unforgettable features, impressing our minds as vigorously as the

---

[1] *The Engineer's Thumb*, HOL. II, p. 205.
[2] *The Musgrave Ritual*, HOL. II, p. 396.
[3] *The Man with the Twisted Lip*, HOL. II, p. 142.
[4] *The Red-Headed League*, HOL. II, p. 43.

drawings of *Punch* which flowed from Dicky Doyle's pen. Holmes is right when he says, 'art in the blood is liable to take the strangest forms'.[1]

However, neither of these two aspects of this outline are so much heroic, in the true sense of the word, as picturesque and remarkable. Holmes's vocation as a fictional character, willed and designed by his creator, destines him to follow a certain career and play a certain part, even though the stages and episodes in it are only potential. He must therefore possess a certain number of attributes, and his figure must be set against an aesthetic or ethical background which brings out its essentially heroic quality, independent of the heroism of the adventures themselves.

One of these is his herculean strength, whether of muscle or endurance. We see Holmes being engaged as a stable-boy in order to get information about Irene Adler, and verifying a hypothesis with a harpoon. We see him twisting a poker in his powerful hands, and intimidating enormous men; and in *The Sign of Four* a professional boxer greets him as a colleague and regrets that he never became a pugilist. He is probably not addicted to any one sport (how could he possibly find time?) nor to any form of physical training; yet the drain upon his energies involved in the investigations in *The Hound of the Baskervilles* and *The Final Problem* is never too much for his strength. The opening of *The Reigate Squires* gives Watson the chance to talk of his friend's 'iron constitution', which 'however had broken down under the strain of an investigation which had extended over two months, during which period he had never worked less than fifteen hours a day, and had more than once, as he assured me, kept to his task for five days at a stretch'.[2]

Holmes's physical energy is backed up by his quite exceptional acuteness of the senses. His sensitive ear, which partly explains his love of music, enables him always to be the first to detect the approach of some criminal for whom he and Watson are lying in wait. In *A Scandal in Bohemia* he recognises the disguised voice of Irene Adler wishing him a rapid and ironical good-night, even though it is only slightly familiar to him. But his piercing sight is his most precious possession. From tobacco-ash to mud-stains, there is nothing he cannot identify, read and decipher with speed.

[1] *The Greek Interpreter*, HOL. II, p. 478.
[2] *The Reigate Squires*, HOL. II, p. 417.

His deductions from objects in the Adventures are not always vital to the investigation. But their very superfluity only emphasises how superior Holmes is to the task he is carrying out and the society he has chosen to serve, and reveal his natural brilliance as a detective to every observer. They also contribute to the popularity of the Adventures, by turning them into a sort of parlour game. This aspect of the Holmes stories is not incompatible with their epic quality. Heroes start a fashion: Holmes has as many eager imitators as Robinson Crusoe. Even in the text itself Sherlock is imitated by his brother Mycroft or by Dr. Watson, with varying degrees of success. Holmes invariably exercises his powers of deduction on commonplace objects. A hat in *The Blue Carbuncle* leads him to hazard a good many opinions about the health, age, habits and character of its owner, as well as his financial and family situation. In *The Yellow Face* he 'reads' a pipe and in *The Golden Pince-nez* a pair of pince-nez, by means of which he is able to give an accurate description of an unknown man and woman—what modern detectives call an identikit. *The Hound of the Baskervilles* begins with his 'reading' Dr. Mortimer's walking-stick, and this leads on to a playful dialogue of five pages in the course of which Holmes and Watson analyse the object according to the rules of the 'method'.

More often than not, it is the Doctor who gives his friend opportunities to display his deductive skill. In *The Sign of Four*, Watson's watch is the point of departure for a description of his deceased brother. In *The Stockbroker's Clerk* the detective takes a look at his friend's slippers. He notices that although they are new the soles have been slightly scorched. Did Watson perhaps get them wet and then put them in front of the fire? No, because in that case the label near the instep would have come unstuck from the damp. Watson must therefore have been sitting close to the fire, and since it is midsummer, it is obvious that he has had a cold. At the beginning of *The Crooked Man*, Holmes deduces, from Watson's boots, that his patients are keeping him very busy and, also from his boots, in *The Disappearance of Lady Frances Carfax* that he has been to a Turkish bath. 'Reading' objects and clothes is often merely a branch of 'reading' their owners. The numerous instances to be found in *A Study in Scarlet* follow much the same plan as the anecdote about Joseph Bell quoted above. Holmes's first words to Watson after they are introduced come straight from the scene when Bell deduced that his patient was a veteran from Barbados: 'You have been in Afghanistan, I perceive.' An incident a little further on, where he identifies a commissionaire as an ex-sergeant of Marines, is a variation on the same theme. With *A Case of Identity* we gradually move on a little, and it is the profession of his client, Miss Mary Sutherland, that the detective spots at first sight. But Sherlock Holmes's most spectacular deduction makes the person concerned faint, because it brings back the memory of his troubled and threatening past.[1]

Like the Chevalier Dupin, Holmes practises reading other people's thoughts, and here again Watson is very useful to him: ' "So, Watson," said he suddenly, "you do not propose to invest in South African securities?" '[2] Afterwards he reveals his train of reasoning in six sentences. In another passage he guesses that Watson is speculating about the consequences of the American Civil War.[3]

His deductions lead Holmes to make revelations which appear almost magical. And his fondness for doing chemical experiments adds to the air of mystery surrounding him. Watson tries to explain Holmes's two-sided nature in rational and intelligible terms: ' . . . his extreme exactness and astuteness represented, as I have often thought, the reaction against the poetic and contemplative mood which occasionally predominated in him'.[4] But he soon gives up this theory and declares that his friend is superhuman, 'a man whose knowledge was not that of other mortals'.[5]

It is clear that Watson is not thinking of the range of his knowledge so much as of his means of acquiring it. After all, the detective has confided his ambitions to him. Holmes's desire for power takes the form of a desire for knowledge. Like Le Sage's Asmodée he conjures up a view of the great city which is the field of operations assigned to him:

> If we could fly out of that window hand in hand, hover over this great city, gently remove the roofs, and peep in at the queer things which are going on, the strange coincidences, the plannings, the cross-purposes, the wonderful chains of events, working through generations, and leading to the most *outré* results, it would make all fiction with its conventionalities and foreseen conclusions most stale and unprofitable.[6]

[1] *The 'Gloria Scott'*, HOL. II, p. 374.
[2] *The Dancing Men*, HOL. II, p. 610.
[3] *The Cardboard Box*, HOL. II, p. 924.
[4] *The Red-Headed League*, HOL. II, p. 45.
[5] *Ibid.*, HOL. II, p. 46.   [6] *A Case of Identity*, HOL. II, p. 55.

Although this dream is impossible to realise, Holmes has never-theless travelled widely in the course of his career, not only in Europe but also in Asia, especially Tibet. This touch of the exotic in him, together with what might be called his Byronic side, helps convince us of his world-wide reputation and intimate knowledge of interna-tional criminal circles—an important point, because the first of the Holmes stories refers to similar cases with which Holmes was familiar when Watson got to know him: 'There was the case of Von Bischoff at Frankfort last year. He would certainly have been hung had this test been in existence. There was Mason of Bradford, and the notorious Muller, and Lefevre of Montpellier, and Samson of New Orleans. I could name a score of cases in which it would have been decisive.'[1] And again: 'I have notes of several similar cases . . . There was a parallel instance in Aberdeen some years back, and something on very much the same lines at Munich the year after the Franco-Prussian War.'[2]

His travels, his reading, his tastes have all helped him acquire those 'vast stores of unconnected knowledge' described by Steven-son's character Somerset as being indispensable to 'a complete detective'. A brilliant talker when opportunity offers, he dazzles Dr. Watson just as much by his erudition as by his descriptions of travels in far countries:

> Our meal was a merry one. Holmes could talk exceedingly well when he chose, and that night he did choose. He appeared to be in a state of nervous exaltation. I have never known him so brilliant. He spoke on a quick succession of subjects—on miracle plays, on mediaeval pottery, on Stradivarius violins, on the Buddhism of Ceylon, and on the warships of the future—handling each as though he had made a special study of it.[3]

Thus, while giving expression to the two chief trends of his creator's mind—his need for action and his need to dream—Sherlock Holmes developed a personality which roused a thrill of response in the latent romanticism of the reading public.

[1] *A Study in Scarlet*, HOL. II, p. 11.
[2] *The Noble Bachelor*, HOL. II, p. 237.
[3] *The Sign of Four*, HOL. I, p. 199.

Chapter 13

SHERLOCK HOLMES: THE ORIGIN AND STRUCTURE OF THE CYCLE

The Adventures of Sherlock Holmes are separated sharply from the rest of Sir Arthur Conan Doyle's very varied output by the great social and literary success his detective achieved. The distinction has gradually been accepted both by public and publishers, and today no one would be likely to confuse an extract from one of the Holmes stories with a passage from any of the other books. Yet it is a distinction that has resulted from circumstances. Conan Doyle must have been unconscious of it when he was writing the first of the Sherlock Holmes stories, *A Study in Scarlet*, nor could he for a moment have imagined that fifty-nine other stories were to follow. So that what today seems to us a cycle or a saga, was not deliberately planned. When later on he spoke of the first of his Sherlock Holmes stories, Conan Doyle made no attempt to attribute revolutionary significance to it *a posteriori*. *A Study in Scarlet* was just another new book: 'I felt now that I was capable of something fresher and crisper and more workmanlike,' he tells us in his autobiography.[1]

In what circumstances did Conan Doyle begin to write? Without the slightest pretension to being an artist, for one thing; if anything he under-estimated the intrinsic value of his first efforts: ' They served their purpose in relieving me a little of that financial burden which always pressed upon me.'[2]

These anonymous published stories, which brought their author about £4 each, could have been taken for the work of Bret Harte. Conan Doyle half-seriously suggested the likeness himself, and soon afterwards found himself in the same predicament as the American short story writer, who 'was always like one of his own goldminers, who struck a rich pocket but found no continuous reef'.[3]

The story called *Crabbe's Practice* is partly drawn from his own

---

[1] AUT., p. 89.   [2] *Ibid.*, p. 87.
[3] *Through the Magic Door*, p. 116.

life, and concerns a young, eccentric and unscrupulous doctor, the first literary incarnation of Dr. Budd, who was to reappear as Cullingworth in *The Stark Munro Letters* and also in Sir Arthur's autobiography. After this, his literary reputation began to bear fruit: in 1884 *The Cornhill Magazine* published *Habakuk Jephson's Statement*. It was still an anonymous reputation however, and some readers and critics took the story to be by Stevenson. Taking his inspiration from the discovery of the mysterious *Marie-Celeste*, he made use of the same methods of fictitious realism that had been used by Stevenson and Poe—particularly by the latter in *The Balloon Hoax*. Conan Doyle's story had the same fate as Poe's. Several readers, particularly James Payn, wanted to know if it was true. Thus, before Sherlock Holmes had ever been thought of, Conan Doyle had already given proofs of his power to make imagined things seem real. *A Literary Mosaic*, published in 1886, seems to show a different orientation. It is a pastiche, taking for its pretext a conversation between Defoe, Smollett, Scott and other English novelists in a sort of writers' paradise. But there is no trace of detection in these first works. When asked how the idea for *A Study in Scarlet* came into his head, Conan Doyle told journalists in December, 1900:

> At the time I first thought of a detective—it was about 1886—I had been reading some detective stories, and it struck me what nonsense they were, to put it mildly, because, for getting the solution of the mystery, the authors always depended on some coincidence. This struck me as not a fair way of playing the game, because the detective ought really to depend for his successes on something in his own mind and not on merely adventitious circumstances which do not, by any means, always occur in real life.[1]

What are we to understand from this statement? That, like a portrait-painter, Conan Doyle first 'saw' and posed his hero, and afterwards designed the plot and decor. Other detective-stories of the period certainly seem to be the result of diametrically opposite processes, and put much more emphasis on the intricacies of the plot than on the detective's personality. But what books was Conan Doyle referring to? His notebooks from 1885 and 1886 tell us what he was reading, and among the novels almost the only detective stories were by Gaboriau, whose work impressed him favourably. On the very page where Gaboriau's name figures, he wrote some

[1] *The Westminster Gazette*, 13 December 1900, and *Tit-Bits*, 15 December 1900.

interesting notes about the genesis of Dr. Watson's character. As
we know from *A Study in Scarlet* he had been an army doctor during
the second Afghanistan campaign and wounded by the Gylzies or
Ghazis, from whom he narrowly escaped at the battle of Maiwand.
Southsea Notebook No. 1 reads:

> Afghan campaign of 1840 undertaken to put Shah Soojah upon the
> throne. Successful at first and under Sir John Keane and Elphinstone,
> with McNachten and Burns, we occupied Kaubul. Then came the great
> rising of the Gilzyes and the Barukzirs and the Douranees. Murder of
> Burns and McNachten. Retreat from the Kaubul cantonments and
> massacre in the mountain passes. Dr. Bryden alone escaping to
> Jellabad. Then came the turn of the tide when Nott, Pollock and Sale
> took Kaubul once more.[1]

Except for Gaboriau, the notebooks make no reference whatever
to any detective-stories read by Conan Doyle at this time or earlier.
Although we know what books were probably in his library, from
the list he made of works on criminology and detective fiction before
selling them in 1930, and also from the books still remaining in the
biographical archives, it is impossible to be sure what works he was
referring to in his statement to the journalists in 1900. Nor does his
autobiography make the matter clearer. Had he read the very feeble
stories published under the name of 'Nick Carter' first in the United
States, afterwards in England, from 1884 onwards? It is extremely
unlikely. Since they went on appearing until the beginning of the
present century, Conan Doyle would hardly have spoken of them in
1900 as books that had fallen into neglect. Later on, after the publication of *A Study in Scarlet*, Conan Doyle must have read *The
Mystery of a Hansom Cab* by Fergus Hume. In fact he wrote of it in a
letter to his mother as 'one of the weakest tales I have read, and simply
sold by puffing'. So that Conan Doyle's statement does not seem to
give us the true explanation of the origins of the Sherlock Holmes
cycle. *A Study in Scarlet* has not got the quality and significance of a
protest against the poverty of contemporary detective fiction. It does
not show any completely new orientation of the writer's mind, nor
does it pretend to disown the literary influences with which it is
visibly impregnated. It was a question of climbing a little higher or a
little further along an as yet inadequately blazed trail.

As with Gaboriau's novels, we find *A Study in Scarlet* divided into

[1] Unpublished (C.D.B.A.).

two symmetrical parts, each subdivided into the same number of chapters. The two introductory chapters of the first part correspond to the two concluding chapters of the second. Only the first part follows the plan of the later Sherlock Holmes stories. It is here that the Baker Street saga begins, with the memorable meeting between the detective and Dr. Watson, the story of their setting up house together and their first conversations. As the scope of the Adventures widens, these pages gain in significance. But this effort of perspective could not of course have been apparent to the first readers of *A Study in Scarlet* in 1887. The detective element appears in the third chapter and ends with the arrest of Jefferson Hope, an American on his way through London. The first part serves simply as a prelude to the long adventure story contained in the second. Later on, in the short stories of the Sherlock Holmes cycle, such a narrative as this would have been subordinated to detection. But we cannot merely take this long second part as the explanation or justification of Jefferson Hope's behaviour; its apparent digressiveness comes from the fact that Watson and Holmes leave the stage and the story is taken over by an anonymous narrator. The reader finds himself suddenly jolted out of time and place and landed in America, about forty years before the events described in the first part. Along with two travellers wandering in the Far West, John and Lucy Ferrier (still a little girl), we meet Brigham Young's Mormons from Illinois; the Ferriers join the Mormons. A few years later they are living near the Great Salt Lake, and John's prosperity and Lucy's beauty excite the covetousness of their neighbours. Two suitors dispute for Lucy's hand, but she rejects them both out of love for Jefferson Hope, a young farmer from Nevada. Ferrier and Lucy are forced to escape in secret from the persecution and threats of the Mormon colony. With Hope's help the fugitives get past the sentinels, but they are caught soon afterwards, when Ferrier is murdered and Lucy is forced to marry Drebber, one of her suitors, and dies soon afterwards. Hope manages to escape from his pitiless pursuers, and devotes his life to avenging his betrothed. The epilogue of *A Study in Scarlet* takes us back to Baker Street, with Hope explaining how he followed Drebber and Lucy's other suitor to London, and made them both expiate the deaths of Lucy and John Ferrier.

Holmes now describes the stages of his investigation and the deductive processes which led him to the solution. The second part of

A Study in Scarlet thus takes the story into the realm of history, but there is no justification for thinking that Conan Doyle attached less importance to it than to the first. We only feel this because Holmes and Watson were to reappear in innumerable subsequent adventures and because three years later Conan Doyle makes Sherlock Holmes refer in *The Sign of Four* to his first investigation: 'you have yourself had some experience of my methods of work in the Jefferson Hope case'. But in 1887 it was probably the American episode that held the reader's interest. It is even quite uncertain whether Conan Doyle ever intended to give Sherlock Holmes any sequel at all. *A Study in Scarlet* still shows the influence of Bret Harte, and its historical treatment and the serious or even solemn tone of certain passages show that he was thinking in terms of the historical novel. In 1889, just before *The Sign of Four*, Conan Doyle had published *Micah Clarke*, an historical novel concerning the fate of a group of English Puritans, who lived like the Mormons of America on the fringes of ordinary society. It is true that in 1888 Conan Doyle also wrote an adaptation of *A Study in Scarlet* for the stage, but this only confirms the impression that Sherlock Holmes had not yet really taken up his dominant position in Conan Doyle's work. This unpublished adaptation was called *Angels of Darkness* and, although Dr. Watson appears in it, Holmes has simply been jettisoned; it merely reproduces some of the scenes of the second part of the book in dialogue form. The title and the episode to which it alludes suggests the source whence *A Study in Scarlet* had come. Conan Doyle had always expressed his admiration for Stevenson, and about 1882 he became a devotee of *The New Arabian Nights* and thought *The Pavilion on the Links*: ' . . . the very model of dramatic narrative. That story stamped itself so clearly on my brain when I read it in *Cornhill* that when I came across it again many years afterwards in volume form, I was able instantly to recognize two small modifications of the text—each very much for the worse—from the original form.'[1]

In 1885 Stevenson published *The Dynamiter*, and the Mormon episode called 'The Story of the Destroying Angel' in this book provides the source not of the whole Holmesian saga, of course, but of the plot of *A Study in Scarlet*. Conan Doyle took from it the Mormons as a subject, the atmosphere of some of the incidents, and perhaps the heroine's name.

[1] *Through the Magic Door*, p. 117.

Where essentials were concerned, however, particularly the basic ingredients of the plot, Jefferson Hope's character and the rapid, muscular development of the action, Conan Doyle's quality as a writer is revealed with a distinction not to be seen in his earlier stories: so that *A Study in Scarlet* turned Conan Doyle's mind in the direction of the historical novel and also of a new exploitation of detective themes, although Holmes himself occupied such a modest position in his creator's esteem. He found some difficulty in placing the manuscript of this story which was to play such an important if indirect part in his career as a writer; it spent six months shuttling to and fro between different publishers. Professor Bettany, one of the directors of Ward, Lock & Co., was sufficiently interested to get his wife to read it. Mrs. Bettany was enchanted by the book and pressed her husband to give the public the benefit of this new novelist's talent, somehow guessing instinctively that he was a doctor. Ward, Lock & Co. offered £25, and Conan Doyle accepted for the sake of peace and quiet. A final insult: the story was only published a year later, at the end of 1887, in *Beeton's Christmas Annual* together with 'two original drawing-room plays'. It was twice reprinted, in 1888 and 1889, showing that it had not passed unnoticed, although *The Sign of Four* and *Scandal in Bohemia* (the first of the Adventures of Sherlock Holmes) had not yet appeared.

However Conan Doyle made up his mind to try his luck in a literary form that attracted him more. The manuscript of *Micah Clarke* also suffered some reverses before being published in 1889. This novel had a greater success than *A Study in Scarlet*, and was reprinted three times that same year and nine times between 1890 and 1893. During this period, the absence of copyright laws in the United States made it possible to publish pirated editions of work by foreign authors there. *A Study in Scarlet* was one of these and met with an enormous success. The American public appreciated it not only as good 'magazine' fiction, reminiscent of Poe, but also for its romantic presentation of the past and of certain current problems. Lippincotts, a firm of Philadelphia publishers who published a rival magazine to *The Atlantic Monthly* in which English writers were well-represented, became interested in Conan Doyle, and in 1889 one of their agents invited him to dinner in London. This was the occasion of his famous meeting with Oscar Wilde. Both writers agreed to write something for *Lippincott's Magazine*. *The Sign of Four* appeared in February and

The Picture of Dorian Gray in July. 'Eighteen-ninety was a good year for Lippincotts,' remarks Charles Carrington in *Rudyard Kipling, his Life and Work*: 'it began with Conan Doyle's *Sign of Four*, went on with Oscar Wilde's *Dorian Gray*, and finished with the number containing *The Light that Failed*, which was five times reprinted in January 1891.'

Sherlock Holmes appears on the scene in the very first lines of *The Sign of Four*, giving it a more distinctive, lively opening than that of *A Study in Scarlet*. Dr. Watson pretends to let the reader into the secret of his first meeting with the detective, which is in itself a serial-writer's device. This retrospective account is short, and the plot unrolls as we follow the detective to the solution of the problem, our participation sharpening the dramatic tension. The four men referred to in the title are doing time for murder in a military prison on the Andaman Islands in the Indian Ocean. Before they were arrested they just had time to conceal the treasure they had stolen from Agra in a safe hiding-place. One of them, Jonathan Small, had succeeded in bribing two of the officers in charge of the prison, Captain Morstan and Major Sholto, to help them escape in return for a share of the booty. However, on the pretext of verifying Small's directions, Sholto removes the treasure from its hiding-place and goes back to England. A few years later Morstan mysteriously disappears at the very moment of arriving in London on leave. Later still, the dying Sholto tells his two sons, Bartholomew and Thaddeus, about the existence of the treasure, Morstan's death and the rights of his daughter to a share of it. But he dies before he has had time to say where the treasure is hidden or admit to his own greedy and cowardly behaviour. Finally Bartholomew discovers the treasure in his own house, and it is at this point that the story really begins. Faithful to his father's dying wish, Thaddeus invites Miss Morstan to come and see him, bringing two witnesses, who are of course Holmes and Watson. After explaining the facts to Miss Morstan, Thaddeus Sholto begs her to come with him to see Bartholomew; but when they arrive with Holmes and Watson they find him murdered and the treasure stolen. Holmes deduces that the assassin must have been no larger than a child and as agile as a monkey: there is an echo here of Poe's *Murders in the Rue Morgue*. Holmes and Watson hurry off in pursuit of the murderer, and after many adventures the last act takes place on the river Thames. Jonathan Small is caught and his accomplice, a pygmy Andaman islander, is killed. The disappearance of the treasure into the river is compensated for by Watson's joy at getting Miss Morstan to accept him. The Indian sub-plot, and theme of the treasure with a curse on it bringing disaster in its train, belong to the stock-in-trade of many of Conan Doyle's predecessors, particularly Wilkie Collins and Stevenson. Perhaps the latter again provided the source of some of the plot.

> 'An officer', began Prince Florizel, (in *The Rajah's Diamond*), 'a man of courage and conduct, who had already risen by merit to an eminent rank . . . visited . . . the collection of an Indian Prince. Here he beheld a diamond so extraordinary for size and beauty that from that instant he had only one desire in life: honour, reputation, friendship, the love of country, he was ready to sacrifice all for this lump of sparkling crystal. . . . At a time of great danger for his native land, he betrayed a body of his fellow-soldiers, and suffered them to be defeated and massacred by thousands. In the end he had amassed a magnificent fortune, and brought home with him the coveted diamond.'

Conan Doyle's chief concern is to create an atmosphere of dramatic tension subtly calculated to make the reader thrill with horror or suspense, as even Stevenson could not do without recourse to the supernatural (*Doctor Jekyll and Mr. Hyde*). He leads us to the frontiers of the supernatural but does not cross them. The description of Thaddeus Sholto's unexpectedly sumptuous drawing-room and the uneasiness it provokes, accentuates the forebodings of both fictional characters and reader:

> The richest and glossiest of curtains and tapestries draped the walls, looped back here and there to expose some richly-mounted painting or Oriental vase. The carpet was of amber and black, so soft and so thick that the foot sank pleasantly into it, as into a bed of moss. Two great tiger-skins thrown athwart it increased the suggestion of Eastern luxury, as did a huge hookah which stood upon a mat in the corner. A lamp in the fashion of a silver dove was hung from an almost invisible golden wire in the centre of the room. As it burned it filled the air with a subtle and aromatic odour.[1]

The subjective power of objects, the implication that they are dangerous traps or masks, of which the cinema has made such potent use more recently, stands out from this description with fascinating and forceful suggestiveness, and one would look in vain, even in Poe, for a more spell-binding description, a better demonstration of

[1] HOL. I, p. 143.

the importance of décor, of stage-production rather, in the art of creating uneasiness. The author skilfully avoids setting the action in motion immediately, so as to prolong the reader's suspense and prepare for the humorous relaxation provided by the remarks of Thaddeus Sholto, a caricature of the *fin de siècle* aesthete:

> I am a man of somewhat retiring, and I might even say refined, tastes, and there is nothing more unaesthetic than a policeman. I have a natural shrinking from all forms of rough materialism. I seldom come in contact with the rough crowd. I live, as you see, with some little atmosphere of elegance around me. I may call myself a patron of the arts. It is my weakness. The landscape is a genuine Corot, and, though a connoisseur might perhaps throw a doubt upon that Salvator Rosa, there cannot be the least question about the Bouguereau. I am partial to the modern French school.[1]

Sherlock Holmes's appearance in *The Strand Magazine* was the actual starting-point of the cycle, or at least of the phase leading to its success. From now on the plots were drawn less from the author's memory of books he had read, and the treatment became simpler, as befitted the shortness of the stories. George Newnes, who had handed over the editorship of *The Review of Reviews* to William Stead, decided that his new monthly magazine must have an illustration on every page, thus firmly staking all on a formula which was to have an incalculable effect on literature, directly or indirectly. *The Strand Magazine* was an immediate success. It is difficult today to separate the triumph scored by Holmes from the popularity of the magazine itself, and of the image created by Sidney Paget's illustrations. We should not conclude from this that *The Strand Magazine* contributed to any great extent to Conan Doyle's success. It was Conan Doyle who made the fortune of *The Strand Magazine*. We know that the editors offered him large, afterwards fabulous sums of money. Less concrete perhaps, but just as eloquent, is the evidence of Basil Hastings, the editor-in-chief:

> Alone of all the great and popular authors in that astonishing flowering of letters which marked the beginning of this century, and the beginning of the popular illustrated magazine, Conan Doyle writing Sherlock Holmes, was the only one—Kipling and Wells *not* excepted—whose name on the cover as a contributor was sufficient to justify the publisher in increasing by many thousands the print run for that particular issue. I can think of only one contributor who, if we had the paper, and the

[1] HOL. I, p. 145.

author were willing, could put thousands on the sales of any one issue of a magazine to-day. And that is Winston Churchill.[1]

Of course it is more difficult to analyse the multiple factors contributing to an artistic success than to treat the artist like a tradesman in terms of supply and demand. 'He was greatly admired by the intelligentsia', wrote Somerset Maugham of Conan Doyle, 'they couldn't help enjoying his stories, but felt that it was hardly literature'.[2] Conan Doyle was to some extent the victim of the prejudice against detective fiction, a prejudice he shared himself; and he maintained a somewhat ambiguous modesty about this part of his work. Perhaps he did his reputation a disservice by attracting our attention to the formula he believed he had invented:

> It had struck me that a single character running through the series, if it only engaged the attention of the reader, would bind that reader to that particular magazine. On the other hand, it had long seemed to me that the ordinary serial might be an impediment rather than a help to a magazine, since, sooner or later, one missed one number and afterwards it had lost all interest. Clearly the ideal compromise was a character which carried through, and yet instalments which were each complete in themselves, so that the purchaser was always sure that he could relish the whole contents of the magazine. I believe that I was the first to realize this and the Strand Magazine the first to put it into practice.[3]

Conan Doyle was unaware that this last statement was not exactly true, and that others before him, Dickens in particular, had thought of a similar formula.[4]

Nor do his reflections really explain why Sherlock Holmes continued to flourish in the pages of *The Strand Magazine* until as late as 1927, nor why in two cases, *The Hound of the Baskervilles* and *The Valley of Fear*, published respectively in 1901 and 1914, the formula was abandoned without the slightest ill effect. It had already been exploited before the founding of *The Strand Magazine* in *The Sign of Four*, a story about the same characters who had appeared in *A Study in Scarlet*. The only appreciable result of transferring the Sherlock Holmes stories to the restricted area of a monthly magazine was to reduce them in scale. In its turn, this necessary reduction

---

[1] *John O'London's Weekly*, 4 February 1949.
[2] Letter to Pierre Nordon, 15 March 1960.
[3] AUT., pp. 113–14.
[4] Cf. Original Preface to the *Pickwick Papers*.

simplified the plots and directed Conan Doyle's mind towards less impersonal subjects than those of the two previous stories.

It is difficult to analyse the sources of a writer who is both very imaginative and a great reader. The simplest plot lends itself to innumerable comparisons. For instance that of *The New Catacomb*, published in 1898, could be traced to the influence of three separate authors, as well as to a theme already treated by Conan Doyle and an incident from his own life.

From 1891 on, however, literary reminders are very few; the similarities that can be traced between Conan Doyle and Poe in *The Musgrave Ritual* or *The Dancing Men* are inherent in the cipher theme as Conan Doyle himself pointed out.

> Not only is Poe the originator of the detective story; all treasure-hunting, cryptogram-solving yarns trace back to his *Goldbug*, just as all pseudo-scientific Verne-and-Wells stories have their prototypes in the *Voyage to the Moon*, and the *Case of Monsieur Valdemar*. If every man who receives a cheque for a story which owed its springs to Poe were to pay a tithe to a monument for the master, he would have a pyramid as big as that of Cheops.[1]

We can therefore definitely say that many more of the plots came from life than from books, and the origin of a story will often be found in some incident experienced or observed by the author, some echo of a suggestion or memory of a conversation.

Can the first of the Sherlock Holmes Adventures to appear in *The Strand Magazine* be said to have a plot at all? The beautiful adventuress Irene Adler has in her possession compromising letters from the King of Bohemia (as imaginary a figure as Shakespeare's dukes), who is afraid that the scandal created by their publication will prevent his proposed marriage to a 'Scandinavian' princess. He begs Sherlock Holmes to help him get back the letters, which Irene Adler refuses to return. It is a situation slightly reminiscent of *The Purloined Letter*, but Conan Doyle projects a very different light on it. Not only do the incidents have no relation to those in Poe's story, but the reader's interest is gripped by Irene Adler's character and Sherlock Holmes's deductions: 'To Sherlock Holmes she is always *the* woman. I have seldom heard him mention her under any other name. In his eyes she eclipses and predominates the whole of her sex.'[2]

---

[1] *Through the Magic Door*, p. 115.
[2] HOL. II, p. 3.

Conan Doyle has not made her a commonplace adventuress, influenced by sordid motives. She in fact refuses to sell the letters, and once she realises that her feelings for the King have changed she is ready to give up any attempt to interfere with his marriage plans. Although at the mercy of her own impulsive but generous nature, she never becomes unreasonable; and she shows Sherlock Holmes that she is an adversary worthy of his steel. She succeeds in frustrating his plans—no mean success. In a word she is as nearly as possible the detective's feminine counterpart, as he freely admits. The concise irony of his comment on the subject escapes his clumsy and obtuse client: ' "From what I have seen of the lady, she seems, indeed, to be on a very different level to Your Majesty," said Holmes, coldly.'[1]

Irene Adler's personality is the pivot of the story, and it is unnecessary to look far for the model Conan Doyle took her from. She was Lola Montès. Born in 1818, this adventuress had appeared on the London stage before she became the mistress of Louis of Bavaria. Her political influence alarmed the Jesuit party, and the King was forced to part from her. For the purposes of his story Conan Doyle shifted the events to a time forty years later, but the similarity between Irene Adler and his model remains. Both are English by birth and connected with the theatre. Like Lola Montès, Irene Adler is the mistress of a central European sovereign, whose heart has to submit to considerations of State. Both become exiles. Why should the romantic legend of Lola Montès have induced Conan Doyle to make Irene Adler the incarnation of the eternal feminine in Sherlock Holmes's eyes? Of course the story of Lola Montès would have made an impression on him as an adolescent, and it will be remembered that at seventeen he was in Austria in the Jesuit school at Feldkirch. It is permissible to suppose that in this small world and in this small town the amazing story of Lola Montès could still be the subject of conversation in 1876, particularly among school-boys: and in 1891 Conan Doyle and his wife spent the winter in Vienna. This new taste of Austrian life may well have revived his adolescent memories, and *Scandal in Bohemia* was probably written in Vienna. In any case the story was published a few weeks after his return.

The next Adventure introduces a new dramatic element—mystification. In *A Case of Identity* the detective finally discovers that the man he is looking for, who is supposed to have disappeared, never in

---

[1] HOL. II, p. 28.

fact existed at all. Instead of the incidents being scattered through the story, the surprise is reserved entirely for the conclusion; and in order to make it as sensational as possible Conan Doyle makes the enquiry begin in the most colourless and ordinary way. The plots of the stories were gaining in simplicity and consequently in aesthetic perfection. This led to their being based on current events, and we already notice a prosaic quality in *A Case of Identity*, both in the characters and the problems they set Sherlock Holmes. We find the inspiration for many of the stories in the newspapers for the year 1890. It has been shown for instance that the young Earl of Arundel and Surrey, who had been forced by illness to live in isolation at Norbury not far from South Norwood where Conan Doyle was living at the time, may well have given him the idea for *The Yellow Face*.[1]

In *The Stockbroker's Clerk*, Conan Doyle seems to have been thinking of the case of a swindler called Isidor Gilka in November 1888; and in *The Naval Treaty* of Charles Marvin, a Foreign Office official who sold the text of a secret treaty between England and Russia to *The Globe*. Among other references to current events, one should include a photograph of a false horse-shoe in *The Strand Magazine*, or a figure seen more than once in the City, or a house whose situation made it of interest to bank robbers in *The Red-Headed League*. Real-life memories also throw light on some of the plots: the harpooners in *Black Peter* are the men Conan Doyle lived with on board the *Hope*. In the same way the village of Birlstone and its manor-house described in such detail in *The Valley of Fear* are the village and manor-house of Groombridge, seven miles from Crowborough, where Conan Doyle had several times stayed. Other stories were inspired by conversations or correspondence with friends. In 1903 Sir Arthur accepted a device suggested by Jean Leckie to account for Holmes's return after his long absence and apparent disappearance in the falls of Reichenbach. *The Hound of the Baskervilles* arose from a conversation followed by a visit to Dartmoor. Fletcher Robinson, a friend he had made in South Africa, was intrigued by a legend about a phantom dog told him by Max Pemberton; he passed it on to Conan Doyle, who dedicated the book to him. There was some question of a collaboration, but Robinson backed out, though Conan Doyle took him with him for long days on the moors. Hearing that an escaped Dartmoor convict was hiding

---

[1] Cf. M. Harrison, *In the Footsteps of Sherlock Holmes*, pp. 116–20.

in this remote region, he organised his different impressions and observations round an old local legend about a certain Richard Cabell.

Any anecdote, however unexpected and comical, could be the germ of one of Sherlock Holmes's Adventures. Soon after the famous occasion when General Humbert asked if Sherlock Holmes was a private in the British Army, Conan Doyle replied by writing the story which brought his hero's career to an end. This was *His Last Bow*, first published in *The Strand Magazine* with the sub-title *The War Service of Sherlock Holmes*.

How can one sum up the sources of the Sherlock Holmes Adventures? The formula he used to make them suitable for a magazine resulted in a success he had never dreamed of, nor even perhaps desired. As the cycle grew he came under more and more pressure from his own creation, and for a great many years the thread on which his days were strung was tightened by the fact that his imagination was caught in a trap. The intimacy this wove between the author and this series of stories during nearly forty years, gave them very visible organic unity. Technically speaking, the need for the plots to be as short and lucid as possible helped to build up the character of Holmes—the central point where all the threads met. But we must now go on to study the background, which will raise the question of the nature of detective fiction in general.

Every novel in which police and detectives play an important part is not necessarily a detective-story. One might mention works as different from each other as *Moll Flanders, Les Misérables, Crime and Punishment, Le Procès, Sanctuary* and a great many more. What is it about the Sherlock Holmes stories that makes them so typical of detective fiction? Firstly, it would seem, that everything to do with the investigation is given primary importance, to the detriment of the rest of the action and descriptions of persons and places. Also that in the detective story in general, and the Sherlock Holmes cycle in particular, time factors, characters and plot are controlled by aesthetic considerations belonging more to the domain of the theatre than the novel. We have to do with several hundred characters, almost all of whom appear in only one of the stories. What they are and what they do only interests us in so far as it concerns the hero. Later on we will describe Conan Doyle's treatment of his characters; for the moment we will confine ourselves to making clear that whatever their status in the action, whether the plot requires them to be princes or pariahs, they are technically speaking mere satellites. They fall into two groups or camps, according as to whether the hero is on their side or against them—a dualism that inevitably results in an almost Manichaean simplification of their psychological make-up. To know all is to forgive all: but criminals cannot be allowed to justify their crimes, the plot requires them to remain as they are. All that is necessary is to attribute their actions to one of the two motive forces to which all behaviour can be reduced—love or gain.

Let us consider the whole cycle of fifty-six short and four long stories, disregarding the distinction between innocent and guilty. In twenty of them either the central or subsidiary action depends on a love affair. Among eight murders motivated by jealousy, the rival is the victim in six and the unfaithful spouse in two. In these two last, one of the murderers is the husband (*The Retired Colourman*) and one the jilted fiancée (*The Musgrave Ritual*); but the crime of passion plays only a secondary part in the plots. In only one story, *The Abbey Grange*, do we find a drama of jealousy of the traditional type, and the victim is presented in such an unfavourable light that Sherlock Holmes allows the criminal to escape from justice.

If we examine these twenty plots we find that it is generally the victims who are involved in love affairs, whereas the criminals are invariably inspired by more sordid motives. We see from this that love is treated extremely unrealistically, never losing its pure and even sacred character, and in one case it is allowed to triumph over the law of the land. It must not therefore dominate the action. More often than not, whenever the plot seems to hinge upon a love affair, the final explanation brings more sordid motives to light. However there is one story, *The Missing Three-Quarter*, in which exactly the opposite happens, and any reader familiar with the previous stories is as much surprised as the author evidently intended him to be.

The great majority of Holmes's adversaries are in complete control of their emotions, perfectly aware of what they are doing and therefore responsible; at least this is so in all the stories written before 1910. They represent the most formidable threat to the safe and well-organised class who profited from the established order in Great Britain before the First World War—the threat to property. Sometimes they are ordinary burglars, counterfeiters, or treasure-seekers; sometimes blackmailers, hired thieves or swindlers. It is not surprising that such characters as these should often have scores to settle among themselves, nor that three of the novels and nineteen of the Adventures should centre round the essentially dramatic theme of revenge.

The cycle is concerned with crimes of blood, but we never have to face unbearable scenes of slaughter, nor do we come across those 'chain' murders so commonly found in detective-stories written after 1930. Some of the stories even make do without a corpse. Among the twelve stories of the first series of Adventures, nine contain no bloodthirsty crime at all. It is true that they become more common in the later stories, figuring in nine out of eleven stories in the *Memoirs* and ten out of thirteen in the *Return*. But the murders are used to give accent, or are too episodic in character to create a macabre atmosphere. It is rare to find Holmes's investigations beginning with a bloody crime. Only seven stories start with a murder; the story called *Thor Bridge* seems to be an eighth but in reality is not.

Holmes's task is not therefore always to unmask or arrest a murderer. Very often the problems he is given to solve are nearer comedy than tragedy. Perhaps this is why Sherlock Holmes is so ready to describe them as 'grotesque'—by which he means tragi-comic. For instance the criminal may use a deliberate confusion of identity to achieve his ends: someone is forced to play the part of victim (*The Copper Beeches, Shoscombe Old Place*), or else the crimi-nal passes himself off as the victim (*A Case of Identity, The Man with the Twisted Lip, The Stockbroker's Clerk, The Norwood Builder*) and deceives the reader, as well as Holmes and Watson. Or the detective may be asked to find a valuable piece of jewelry or a stolen docu-ment. But whether it is a question of finding insufficiently well guarded State secrets (*The Naval Treaty, The Second Stain, The Bruce-Partington Plans*) or of acting for private individuals, we find ourselves accompanying Holmes on a treasure-hunt that is exciting rather than really dangerous.

The unexpected appearance of someone after a long absence in a remote country is a specifically theatrical device, and Shakespeare, Molière, Racine and Beaumarchais among others have accustomed us to it. Whether he is the criminal, an inconvenient witness, or a redresser of wrongs, this individual is always a 'skeleton in the cup-board' for the other characters, and the *deus ex machina* of the story. It will be noticed how frequently this theme occurs in the stories published between 1900 and 1910, when the author was having to make an effort to renew the series, and most of all in the *Return* stories, the first of which brings the detective once more on the scene. Perhaps it is too convenient a contrivance to satisfy aesthetic principles, but it at least allows Conan Doyle to conjure up an exotic and romantic background and give the Holmes cycle its epic quality.

The mysterious confines of the criminal world sometimes contain secret societies, whose activities do not escape Sherlock Holmes's vigilance, and introduce a disturbing note, as also do the cases of kidnapping he exposes in the course of his investigations. The criminal may perhaps want to get by force the services of someone with a particular skill (*The Engineer's Thumb*, *The Greek Interpreter*), or conceal the victim of some infirmity from inquisitive eyes (*The Yellow Face*, *The Blanched Soldier*). And there are five stories in which a guilty or innocent person tries to remain hidden or else pass for dead. Critics have amused themselves by pointing out the classical treatment of plots and situations; with this we find an atmosphere belonging more to the theatre than to the novel. It is hardly surprising that within the very narrow scope of these plots, Conan Doyle has only rarely introduced a sub-plot; but with the exception of *The Musgrave Ritual* (perhaps the most successful and characteristic of all the stories) when he does so this second plot spoils the balance. He nearly always preserves the unity of action, and this does not interfere with the intricacies of the plot, but facilitates them. Since these involve Holmes's adversaries as well as himself, an apparent equilibrium is maintained between the different forces in play. To destroy this equilibrium long before the *dénouement* would be to deprive it of all tension and therefore of interest.

The simplest stratagem used by Holmes is disguise. Dr. Watson, who is taken in every time, insists that his friend is a gifted actor with a talent for changing his walk or tone of voice. Holmes's love of disguise and stage-production even leads him to use a wax image of himself as a bait. But other characters in the stories share his taste for disguise. Some of his enemies use camouflage of a different sort, for instance in *Silver Blaze*. Hiding-places also play an important part in their plans, and so sometimes do houses that have been faked, rather like boxes with double bottoms. Holmes never hesitates to fight his adversaries with their own weapons, force his way into a private house in disguise, or arrange a false alarm with or without the help of the official police (*Scandal in Bohemia*, *The Norwood*

Builder). If the criminals set a trap to get him out of the way, Holmes and his devoted friend Watson divert their suspicions by pretending to follow the false trail. His sense of artistic perfection makes him aim at ingenious or spectacular *dénouements* (*The Dancing Men*), or indulge in the innocent pleasure of mystifying his own clients. The *dénouements* are particularly dramatic, and all with two exceptions (*The Yellow Face* and *The Missing Three-Quarter*) turn out favourably for Holmes.

The aesthetics of the Holmesian cycle have the same advantages and disadvantages as those of the theatre. The psychological field is strictly limited, but situations and incidents can be exploited by good organisation and balance. A writer like Chesterton may have greater aesthetic subtlety, but whatever the merits of his detective-stories they have not the formal perfection we find in Conan Doyle. The danger of the theatrical treatment is that it may end in melodrama or *grand guignol*. It must be admitted that some of his *dénouements* are not free from melodrama—those of *The Yellow Face* or *The Beryl Coronet* for instance—but this is exceptional. As for *grand guignol*, it is hardly apparent in the stories written before 1910, which contain few scenes of horror, and those strictly subordinated to the needs of the action. However, after 1910 this element becomes much more common; the last fifteen stories are different from the rest both in their atmosphere and the part Sherlock Holmes plays in them.

In contrast to the problems in the earlier stories, we now find some actually morbid ingredient in the plots: for instance, a disease having all the appearance of leprosy (*The Blanched Soldier*), a case of mental abnormality in a child (*The Sussex Vampire*), a fantastic physical mutation of a Jekyll and Hyde description (*The Creeping Man*), a horrible mutilation (*The Veiled Lodger*). Some of the other Adventures are burdened with scenes of violence quite disconnected with the action. More or less imaginary poisons are used in some of the murder stories, and there are scenes involving gruesome discoveries. Conan Doyle only returns to his normal manner in the novel *The Valley of Fear* and the story of *Thor Bridge*; the investigation develops in a similar way in both of these, and ends with the discovery of important evidence in a moat and a lake. Except for these two, the detection has lost some of its dramatic tension, the incidents are shorter and less numerous. The analysis is generally longer however, and in four of the stories Dr. Watson is no longer the narrator. We leave the glare of the footlights and move into a region of disturbing semi-obscurity, with something of the atmosphere of modern science-fiction about it. Holmes's personality suffers from these developments. He now gives us the impression of being a passive witness of events, rather than dominating and directing them. Henceforth we do not feel sure of his omnipotence. Of course he has sometimes been outwitted before (*Scandal in Bohemia, The Missing Three-Quarter*), but at least he did not then give the impression of having lost the initiative.

The plots of some of the final stories of the cycle are so paradoxical that he is obliged to be relatively inactive. In *Shoscombe Old Place* and *Thor Bridge*, for instance, though there are apparently two murders to be solved, they in fact turn out to be natural death and suicide. The situation in *The Three Gables* corresponds with that of the first story of all, *Scandal in Bohemia*, but Sherlock Holmes's role is reversed. Instead of being commissioned to find papers which would compromise his client, he is asked to forestall a burglary organised by an adventuress, far less attractive and alive than Irene Adler, in search of a document incriminating her. Moreover the story is bathed in an extremely changeable atmosphere, at times almost scabrous, at others frankly improbable. It is as if Sherlock Holmes's dwindling stature had thrown the story out of balance, with the result that these last stories do not have the eminently reassuring quality his resplendent presence conferred on the Adventures of the great period.

Chapter 14

SHERLOCK HOLMES AND THE READING PUBLIC

The thing is no longer a string of incidents; it is a cycle of incidents.

G. K. CHESTERTON: Introduction to *Bleak House*

The boldly drawn outlines of their hero's character and destiny do not entirely explain the phenomenal success of these stories, published at intervals and under more or less direct pressure from this very success itself; it is necessary to look for some correlation between the works and the social life of the period. First we must anticipate our conclusion, and give our reasons for comparing the Holmesian cycle to an epic. Does this seem unjustified, or even sacrilegious? Is it too audacious to compare a series of prose stories, written without the slightest literary pretensions and with complete detachment, to a poetical and intellectual unity such as *Paradise Lost*, for example? The Holmes cycle has neither the grandeur of subject nor the rhetorical richness of epic poetry. None the less, all judgement of value apart, the epic treatment of the Adventures of Sherlock Homes is sufficiently striking. The heroism of the detective, the moral theme giving unity to the whole, the place occupied in it by discourse, changes of fortune, disasters, humour and the scientific aspect of the marvellous: are not these all characteristics of the epic? But above all the work satisfies certain ideological requirements, and expresses the sensibilities of a comparatively recent period, in which the roots of present-day England are still firmly embedded, although its more obvious features no longer exist. 'What most makes the epic kind is a communal or choric quality,' writes E. M. W. Tillyard. 'The epic writer must express the feelings of a large group of people living in or near his own time.'[1]

Is it not in the person of Sherlock Holmes, amongst all his other

[1] *The Epic Strain in the English Novel*, 1958, p. 15.

creations, that Conan Doyle reveals himself as the spokesman of his generation? He may have exaggerated the influence of Dr. Bell on the genesis of these stories; but whether that influence was real or imaginary, the Holmesian cycle from the very beginning stimulated the interest the public already felt in science, and increased its hold on their imaginations and intellects. Its hold has perhaps not greatly decreased since then, but each period makes its own image of the scientist according to its attitude to learning. The alchemists' image exorcised the terrors of Christianity at a time when men could only be saved by submitting to dogma. At the other extreme, the twentieth-century research-worker has been endowed with all our scepticism, modified hopes and disillusionment.

The scientist of the late nineteenth century was the product of a society which believed almost unanimously in its own values, resources and future. Readers of *A Study in Scarlet* will remember their first meeting with Holmes. We are in the laboratory where he has just discovered a chemical reaction capable of proving the existence of haemoglobin in a given solution more definitely than had been possible before. Thus, thanks to him, criminal investigation enters a new 'positive' phase. The discovery the detective has made almost in front of our eyes is not the result of happy chance. Holmes does not differ from his predecessors, particularly Dupin, so much in intelligence, acumen and tenacity, as in having had a really scientific training. The years he spent in the faculties of Medicine and Science have fitted him to bring an increasingly exact scientific technique to criminology. In the same story Dr. Watson makes a list of the different subjects Holmes has studied; it might serve as a syllabus for the theory and practice of criminology. Chemistry has the place of honour, next come law, anatomy, the arts of defence, and lastly elementary geology and botany—but (Watson notes characteristically) he knows little about horticulture. Such an ambitious programme was only possible because of the progress made by chemistry and the natural sciences round about 1880. By creating a new branch of applied science Holmes was following the advice Lord Kelvin gave to his students: 'There cannot be a greater mistake than that of looking superciliously upon practical applications of science; the life and soul of science is its practical application.'[1]

If it is true, as the experts in Holmesian studies maintain, that

[1] Lecture reprinted in *Popular Lectures and Addresses*.

Sherlock Holmes was born in 1854, he must have been the contemporary within two years of the greatest chemist of his day, Sir William Ramsay; and judging by F. G. Donnan's article on Ramsay in the *Dictionary of National Biography*, the two men had various points in common: 'He was gifted with rare scientific insight and imagination, and was the possessor of a most wonderful skill and dexterity in the devising, constructing and use of apparatus . . . A man of sanguine and courageous temperament, of tireless energy, and power of instant action, he fearlessly attacked problems the experimental difficulties of which could have dismayed and deterred most men.'

On more than one occasion, Holmes describes a method of reasoning founded on a rationalistic conception of the universe. In spite of his pretended ignorance of astronomy, he talks like a follower of Le Verrier, the mathematician who put astronomers on the track of the planet Neptune: 'From a drop of water . . . a logician could infer the possibility of an Atlantic or a Niagara without having seen or heard of one or the other. So all life is a great chain, the nature of which is known whenever we are shown a single link of it.'[1] Or again: 'As Cuvier could correctly describe a whole animal by the contemplation of a single bone, so the observer who has thoroughly understood one link in a series of incidents, should be able accurately to state all the other ones, both before and after.'[2]

We also find him stressing the importance of mathematics and the authority of Euclid. He feels an inventor's pride in his 'methods', ('You know my methods, Watson' is one of the leitmotivs of the Adventures), and insists on the importance of observing details: 'Never trust to general impressions, my boy, but concentrate yourself upon details. My first glance is always at a woman's sleeve, in a man it is perhaps better first to take the knee of the trouser.'[3]

His skill in reading objects, character and thoughts, confirms the excellence of this rule, and it must be said that in practice he gets much more conclusive results from observation than from logical processes. Perhaps a problem such as that of *The Beryl Coronet* offers somewhat unsystematic proof of the value of the study of foot-prints; nor does it justify the distinction Holmes tries to make between his own methods and those of his predecessors. He shows his superiority over the Scotland Yard detectives less by the origi-

[1] *A Study in Scarlet*, HOL. I, p. 20.   [2] *The Five Orange Pips*, HOL. II, p. 116.
[3] *A Case of Identity*, HOL. II, p. 66.

nality of his methods than by his greater skill in analysing the clues. Thus for example, in *The Norwood Builder*, a thumb-print leads him to make an exactly opposite deduction to Inspector Lestrade's: ' "The thumb-mark, Lestrade. You said it was final; and so it was, in a very different sense. I knew it had not been there the day before. I pay a good deal of attention to matters of detail, as you may have observed, and I had examined the hall, and was sure that the wall was clear. Therefore, it had been put on during the night." '[1]

As though the events of the plot were not enough to show the importance of apparently insignificant details, a certain number of allusions to imaginary cases are used to show off the acuteness of Holmes's powers of observation. For instance: 'You will remember, Watson, how the dreadful business of the Abernetty family was first brought to my notice by the depth which the parsley had sunk into the butter upon a hot day.'[2] Humorous though these often are, they still serve to stress the subtlety of the famous 'methods'. And it is almost always under a veil of humour that Conan Doyle describes Holmes lecturing his listeners on objectivity. In *The Noble Bachelor* a message scribbled on the back of a hotel bill puzzles the detectives. Holmes puts them on the right track by showing them that the bill itself contains much more useful evidence.

We have already remarked on the restraint and lack of bloodshed in the plots. Sherlock Holmes is not interested in notorious crimes alone; he also sets himself to end scandals and solve problems, whether criminal or no. He admits to a special taste for unimportant cases, when he can indulge his curiosity without anxiety. In his search for clues and documents, his efforts to extract evidence from them and reconstruct the situation objectively, he shows the attitude of an archaeologist or historian. But where the archaeologist makes old records or inscriptions 'speak', Sherlock Holmes asks questions of objects that appeal to the popular imagination, like the stone used by the criminal as a weapon, or the disguised handwriting on an envelope. From the point of view of the mental processes brought into play by both author and reader, the Sherlock Holmes stories have something in common with Conan Doyle's historical novels and also with the movement to popularise science which was already beginning to appear in the last years of the nineteenth century, as only one of the forms taken by the general spread of education and culture,

[1] HOL. II, p. 608. [2] *Ibid.*, II, p. 743.

notably in the illustrated magazines, with *The Strand Magazine* well to the fore.

On the pretext that Sherlock Holmes's 'deductions' are really 'inductions', that chance is too often on his side and that his hypotheses are not always flawless, there have been attempts to minimise the influence of science on the Holmes stories. They may not have much to do with the actual content of scientific thought, but that does not prevent their showing a debt to the preoccupations of the period. The fictitious world, to which Sherlock Holmes belonged, expected of him what the real world of the day expected of its scientists: more light and more justice. As the creation of a doctor who had been soaked in the rationalist thought of the period, the Holmesian cycle offers us for the first time the spectacle of a hero triumphing again and again by means of logic and scientific method. And the hero's prowess is as marvellous as the power of science, which many people hoped would lead to a material and spiritual improvement of the human condition, and Conan Doyle first among them.

As with every other heroic figure, the reader is tempted to identify himself with Sherlock Holmes, as the incarnation of the spirit of his age. The setting and the details of the stories also facilitate identification. The public, particularly the London public, could live through Sherlock Holmes's Adventures in imagination, without making any great change in their normal way of life. The cycle may be said to be an epic of everyday events. The reader can put himself in the hero's place without much difficulty, and be actor and spectator at the same time in an adventure that he knows will turn out well.

What were the social circumstances of the readers who entered the imaginary world of Holmes and Watson? Who were the readers of *The Strand Magazine*? What motives influenced them? What did literature mean to them? As a result of unprecedented economic and social developments, its object and function had undergone a violent change. Until the middle of the century, prose had been much less democratic than it is today and a large section of the population was illiterate. Of course, the minority for whom books were written had left their impress on the economic and social life of the nation; they probably included relatively few of the aristocracy and more from the landed gentry, church, trade and industry. It was none the less a well-read and cultured minority. The fact that literature was necessarily addressed to a few does not imply that it did not recognise the existence, conditions and needs of the proletariat, but only that we must accept the picture it gives of that proleteriat with the greatest possible reserve.

During the nineteenth century the English economy had ceased to be agricultural and rustic, and become industrial and urban. This development was virtually completed between 1870 and 1880. The importation of American corn and foodstuffs during Disraeli's ministry between 1875 and 1880 gave English agriculture its death blow. In 1881 only 12% of the population was actively employed on the land and this proportion went on declining.

The masses of workers employed under the new economy gradually became organised. Too long disabled by social inequalities, they now quickly achieved more privileges and a better standard of living. The length of the working day was fixed, and in 1870 the Forster Act instituted elementary education on a national scale. 'Look at those big, isolated clumps of buildings rising up above the slates, like brick islands in a lead-coloured sea,' says Holmes. 'The Board Schools—Lighthouses, my boy! Beacons of the future! Capsules, with hundreds of bright little seeds in each, out of which will spring the wiser, better England of the future.'[1]

These two factors soon led to a reduction in illiteracy and also to daily periods of leisure for everyone; however short these might be they were sharply separated from the working hours away from home. A greater number could enjoy the pleasures of reading. Up till now literature had been addressed almost exclusively to a class which valued reading and culture as a part of family life and the education of their children. But the mass of new readers, most of them from illiterate homes, made up what might be called a proletariat of culture. The earliest popular newspapers and illustrated magazines provided these newcomers with a miscellaneous collection of news and entertainment. Artistic merit was probably therefore not the sole factor contributing to the success of Sherlock Holmes's Adventures. Perhaps some readers may have got more enjoyment from the mental gymnastics the stories provided. The way the public received Holmes's disappearance at the end of *The Final Problem* illustrates this point. The letters of dismay written by some readers to Conan Doyle do not merely show to what extent they had adopted Sherlock Holmes: they seem to express personal grief of an identical sort as is provoked

[1] *The Naval Treaty*, HOL. II, p. 515.

today by the breaking off of some favourite television programme. Concerned as he was to preserve the dignity of literature, Conan Doyle could only deplore this unexpected phenomenon. It shows us what a debt that marginal but functional literary form the modern detective-story owes to Sherlock Holmes.

One of the most important social factors on which the success of Sherlock Holmes depended was the spread of the towns and especially of London. Coinciding with the Industrial Revolution, pre-romantic and romantic literature on the whole appears indifferent to the picturesqueness of great man-made cities, and prefers the country, handiwork of God. Wordsworth had never lived in London, though he did once have a glimpse of its majestic splendour. But Byron denounced 'the hum of human cities torture' and made fun of the author of the *Lines written on Westminster Bridge*. Shelley described London as a sewer, and Keats as a hideous prison, full of groans, disease, despair and death. It was left to the prose-writers to rehabilitate London; Lamb led the way and Charles Dickens of course takes pride of place. But by 1870, when Dickens died, London had lost the 'parochial' character it has in many of his works. In 1820 London was comfortably contained within the quadrilateral bounded by the Edgware Road and Chelsea to the west and Bethnal Green and Bermondsey to the east. Fifty years later the city had stretched its tentacles as far as Ealing, Twickenham and Wimbledon to the west, Ilford, Charlton and Lewisham to the east, and had at least tripled in size. In 1891 the census showed a population of 4,300,000 or approximately one-seventh of that of the British Isles.

It is interesting to see how the Sherlock Holmes cycle reflects London's increasing population, and even anticipates the facts: although a story published in January 1892 gives the correct figure of 4,000,000, another published exactly a year later adds an extra million. Dr. Watson enjoyed picturing this vast population in all its infinite variety: 'For three hours we strolled about together, watching the ever-changing kaleidoscope of life as it ebbs and flows through Fleet Street and the Strand.'[1]

The picture drawn for us, of Sherlock Holmes crouching in the very centre of the city, is an example of the modern character given to urban civilisation in the Adventures. London is no longer, as in Dickens's earlier novels, a collection of parishes and suburbs, each

[1] HOL. II, p. 459.

with its own life and character. Conan Doyle paints it in almost sociological terms, suggesting an enormous complex spider's web, with every thread leading to his hero in the centre. Holmes speaks of spinning a web round his adversaries, and the image is exact. Does he not use every means of collecting or communicating information that was available at that time? First there are the 'Baker Street Irregulars' those invaluable little agents who can pass unnoticed in the great town. Then there are telegrams (the Postmaster-General had instituted the national system in 1870); the morning papers and their personal columns, through which personal messages can be immediately conveyed to anyone. And London is full of archives such as those of Lloyd's Register, where Holmes can get any information that his own records do not provide.

We are often shown the worldly side of London life: 'At the Lyceum Theatre the crowds were already thick at the side-entrances. In front a continuous stream of hansoms and four-wheelers were rattling up, discharging their cargoes of shirt-fronted men and beshawled, be-diamonded women.'[1]

The Adventures often allude to these dense streams of four-wheelers and hansoms, sometimes also to river transport—in the man-hunt in *The Sign of Four* for instance—and the Underground already figures as the scene of the crime in *The Bruce-Partington Plans*. Many of the stories take us to stations or railways leading out of London, and describe the new attraction of speed with a technique now familiar to us through the cinema.

Travellers from distant lands are always arriving in the capital of the Empire, and our attention is called to the mysterious anonymity of great modern hotels. London cannot help being a centre of international crime, and a meeting-place for various shady societies, like the Carbonari, Nihilists or Ku-Klux-Klan. The criminal context is unimportant: the Adventures conjure up an image based on those imperialistic ideals so dear to the English public during Queen Victoria's Jubilee years.

The high reputation of science and the excitement of town life could find no better literary expression than in the setting of a detective-story. Stevenson clearly envisaged this sort of writing:

> Chance will continually drag before our careless eyes a thousand eloquent clues, [says one of his characters], not to this mystery only,

[1] HOL. I, p. 140.

but to the countless mysteries by which we live surrounded. Then comes the part of the man of the world, of the detective born and bred. This clue which the whole town beholds without comprehension, swift as a cat, he leaps upon it, makes it his, follows it with craft and passion, and from one trifling circumstance divines a world.[1]

Sherlock Holmes answers this description perfectly. But it is hardly necessary to say that this 'whole town' to whom Conan Doyle offered a romantic picture of their city, were very far from being a homogeneous group. In the year 1880 no one attempted to deal with anything but concrete realities. Careful social analyses, such as Mayhew's exhaustive enquiry into the population of London,[2] and Charles Booth's researches a generation later, led in the long run to effective and disinterested reforms. Booth's enquiry established the fact that at the period we are interested in, about 30% of the London population were living below the poverty line.[3]

The modern historian David Thomson has shown how unemployment in rural areas drove many to look for work in the towns.[4] A study of social classes in England in the middle of the twentieth century came up against obvious difficulties in differentiating them objectively and quantitatively, and finally had to give up the attempt.[5] In 1880, on the contrary, it was easy to distinguish two groups— those possessing an income and those without, the first group including not only the rich, but also all those, however low and precarious their level of life, who depended on an employer more prosperous than themselves. From instincts of solidarity and self-preservation they were opposed to the other group, the outcasts of fortune, whose grudge against the privileged was a permanent threat to property-owners. The reformer Samuel Barnett wrote of the 're-criminations of London's pariahs', and the animosity felt by the poor against the rich, which he believed might even have been an aggravating cause of poverty.[6] The Holmes cycle in a sense takes advantage of the psychological consequences of this state of things. Addressed to the privileged majority, it plays on their fears of social disturbance and at the same time makes use of Sherlock Holmes and what he stands for to reassure them.

[1] *The Dynamiter.*
[2] H. Mayhew, *London Labour and the London Poor*, 4 vols., 1851–2.
[3] C. Booth, *Life & Labour of the People in London*, 17 vols., 1889–1903.
[4] D. Thomson, *England in the Nineteenth Century*, 1950, p. 195.
[5] R. Lewis and A. Maude, *The English Middle Classes*, 1949.
[6] *The Bitter Cry of Outcast London*, 1883. *The Nineteenth Century* for November 1886.

This was quite enough to ensure the Sherlock Holmes cycle being attacked by the U.S.S.R. as 'bourgeois literature'. But the Adventures are in much greater harmony with contemporary ideology than these virtuous critics seem to realise. We find in them a continuous panorama of social conditions, as well as a picture of London itself. The field covered is certainly very large and involves men and women from a great many different walks of life—cabinet ministers, doctors, tradesmen, workmen, governesses, priests, dandies, boxers and of course police inspectors. But there is one point—and a very important one—where Holmes's world fails to coincide with reality: it completely ignores the thousands of unemployed or manual workers who constituted such a large part of London's population. The criminals we meet are either professionals or members of the class we call privileged, for want of a better word. The anxiety aroused by the proximity of crime is reduced by the fact that threats against property and the social order do not come from those who might have deep-rooted reasons for making them, but from immoral individuals. Neither victims nor criminals question the established order. In the same way, though there are allusions to terrorist societies, a danger much nearer home and more real than the Ku-Klux-Klan, the activities of the Irish nationalists, is passed over in silence. These are not defects. Such restrictions allow the Holmes stories, in spite of their modernity, to preserve the basically romantic character their author delighted in. But by failing to establish the distinction between the real London of 1880 and the carefully selective pictures we find in the Holmes cycle, we are in danger of mistaking one for the other, and trying to attach our eternal nostalgia for the golden age to an extremely hypothetical *belle époque*. However, the case of the novelist Orwell shows to what extent the legend of a Holmesian London has been accepted. He believed that, 'during the peaceful years of the end of the last century, society had been assumed to consist essentially of good people, whose peace was only troubled by criminals. To the eyes of his contemporaries Professor Moriarty was as diabolical a character as Hitler is to ours and his vanquisher a knight-errant or a national hero. When Conan Doyle described the death of Holmes at the end of the Memoirs, he made Watson use Plato's words of farewell to Socrates, without any fear of ridicule.'

Though the last years of the century may have been infinitely less peaceful for everyone than Orwell liked to believe, Holmes's world is also much more complicated. Sherlock and the other characters are completely three-dimensional, but we can only see their third dimension through the eyes of their contemporaries. The character of Professor Moriarty is the worst example Orwell could have chosen. He is one of the few cerebral criminals in the cycle who are specialists in the most delicate techniques, and have potent agents at their disposal. Three such men figure in the Adventures: Charles Augustus Milverton in the story of the same name, Baron Gruner in *The Illustrious Client*, and Professor Moriarty himself, who eclipses the first two by the variety, daring and difficulty of the enterprises he plans, but leaves them to mercenaries to carry out. Naturally some people wanted to have it that Conan Doyle had drawn Moriarty from life. The name of one of the most notorious criminals in America, Adam Worth, was mentioned. There is no objection to this identification except that it seems very hypothetical. Worth is much more likely to have been the model for the Chicago gangsters of 1930 than for Moriarty, who is no more nor less than a caricature of Sherlock Holmes in reverse. He is the super-criminal just as his adversary is the super-detective. But above all he owes his existence to the exceptional character of the story in which we first meet him, *The Final Problem*.

As soon as Conan Doyle had decided that Sherlock Holmes must disappear, he had to find a suitable setting for his disappearance. It could not happen anywhere, nor be the work of anyone. Just as he chose the Byronic background of the Swiss Alps, he found an adversary worthy of his hero. Holmes's resurrection gave Conan Doyle the chance to make a further reference to Moriarty at some length in *The Valley of Fear*, which was written after a visit to the United States. Something he heard while there may have inspired Conan Doyle to let drop Worth's name, so as to satisfy the curiosity of a journalist perhaps. But the work itself implicitly gives the lie to this identification, for in it we find Moriarty compared to Jonathan Wild. It is just as possible to see the latter as the model for Moriarty, particularly in view of Conan Doyle's often expressed admiration for Fielding and familiarity with his work. To confuse the social life of the period with the caricature of it contained in the contest between Holmes and Moriarty, as Orwell invites us to do, is to fail to understand the dual aspect of reality—historical and literary. The crowded social scene in the Holmesian saga is taken from a cross-section of London life, and is seen from the point of view of the eminently middle-class Watson. If we borrow that point of view we see a pyramid with the ruling aristocracy at its apex and domestic servants at its base, but altogether excluding the urban proletariat.

It is clear that all the inhabitants of this world are keenly aware of where they belong—are 'class-conscious' in fact. It is rare for this to be explicitly remarked on—it would be out of keeping with Watson's style; but it is implicit in the way the characters reveal themselves in the dialogue, or by the choice of their surnames. The aristocracy are represented by Holdhursts, St. Simons, Holdernesses, Musgraves, Mount-Jameses, Baskervilles, Brackenstalls or Prendergasts. Such resounding names are not allowed to the lower orders, among whom we find housekeepers called Porter or Warren (who must not be confused with Bernard Shaw's heroine); a grocer named Francis Prosper; Mrs Oakshott, a poultry-seller; Morton, an electrician; and Pycroft, a young bank clerk:

> The man whom I found myself facing was a well-built, fresh-complexioned young fellow with a frank, honest face and a slight, crisp, yellow moustache. He wore a very shiny top-hat and a neat suit of sober black, *which made him look what he was*—a smart young City man, *of the class who have been labelled Cockneys, but* who give us our crack Volunteer regiments, and who turn out more fine athletes and sportsmen than any body of men in these islands.[1]

Watson's 'but' is admirable, and this portrait reveals from what a distance the members of his world observed the rest. The narrator practically tells us what rank young Pycroft may hope to reach—but not to pass—as a volunteer.

Between the aristocrats by birth and the almost anonymous but numerous group of 'little men', we find the true middle-class as represented by Dr. Watson—and they are the majority. Holmes stands for the landed gentry. From the point of view of their criminal guilt the different worlds are treated with complete impartiality. Each has its honest and dishonest members. It is not surprising that there are fewer dishonest men among the aristocracy, nor is it grounds for charging the Adventures with being perversely 'bourgeois'. Quite the reverse, for it is the representatives of the aristocracy in the stories who are judged most severely. But by the end of the last century they

---

[1] HOL. II, p. 357. The italics are mine.

had lost the aura of absolute respect which surrounded them forty or fifty years earlier.

The historian G. M. Young writes that in 1890: 'It would have been hard to find even a Conservative who felt for a rich man, or a titled man, as such, the respect which Early Victorians had, not wrongly, paid to the founders of great industries or the heads of historic houses, on whose capacity they depended for good government and progress.'[1]

Except for an extremely discreet allusion to Queen Victoria at the end of *The Bruce-Partington Plans*, royalty is only represented by the King of Bohemia in *A Scandal in Bohemia*. He gets somewhat rough treatment, but he is after all only a foreign sovereign. Baron Gruner and Count Sylvius are the only representatives of the foreign nobility, and Watson's portraits of them lack indulgence to say the least of it. The aristocrats we are asked to judge severely are never those with political power. The Prime Minister and Secretary of State in *The Second Stain* (their names are Lord Bellinger and the Right Honourable Trelawney Hope) are both likeable and in the highest degree honourable men. But whenever the taboo on affairs of State is removed, the Adventures show great freedom of judgement, and describe, as G. M. Young puts it: 'The supersession of the aristocracy by the plutocracy, a process masked by the severe and homely court of Victoria, but growing precipitate, after the agricultural depression, with the influx of South African money and American brides.'[2]

As well as the tyrannical and degenerate Lord Brackenstall, John Clay, the black sheep grandson of a royal prince, and the Duke of Holdernesse (who is involved in kidnapping his own son), we have the vulgar Lord St. Simon, younger son of the Duke of Balmoral, announcing his marriage to Miss Hetty Doran, 'the fascinating daughter of a Californian millionaire'. Holmes reads *The Morning Post*'s significant comment aloud to Watson: 'There will soon be a call for protection in the marriage market, for the present free-trade principle appears to tell heavily against our home product. One by one the management of the noble houses of Great Britain is passing into the hands of our fair cousins from across the Atlantic.'[3]

All the fore-mentioned characters in their different ways exemplify the only reproach levelled at the aristocracy by their admirers the middle-classes: they sometimes fail to set a good example.

[1] *Victorian England, Portrait of an Age*, 1936.   [2] *Ibid.*   [3] HOL. II, p. 227.

The Holmesian cycle pays much less attention to the social behaviour of the lower orders. Watson lets them voice their feelings and ideas themselves, and they do so in a very characteristic manner, but also so prosaically and with such vapidity, that we begin to wonder whether the Southsea doctor is having his revenge, at Holmes's expense, for the interminable and confused confidences he may have had to put up with from some of his patients. Watson hits the nail on the head when he says: 'I had expected to see Sherlock Holmes impatient under the rambling and inconsequential narrative.' In Holmes's world, as in our own, the surest sign of social stability is the rarity or complete absence of people who have changed class— either upwards, by becoming *nouveaux riches*, or downwards, by becoming new poor. The aristocratic young criminal in *The Red-Headed League* belongs rather to the type of 'gentleman cracksman' whose exploits were described by Conan Doyle's brother-in-law, William Hornung. Jonathan Small in *The Sign of Four* is a much more interesting character. It will be remembered that he is the villain of the story and that Holmes eventually arrests him after an exciting chase on the river Thames. In the last chapter Small tells us his own life story. He was guilty of taking advantage of the general confusion during the Indian Mutiny to become involved in the murder of a rich merchant whom it was his duty to protect. He describes his long years of suffering in a convict settlement to Holmes and Watson: 'Twenty long years in that fever-ridden swamp, all day at work under the mangrove-tree, all night chained up in the filthy convict-huts, bitten by mosquitoes, racked with ague, bullied by every cursed black-faced policeman who loved to take it out of a white man.'[1]

Small deserved to be sent to this hell upon earth, not only because of the blackness of his crime, but also because, by agreeing to be an accomplice in a native plot, he had debased his status as a 'sahib'. However his downfall has not entirely obliterated his sense of honour: it was his loyalty to his companions in crime that destroyed him and also explains the significance of 'The Sign of Four' of the book's title. He is a figure reminiscent of Conrad—the exception that confirms the rule of solidarity with class and way of life.

Censoriousness about morals was another characteristic of the Victorian mentality. In Conan Doyle's works it is an expression of his own personal chastity. The shattering entry of the deplorable

---

[1] HOL. I, pp. 215–16.

prostitute in *The Illustrious Client* must be attributed to Conan Doyle's efforts to start a new series of Adventures. The story was written in 1925 and shows what vain attempts he made to distort his own fastidiousness. In a page of literary criticism, Conan Doyle tells us what a fascination the female characters in Richardson's and Fielding's novels had for him. Can all eighteenth-century women have had the piquant charm of Pamela, Harriet Byron, Clarissa, Amelia and Sophia Western? he asks. He sets against their attractions the 'negative charm' of that innocent and insipid creature the amiable doll of the nineteenth century. We can be more objective than Conan Doyle here, and ask whether the difference does not come from the eye of the beholder rather than the subject seen. Except for Lady Hilda Trelawny Hope, quivering with a sense of her own aristocratic grandeur, most of the women in Holmes's world are in fact very insipid and incredibly innocent. The author does not seem to want to interest us in them. They merely perform the dramatic function of being 'young girls in danger', and Conan Doyle shows his casualness about differentiating them even in the choice of their Christian names: Violet Smith, Violet Westbury, Violet de Merville, Violet Hunter. This name is as common in the stories as dukes in Shakespeare's comedies.

Perhaps the fact that these young women seem almost disembodied conduces to their intuitive awareness of their fate. Holmes remarks on the spirituality of Violet Smith's features. Helen Stoner foretells her twin sister's tragic fate: 'A vague feeling of impending misfortune impressed me. My sister and I, you will recollect, were twins, and you know how subtle are the links which bind two souls which are so closely allied';[1] while Mrs. St. Clair is sure that her husband is alive, despite all appearances to the contrary: 'There is so keen a sympathy that I should know if evil came upon him.'[2]

Just as the Holmes cycle depends on a Victorian view of the social order, it appeals also to a corresponding moral code. The Holmesian ethics are revealed in the judgements the reader is invited to make, and also in Holmes's character considered as a model of conduct.

Watson's character will be considered later; he is much more than a mere narrator. His credulity, his unreserved admiration for Sherlock Holmes, the judgements he makes, have not been left to chance. He is implicated in the saga on the same footing as the other char-

---

[1] HOL. II, p. 180. [2] *Ibid.*, II, p. 141.

acters, not merely as narrator. But whereas Holmes appears to be much above the common level of humanity, Watson is intentionally made a perfect representative of the middle-class and of everything that is mediocre. If there is such a thing as a 'man in the street' it is Watson, and Sherlock Holmes speaks for his creator when he declares: 'Watson, you are a British jury, and I never met a man who was more eminently fitted to represent one.'[1]

Holmes has to be the defender and champion of the highest moral values. He is fond of saying that it is his duty 'to uphold the law'. If this means that he is not content merely to make up for the inadequacies of the police but sets store by maintaining law and order, it is contrary to his practice: over and over again we find him breaking into private houses intentionally and with premeditation. 'Of course, legally, we are putting ourselves hopelessly in the wrong,' he says to Watson.[2] Then again, with the help of a complete burglar's outfit, 'with every modern improvement that the march of civilisation demands', he takes his companion on a highly compromising expedition, saying in a bantering tone: 'We have shared the same room for some years, and it would be amusing if we ended by sharing the same cell.'[3] They break the law again together in *Wisteria Lodge* and *The Illustrious Client*. At the conclusion of the latter affair Holmes has a narrow escape: 'Sherlock Holmes was threatened with a prosecution for burglary, but when an object is good and a client is sufficiently illustrious, even the rigid British law becomes human and elastic.'[4]

Can one say that Holmes sacrifices the means to the ends and always arranges that the law shall have the last word? No: under the influence of the Christmas spirit or the spectacle of love triumphant, he is quite capable of saving a thief and a murderer from justice. What does he mean then by upholding the law? He is not defending legality in the strict sense of the word, nor is he a reformer, whose object is social justice. He must be referring to some conflict within the social order, some moral conflict. There is nothing radical about Holmes's social and moral judgements, they do not threaten the established order, but strive to consolidate it. When he reproaches some nobleman, he is not questioning the rights of the aristocracy; on the contrary he is trying to preserve them. And when he jeers at

---

[1] HOL. II, p. 858.　　　　　　　[2] *The Yellow Face*, HOL. II, p. 350.
[3] *Charles Augustus Milverton*, HOL. II, p. 728.　　　　[4] HOL. II, p. 1117.

the police, it is not the organisation he is deploring, but its inefficiency. From the moral point of view, in fact, Holmes's actions and judgements invite his fellow citizens to reform, not to repudiate existing values. Thus, in spite of his faith in science and his modern outlook, the cycle has a messianic value reminiscent of the Carlylian gospel of two generations earlier. But like Carlyle's ideal hero, Holmes was preaching to a society that persisted in its love for individualism. The spirit of English democracy makes one of its most serious denunciations of anything approaching totalitarianism, in the person of Holmes. The police are not corrupt, but they must constantly be encouraged to do better. The chosen few who maintain the social order are in danger of degenerating if there is no one prepared to remind them of their duty.

Spare the rod and spoil the child: Holmes's severity towards the 'chosen few' finds its counterpart in the movements which put an end to the careers of Parnell and Dilke at the same period.

Sherlock Holmes's cavalier attitude towards the representatives of authority gives artistic expression to his individualism. 'Fancy his having the insolence to confound me with the official detective force!' he says to Watson. As an amateur with a perfect understanding of his mission, he contributes to the defence of society, just as Conan Doyle's Rifle Clubs did on the eve of the Boer War. The approval both received from Conan Doyle's fellow-citizens was based on the feeling that in the last resort the nation's safety depends less on some permanent organisation than on the devotion and skill of individuals. Here we have one of the fundamental assumptions of Toryism.

Sherlock Holmes is all the better fitted to function efficiently as a trained amateur because he has sacrificed almost all his family and social ties to his mission. His celibacy and his indifference to all sport except the arts of defence do not imply that he is insensible to feminine charm[1] and ignores the essentially sporting virtue of 'fair play'. Describing how he has solved the problem in *The Devil's Foot*, he tells Watson:

> 'There, sure enough, I perceived a number of flaky ashes, and round the edges, a fringe of brownish powder, which had not yet been consumed. Half of this I took, as you saw, and I placed it in an envelope.'— 'Why half, Holmes?'—'It is not for me, my dear Watson, to stand in the way of the official police force. I leave them all the evidence which

[1] Cf. *Scandal in Bohemia*.

I found. The poison still remained upon the talc, had they the wit to find it.'

Nothing would be further from the truth than to represent Holmes as an anchorite in the desert of crime. He is in the highest degree Stevenson's man of civilised tastes. We must remember that he is no enemy to good food, wines and cigars, and much more of a connoisseur of works of art than Watson. He enjoys pictures, music and the opera, plays the violin for hours at a time, and is even something of a musicologist: 'As to Holmes, he returned refreshed to his monograph upon the Polyphonic Motets of Lassus, which has since been printed for private circulation, and is said by experts to be the last word upon the subject.'[1] He has in fact all the distinguished restraint of a gentleman, although he has little leisure or inclination to bother about such things. Holmes is a wit, whose sayings Watson delights to record. Finally, though he certainly does not despise money, he has an aristocratic detachment towards it, perhaps thrown into relief by Watson's modest financial transactions. 'So, Watson,' says Holmes suddenly 'you do not propose to invest in South African securities.'[2] But such indications as these are not enough to reveal what part his gifts and education would have induced our hero to play if he had put them at the disposal of the public. The enigmatic and subtle character of his brother, Mycroft Holmes, is intended to fill in this gap.

Mycroft Holmes only makes two appearances in the Adventures, neither of which is necessary to the plot. He is in fact a mere extension of Holmes's personality, and an incarnation of his qualities. Sherlock's fleeting moods of listlessness become permanent in his brother—the price he pays for even greater intellectual ability. His extraordinary memory makes Mycroft indispensable to the Government. He is a living encyclopedia for the exclusive use of Whitehall. But in spite of his immense influence, Mycroft's inability to overcome his diffidence, and disconcerting absence of ambition, doom him to obscurity: 'Mycroft draws four hundred and fifty pounds a year, remains a subordinate, has no ambitions of any kind, will receive neither honour nor title, but remains the most indispensable man in the country.'[3]

We have seen what an elevating influence Sherlock Holmes has

---

[1] HOL. II, p. 1000.　　　　　　　　[2] *The Dancing Men*, HOL. II, p. 610.
[3] HOL. II, p. 970.

on the reader's mind. The motives controlling his behaviour, his heroism and the character-traits connecting him with his period, all hark back to the ideal of the gentleman. And indirectly, through Mycroft, Sherlock Holmes flatters our good opinion of ourselves by sharply dissociating what is from what ought to be. The opposition he so forcefully suggests, between the power of money and of feudal ethics, makes him an eminently moral hero.

The major theme of this deeply significant work concerns the intellectual, aesthetic, social and moral ideas of the dying Victorian era. On a slightly lower level, and in a minor key, we find what might be called 'The Watson chronicle', in contrast to 'the Holmes saga'. Here science and heroism have been exchanged for facts and domesticity. Instead of a wide but impersonal vision of city life, we have the picturesque aspect of London and Baker Street which appealed to Dr. Watson. The Adventures of Holmes and Watson sometimes take them out of London for a longish period, as in *The Hound of the Baskervilles*; occasionally it is only for a few hours, as when they visit Birmingham in *The Stockbroker's Clerk*. But in more than half the stories the whole investigation takes place in London. London is never forgotten; every enquiry begins in the Baker Street flat, and we are brought back to Baker Street at its conclusion. Holmes and Watson are such complete Londoners that we even share their sense of exile during their trips to the country. Let us listen to the reflections the sight of the countryside inspires in Holmes in *The Copper Beeches*:

> 'Good heavens!' I cried. 'Who would associate crime with these dear old homesteads?'
> 'They always fill me with a certain horror. It is my belief, Watson, founded upon my experience, that the lowest and vilest alleys in London do not present a more dreadful record of sin than does the smiling and beautiful countryside.'
> 'You horrify me!'
> 'But the reason is very obvious. The pressure of public opinion can do in the town what the law cannot accomplish. There is no lane so vile that the scream of a tortured child, or the thud of a drunkard's blow, does not beget sympathy and indignation among the neighbours, and then the whole machinery of justice is ever so close that a word of complaint can set it going, and there is but a step between the crime and the dock. But look at these lonely houses, each in its own fields, filled for the most part with poor ignorant folk who know little of the law. Think of the deeds of hellish cruelty, the hidden wickedness which may go on, year in, year out, in such places, and none the wiser.

Had this lady who appeals to us for help gone to live in Winchester, I should never have had a fear for her. It is the five miles of country which makes the danger. Still, it is clear that she is not personally threatened.'[1]

London is the focus of the Adventures, but it also reassures the town-dwelling reader about the moral context of his society. It is impossible not to remember the very different charges James Joyce levels against town life in *Dubliners*!

In the purely London stories, the topography is usually so precisely indicated that certain passages will give anyone who knows the city well the pleasure of re-discovery. With Watson as guide we visit in turn fashionable London, the London of hotels and theatres, literary London, business London and finally London the sea-port. Stories like *The Sign of Four*, *The Red-Headed League*, *The Blue Carbuncle*, *The Greek Interpreter*, *The Hound of the Baskervilles*, *The Six Napoleons* and *The Bruce-Partington Plans* bring out these different aspects of London in a panorama as kaleidoscopic as Watson's view of Londoners themselves. Long descriptions are unnecessary: a few impressionistic notes are quite enough to revive the very endearing and individual personality of the vast city: 'At half-past five a cab deposited us outside 104 Berkeley Square, where the old soldier resides—one of those awful grey London castles which would make a church seem frivolous.'[2]

One of Holmes's most picturesque 'readings' of objects takes place in a cab carrying our two friends to an unknown destination:

> Sherlock Holmes was never at fault, and he muttered the names as the cab rattled through squares and in and out by tortuous by-streets.
>
> 'Rochester Row,' said he. 'Now Vincent Square. Now we come out on the Vauxhall Bridge Road. We are making for the Surrey side, apparently. Yes, I thought so. Now we are on the bridge. You can catch glimpses of the river.'
>
> We did indeed get a fleeting view of a stretch of the Thames, with the lamps shining upon the broad, silent water; but our cab dashed on, and was soon involved in a labyrinth of streets upon the other side.
>
> 'Wandsworth Road,' said my companion. 'Priory Road. Larkhall Lane. Stockwell Place. Robert Street. Coldharbour Lane. Our quest does not appear to take us to very fashionable regions.'
>
> We had indeed reached a questionable and forbidding neighbourhood. Long lines of dull brick houses were only relieved by the coarse glare and tawdry brilliancy of public-houses at the corners. Then came

---

[1] HOL. II, p. 286.   [2] *Ibid.*, p. 1102.

rows of two-storied villas, each with a fronting of miniature garden, and then again interminable lines of new, staring brick buildings— the monster tentacles which the giant city was throwing out into the country.[1]

Here we have that effect of speed so reminiscent of the cinema; it is produced by the rapid succession of Holmes's remarks punctuated by the staccato rhythm of the style. Watson's eyes move more slowly and are more attentive to detail; he analyses what he sees and conveys an eminently pictorial and personal impression to our imaginations.

The people of London are just as briefly, precisely and vividly described. Their habits, the places they frequent, their clothes, never go unobserved. Here is Miss Mary Sutherland in her boa, her straw hat, worn like the Duchess of Devonshire's, her simple plum-coloured dress with collar and cuffs of purple velvet; here is her pseudo-fiancé in black frock-coat, grey Harris tweed trousers, brown gaiters and elastic-sided boots. Here again is that aristocratic bachelor, Lord St. Simon: 'His dress was careful to the verge of foppishness, with high collar, black frock-coat, white waistcoat, yellow gloves, patent-leather shoes, and light-coloured gaiters. He advanced slowly into the room, turning his head from left to right, and swinging in his right hand the cord which held his golden eye-glasses.'[2]

In the heart of the city, and (like Watson) 'the only fixed point in the centre of an ever-changing universe', are the Baker Street rooms which the chronicle has made so familiar. Baker Street is the permanent stage-set in which Watson has granted us the privilege of living in intimacy with his illustrious friend; it is the mute witness of conversations or long silences between the two. Everything in it speaks of Holmes to our imagination: 'There were the chemical corner and the acid-stained deal-topped table. There upon a shelf was the row of formidable scrap-books and books of reference which many of our fellow-citizens would have been so glad to burn. The diagrams, the violin-case, and the pipe-rack—even the Persian slipper which contained the tobacco—all met my eyes as I glanced round.'[3]

Chemist, archivist, artist, dilettante and bohemian—Holmes is all of these; we can use his 'methods' to translate this description at sight, so clearly is his personality given off by it. But these rooms are also an observation-post. Let us follow Watson to the window and watch the London scene beside him:

[1] HOL. I, pp. 141–2.   [2] HOL. II, p. 231.   [3] *Ibid.*, p. 578.

> It was a bright, crisp February morning, and the snow of the day before still lay deep upon the ground, shimmering brightly in the wintry sun. Down the centre of Baker Street it had been ploughed into a brown crumbly band by the traffic, but at either side and on the heaped-up edges of the footpaths it still lay as white as when it fell. The grey pavement had been cleaned and scraped, but was still dangerously slippery, so that there were fewer passengers than usual. Indeed, from the direction of the Metropolitan station no one was coming save the single gentleman whose eccentric conduct had drawn my attention.[1]

In spite of the variable weather, Conan Doyle likes best to show us Baker Street in the morning dimness of all-pervading, mysterious fog:

> It was a cold morning of the early spring, and we sat after breakfast on either side of a cheery fire in the old room in Baker Street. A thick fog rolled down between the lines of dun-coloured houses, and the opposing windows loomed like dark, shapeless blurs, through the heavy yellow wreaths. Our gas was lit, and shone on the white cloth, and glimmer of china and metal, for the table had not been cleared yet.[2]

Among all the kinds of weather that Conan Doyle excels in describing with an ever-alert, exact and restrained pen, the London fog has double significance. Why should the reader so often associate Baker Street with the fog, described even more insistently in *The Bruce-Partington Plans*? asks Gavin Brend.[3] Because it is a feature of the London weather, of course; but also because it belongs to a literary tradition of which the reading public is more or less consciously aware. Ever since the rediscovery of Shakespeare during the romantic period, we have known what a dramatic and moral function fog can assume. It is not necessary to have read *Macbeth* to associate the word 'fog', like the word 'shadows', with the idea of crime, and so with the notion of a blurred, confused and disordered perception of moral values. The idea of fog is inextricably involved with a very rich and complex cultural experience. And the London fog in particular, its aspect and its evocative power, have been enlarged upon by Dickens to such an extent that it has become permanently linked with his novels. So that it is not surprising that Conan Doyle's descriptions of it raise echoes of special significance in every English reader's mind.

A chronicle of London, the chronicle of an epoch, and also of

---

[1] HOL. II, p. 248.   [2] *Ibid.*, p. 276.   [3] *My Dear Holmes*, 1951.

course an impressionistic chronicle. Because he wanted to keep Watson's chronicle distinct from those of the historians, the chronicles of political and current events, Conan Doyle was careful, as we have seen, not to mix reality too exactly and too brutally with fiction. How then did he succeed in making the stories give such a vivid sense of the period? Simple repetition and frequent allusions to the manner and spirit of the age certainly illuminate the whole Holmesian cycle; but are they enough to create such a definite impression? It is difficult to be sure, and we must therefore consider the stories from a purely temporal point of view.

We know that they were published between 1887 and 1927, but that this is not the period covered by the Adventures themselves. We also know that their internal chronology does not correspond to the order in which they were published. It is this internal and fictitious chronology that H. W. Bell amused himself by establishing from direct or implied evidence in the text.[1]

I do not propose to discuss his methods nor the exactness of his conclusions in detail. With certain reserves, due to the extremely fantastic nature of some of his conjectures and the uncompromising precision with which he presses his points, his conclusions are acceptable, and lead to a certain number of assumptions of which he was apparently unaware himself. The story of Sherlock Holmes's first campaign, which Bell places in 1875, is to be found in *The 'Gloria Scott'*. The detective's career ends in 1914 during the first days of the war. But if one amuses oneself by drawing up a diagram of his activities, it soon becomes clear that its intensity varied greatly, and two main phases can be distinguished—one lasting six years, the other nine, the interval between them explained by Holmes's reserve after his duel with Professor Moriarty.

NUMBER OF SHERLOCK HOLMES'S INVESTIGATIONS

1875–9	2	1895–7	14
1880–5	6	1898–1904	11
1886–91	23	1905–14	2
1892–4	2 (*Disappearance of Holmes*)		

This table shows clearly enough the relation between Sherlock Holmes and several generations of his public—those who reached the reading age between 1886 and 1904. These dates indicate the limits

[1] H. W. Bell, *Sherlock Holmes and Doctor Watson: the Chronology of their Adventures*, 1932.

of the social reverberations of the Holmes stories more accurately than do the dates of publication. But if we accept Bell's theories as to the time-lag between the fictitious date and the date of publication, we can construct a very illuminating diagram, showing the mutual fidelity between Sherlock Holmes and his public. In fact we may say that as the dates of publication advanced in time, the interval between them and the fictitious dates steadily increased.

Series	Number of stories	Minimum interval	Maximum interval	Average
Adventures (1892)	12	1 year	10 years	3 years 11 months
Memoirs (1894)	11	2 years	18 years	7 years 8 months
Case-Book (1927)	12	18 years	31 years	24 years

The whole Holmesian cycle is thus concentrated in time in a way that gives readers the illusion of being Sherlock Holmes's contemporaries, and of taking part in the Adventures. The stories have the further attraction of touching their imaginations by appealing to their personal memories. This simple conclusion helps us understand the nostalgia that so many readers of 'Sherlock Holmes's generation' feel for the earlier stories, and the fact of their finding them preferable to those published later. We believe this to be something subjective, and in which aesthetic judgements only play a secondary part. It does not matter if a story published in 1922 is technically better than another published thirty years earlier, if what we feel today is the echo of yesterday's youthful response. For the benefit of his chosen public, Watson's chronicle occasionally refers to some recent event or contains a topical pastiche, to create atmosphere and appeal to all the resources of 'magazine aesthetics'. Holmes and Watson are not the only characters who reappear in the stories. Other old acquaintances turn up at less regular intervals: Moriarty, Mycroft Holmes, Mrs. Hudson, the 'Baker Street Irregulars' and a few more. The stories contain frequent references to one another, sometimes explicitly, sometimes by inference. For example in *The Empty House*, the brief reference to an air-gun reminds one of *The Final Problem*. In this way the Holmes cycle develops that piquant sense of initiation, that enjoyable esoterism which is one of the chief attractions of the 'Holmes Clubs'. Sometimes the stories even presuppose the reader's fidelity or complicity. Some of the dramatic effects are based on this. Our surprise at the *dénouement* of *The Missing Three-Quarter*, for example, largely depends on our having grown accustomed to a very different sort of conclusion. We have seen that a great many different aesthetic elements combine on the epic canvas of the Holmes saga. Whether through the London background or the atmosphere of some of the stories, the Sherlock Holmes cycle draws upon a collective literary inheritance and a sediment of popular ideology without its readers knowing it. Something of the same sort is true of the part played by Dr. Watson.

Chapter 15

WATSON, HOLMES AND CONAN DOYLE

It goes without saying that Dr. Watson's character is technically no less important than that of Holmes. He is Holmes's witness and companion and also his chronicler. In him collective judgements find their expression, he is the incarnation of the *vox populi*. In this democratic guise he has undoubtedly made a definite contribution to the popularity of the stories outside England, particularly in France and the United States. As Desmond MacCarthy so admirably expressed it, Watson is the most representative Englishman of the end of the nineteenth century.[1] In terms of the aesthetic value of the work, Dr. Watson's character has dramatic, psychological and literary significance.

Both as narrator and independent individual he acts as an intermediary between the reader and the dramatic action. From the very first story, his existence bears witness to Conan Doyle's sure instinct in the technique of story-telling. He was aware of the drawbacks of an impersonal narrative on one hand, and of making his hero tell his own story on the other. The first method might have made Sherlock Holmes a less attractive, more remote and appreciably less solid figure, while Watson would have been relegated to the position of a confidant on the stage. The second method would have meant sacrificing most of the dramatic effects designed to emphasise Holmes's heroism. As Conan Doyle shows in *The Exploits of Brigadier Gerard*, a hero cannot sing his own praises without making his readers smile. A narrative by Holmes in the first person would have prevented his being glorified by the narrator. Neither technique was suitable to the epic plan. Conan Doyle chose an intermediate formula, by means of which we pass constantly from first to third person, through the medium of Dr. Watson's narrative. Technically, he has to play a double role for the reader's benefit. Sometimes he reveals what Holmes knows and plans to do, by asking him the same questions the reader is asking himself. In Holmes's absence

[1] *The Listener*, 11 December 1929.

Watson still asks himself questions in the reader's name, so as to make the subsequent elucidation of the problem as coherent and convincing as possible: 'What then? Was he the agent of others, or had he some sinister design of his own? What interest could he have in persecuting the Baskerville family? . . . was that his work, or was it possibly the doing of someone who was bent upon counteracting his schemes?'[1]

Thus he calls the tune, and either provokes a clear statement of the different elements in the plot by his questions, or makes certain that the final explanation throws all possible light on Holmes's actions. Conan Doyle emphasises Watson's naïveté. (The famous 'elementary, my dear Watson' is apocryphal, but we find: ' "It is wonderful!" I exclaimed. "It is obvious." '—' "Excellent!" I cried. "Elementary," said he.'—' "Wonderful!" I ejaculated. "Commonplace," said Holmes.') This trait of Watson's helps the reader participate more intensely in the plot. In fact, when Watson seems excessively admiring we get the flattering illusion of coming closer to Holmes ourselves, since we understand his point of view better than Watson does. Whenever Watson seems almost rudely incredulous, we remember that Holmes does nothing without good reason, and instinctively take sides against his sceptical companion. This happens at the beginning of *A Study in Scarlet*, for instance, when Watson expresses doubts about Holmes's scientific pretensions. The fact that Watson's intelligence functions so inopportunely, as it were, gains the reader's interest, and prepares the way for Holmes's marvellous scientific knowledge to create an impression.

This use of a 'go-between' to endorse the marvellous or supernatural element of a drama is a well-tried device. For instance in the first scenes of *Hamlet*, when Horatio's natural incredulity gives way before the evidence, the spectator is forced to accept the objective reality of the ghost. Watson's role always bears some relation to that of Holmes. One is the statue, the other the pedestal. Even if he happens to complain of Holmes, Watson never ceases to respect his heroic image:

> One of Sherlock Holmes's defects—if, indeed, one may call it a defect—was that he was exceedingly loth to communicate his full plans to any other person until the instant of their fulfilment. Partly it came no doubt from his own masterful nature, which loved to dominate and

[1] *The Hound of the Baskervilles*, HOL. I, p. 301.

surprise those who were around him. Partly also from his professional caution, which urged him never to take any chances. The result, however, was very trying for those who were acting as his agents and assistants.[1]

It is through Watson that we have intimate access to the hero, and he knows how to bring out the endearing as well as the admirable traits of his character. He is the witness of Holmes's failures, his confidant when discouraged, his only friend: ' "What you do in this world is a matter of no consequence," returned my companion, bitterly. "The question is, what can you make people believe that you have done." '[2]

To whom except Watson would Holmes dare speak of his own 'great powers', without fear of ridicule? Holmes's friendship for Watson is characteristically expressed in his special desire for Watson's approval: 'The same singularly proud and reserved nature which turned away with disdain from popular notoriety was capable of being moved to its depths by spontaneous wonder and praise from a friend.'[3]

It also sometimes manifests itself in less egoistic fashion. In *The Three Garridebs*, Watson is wounded by a dangerous criminal. Holmes hurls himself on his assailant and disarms him: ' "You're not hurt, Watson? For God's sake, say that you are not hurt!" It was worth a wound—it was worth many wounds—to know the depth of loyalty and love which lay behind that cold mask.'[4]

But compensations such as these are exceptional. Holmes never hesitates to expose Watson to fits of ill-humour that are sometimes prolonged (in *The Missing Three-Quarter* for example) or to entrust him with delicate and dangerous missions, often obviously beyond his powers. Then Holmes scolds him unmercifully like a schoolmaster. For instance: ' "Your hiding-place, my dear Watson, was very faulty." ... "You really have done remarkably badly." ... "And a singularly consistent investigation you have made, my dear Watson", said he. "I cannot at the moment recall any possible blunder which you have omitted." '

Nevertheless, of all the characters in the stories, Watson is the one who understands Holmes best, as the others realise: ' "But you know him well, Watson. He is such an inscrutable fellow that I never

---

[1] *The Hound of the Baskervilles*, HOL. I, p. 384.
[2] *A Study in Scarlet*, HOL., I, p. 117.
[3] *The Six Napoleons*, HOL., II, p. 760.   [4] HOL. II, p. 1213.

quite know what to make of him. Do you think he is hopeful? Do you think he expects to make a success of it?" "He has said nothing." "That is a bad sign." "On the contrary, I have noticed that when he is off the trail he generally says so." '[1]

If the dramatic element is abstracted from the Adventures, leaving only the human relationship between Holmes and Watson, the cycle seems to be a sort of anecdotal biography. One cannot over-estimate the effect on Conan Doyle and other writers of the comparatively recent popularity of this biographical form. It is to a large extent explainable by an outcrop of scholarly or romantic historical studies, and the interest in history they stimulated. A great reader, especially of history, Conan Doyle knew Lockhart and Froude well, and of course Boswell.

There is a whole chapter on *The Life of Samuel Johnson* in *Through the Magic Door*. Conan Doyle says it is a work that interests, even 'fascinates' him, and we see why in this chapter. Questioning Boswell's accuracy, Conan Doyle tries to form an objective view of Samuel Johnson's character: 'When you have been accustomed to look at him through the sympathetic glasses of Macaulay or of Boswell, it is hard to take them off to rub one's eyes, and to have a good honest stare on one's own account at the man's actual words, deeds and limitations.'[2]

It is as clear as possible that the chief attraction of the *Life*, for the creator of Sherlock Holmes, lay in Samuel Johnson's character and his relationship to his biographer. From trying to separate the real Johnson from Boswell's hero, Conan Doyle is led on to describe Boswell's gifts as a biographer: 'It is just these pen pictures of his of the big, uncouth man, with his grunts and his groans, his gargantuan appetite, his twenty cups of tea, and his tricks with the orange peel and the lamp-posts, which fascinate the reader and have given Johnson a far broader literary vogue than his writings could have done.'[3]

But is not this art of the 'pen picture' exactly what the Holmes cycle so convincingly provides? These lines illumine for us the unexpected transformation of the Johnson-Boswell relationship into that of Holmes and Watson. Holmes's comparison of Watson with Boswell in *A Scandal in Bohemia* is not purely a whim ('I am lost without my Boswell'): it conveys more than a mere symmetry

---

[1] *The Naval Treaty*, HOL. II, p. 528.
[2] *Through the Magic Door*, p. 48.   [3] *Ibid.*, p. 52.

between the relationships, it means that Boswell and Dr. Watson had a similar manner of describing and giving life to their models, in short of giving their portraits permanent artistic value. It is no accident that an authority on Boswell and Johnson, Sir Sydney Roberts, showed a particular fondness for Conan Doyle's work, and is president of both the Johnson society and the Sherlock Holmes Society of London. In his book on Holmes and Watson,[1] Sir Sydney has brought out several similarities between Holmes and Johnson, but without apparently drawing any very definite conclusion from them. He tells us that:

> Holmes found in Watson, as Johnson found in Boswell, the perfect foil . . . Both Boswell and Watson were superbly good listeners . . . In Johnson's and Holmes's general approach to life there is, indeed, a substantial element in common . . . Chemical experiment was, of course, a particular hobby of both men . . . for Nature in the broader sense, neither had a genuine love or interest. . . . Finally: 'It is easy to guess the trade of an artisan by his knees, his fingers or his shoulders.' That is a quotation not from *A Study in Scarlet*, but from *The Rambler* (No. 173).

These comparisons are indications of a close kinship between Boswell's chronicle and Watson's. Conan Doyle's critical acuteness had soon made him aware of the aesthetic richness of Boswell's work, and he had sufficient artistry to make use of it to immortalise his own two imaginary characters. We see how Dr. Watson, as narrator, emphasises the distance between Holmes and himself in order to exalt the detective's heroism. Seen from an opposite direction, this distance gives Watson's character a rich humour reminding us of Boswell's portrait of Goldsmith. By a curious coincidence Watson's character might well have been one of Goldsmith's own humorous creations. Perhaps the fact that Goldsmith and Conan Doyle were both Irishmen may have something to do with it. However that may be, the subtle blend of seriousness and humour and the narrator's way of innocently revealing the finer psychological shades of his own ego, irresistibly draw a comparison between Dr. Watson and the immortal Dr. Primrose. If Holmes is essentially a thinker, Watson is a man of feeling. He feels cold, heat, hunger, thirst and the pain of his old wound. He feels indignation and pity (sometimes at the wrong moments), enjoys the beauties of nature, and regrets being

---

[1] *Holmes and Watson*, 1953, pp. 51–4.

unable to linger among them: 'The trees and wayside hedges were just throwing out their first green shoots, and the air was full of the pleasant smell of the moist earth. To me at least there was a strange contrast between the sweet promise of the spring and this sinister quest upon which we were engaged.'[1]

Invariably loyal and indulgent, unostentatiously brave, even when he is chasing a criminal he cannot help giving his adversary a last chance: 'A lucky long shot of my revolver might have crippled him, but I had brought it only to defend myself if attacked, and not to shoot an unarmed man who was running away.'[2]

We notice the delightful 'lucky': Holmes would never have used such an adjective in similar circumstances!

All these aspects of his character would strike us as humorous if Dr. Watson were not sometimes moved by a devotion and admiration entirely estimable in themselves to transgress the bounds of his natural modesty a little. Doing his best to follow Holmes's example, he decides to show off his own powers of observation and deduction; the discoveries that follow remind us more of Monsieur de la Palice than Sherlock: 'You are hungry,' he says to Holmes, seeing him devouring a piece of stale bread. Or again: 'Quarter of an hour later we found ourselves in what I judged, from the lines of polished barrels behind glass covers, to be the gun-room of the old house.'[3]

In *The Hound of the Baskervilles* Holmes asks him what the letters C.C.H. engraved on the band of a cane stand for. Watson replies that the last letter probably stands for the word 'Hunt', and the two first for its name.

> 'Really, Watson, you excel yourself,' said Holmes, pushing back his chair and lighting a cigarette. 'I am bound to say that in all the accounts which you have been so good as to give of my own small achievements you have habitually underrated your own abilities. It may be that you are not yourself luminous, but you are a conductor of light. Some people without possessing genius have a remarkable power of stimulating it. I confess, my dear fellow, that I am very much in your debt.'
>
> He had never said as much before, and I must admit that his words gave me keen pleasure, for I had often been piqued by his indifference to my admiration and to the attempts which I had made to give publicity to his methods. I was proud, too, to think that I had so far mastered his system as to apply it in a way which earned his approval.[4]

[1] *The Speckled Band*, HOL., II, p. 187.
[2] *The Hound of the Baskervilles*, HOL. I, p. 335.
[3] HOL. II, p. 1316.　　　　　　　　　　[4] HOL. I, p. 243.

Unfortunately poor Watson sees his illusions crumbling a few moments later, when his cruel friend proves that the mysterious initials stand for Charing Cross Hospital! Watson's human and entertaining mediocrity, the banality and triviality of his ideas, his modest needs, indulgent nature, lack of ambition, conventionality and love of order, make up a sort of middle-class Everyman whom it gives us a certain satisfaction to identify with our next door neighbour.

The fact that a literary biographer has found autobiographical significance in Dr. Watson is evidence of his omnipresence: 'While writing my biography of Doyle,' writes Hesketh Pearson, 'I came across the statement in his "Memories and Adventures" that he was not at all observant in the ordinary way and had to get into an artificial frame of mind before he could work out a problem. This convinced me of a conclusion I had already reached that, consciously or unconsciously he had pictured himself as Dr. Watson.'[1]

It was hardly necessary to delve into Conan Doyle's autobiography to arrive at such penetrating conclusions: was not Watson a doctor like Conan Doyle? His patients left him plenty of time to himself, and like Conan Doyle, he was fond of billiards. And finally, as narrator of the story, must he not be considered as the novelist's spokesman? One would prefer not to ask such futile questions, but one must protest against such ridiculous inferences, and literary criticism being reduced to such a puerile caricature. It is surely clear that no writer, even one with a very robust sense of humour, would deliberately try to paint his own portrait in the only character designed to make the reader smile. As for the hypothesis of unconscious identification, it is even less tenable: apart from the title of Doctor and the taste for billiards, which they share with a great many of their fellow-men, it is difficult to think of any significant traits that Watson has borrowed from his creator. John Dickson Carr suggests that a partial model for Watson may have been a certain Dr. James Watson, a colleague of Conan Doyle's at Southsea, and a fellow-member of the Portsmouth Literary and Scientific Society.[2] We know very little about him except that he presided at the farewell dinner given to Conan Doyle by the Society a few days before he and his wife left for Vienna in December 1890. But there is no mention of him in

[1] *The Sunday Times*, 17 May 1959.
[2] *The Life of Sir Arthur Conan Doyle*, pp. 62 and 82.

Conan Doyle's books or letters. Besides which, it seems to us that the use of his name is evidence against Carr's view, and that if the novelist had wanted to create even a partial portrait of his colleague and friend he would have begun by giving him a different name, as other authors do in similar cases. Another real person who has a better claim to pass as the partial model of Dr. Watson is Major Wood. Conan Doyle's son Adrian deserves the credit for this suggestion, but was careful to explain that his father never explicitly mentioned any model for Watson, and that this was his own personal impression.

> ... My father never disclosed the model for Watson [he writes]. It is my own opinion that he used Wood and I think that we have a stronger case than any other to support that supposition. Major Wood was, in common with Watson, a very clear-cut type. He was a thickset moustached Englishman, intelligent without being brilliant, reliable and a keen sportsman. Bearing in mind my father's power of character drawing coupled with my own knowledge of Major Wood, I have no doubt whatever that Wood was the matrix from which Watson was hewn. Wood was a friend of my father's in Southsea when he was first writing the original Holmes book. When my father moved to Norwood, Wood was a frequent visitor and, about 1897, became his secretary. He was working daily with my father at the time of the Edalji, Slater cases, etc., and, as I can confirm from personal knowledge, over a period of years, he was as much a foil to my father as Watson was to Holmes.[1]

The authority and, above all, the objectivity of the witness justify a brief enquiry into the Major's claims. Adrian Conan Doyle tells us that Wood became his father's secretary about 1897, and the autobiography contains a paragraph describing a meeting with him at the front during the Great War.

The text shows that Wood must have been his junior by five years: the two men may well have been old friends. Wood's powers of organisation and method are mentioned—characteristics that are desirable in a good officer, and even more in a good secretary. They are also those Holmes expected to find in his chronicler: and there is a letter written to Conan Doyle in 1910 from James Ryan, one of his oldest and most intimate friends, which refers to Wood in terms entirely supporting Adrian Conan Doyle's evidence: 'As for Wood, I love to think of that genial personality—no edges on it.'[2]

[1] Letter to Pierre Nordon, 15 February 1957.
[2] 3 November 1910 (C.D.B.A.).

The resemblance between Watson and Wood becomes even more striking if we compare a photograph of the Major in uniform with the brief description of Watson at the end of *Charles Augustus Milverton*: 'He was a middle-sized, strongly built man—square jaw, thick neck, moustache.' To complete the comparison there are frequent reminders of Watson's military career in the Holmes cycle, as well as the little idiosyncrasies he acquired during it: 'It's easy to tell that you've been accustomed to wear a uniform, Watson; you'll never pass as a pure-bred civilian as long as you keep that habit of carrying your handkerchief in your sleeve.'[1]

Without amounting to absolute confirmation, these similarities strengthen a perfectly tenable hypothesis. It seems also that in the stories published after 1900, that is to say after Major Wood became Sir Arthur's secretary, Watson's character gains in dignity. Up till then he was mainly the narrator of Sherlock's exploits. Afterwards he began to take a more active part as his collaborator. This emerges very clearly from a reading of *The Hound of the Baskervilles* (1901), *Charles Augustus Milverton* (1904) and *The Disappearance of Lady Frances Carfax* (1911). When Wood became Sir Arthur's assistant, Watson was promoted.

Since Major Wood may have been the original for Watson, it is natural for us to wonder whether Holmes's character does not owe something to Sir Arthur's. We know that the novelist was always curiously reserved about his most popular works. Why was this? Conan Doyle was both a democrat and an aristocrat. The democrat appears in his confidence that his fellow-citizens would use their votes wisely and fairly; it explains the part he took in public affairs, his statements to the press, his defence of the oppressed, his efforts on behalf of sport, important national and humanitarian causes and spiritualism. His life and career show an increasingly firm and effective determination to devote himself to the public good and safety. But Conan Doyle was very far from being 'the man in the street', and whether this is a fault or a virtue, it explains some of his failures. As an aristocrat, his warm attachment to the past cannot plead the alibi of egoism; it does not arise from submissive respect for tradition nor cover any form of vanity. The causal connections Conan Doyle traced in the sequence of events, the genetic or genealogical standards he applied in his judgements of men, the significance history had for

---

[1] HOL. II, p. 439.

him, the spiritual values he invoked—these are the mental categories of a man for whom tradition was the definition of life itself. This was why he was more surprised than anyone at Sherlock Holmes's success. He could not understand the reason for it, and in spite of his pleasure at finding himself rich and famous, it went on worrying him. Hoping to win literary fame by his historical novels, he had gained it instead by a popular work, written with his left hand as it were. The ease of his success also inclined him to under-estimate the value of the work that had achieved it. He began at once to feel that this success was at cross-purposes with his ambitions and would distract attention from work that was in an infinitely more serious and ambitious tradition. He alone could feel the full irony and ambiguity of the fact that he was known as 'the creator of Sherlock Holmes'. This was why he killed off Holmes so light-heartedly; and when he came to resurrect him, his letters show that he did so with 'all passion spent', like Milton's Samson.

This indifference was not the mood of a moment. Twenty years later, he wrote as follows to Vincent Starrett, Holmes's first 'biographer':

> Dear Mr. Vincent Starrett,
> It was really very kind of you to write so heartily about Holmes. My own feelings towards him are rather mixed, for I feel that he has obscured a good deal of my more serious work, but that no doubt will right itself in time—or if not, it does not really matter.[1]

This attitude explains why, apart from paying homage to Dr. Bell's influence, Conan Doyle was always extremely discreet about everything that might reveal his own face behind the mask of Holmes. Of course Sherlock Holmes was never intended to be a self-portrait; of course, too, Conan Doyle's reservations about his detective only applied to his interference with his more serious literary ambitions; but it is entirely untrue to say that he 'hated' Sherlock Holmes.

Quite the reverse: the evidence of kinship was far too plain for there to be the smallest doubts about his true feelings for his problem child. Holmes has not Conan Doyle's build nor his features, but like him he is tall and immensely strong. The man who tackles the formidable harpooner in *Black Peter* and disarms his enemies with his bare hands is as tough as we imagine his creator was when he sailed on the *Hope*. Like Conan Doyle, Holmes has robust health;

[1] 1918, unpublished. (Copy in C.D.B.A.)

Watson talks of his 'iron constitution'. Sherlock speaks of 'the good old British sport of boxing', and Conan Doyle of 'the noble old English sport of boxing' and 'the finest single man sport'.[1]

In *The Sign of Four* an ex-professional boxer regrets that Holmes did not take up boxing more seriously. Conan Doyle tells us in his autobiography: 'As I was just over six feet high, and was forty three round the chest, weighing over 16 stone in the buff, I was well qualified for the heavy-weight division, and I came of that brown-haired, grey-eyed stock which George Borrow declares to be apt at the game.'[2]

We know that he sang the praises of boxing in *Rodney Stone* and had tasted its pleasures. Nothing could have been more acceptable therefore than an invitation to go to the United States and judge the world heavy-weight championship. Like Conan Doyle, Holmes was reluctant to display his physical strength without due cause; when he did so it was to show his disapproval of some particularly disgraceful act. Sherlock Holmes thrashing Windibank in *A Case of Identity* is the young Conan Doyle, recently arrived at Portsmouth, forgetting his dignity as a doctor to rush to the help of beauty in distress:

> On the very first night, with that curious faculty for running into dramatic situations which has always been with me, I became involved in a street fight with a rough who was beating (or rather kicking) a woman. It was a strange start, and after I began my practice one of the first people to whom I opened my door was this very rascal. I don't suppose he recognized me, but I could have sworn to him. I emerged from the fray without much damage, and was very glad to escape some serious scandal. It was the second time that I had got knocked about in defence of beauty in distress.[3]

He is also the septuagenarian enraged by the outrageous accusations of a stranger: 'Even at the age of 70, my father sallied out in a capital city of the Empire with the express purpose of thrashing with his favourite umbrella the rascal who had publicly stated that he was making psychic propaganda from the death of his eldest son.'[4]

And at a more frivolous level, Holmes reflects Sir Arthur's taste for certain delicious dishes or his fondness for mystification and disguises. As G. Brend points out:

> We know that Holmes could never resist a disguise. At different times we find him masquerading as a plumber with a rising business

[1] AUT., pp. 316 and 321.   [2] *Ibid.*, p. 316.
[3] *Ibid.*, p. 76.   [4] Adrian Conan Doyle, *The True Conan Doyle*, p. 15.

(*Charles Augustus Milverton*), a loafer (*The Beryl Coronet*), an old salt (*The Sign of Four*), a drunken groom (*Scandal in Bohemia*), an opium addict (*The Man with the Twisted Lip*), a venerable Italian priest (*The Final Problem*), a crippled bookseller (*The Empty House*), an unshaven French 'ouvrier' in a blue blouse (*Lady Frances Carfax*), a workman looking for a job (*The Mazarin Stone*), and an old woman (*The Mazarin Stone*).[1]

John Dickson Carr reminds us of the practical joke Conan Doyle played on his brother-in-law, Hornung; this taste, also, we find in Holmes: ' "Too bad, Lord Cantlemere, too bad!" cried Holmes. "My old friend here will tell you that I have an impish habit of practical joking. Also that I can never resist a dramatic situation." '[2] A few years later the novelist posed for a press photographer disguised as Professor Challenger. Holmes and Conan Doyle are both indulgent towards untidiness and muddle, yet they also share a love of exactness and an extraordinary attention to detail. Holmes's meticulousness appears in his investigations, Conan Doyle's in his historical novels or the military history of the Great War.

At the opposite extreme from Holmes the boxer we find Holmes the archivist, with 'a horror of destroying documents, especially those which were connected with his past cases'.[3] In just the same way Conan Doyle accumulated notebooks, press-cuttings and albums of odds and ends, and kept a regular record of his literary output in letters or journals.

Even more significant is the similar rhythm of work in detective and writer. For two months, so Watson tells us, Holmes 'never worked less than fifteen hours a day';[4] it was the same with Conan Doyle when he was writing *The White Company* in his hermitage in the New Forest. Beside such traits which may well have formed part of Conan Doyle's image of himself, Holmes has other more profound aspects, less clearly elucidated by his creator. He is extremely prudish, and ill at ease in feminine society, which he avoids as much as possible. His attitude to money is the same as Conan Doyle's. He does not of course run away from it, but when he has it he is extremely generous. We also see him doing in the Adventures some of the things Conan Doyle did in real life. When Holmes buys a practice for his friend Watson with a distant relation as intermediary, he is

---

[1] *My Dear Holmes*, p. 114. [2] HOL. II, p. 1158.
[3] HOL. II, p. 396. [4] *The Reigate Squires*, HOL. II, p. 417.

repeating Conan Doyle's transaction with the American publisher Samuel McClure. He also reflects his creator's culture and opinions. His first name, Sherlock, may have been chosen in deference to Conan Doyle's Irish origins, for a village called Sherlockstown exists in County Kildare. As for the surname, there is little doubt that he was thinking of the American writer Oliver Wendell Holmes, of whom he wrote: 'Never have I so known and loved a man whom I had never seen.'[1]

Like Conan Doyle, Holmes knows German and quotes Goethe. He alludes to authors read by the novelist: Shakespeare, Darwin, Carlyle and above all Winwood Reade. He boasts of being an 'omnivorous reader'. In 1891 he echoes Conan Doyle's interest in the work and personality of George Meredith. Sherlock Holmes also shows signs of the traditional francophilia of the Doyle family. As great-nephew of the painter Horace Vernet, he is not interested in any painters except those of the French school, like Greuze, or in other schools of criminology than the French one represented by Bertillon. He also has some knowledge of French music, shown by his study of Roland de Lassus, as well as of the military history of France; and he knows French literature through Boileau, La Rochefoucauld and Flaubert, as well as Gaboriau. His conversation is sprinkled with French expressions. The only investigations in which we see him at work outside the British Isles take place in France and Switzerland.

His desire for the eventual union of the United Kingdom and the United States coincides with that expressed in the dedication of *The White Company*: 'To the Hope of the Future, the Reunion of The English Speaking Races This little Chronicle of our common Ancestry is inscribed.' It anticipates the exact words of Joseph Chamberlain's famous speech in 1898.

We notice another curious parallelism between Holmes and Conan Doyle. Holmes might well have taken no interest in Watson's chronicle. Nothing could be further from the truth. He attaches the greatest importance to the way in which his collaborator presents the story of their adventures and his own exploits to the reader. He has no desire to appear as the hero of a 'cloak and dagger' novel, but he insists on Watson bringing out his gifts as a logician and violinist— his artistic rather than his epic abilities. So that, like Conan Doyle, he is far from indifferent to the verdict of posterity in the light of which

[1] *Through the Magic Door*, p. 255.

his image will take shape. We see his own view of his work in the fact that Holmes begs Watson to draw the attention of readers to his 'methods' for their own instruction and enlightenment. In spite of his occasional disclaimers, Conan Doyle's literary ideas were also sometimes didactic and normative. His attitude to the Holmes stories was no exception; it is amusing to note that there was nothing apologetic about it: 'Ward, Lock & Co. wrote to ask me to write a preface for *A Study in Scarlet*,' he wrote in 1891. 'I refused. Then they wrote for leave to use a subtitle with the name of Sherlock Holmes. I refused again.' [1] Why did he refuse? He gave the answer ten years later—in the name of the dignity of literature. When he had finally agreed to write a preface for the Sherlock Holmes stories in the complete edition of his works, he began: 'So elementary a form of fiction as the detective story hardly deserves the dignity of a Preface.'

This proud statement of his literary convictions went on: 'I can well imagine that some of my critics may express some surprise that, in an edition of my works from which I have rigorously excluded all that my literary conscience rejects, I should retain stories which are cast in this primitive and conventional form.' Conan Doyle also raised the question of Holmes's influence. He admitted that it was unhealthy for the young to contemplate crime. What justification could the author find?

Aware of having realised an 'honourable' aesthetic aim, and feeling that he had done the best he could with his talents within the limits prescribed by his chosen form, he declared: 'My own feeling upon the subject is that all forms of literature, however humble, are legitimate if the writer is satisfied that he has done them to the highest of his power.'

This distinction between literary form and content is also made by Holmes, who holds that Watson's chronicle can truly be useful if it underlines the precision and practical effectiveness of his deductive methods.

Did Conan Doyle realise how much of a self-portrait he had painted in his detective? We cannot tell. But he was certainly aware of it to some extent. We first find evidence of an intentional assimilation of Sherlock Holmes to himself in *The Musgrave Ritual* (May 1893). Holmes tells Watson that when he first arrived in London he

[1] Letter to Mary Doyle, 14 October 1891 (C.D.B.A.).

took rooms in Montague Street, close to the British Museum. 'Every morning I walked from the lodgings at Montague Place', wrote Conan Doyle in his autobiography, 'and reached my consulting-room at ten.'[1]

The atmosphere of *The Musgrave Ritual* is appropriate to this note of intimacy. In the character of Reginald Musgrave, a friend of Sherlock Holmes's and curiously like him, in the allusions to the traditions of a modest but very ancient family, and also in the re-strained dignity of this fine story, we detect a confidential nostalgia. One seems to glimpse Undershaw behind the description of the Manor of Hurlstone: 'In order to reach the billiard-room I had to descend a flight of stairs, and then to cross the head of the passage which led to the library and the gun-room. . . . The corridors at Hurlstone have their walls largely decorated with trophies of old weapons.'[2] And the way is prepared for the announcement in *The Greek Interpreter* (September 1893): 'My ancestors were country squires, who appear to have led much the same life as is natural to their class. But, none the less, my turn that way is in my veins, and may have come with my grandmother, who was the sister of Vernet, the French artist. Art in the blood is liable to take the strangest forms.'[3]

These three short sentences are packed with significance. To begin with they identify Holmes and Conan Doyle by their common social origin. ('The penal laws became so crushing upon landed gentry that my great-grand-father was driven from his estate,' Conan Doyle was to write later on.)[4] Next they identify them through their artistic inheritance, and by allusion to the painter Vernet in particular. Vernet's name was certainly not a chance choice, for Conan Doyle knew that his work had been much admired by his uncle, Richard Doyle. So that he stands at the same time for artistic traditions, francophilia strengthened by remote French ancestry, and finally, a secret relationship between Holmes and the Doyles, whose views on painting he has taken over. Holmes's remarks also show how much he agreed with his creator about the importance of heredity, and his interest in ancient manuscripts. In *The Hound of the Baskervilles* he dates an eighteenth-century document at first glance; in *The Three Students* we learn that he is doing research on the earliest English

---

[1] AUT., p. 113.   [2] HOL. II, p. 402.
[3] *Ibid.*, p. 478.   [4] AUT., p. 13.

charters; while the introduction to *The Golden Pince-Nez* shows him absorbed in the study of a palimpsest.

He appeals to genetics to explain Professor Moriarty's 'hereditary tendencies of the most diabolical kind', and formulates a hypothesis obviously reflecting some passing train of thought of Conan Doyle's: 'I have a theory that the individual represents in his development the whole procession of his ancestors, and that such a sudden turn to good or evil stands for some strong influence which came into the line of his pedigree. The person becomes, as it were, the epitome of the history of his own family.'[1]

After the unmistakable identification between author and hero given us in *The Greek Interpreter*, Conan Doyle seems to take a mischievous delight in slipping in other clues connecting Holmes with his own life. In *The Six Napoleons* (1904) the words of gratitude expressed to Sherlock Holmes by Inspector Lestrade on behalf of Scotland Yard are modelled on a letter Conan Doyle received in 1900 from an old sailor from Peterhead called James Brown, who was writing to him, not as an author, but to wish a fellow member of the crew of the *Hope* the best of luck in South Africa. At first glance there seems little connection, but the words of Lestrade and Brown show the same warm simplicity, sincerity and kindly awkwardness; while the recipient's reactions are equally characteristic. Conan Doyle valued this touching letter for the deep emotion it expressed; Holmes, who refuses the knighthood which Conan Doyle finally accepted, gives way to emotions which greatly surprise Watson.

Among other similarities, may be mentioned their interest in the Cornish language, the choice of 'Altamont' as a pseudonym,[2] and a taste for Turkish baths. Except for the passage about Anglo-Saxon unity referred to above, Conan Doyle preferred not to make systematic use of Sherlock Holmes as a mouthpiece, and uses less important characters whenever he wants to express an opinion he has much at heart. Lady Brackenstall and Dr. Sterndale[3] reflect his ideas about the need for divorce law reform. Von Bork's companion, Baron Von Herling, justifies his fears about Irish terrorism and the suffragette agitation: 'How then can England come in, especially when we have stirred her up such a devil's brew of Irish civil war,

---

[1] HOL. II, p. 580.
[2] *His Last Bow.* Altamont was the second name of Conan Doyle's father.
[3] *The Abbey Grange* and *The Devil's Foot.*

window-breaking Furies, and God knows what to keep her thoughts at home?'[1]

Von Herling also acts as spokesman for Conan Doyle by antiphrasis when he says: 'We live in a utilitarian age. Honour is a medieval conception.'[2]

The remarks Holmes makes about Germany, after he has captured Von Bork, seem to apply less to himself than to Conan Doyle; they remind us what a long time he spent in that country, and of the warnings he addressed to his fellow-countrymen in the years before the outbreak of the First World War.

Nor shall we be surprised to find Holmes indistinctly echoing certain of Conan Doyle's religious and ethical views. At the end of *The Cardboard Box* he poses the problem of evil in terms which imply the novelist's fundamental optimism: 'What object is served by this circle of misery, of violence and fear? It must tend to some end, or else our Universe is ruled by chance, which is unthinkable. But what end?'[3] A rationalist perhaps, but obsessed with the need to prove the existence of God, he takes refuge in arguments unworthy of a scientific mind. For Holmes, flowers are the supreme evidence of the existence of a divine Providence. The scent and colour of a rose, he says in fact, are both unnecessary, they benefit neither the flower nor the universal order. Here is proof of the goodness of Providence. An argument more reminiscent of Bernardin de Saint-Pierre than Descartes, and which confirms our belief that, like his creator, the detective is at heart less the logician he pretends to be than an artist given to moral speculation. In spite of his denunciation of utilitarianism, he cannot make up his mind to accept the senselessness of war, and sees it as a means used by Providence, a test imposed on us by fate: 'There's an east wind coming all the same, such a wind as never blew on England yet. It will be cold and bitter, Watson, and a good many of us may wither before its blast. But it's God's own wind none the less, and a cleaner, better, stronger land will lie in the sunshine when the storm has cleared.'[4]

Even in the final stories, Holmes shows that he believes in the beneficence of the laws of nature, that there will be compensations in the next world, and that the human condition would be insignificant and unbearable if God did not exist.

---

[1] *His Last Bow*, HOL. II, p. 1072. [2] *Ibid.*, p. 1071.
[3] HOL. II, p. 946. [4] *His Last Bow*, HOL. II, p. 1086.

The authenticity of Sherlock Holmes as a human being does not therefore depend upon this or that subsidiary characteristic, gratuitously invented by his creator—like his violin or his hypodermic syringe. Conan Doyle was not a musician, nor did he take laudanum or cocaine; and it would never have occurred to him to describe himself as 'the best and the wisest man', as Watson describes Holmes in his obituary tribute in *The Final Problem*. But in the deepest fibres of his being, his dominant ideas, Holmes is certainly fashioned in Conan Doyle's image. His achievement consists not so much in solving the mystery of appearances as in defending the innocent—we think of the Edalji affair; in righting wrongs—and we think of Slater, the Congo, Divorce reform, Casement; in giving a new value to his creator's ideas of chivalry—and we think of *Sir Nigel* and *The White Company*. In the Adventures, Sherlock Holmes is fighting a spiritual campaign designed to startle consciences and hearts, just as Conan Doyle did in his life. Because he is like Conan Doyle, because he is Conan Doyle, Sherlock Holmes is much more than a portrait: he is one of the last incarnations of chivalry in the literature of the English language.

Chapter 16

THE HISTORICAL NOVELS: MICAH CLARKE

A certain contradiction is apparent in Conan Doyle's judgements of his own work. He owed his fame essentially to the Sherlock Holmes cycle, but subscribing as he did to traditional literary values this fame gave him only slight pleasure. His sense of hierarchy intervened in his literary judgements, and all the more vigorously because it was backed up by the artistic and social traditions of the Doyle family. Two generations of his ancestors had devoted their lives to art. Although their work was anything but academic, the pressure of their period and the world in which they lived had induced some degree of conformism. Mid-nineteenth-century England was a period when power, fashionable society and the artistic élite mingled freely—in the persons of Disraeli, Macaulay and Tennyson for example. The traditions of the Doyle family tended in two directions towards dogmatic religion and art, and although Conan Doyle broke loose from them on the religious plane, he remained faithful to their esteem for the arts, in which his mother as well as his uncle Michael Conan had shared. His respect for tradition thus bound him more closely to the generation of 1850, or even 1820, than to that of 1880.

The preferences of the generation of 1850 were for prose and the novel, and the historical novels in particular. The names mentioned at the Doyle dining-table—with admiration unaffected by personal knowledge of the writers in question—were Bulwer Lytton, Thackeray, Macaulay and Walter Scott. In 1880 these writers were still influencing the work of novelists and historians, although their conception of the historical novel did not correspond with the changes that had taken place in social life or find an echo in current ideology. Throughout the eighteenth century and a large part of the nineteenth, the middle-classes had reigned supreme. But the ideology of the middle-classes was an essentially 'national' one, in the sense that Napoleon said that he was and wished to be 'national'; it was not only that the interests of the entire country were identified with those of the middle-classes, but also that there was an implicit solidarity between the social classes, a tendency to exalt community of ideals, liberal principles, and political and religious institutions founded on the voice of the people. But about 1880 a new ideology was formed, independent of Marxism but not of the economic and social evolution Marxism described. 1884, the date when the Fabian Society was founded, is a landmark: this was the moment when the English intelligentsia became involved in the Labour movement. The new ideology tended to stress conflict between the classes, because it was based on an analysis of their different interests. We soon begin to see traces of this influence in the work of novelists whose outlook might have drawn them to the historical novel, but who confined their works to the doings of a single social class instead. The names of Wells, Galsworthy and Arnold Bennett spring immediately to mind.

Anchored as he was to a respectable but old-fashioned literary tradition, Conan Doyle did not feel any need for a change in the school of historical novel writing founded by Walter Scott. This is only another aspect of his neo-Conservatism, and his later development made his inability to adapt himself to his age even more obvious. His contribution to Scott's tradition was not a matter of kind but of degree: he himself preferred to show originality as a disciple than to be an innovator. Nor is there any essential division between the ideology and aesthetics of Conan Doyle's historical novels and those of the Holmes stories, in spite of differences of genres and values. In the historical novels we again find the aesthetics of the theatre, and action that is essentially episodic and cinematic, so to speak. We also find the same angle of incidence, the same cross-section through the different social classes existing at a given period in the history of the country, the same careful identification of the characters and their respective categories, the same apologia for the solidarity between the different members of society.

1859, the year in which Conan Doyle was born, ended with the death of Macaulay. We cannot be sure that Conan Doyle was indifferent to this double anniversary. What is certain is that his vocation as a serious novelist owed much to the impressions engraved on his mind by his literary pilgrimages during adolescence:

> I can remember that when I visited London at the age of sixteen the first thing I did after housing my luggage was to make a pilgrimage to Macaulay's grave where he lies in Westminster Abbey, just under the

shadow of Addison, and amid the dust of the poets whom he had loved so well. It was the one great object of interest which London held for me. And so it might well be, when I think of all I owe him. It is not merely the knowledge and the stimulation of fresh interests, but it is the charming, gentlemanly tone, the broad, liberal outlook, the general absence of bigotry and of prejudice. My judgement now confirms all that I felt for him then.[1]

While with his left hand he somewhat casually created the immortal Sherlock Holmes, his right hand was lovingly engaged on work more in keeping with his sincerest literary ambitions. 'I wish Macaulay had written a historical novel,' he was to write later on.[2] *Micah Clarke* raised a preliminary echo of this nostalgic reflection. Without losing his own identity, Conan Doyle virtually modelled himself on the brilliant historian of the English Revolution, even adopting Macaulay's view of the events in his history. This was the longest of all the historical novels. It was published in February 1889, although he had finished writing it in 1887. But as one of his letters show, he devoted two years to a study of the subject, and the project itself must have been conceived in 1885 or even earlier. As he wrote to the mother of his friend James Ryan: 'I don't know whether *Micah Clarke* happened to drift your way. He has only been out two months and the first English edition is exhausted. I believe the American edition is selling well also—, so, though I may make very little pecuniarily it may possibly make a literary opening for me. I wrote the book in about five months, but it took me about two years to collect my materials.'[3]

Micah Clarke enjoyed an immediate and prolonged success. The second edition followed only a few days after the first; the third appeared in May and the fourth in August. The next four years saw the publication of three, one, one and three more reprints respectively.

The character who gives his name to the novel is both hero and narrator; but in the interests of historical truth Conan Doyle has explained in a long sub-title written in archaic style that the book is less an historical novel than a statement in fictional form:

> *Micah Clarke*, His Statement, As made to his three grandchildren Joseph, Gervais, Reuben, During the hard winter of 1734 Wherein is contained A full report of certain passages in his early life, Together with some account of his journey from Havant to Taunton with Decimus Saxon in the summer Of 1685. Also of the adventure that

---

[1] *Through the Magic Door*, p. 11.   [2] *Ibid.*, p. 9.   [3] N.d., *circa* 1889.

befell them During the western rebellion & of their intercourse With James Duke of Monmouth, Lord Grey and other persons of quality. Compiled day by day, from his own narration by Joseph Clarke & never previously set forth in print, Now for the first time collected, corrected & re-Arranged from the original manuscripts By A. Conan Doyle.

In spite of this precaution many readers compared it to *Lorna Doone*, which was still very popular and was also set against a background of Monmouth's rebellion. But whereas in Blackmore's novel the historic setting is a mere pretext for a romantic plot, the reverse is true of *Micah Clarke*, which consists of episodes, some based on tradition, others invented by Conan Doyle, strung together on the thread of the historical narrative. It has the charm of a chronicle rather than of a novel. The climax is reached with the battle of Sedgemoor, and perhaps we may recognise some idea of commemoration in the coincidence between the dates 1685 and 1885. It was written entirely at Southsea, and combines local history with that of Monmouth's partisans. Micah Clarke was not a native of the West of England but of Havant, a Hampshire village four or five miles from Portsmouth. For his historical background Conan Doyle went to Macaulay:

> I now determined to test my powers to the full, and I chose a historical novel for this end, because it seemed to me the one way of combining a certain amount of literary dignity with those scenes of action and adventure which were natural to my young and ardent mind. I had always felt great sympathy for the Puritans, who, after all, whatever their little peculiarities, did represent political liberty and earnestness in religion. They had usually been caricatured in fiction and art. Even Scott had not drawn them as they were. Macaulay, always one of my chief inspirations, had alone made them comprehensible—the sombre fighters, with their Bibles and their broad-swords.[1]

The book falls into six different sections. The first (chapters 1 to 7) is a long introduction describing Micah's childhood. He tells us about the short time he spent at a private school in Petersfield; about his friends (Reuben Lockarby who joined Monmouth's army with him; the carpenter Zachary Palmer, who was fond of philosophical and theological speculation; and Solomon Sprent, the sailor), about his parents and above all about his father, Joseph Clarke the tanner, a veteran of Cromwell's army and ex-standard-bearer to his regiment.

[1] AUT., p. 91.

Micah and Reuben pick up a strange shipwrecked man off the Isle of
Wight and bring him back to the village. He is a soldier of fortune,
Decimus Saxon, who has come from Holland charged by the con-
spirator Richard Rumbold with the mission of getting in touch with
some of Monmouth's supporters. Saxon's message is in fact for
Joseph Clarke himself, and the tanner asks his son to take his place
and go with Saxon to Somerset, where Monmouth has already set up
the standard of revolution. We therefore take the Taunton road with
Micah, and the second part of the book (chapters 8 to 16) has sur-
prises of many different kinds in store for us. Fortunate and unfortunate meetings, brawls and quarrels in inns, battles, pursuits, all
give the novel a typically picaresque charm. Two individuals who
could hardly be more different from each other join Micah and his
companion. One is a fanatically zealous preacher, the other, Sir
Gervas Jerome, is an eccentric courtier caught up in events he does
not understand. The third part (chapters 17 to 22) deals with the
history of the town of Taunton, and describes the preparations made
by Monmouth's supporters and his triumphant arrival. A romance
springs up between Reuben and the daughter of the mayor of the
town, Master Stephen Timewell. During a dinner given in honour of
Saxon and Micah, Timewell tells the story of his misfortunes on a
recent visit to London. The fourth part (chapters 23 to 26) is entirely
devoted to a subsidiary episode. Micah, who has quickly gained
Monmouth's confidence, is entrusted by him with an especially
delicate mission. He is to go and sound the intentions of the Duke of
Beaufort, President of Wales. Micah travels from Taunton to Bad-
minton, not far from Bristol, is captured by smugglers on the way, but
released again. He is very badly received by Beaufort, who throws
him into a dungeon, but as soon as night falls the duke comes and
sets his prisoner at liberty and gives him an extremely ambiguous
reply to take back to Monmouth. With the fifth part (chapters 27 to
32) we are back in the insurgents' camp, and witness the beginning of
military operations between Bristol and Bridgwater as well as acts of
vandalism by fanatical iconoclasts in Wells Cathedral. We meet a
picturesque highwayman, who in his turn relates some of his adventures. Then at last comes the battle of Sedgemoor, the defeat of the
rebels and flight of their leader. The epilogue (chapters 33 to 36)
describes Micah's tribulations and his capture by Kirke's soldiers.
He gets a summary trial from the sinister Judge Jeffreys, is declared

an outlaw and condemned to be sold as a slave to the West Indies. But at the last moment his friend Decimus Saxon procures his release. Until happier times make it possible for him to return home, he decides to go and seek his fortune as a soldier in Europe.

It is easy to see how much Conan Doyle borrowed from Macaulay. Chapter 3 of the *History of England*—one of the novelist's favourites —not only provided him with the facts from which he built up his historical picture, but also the idea for the story told by Timewell, whose unfortunate adventures in London bring out with considerable humour the gulf dividing the political capital of the kingdom from the jolly life of rural England. As for the account of the rebellion itself, it is based on Macaulay's fifth chapter. But Conan Doyle deviates from his source in three places for the purposes of the plot. The historian tells us that, on the eve of the battle of Sedgemoor, a young girl who was devoted to the royalist cause left Bridgwater and informed the loyalist army that Monmouth was preparing to attack them.

Conan Doyle has modified this incident rather curiously, so as to get rid of one of his minor characters, the unglamorous John Derrick. He is made to take the place of Macaulay's young girl, and Conan Doyle explains his treachery by his desire to get his own back for a disappointment in love. More serious from the point of view of historical accuracy are the changes he has made in the character of Henry Somerset, Duke of Beaufort. Like Macaulay, Conan Doyle stresses the feudal power of this great nobleman, and enjoys describing his magnificent way of life. Macaulay leaves us in no doubt as to Beaufort's loyalty to James II. ('He would see Bristol burned down, he said, nay he would burn it down himself, rather than it should be occupied by traitors.') Conan Doyle, on the contrary, depicts him as a double-dealer, giving pledges to both sides and waiting to see which is successful in battle. The reasons for the transformation are plain. Having placed his hero in an impossible situation in the fourth part of the book, Conan Doyle has the idea of making the Duke of Beaufort the *deus ex machina* who will arrange matters. In the final phase of the story Beaufort is again made to play a convenient part, when his own duplicity obliges him to give Saxon the necessary sum of money to liberate Micah, whether he likes it or not. Finally, so as to justify the presence of his hero in the rebel's camp, Conan Doyle has brought up the question of Monmouth's legitimacy. Macaulay is categorical on this point: 'That Monmouth was legitimate, nay, that he thought himself legitimate, intelligent men could not believe. He was therefore not merely an usurper, but an usurper of the worst sort, an impostor.' Yet Conan Doyle several times suggests, both in the course of the narrative and in the epilogue, that Monmouth may perhaps have possessed evidence in writing of a marriage between his father, Charles II, and his mother, Lucy Walters.

In spite of the density of the historical narration and the realism conveyed by its colour and contrast—Conan Doyle here shows himself an excellent pupil of Defoe's—some of the episodes, particularly in the fourth part of *Micah Clarke*, have a 'cloak and dagger' flavour. The necessity for this part is not very clear, for it is in fact a long digression. The most memorable scene of this huge canvas is without doubt the battle of Sedgemoor. Conan Doyle has here made good use of detailed topographical and military exactness and truly remarkable descriptive virtuosity. His instinctive eye for picturesque detail, and his gift for dialogue, give the narrator's story all possible realism, without sacrificing the vision of the whole which enables us to grasp the movements of armies and the different stages of the conflict. His incidents are always vivid and have an air of complete authenticity. Against the background of this sometimes exact and sometimes romantic page of national history, Conan Doyle has created several characters in whom the artistic purpose of the novel is realised and justified. 'To me it always seems,' he writes in his preface, 'that the actual condition of a country at any time, a true sight of it with its beauties and its brutalities, its life as it really was, its wayside hazards, and its odd possibilities are of greater interest than the small aims and petty love story of any single human being. The lists, the woodlands, and the outlaws are more to me than Rebecca and Rowena.'

His picture of the 'actual condition' of England begins in the very first pages with his vigorous portrait of Joseph Clarke; and the story of his youth allows us to make a necessary journey into the past, which broadens the scope of the narrative and grips the reader's imagination: 'I can well believe what I have heard, that when he chanted the Hundredth Psalm as he rode down among the blue-bonnets at Dunbar the sound of the hymn rose above the blare of trumpets and the crash of guns, like the deep roll of a breaking wave.'[1]

[1] HIS., p. 790.

It is with touches of this sort that Conan Doyle brings a character or an epoch to life. And a certain number of other typical scenes help to recreate the atmosphere of a very different world, without a single false note—for instance when Joseph, in a state of ecstasy, tells his family to be ready to receive a heavenly visitor. Beside this militant Puritan, we have an example of one of the pedantically theoretical variety in the preacher Pettigrue. Micah Clarke's latitudinarian sympathies—or else those of Conan Doyle himself—are shown here in a preference for action rather than words. Joseph Clarke's biblical style of speech has convincing human warmth and power to communicate; whereas the preacher's cant leaves an impression of artificial and ridiculous aridity: 'I am an unworthy worker in the Lord's vineyard, testifying with voice and with arm to His holy covenant. These are my faithful flock, whom I am bringing westward that they may be ready for the reaping when it pleases the Almighty to gather them in.'

The martial Decimus Saxon, for his part, belongs to no clan and no class. He is nevertheless very much alive. An exuberant, unscrupulous rake, recognising no master but himself, he is instinct with the need to act and to fight, and expresses decisive opinions on every subject—whether the art of warfare, the fair sex or literature. He seems to know *Hudibras* almost by heart and quotes it on every occasion, making some of his companions rather uneasy. But on the battlefield his ardour is a match for theirs. His zealous independence, cynical opportunism and indifference to religion (did he not become a Moslem when he was in the East?) link him with the eighteenth century, and one can see him as the contemporary of some of Defoe's characters, or perhaps of Smollett's. Sir Gervas Jerome is also a representative of a new age, although he belongs to a restricted and short-lived class. Conan Doyle has modelled him on the character of Fashion in Vanbrugh's comedy *The Relapse* (1696). As for the London atmosphere which floats in Sir Gervas's wake, it has been taken from John Ashton's *Social Life in the Reign of Queen Anne* (1883).

The unexpected appearance of this fop in the ranks of Monmouth's army naturally leads to comic situations which Conan Doyle brilliantly exploits. Jerome's urban way of life, his extravagances and his mistakes, add a touch of fantasy to an otherwise serious group of characters. Whether it is Sir Gervas's kinship with Beau Didapper in *Joseph Andrews*, or the picaresque element, or the sharp contrast between fashionable town life and the rural world, or the specifically dramatic humour of certain passages, this novel takes us straight back to Fielding. If Sir Gervas introduces us to the tribulations of a courtier in the country, Stephen Timewell, mayor of Taunton, makes us share in the disappointments of a provincial in London and at court. In these two creations Conan Doyle has given free rein to his verve and humour, and forgotten Macaulay for a while . . . But as soon as he begins to describe historical characters for us, how much less freely he writes! It is not so much that his portrait of Monmouth conforms docilely to tradition, as that his narrator, Micah Clarke, seems to parody Macaulay's manner and style.

In the same way, in the latter part of the book, Conan Doyle portrays Judge Jeffreys as if he were adapting his character for the stage, and putting historical fact into dialogue. If the result is defensible on the grounds of historical accuracy, it is less so in its effect on the aesthetic unity of the novel, for the macabre scenes of the 'Bloody Assizes' distract our attention from the hero's fate. We get the impression that Conan Doyle has stopped taking Micah Clarke seriously, and the too artificial *dénouement* does not help to dispel this impression. Jeffreys becomes a sort of stage devil, whose 'asides' add to the melodramatic unreality of the scene.

Among the minor figures taking part in the picaresque episodes, one of the happiest creations is Hector Marot, the highwayman. His brief appearance serves as pretext for an anecdote whose delicate humour reminds us of Richard Doyle's drawings. One fine morning, when he was in search of adventures, Marot caught sight of three farmers, energetically pursuing a harmless little rabbit. He joined them at once: 'Away went my gentlemen, whooping like madmen, with their coat-skirts flapping in the breeze, driving the dogs, and having a rare morning's sport.'[1] He caught up with them just as they had triumphed over their wretched adversary: 'With that I lugged out my persuaders, and made the thing clear in a few words, and I'll warrant you would have laughed could you have seen their faces as they slowly dragged the fat leather purses from their fobs. £71 was my prize that morning, which was better worth riding for than a hare's ears.'[2]

Here and elsewhere, the digressions, inn scenes and chance meetings are in tune with the spirit of the period and world Conan Doyle had set himself to bring to life. It is not surprising to find a certain

[1] HIS., p. 1157.   [2] *Ibid.*, p. 1158.

number of enigmatic and disturbing characters in *Micah Clarke*, as we do in Fielding's novels. The old woman keeping watch beside a gibbet, who is taken for a witch by the travellers, is there to remind us (as the author does in his preface) that although old England was in process of disappearing, she had not quite disappeared. The digression contained in the second part, when the travellers stop with Sir Jacob Clancing at Snellaby Hall, has several things in common with the episode of the Man of the Hill in *Tom Jones*. It will be remembered that he tells Jones and Partridge the story of his adventures during Monmouth's rebellion, and how he fought at Sedgemoor and was taken prisoner by James II's army. But the similarity to Fielding is not merely a question of subject. Both storytellers are disappointed men. In both Conan Doyle and Fielding we find the same curious discord between this fact and the generally optimistic tone of the narrative, with the same gratuitously absurd effect. Through the old sailor, Solomon Sprent, Conan Doyle varies the description of the village of Havant and its inhabitants by introducing images of life at sea. Having made up his mind to settle down and choose a wife, Solomon, who is not at all at home in such matters, writes a proposal of marriage in technical jargon which the peasant girl will certainly never understand; once again Conan Doyle gets his best humorous effects from an ingeniously arranged comic situation. The carpenter Zachary Palmer, who also belongs to the little world of Havant, is Micah Clarke's confidant and mentor as well as his friend.

Conan Doyle has seized the chance offered by the theme of his first novel to attempt a dialogue with himself about the religious doubts which still attacked him. As the son of an independent puritan father and a conformist mother, Micah Clarke finds himself at the crossroads. While respecting his father's religious convictions, he himself chooses the least dogmatic religion possible—latitudinarianism: 'I was no keen religious zealot. Papistry, Church, Dissent, I believed that there was good in all of them, but that not one was worth the spilling of human blood.'[1]

If *Micah Clarke* can be said to contain a message, it is that since religious dissension is merely a form of civil unrest and an excuse for unleashing cruel passions, the reader of 1885 is entitled to be complaisant about the progress made since 1685. As for Conan Doyle, he adhered more closely and completely than his ancestors had done to

[1] HIS., p. 839.

his belief in progress, and found justification in it for his religious faith: Micah Clarke, like Conan Doyle, separates faith from morality and rejects the one in order to defend the other more effectively. And although Zachary Palmer is described as a venerable village philosopher, we are aware that he reflects the personality, thoughts and influence of Dr. Waller, who had once led the young novelist along the path of religious neo-positivism.

The division of the narrative into two parts prejudices the unity of Micah Clarke's character. We easily accept the frank, courageous village lad given us in the first chapter, and we are equally ready to accept him as narrator, since the energy and liveliness of his style fits in with this image. But he becomes much less convincing when he takes the tone of a professional historian. Some pages smack too much of a historical synopsis, while in others the prophetic tones of the author emerge too clearly from the text.

Thus, in spite of the undeniable power of some scenes, the varied action, and the skill with which the young novelist has made use of his characters to carry out his purpose and bring alive in all its picturesque detail the spirit and conditions of a past age, this work does not perhaps possess the necessary homogeneity to make it a truly great historical novel. It would have been better to prune away certain scenes, such as the episodes with the smugglers in the fourth part, and to modify others. Conan Doyle was aware of this, and considered making cuts, but seems never to have made up his mind to it. In January 1889 he wrote to his sister Lottie: '. . So glad you continue to like "Micah". I think it drags in places, and am inclined to cut it down in the final revise. Lang is of that opinion, and I think Mrs. Prideaux is also. However, I have asked that all the proofs should be sent down to me, when I will go over them with care . . .'[1]

The disappearance of the traitor John Derrick in the quicksands, in the thirty-first chapter, was repeated with much greater dramatic effect in the more appropriate context of *The Hound of the Baskervilles*. There is no need to study this book very long, however, to realise how much maturity and facility its author had already achieved, and his manner is entirely suitable to an historical novel of more than four hundred pages. It is curious that the book was not published in three volumes according to the fashion of the time

[1] Unpublished (C.D.B.A.).

which was adopted with *The White Company* (1891) and *The Refugees* (1893), both shorter books.

Micah Clarke is a fresco, whose detail is less important than the whole composition; its unity is not built up of chapter and sentence, but of episode and paragraph. This somewhat monumental treatment —and we shall see that it was not altogether in accord with Conan Doyle's genius—allows of great flexibility and subtlety in the narrative, and the use of a great variety of rhythms and tones. In his few, very restrained descriptions, Conan Doyle gives rein spontaneously and in the simplest manner to rhythmic, colourful prose:

> My course ran along by the foot of the beautiful Quantock Hills, where heavy-wooded coombes are scattered over the broad heathery downs, deep with bracken and whortlebushes. On either side of the track steep winding glens sloped downwards, lined with yellow gorse, which blazed out from the deep-red soil like a flame from embers. Peat-coloured streams splashed down these valleys and over the road, through which Covenant ploughed fetlock-deep, and shied to see the broad-backed trout darting from between his fore feet.[1]

The dialogue naturally plays an essential part, by allowing the characters to display themselves in the liveliest way and consistently with the images that are impressed on the reader's memory. Conan Doyle was always careful that his conversational style should be true to life, and even in his earliest books he avoided the error of which Goldsmith accused Dr. Johnson, of 'making his little fishes talk like whales'. The dialogue has an almost descriptive effect when someone like Sir Gervas, Joseph Clarke or Decimus Saxon is speaking, whereas a character like Solomon Sprent achieves deliberately comic effects by exaggeration.

Conan Doyle took the success of *Micah Clarke* as encouragement to go on writing historical novels. He was to return to the religious conflicts of the seventeenth century in *The Refugees*, an account of the tribulations of the Huguenots, the French Puritans. But before he even had the idea for this novel, he followed his own personal preferences by resolutely returning further into the past and trying to produce a historical portrait of the English bowman, as Scott had done for the English knight nearly a century earlier.

[1] HIS., p. 1053.

Chapter 17

THE NOVELS OF CHIVALRY

Like *Micah Clarke*, *The White Company* is set in Hampshire, and tells of the history of that part of England; but this time we have been carried further back into the past. Although the period of Monmouth's rebellion in his first historical novel had a picturesque variety which stimulated his imagination, it had been distressingly agitated by civil and religious troubles. In *The White Company* Conan Doyle returned to the Middle Ages, a period which appealed both to his heart and his imagination. To his heart—a story about the age of chivalry was first of all a tribute to his mother, and the legends she had told him as a child. To his imagination—although the battle of Sedgemoor had no special appeal for him, the idea of a tournament touched him much more closely. It could not fail to suggest the figure of a knight bearing a shield with three bucks' heads, the arms of Sir Foulkes d'Oyley, who fought with Richard Cœur de Lion at Acre during the Third Crusade, or of Baldwin de Oyley, mentioned by Walter Scott in *Ivanhoe*. A novel set in medieval times thus gave Conan Doyle the chance to make a pilgrimage to the springs that had nourished his childhood, the sources of family traditions; to return to the first French texts he had ever read and to certain ideals and certain visions of existence which had crystallised for him at the threshhold of maturity.

In the spring of 1889, at the end of April to be exact, Conan Doyle took a short holiday in the New Forest with three Portsmouth friends—Boulnois, General Drayson and the oculist Vernon Ford. As soon as they had found rooms in Emery Down, near Lyndhurst, they set off to explore the paths through the surrounding forest. At Castle Malwood they saw the stone commemorating the murder of William Rufus, and a little further on the ruins of the Cistercian abbey of Beaulieu. The destruction carried out under the Reformation had spared the refectory, and Conan Doyle was able to see the stone chair from which a friar used once to read to the white-clad monks as they sat at table. His imagination peopled the abandoned hive with invisible figures. Another day he adventured on the road to Christ-church, to Burley, or into the heart of the forest, to Brockenhurst and Whitley Ridge. And while he followed the paths between gnarled oaks and mossy beeches, he looked and listened, and soon began to summon up an imaginary scene from the past:

> As they advanced, the path still trended upwards, running from heath into copse of holly and yew, and so back into heath again. It was joyful to hear the merry whistle of blackbirds as they darted from one clump of greenery to the other. Now and again the peaty amber-coloured stream rippled across their way, with ferny overgrown banks, where the blue kingfisher flitted busily from side to side, or the grey and pensive heron, swollen with trout and dignity, stood ankle deep among the sedges. Chattering jays and loud wood pigeons flapped thickly overhead, while ever and anon the measured tapping of Nature's carpenter, the great green woodpecker, sounded from each wayside grove. On either side, as the path mounted, the long sweep of country broadened and expanded, sloping down on the one side through yellow forest and brown moor to the distant smoke of Lyming-ton and the blue misty channel which lay alongside the skyline, while to the north the woods rolled away, grove topping grove, to where in the farthest distance the wide spire of Salisbury stood out hard and clear against the cloudless sky.[1]

The sight of this English soil into which history had plunged its roots so deeply gave him the idea for the medieval novel he had always wanted to write. But would it not suffer cruelly by comparison with Walter Scott? This thought had long made him hesitate, and he only overcame it now that a better knowledge of his own powers had given him more self-confidence. He set to work as soon as he got back to Southsea and, in order to soak himself in the atmosphere he wanted to recreate, he covered his writing-table with books and documents.[2] At the end of the summer he visited the New Forest

---

[1] *The White Company*, HIS., p. 79.

[2] Cf. (*a*) AUT., p. 96: 'The work needed much research and I have still my notebooks full of all sorts of lore'; (*b*) Letter to Mary Doyle: 'I am still hard at work upon the middle ages, reading Commines' Chronicles and La Chronique Scandaleuse of Jean de Troyes, tho' there is nothing very scandalous therein. Also reading Lacroix's Middle Ages, a very fine French work which will be a great help to me. I hope it will all lead up to something decent'; (*c*) *The Bookman*, May 1892, pp. 50-1, Interview with Conan Doyle by Raymond Blathwayt: 'I read up no less than 150 books in preparation for that novel alone.' However Conan Doyle's notes and exercise-books show that he relied particularly for his documentation on the following works: Lacroix, P., *Mœurs, usages et coutumes, au Moyen-âge et à la Renaissance* (Paris, 1871); *Vie militaire et Vie religieuse au Moyen-âge* (Paris, 1872); Jusserand, J.-J., *Les Anglais au Moyen-âge: la Vie nomade et les Routes d'Angleterre au XIVe Siècle* (Paris, 1884); Strutt, J., *Sports and*

again, alone this time, and worked at his book in the very place whose ancient splendour he was trying to revive. Thus the new novel was begun in circumstances suitable to its special significance and scope. And an incident which occurred when the manuscript was finished is worth recording; it shows how deeply and intensely Conan Doyle had entered into this literary adventure: 'I remember that as I wrote the last words of *The White Company* I felt a wave of exultation and with a cry of "That's done it" I hurled my inky pen across the room, where it left a black smudge upon the duck's egg wallpaper. I knew in my heart that the book would live and that it would illuminate our national traditions.'[1]

This new venture gave him greater latitude as a writer; the problem of historical accuracy was less stringent than in *Micah Clarke*, where the historical events were strictly determined and most readers better informed about them. Here, on the contrary, there was no need for the narrative to be chronologically exact. But Conan Doyle did not take advantage of this to superimpose a romantic plot in the style of Walter Scott on historical foundations. He was probably thinking of this sort of plot when he said that a plot in an historical novel was an insult. The relationship between young Alleyne Edricson and the beautiful Maude, daughter of Sir Nigel Loring, hardly deserves the name: it is merely a necessary concession to romance and nothing could be simpler nor more restrained. As for the purely historical part of the narrative, although it contains an arbitrary number of scenes and episodes, it is free from those digressions which sometimes slow down the movement of *Micah Clarke*. In a more harmonious composition, great care has been given to creating a picture of the manners and daily life of the fourteenth century, yet there is less didactic emphasis. When Conan Doyle had completed his task, he declared this novel to be technically superior to the last, although some of the arguments with which he supported this view in a letter to his sister Lottie, in July 1890, are not entirely convincing:

Dearest Girl,
    You will be pleased, I am sure, to know that I have finished my great labour, and that *The White Company* has come to an end. The first half is very good, the next quarter pretty good, the last quarter

Pastimes of the People of England, 1801; Longman, W., *The Life and Times of Edward III*, 3 vols., 1869.
    [1] AUT., p. 96.

very good again, and it ends with the true heroic note. It is better than *Micah Clarke* for many reasons: (1) because it is in the third person; (2) because it has female interest; (3) because it makes the middle ages interesting, which has very seldom been done before; (4) because the characters are more varied and stronger; (5) because the scene is broader, England, France and Spain; (6) because it deals with the main current of national life, the wars with France and Spain— instead of a mere side issue like Monmouth's affair. So rejoice with me, dear, for I am as fond of Hordle John, and Samkin Aylward and Sir Nigel Loring, as though I knew them in the flesh, and I feel that the whole English speaking race will come in time to be so also. It will be a big hit, I trust and hope . . .[1]

The plot is very simple, and falls into three successive episodes: the formation and departure of The White Company, their crossing and arrival in France, and, finally, fighting on both sides of the Pyrenees. The book opens in the monastery of Beaulieu, whose peaceful hard-working atmosphere is soon disturbed by the expulsion of a novice called Hordle John. This hefty fellow, with his bantering, undisciplined ways, has quickly exhausted the monks' patience by his escapades and his scorn for the rules of the community. At the same time another inmate of the monastery, Alleyne Edricson, is planning to get back the ancestral manor of Minstead from his eldest brother, as soon as he has finished his studies. A few hours later these two very dissimilar men get to know each other better at the inn. They mingle with a large and noisy crowd there. The beginnings of a quarrel are nipped in the bud by the intervention of Sam Aylward, an archer just back from France with valuable booty and even more valuable memories. He dreams only of returning to the scene of his adventures and has very little trouble in persuading Hordle John to go with him. Alleyne arrives at Minstead, has a violent quarrel with his brother, and rejoins his new friends at the manor of Sir Nigel Loring at Christchurch. Sir Nigel commands the White Company, and happens to be looking for a new squire. Alleyne joins him. During preparations for departure the young man spends several weeks as tutor to the beautiful Maude Loring, whom his brother has recently been pestering with his attentions. The delay lasts long enough for the two young people to exchange vows of fidelity; the White Company's expedition will give Alleyne the chance to prove himself worthy of his beloved. The second and third parts of the book are devoted to the

[1] Unpublished (C.D.B.A.).

adventures of the Company, particularly of the four chief characters. Four main episodes can be distinguished: a naval engagement with two pirate ships; a passage of arms at Bordeaux, at which Duguesclin is present; the siege of the château of Villefranche-du-Périgord during a peasant rising; and lastly a murderous battle in the Spanish Pyrenees between the pass of Roncevaux and Pamplona. The different aspects of war at this period are boldly brought to life. As for secondary incidents it is impossible to enumerate them, and also the countless lively minor characters who people the scene. It is clear that Conan Doyle wanted to give the reader as vast and faithful a retrospect of the medieval world as possible. He has succeeded perfectly, not by presenting us with a historian's chronicle of events, but by making us witnesses of warm, living reality. And although much thought and careful documentation has evidently gone to the creation of the characters, although they are essentially mere types, Conan Doyle's creative imagination has succeeded in bringing them convincingly to life. Nor has he sacrificed their individuality to that of the usual historical personages.

It is left to the latter to show us the world of chivalry from within, coloured by the refraction of their different personalities. The Black Prince, Duguesclin, Chandos and Pedro of Castille none of them occupy the front of the stage, and seem—as they probably were—the natural emanation of the communities that produced them. And we see, circulating among them, a cheerful crowd of students and soldiers of fortune, artisans, brigands, monks, peasants, colporteurs, innkeepers, sailors, pilgrims, sellers of indulgences or holy relics. Conan Doyle views this fourteenth-century world from the same angle he has used elsewhere. It is also the viewpoint of Scott and Charles Reade. And his curiosity about the past has a seriousness and a verdant freshness that takes us straight back to Chaucer. Conan Doyle has seen with the eyes of a fourteenth-century poet, and it is not irrelevant that Chaucer's description of Sir Topaz putting on his armour was found among his notes for the book. The irreverence of his allusion to Chaucer in *The White Company* would certainly have enchanted the poet:

'It is well to have a learned clerk in every troop,' said Sir Nigel. 'By Saint Paul! there are men so caitiff that they think more of a scrivener's pen than of their lady's smile, and do their devoir in hopes that they may fill a line in a chronicle or make a tag to a jongleur's romance.

I remember well that, at the siege of Retters, there was a little, sleek, fat clerk of the name of Chaucer, who was so apt at rondel, sirvente, or tonson, that no man dare give back a foot from the walls, lest he find it all set down in his rhymes and sung by every underling and varlet in the camp.'[1]

The direct, concise, vivacious style of this novel has much in common with the spirit of the medieval story-teller. Among the lesser characters, Sir Oliver Buttesthorn, the greedy knight, is an entirely characteristic creation, amusing and full of delicious good humour. The four chief characters are also touched by humour, particularly Sir Nigel and his family. The feelings of Sir Nigel, his wife and daughter for one another are suggested with that lightness of touch that arouses an imperceptible but irresistible movement of gaiety in the reader. A perfect example of a knight-errant, Sir Nigel is also a weak and indulgent father, and an attentive but clumsy husband. He takes advantage of a respite between two exploits to write to his wife, and jumbles together in one long sentence news of the horses' health, his adventures at sea, the losses they have suffered, pirates, the discipline of the men, to end at last with a short and unwonted declaration of conjugal love. This sort of touch makes an appeal to the heart as well as to the imagination. The beautiful Maude and Lady Loring, in spite of being relegated somewhat to the background, have considerable solidity. The former is not a fragile porcelain doll, but an astute, proud amazon. Her mother is clearly a virago.

The novel was finished in the middle of the summer of 1890. It had therefore taken much longer to write than *Micah Clarke*, and Conan Doyle did not conceal his impatience to know how the public would receive the fruit of his labours. Outside the family circle, James Payn was probably the first to express his opinion of it. On 29 October 1891 Conan Doyle wrote to his mother:

My dearest Mam, I hope you got your White Company all right. It looks very neat. There have been no reviews as yet. Payn tells me that he sent the earliest copy to the Times, with a private note to say that he considered it to be the best novel of the kind since Ivanhoe—which was stretching it pretty tight. We'll see how far the reviewer endorses or demolishes the opinion . . .[2]

Payn was editor of *The Cornhill Magazine*, where the novel appeared in instalments from January to December 1891, afterwards

---

[1] *The White Company*, HIS., p. 122.   [2] (C.D.B.A.)

being published in three volumes by Smith Elder and Co. The author sent presentation copies of this first edition to Tennyson, George Meredith, Andrew Lang and William Stead. Although the critics were on the whole favourable, and appreciated the different facets of the novel, Conan Doyle showed in his letters that some of their pedantic or childish comment had irritated him. He wrote to his mother on 11 November 1891:

> I shall send you the cuttings about The White Company when I have accumulated enough of them. So far I have only a few, Scotsman, Telegraph, Daily Graphic, Saturday Review and Observer. They are none of them hostile and yet I am disappointed. They treat it too much as a mere book of adventure—as if it were an ordinary boy's book— whereas I have striven to draw the exact types of character of the folk then living and have spent much work and pains over it, which seems so far to be quite unappreciated by the critics. They do not realise how conscientious my work has been. Says the Saturday Reviewer—'Fancy a carriage in the neighbourhood of Southampton in the year 1367. I wonder what Monsieur Jusserand would say to this!' As it happens the carriage was extracted from Jusserand's book on mediaeval England, where a very elaborate description and picture of it is given. I wrote courteously to the Reviewer and told him so. But that is very typical and somewhat irritating.

And again on 6 January 1892:

> I rely on the general public infinitely more than I do on the Critics. They are really too feeble! They would be depressing if they were unanimous, but as each always contradicts all the others, they form a mutual antidote.

As might have been expected, however, the book had a lively and lasting success. The three-volume edition was quickly exhausted and more than fifty editions in one volume followed without pause. The youthful facility with which the novel is written has for a long time past ceased to hide its permanent value, and professional historians have recognised in it exactly those qualities the novelist had aimed at. '*The White Company*', wrote G. M. Trevelyan, 'gives a spirited and well-informed if somewhat idealised picture of one of these "companies" abroad.'[1]

Idealised? Certainly; Conan Doyle has infused the book with the sympathy he felt for that rough and breezy age. In his preface to *Sir Nigel* he defended himself from the charge of having ignored its less

[1] *History of England*, p. 228.

attractive features: 'It was a sterner age, and men's code of morality, especially in matters of cruelty, was very different. The fantastic graces of Chivalry lay upon the surface of life, but beneath it was a half savage population fierce and animal, with little ruth or mercy. It was a raw, rude England, full of elemental passions, and redeemed only by elemental virtues.' Yet Conan Doyle projects a golden light on those sombre years.

But we must look beyond a sympathy that had its source in childhood dreams and legends of chivalry, and recognise that his interest in the Great Companies was the most valid literary expression of his temperament. Nor need we take Conan Doyle's remarks about the cruelty of the period too seriously. There are fewer painful scenes in *The White Company* than in many other historical novels. The description of the peasants of the Jacquerie, in chapter thirty, seems more justifiable and convincing than that of the Indians in *The Refugees*, or the Spanish bandits in the *Exploits of Brigadier Gerard*.

Is it fair to say that Conan Doyle took an idealised view of the fourteenth century? Something a little different would seem nearer the truth—that he saw it as an age impregnated with idealism, an age throbbing perceptibly and almost palpably with elemental spontaneity. Does that mean that he thought of the men of the fourteenth century as 'noble savages'? No, probably not: the 'noble savage' was a fiction invented by eighteenth-century Europe in an attempt to reformulate the social contract in terms more advantageous to the individual. But medieval society did not hinge upon the individual, as Conan Doyle showed, but on classes, orders, trades and organised groups. The equilibrium of the system depended on gravitation, and that in its turn was engendered by the ideals of the different groups. Of course the picture is a utopian one in so far as it simply ignores the factors which might destroy that equilibrium. Perhaps real worth bows down rather too docilely to noble birth. The archer Aylward never appears to dream for a moment that a coat of arms is within his reach, and Alleyne Edricson knows that he will not be allowed to lead a knight's daughter to the altar while he is without an inheritance: 'Were Minstead yours, Alleyne, then, by Saint Paul! I cannot think that any family in the land would not be proud to take you among them, seeing that you come of so old a strain. But while the Socman lives . . .'[1]

[1] HIS., p. 276.

Naturally, Conan Doyle's chief concern is to depict the military caste, which is fortunate in possessing both noble birth and political power. Without explicitly comparing past and present, as Carlyle did, he none the less applauded the principles he believed to have inspired the Hundred Years War. His treatment of the siege of Villefranche, when French and English nobles became temporary allies against the Jacquerie, is extremely characteristic. He shows how national feeling yielded to the instinct to preserve the social order. No war could have been less imperialist. The White Company and its leaders seem to have obeyed two motives only—the love of sport and the idea of chivalry, and we know what an appeal they both had for Conan Doyle. It was his affinity with the temperament and ideology of a fourteenth-century knight-errant that enabled him to rehabilitate in literature a type usually mistreated in novels through lack of desire or ability to bring it to life. The sporting temperament is manifested in Hordle John, Sam Aylward and their companions in arms, and an example is set by the head of the Company. He has the necessary inspiration and dynamism, and is not so much a chosen and responsible delegate as a hero or 'leader'. Here is another instance of the transcendentalism we have already described in Conan Doyle's life and career. In his picture of monastic life, he has evoked, as Carlyle did, the absolutism which made medieval faith an incomparable means of conquering the self. In the Abbot Berghersh we see the triumph of asceticism over instinct. But, because action seemed to Conan Doyle a more fertile and positive means of testing oneself, he adopts an air of slightly bantering reserve towards the clergy, such as was traditionally shown them by the nobility of the period.

Having drawn a picture of the medieval world in which the ruling aristocracy exalted spiritual power, Conan Doyle seems to suggest that the hope of finding this principle still valid is not after all chimerical. It is here that the deliberate contrast between the spiritual qualities of his characters and their physical appearance makes itself felt. In contrast to Hordle John, who is a natural force, and the athletic Aylward, Alleyne is a delicate looking and quiet young man. Sir Nigel's appearance is even more misleading. Sickly and ageing, his imperfect sight and hearing seem hardly to affect him, and certainly do not prevent his playing an important part in the military history of his day. It is the same with Duguesclin and Chandos. His study of English military traditions has not led Conan

Doyle to exalt brute force or intolerant racialism, as it might so easily have done. It is undeniable that the regeneration he dreamed of had a gymnastic aspect but a revival of spiritual values and the code of chivalry was far more important to him. How could this be achieved except by good example? It cannot at least be said of Conan Doyle that he refused to take his own medicine. Beneath his forceful exhortation, beneath his generous nationalism, beneath the hymn dedicated to the most glorious period in English history, it is possible to detect a precise and concrete intention.

The insistence with which he returns to the importance of English archers in the campaigns of the fourteenth century prepares the way for the modern commando theory he formulated ten years later in his thoughts on the Boer War. Archers were the forerunners of the crack shots Conan Doyle wanted to provide for the British Army at the beginning of the twentieth century. They too would use accurate weapons with perfect skill; they too would know how to exploit those weapons on the battlefield. Finally, the White Company's exploits stress the importance of team spirit; and since the story this novel has to tell is an integral part of the nation's history, it foreshadows several works inspired by the Second World War in spite of its medieval setting. Consciously or no, Monsarrat, Cecil Forester and Eric Williams all emulated Conan Doyle. It is not surprising that the British public of today should salute Conan Doyle not only as the creator of Sherlock Holmes, but also as the author of *The White Company*, as did their great man Sir Winston Churchill in particular.

The great patriotic theme of this novel is matched by a consistent and sincere style; and, particularly in the first part, Conan Doyle has tapped a lyric vein which is rarely found in his writings. Already in the introduction we are transported in sonorous, simple and restrained terms to the borders of the great Hampshire forest:

> The Great Bell of Beaulieu was ringing. Far away through the forest might be heard its musical clangour and swell. Peat cutters on the Blackdown and fishers upon the Exe heard the distant throbbing rising and falling upon the solitary summer air. It was a common sound in those parts—as common as the chatter of the jays and the booming of the bittern. Yet the fishers and the peasants raised their heads and looked questions at each other, for the Angelus had already gone, and Vespers was still far off. Why should the Great Bell of Beaulieu toll, when the shadows were neither short nor long?[1]

[1] HIS., p. 3.

Conan Doyle next shows us the active life of a great monastery, with a wider and more detailed pageantry even than Carlyle's. Carlyle has left his mark on this part of *The White Company*, and it was to be seen again in *Sir Nigel*. There is first of all the relationship between the Abbot Berghersh in the former, Abbot John in the latter and Carlyle's Abbot Samson in *Past and Present*. There is also the mystical leitmotiv. But let us compare Carlyle's:

> Heaven lies over him wheresoever he goes or stands on the earth; making all the Earth a mystic Temple to him, the Earth's business all a kind of worship. Glimpses of bright creatures flash in the common sunlight; angels yet hover doing God's messages among men: that rainbow was set in the clouds by the hand of God! Wonder, miracle encompass the man; he lives in an element of miracle; Heaven's splendour over his head, Hell's darkness under his feet.[1]

with:

> Heaven, too, was very near to them in those days, God's direct agency was to be seen in the thunder and the rainbow, the whirlwind and the lightning. To the believer, clouds of angels and confessors, and martyrs, armies of the sainted and the saved, were ever stooping over their struggling brethren upon earth, raising, encouraging, and supporting them.[2]

and:

> In those simple times there was a great wonder and mystery in life. Man walked in fear and solemnity, with Heaven very close above his head, and Hell below his very feet. God's visible hand was everywhere, in the rainbow and the comet, in the thunder and the wind.[3]

Various stylistic features will also be noted, such as the emphatic use of adjectives: 'Great news this for that fierce old country, whose trade for a generation had been war, her exports archers and her imports prisoners.'[4]

Conan Doyle's style is the more alive of the two and always maintains a balance between description and dialogue. Then he leads us into the heart of the New Forest with Alleyne Edricson. The forest seems to symbolise in natural form the magical element vibrating in the minds of all the characters. It is always present in the first part of

---

[1] *Past and Present.*
[3] *Sir Nigel*, HIS., p. 436.
[2] *The White Company*, HIS., p. 18.
[4] *The White Company*, HIS., p. 140.

the book; its gothic and golden light seems to put a halo of inexhaustible and holy joy around ordinary daily life: 'The sun shining slantwise through the trees, threw delicate traceries across the road, with bars of golden light between.'[1] The luxuriant vegetation impregnated with varied scents, the undergrowth rustling with wings, the trembling leaves, the babbling brooks, the richly coloured fauna of the forest—all bring the background to life for us. And in these twelve chapters, Conan Doyle the painter of animals, the poet in prose, takes over from the story-teller and historian. In the twelfth chapter narrative and poetic description are blended in a page celebrating his native land in all its eager vitality:

> Through the late autumn and the early winter every road and country lane resounded with nakir and trumpet, with the neigh of the war horse and the clatter of marching men. From the Wrekin in the Welsh marshes to the Cotswolds in the west, or Butser in the south, there was no hill-top from which the peasant might not have seen the bright shimmer of arms, the toss and flutter of plume and of pensil. From by-path, from woodland clearing or from winding moorside track, these little rivulets of steel united in the larger roads to form a broader stream, growing ever fuller and larger as it approached the nearest or most commodious seaport. And there all day, and day after day, there was bustle and crowding and labour, while the great ships loaded up, and one after the other spread their white pinions and darted off to the open sea, amid the clash of cymbals and rolling of drums and lusty shouts of those who went and of those who waited. From Orwell to the Dart there was no port which did not send forth its little fleet, gay with streamer and bunting, as for a joyous festival. Thus in the season of the waning days the might of England put forth on the waters.[2]

How is it possible to be indifferent to the resonance of this simple but great vision, and to the alliterations like a flourish of trumpets accompanying the departure of the volunteers? How can one fail to find metre in this sober, muscular prose ('the toss and flutter of plume and pensil'), nor retain its free but suggestive rhythm in one's mind?

The departure of the heroes is greeted with a hymn to English strength, a declaration of faith in the spiritual benefits of action, whose percussive force remains with us until the last page of the book. Conan Doyle was to try in vain, later on, to recapture the practical inspiration which runs through this novel, in his three volumes of rhymed verse: *Songs of Action*, 1898, *Songs of the Road*, 1911, and *The Guards Came Through*, 1919. Anecdotes, ballads, odes, comic verse

[1] HIS., p. 19.   [2] *Ibid.*, p. 140.

or doggerel, their unpretentiousness charmingly excuses their insignificance. But if they mark the lowest level of Conan Doyle's inspiration, they also stress the diversity of his ambitions and literary activities.

None of his other works vibrates with so much seriousness and enthusiasm as *The White Company*. Of all his literary achievements it must remain the most memorable. In 1921, the journalist Herbert Ashley asked him which of his books he had most enjoyed writing. It was *The White Company*, Conan Doyle told him: 'I was young and full of the first joy of life and action and I think I got some of it into my pages.'[1] In his other novels he may have sought after a more complicated dramatic design or a less traditional theme. But its personal significance makes *The White Company* the most attractive of them all. This is because the writer's ego appears there in its most permanent aspect, dissociated from biographical contingencies. The magic, the fervent idealism and tenderness which envelop the characters, reveal for us, as nowhere else, the face of the knightly author with his visor raised.

* * * * *

A gap of fifteen years separates the two novels of chivalry—a gap that must be interpreted in a different light, according to whether one is concerned with the order of publication of the novels or their historical context. With *Sir Nigel*, Conan Doyle takes us further into the past, plunging even more boldly into the age of chivalry. His perseverance is amply justified by his success. At the very heart of his works we find a lively awareness of the differences dividing one generation from another. In order to create an effect of perspective and give his narrative greater depth of focus, Conan Doyle liked to set it against a background evoked by means of the minor characters and their conversation. In *Micah Clarke*, Joseph Clarke takes a backward glance from the main body of the narrative, letting us see the Cromwellian era through his eyes and from a generation's distance. This gives the reader a sense of history and tends to glorify the past, so that Cromwell's wars have a grandeur scarcely to be found in Monmouth's rebellion. *The White Company* adopts the same method. Alluding to the beginning of the Hundred Years War, Sir Oliver Buttesthorn

[1] Letter to H. Ashley, 14 November 1921 (C.D.B.A.).

remembers how the knights used to swear to wear a black patch over one eye until they had accomplished some daring deed:

> 'In truth, you take me back twenty years, Nigel,' quoth Sir Oliver as they mounted and rode slowly through the water-gate. 'After Cadsand, I deem that the French thought that we were an army of the blind, for there was scarce a man who had not closed an eye for the greater love and honour of his lady.'[1]

After writing his first novel of chivalry with such enthusiasm, why did Conan Doyle let so long a time elapse before embarking on a second? Probably because his private worries, his travels and his public activities left little scope for such a long and exacting task. However, this period was far from sterile, for it saw the appearence of *Rodney Stone*, the *Adventures of Gerard* and more than twenty short stories—all works bearing signs of compression. Then, at the beginning of the summer of 1899, after reading a book on the wars of the Middle Ages, he wrote to his mother that he was about to start work on a novel: 'I have only one short story to do, and then I shall be clear and ready to turn to that Mediaeval novel which I have had in mind for some time.' But the outbreak of the Boer War interrupted his plans, and *Sir Nigel* did not finally see the light until 1905. It was published in instalments in *The Strand Magazine* between July 1905 and December 1906, and afterwards in book form by Smith, Elder and Co.

As we have seen, historically speaking, *Sir Nigel* is not a sequel but a prelude to *The White Company*. Assuming with reason that his second novel would reach the same public as the first, Conan Doyle preferred not to create a completely new set of characters, but to reintroduce some of those from *The White Company*, particularly Nigel Loring and Aylward the archer. But *The White Company* is not a convincing sequel to S*ir Nigel*, for there are flagrant discords in the connections between the two works. In *Sir Nigel* the action ends in 1356 after the battle of Poitiers, and the curtain falls on the wedding of Nigel and Mary. But the story of *The White Company* begins only ten years later, and these two characters have aged to an altogether unexpected degree in the time. Here we find them parents of a damsel of twenty, Maude, who in her turn marries the knight she loves, Alleyne Edricson, at the end of the story. *Sir Nigel* tells us, also, that Mary is the daughter of Sir John Butteshorn and Sir Oliver's sister. But there is nothing in *The White Company* to suggest any relationship

[1] *The White Company*, HIS., p. 203.

whatever between Sir Nigel and Sir Oliver. The seam joining the two books is thus plainly visible, and rather than take one as the sequel of the other, it is better not to pay too much attention to the fact that the same characters occur in both. *Sir Nigel* is in fact a new medieval novel, a new interpretation of the romantic ingredients already present in *The White Company*. One may be struck by the resemblances at first sight, both in the general style of the narrative and in the details. There is the same historical background, the same conventional development of the love story; both stories, also, describe the apprenticeship to a knightly career. Both novels are ballads in prose, some thirty chapters long. As for detail, both begin with scenes of violence and confusion in a monastery, followed by the trial of the culprit— Hordle John in *The White Company*, and young Nigel Loring here. We notice too that in both books the hero fights a scoundrel in defence of beauty in distress; in one it is the lord of Minstead, in the other the hunchback Paul de la Fosse. A crossing of the Channel leads to an unexpected adventure at sea in both books. Yet, in spite of these incidental resemblances, if one takes the trouble to study the two books more closely, one becomes aware of profound differences in spirit and treatment. In *The White Company* Conan Doyle accepts a picturesque view of history, radiant with lyrical patriotism. In *Sir Nigel* we have something more precise and deliberate. Instead of the adventures of a group of men whom chance has thrown together and involved in the events of their time, we are here concerned with a single hero who gives us the impression of controlling his own fate to the fullest limits allowed by freedom of the will. It is the man we are interested in, not the events he is involved in. Secondly, *Sir Nigel* is not a novel of the open road. Except for a picaresque episode in the seventh chapter, and another rather unfortunate one in the thirteenth, it is a novel of chivalry. (The meeting with William Langland is actually an anachronism. Conan Doyle makes the poet say that he has finished *Piers Plowman*. But it is the year 1349, when Langland must have been about twenty, and according to the accepted view *Piers Plowman* was written between 1360 and 1399.)

Incidents, situations and characters are designed less to take us into the heart of fourteenth-century England or France than to show us the code of chivalry in action, without appearing to over-exalt it.

Young Nigel Loring is burning with impatience for his first encounter. The unexpected visit of the king to the family manor at last gives him his hoped-for chance. While the royal train is advancing towards Tilford Manor, Nigel has posted himself, armed from head to foot, in front of the drawbridge and informs his guests that he would like to match his skill against anyone who will deign to do him that honour. They are rather surprised, more at the appearance of this strange knight who is challenging them out of courtesy, than at his action:

> His build was strange, and so also was his figure, for the limbs were short for so tall a man. His head also was sunk forward as if he were lost in thought or overcome with deep dejection.
> 'This is surely the Cavalier of the Heavy Heart,' said Manny. 'What trouble has he, that he should hang his head?'[1]

Nigel triumphs over the first two adversaries who come forward; but the third manages to unseat him and his basinet rolls on the ground, making him look as if he had been decapitated! Then it is discovered that young Nigel, being too poor to have a suit of armour of his own, has dressed himself in an old one belonging to his father, which is much too big for him. A little later, when he is off to the war, with his own armour this time, Nigel catches sight of a fully-armed knight some way off. In the hopes of engaging him in single combat the young man leaps to the ground and hastily arms himself. From inexperience, he is unfortunately still not ready, when a disdainful knight comes up and passes him by without so much as a glance. In several similar passages, humour comes to the rescue and prevents the picture of knightly behaviour becoming too stilted or solemn. With objectivity and realism, the novels show not only the somewhat comic aspects of chivalry but also its excesses. Sir James Astley, for example, exposes his companions and his men to unnecessary danger in order to satisfy his desire to perform feats of valour. In contrast to this undisciplined nobleman, characters like Sir Walter Manny or Sir Robert Knolles display less spectacular and more difficult military virtues. It is left to the Black Prince, Chandos and Nigel himself to prove that the highest justification of war is that it is a school teaching greatness of soul.

Although Nigel's own exploits occupy the centre of the stage, they do not prevent Conan Doyle's interest in military history being more apparent that in his previous novels. He can describe a fourteenth-century naval battle, its incidents and atmosphere with genuine

[1] HIS., p. 521.

historical sense. And if his description of the battle of Poitiers is not more powerfully evocative than that of the battle of Sedgemoor in *Micah Clarke*, it at least shows a firmer and more scholarly grasp of the strategic situation. One cannot be indifferent to the restraint and lucidity this gives to the narrative. It is not so much a question of talent as of experience—and personal experience at that. This is no battle seen through Macaulay's eyes; it has been understood, interpreted and analysed in the light of his own real memories of the South African Campaign:

> The two bodies of horsemen had moved slowly over the plain, with a space of nearly a quarter of a mile between them. Now, having come two bow-shots from the hostile line, they halted. All that they could see of the English was the long hedge, with an occasional twinkle of steel through its leafy branches, and behind that the spearheads of the men-at-arms rising from amid the brushwood and the vines. A lovely autumn countryside with changing peaceful sunshine, and nothing save those glittering fitful gleams to tell of the silent and lurking enemy who barred their way. But the bold spirits of the French cavaliers rose the higher to the danger. The clamour of their war-cries filled the air, and they tossed their pennoned spears over their heads in menace and defiance. From the English line it was a noble sight, the gallant, pawing, curvetting horses, the many-coloured twinkling riders, the swoop and wave and toss of plume and banner.[1]

In the same way, the social background may not have the breadth so characteristic of *The White Company*, but the details of the way of life of the nobility, their interests and distractions, are drawn in with even more scrupulous exactness. *Sir Nigel* contains a vivid picture of hunting, falconry and archery. The descriptions of armour persuade us of its attraction for young noblemen; and the conversations bring to life courtly arguments about the formalities of duels and tournaments.

Characters, setting and situations all bear the stamp of a personal message, not indeed more profound but apparently more deliberate than any in the preceding novels. A Nigel or Nele Lorying was present at the battle of Poitiers and afterwards fought in France and Spain. But it was at Sluys in 1340, not at Poitiers in 1356, that this Nigel won his spurs. Conan Doyle has made him younger than he really was, not only to suit his conventional love story, but also so that he can tell us about Nigel's adolescence, and introduce us to his

[1] HIS., p. 762.

grandmother, Dame Ermyntrude, who is as we know a portrait of Mary Doyle. As for the setting, Conan Doyle has brought it with him, so to speak. We have left the New Forest for Hindhead. The English part of the story, which occupies almost half the book, takes place in a triangle of about thirty miles, with Hindhead as the southernmost point. The first twelve chapters are thus set in the neighbourhood of Tilford, Waverley Abbey, Shalford and the North Downs.

Before mingling his hero's adventures with the history of the nation Conan Doyle interests us in a private, but bitter and passionate quarrel, that has been raging ever since its foundation between the Cistercian monastery of Waverley and the Loring family. This unequal contest, leading to the slow but inevitable eviction of the occupants by a powerful and obstinate organisation, reminds one of the history of the Irish Doyles.

So, *mutatis mutandis*, Waverley represents the implacable curse of the 'penal laws'; and Nigel's attacks on the property of the monastery, such as the destruction of the fish-pond, stand for the resistance put up by the small Irish landowners. Nigel therefore has a unique part to play among Conan Doyle's autobiographic characters: he represents the author's solidarity with his own ancestors. In *Micah Clarke* we saw this solidarity questioned in the religious sphere. The sense of conflict persists in *Sir Nigel*, and is expressed in clear symbolic terms in the third chapter, whose hero is 'the yellow horse of Crooksbury'. The monks have seized a superb thoroughbred from the farm at Crooksbury. They soon regret their action because several of them are injured or put to flight trying to control the animal. Attracted by the commotion, Nigel intervenes and saves the life of one of the monks. But he receives the abbot's thanks with bitter and provocative words. The admirable ambiguity of justice speaks through the voice of the bursar of the abbey. He suggests that the horse be given to Nigel: 'Man or beast, one will break the other, and the world will be the better for it.'

Nigel does not try to avoid the implied challenge, and there follows the superb passage dealing with breaking in the horse, six pages of savage poetry. But this victory of rider over his mount is also the beginning of Nigel's rise to fame. We see how he deliberately accepts the challenge and determines to take the consequences, and here we have Conan Doyle's own affirmation of independence of conscience, and refusal to accept patronage at the beginning of his medical career. But this episode may be given a deeper and more permanent interpretation. Nigel's victory over the terrifying animal—one of the monks thought it was the devil—has the value of an act of exorcism or initiation. It represents a victory over the destructive anarchy of the passions, the birth of the self through ordeal, the choice of one's own destiny, and freedom chivalrously won by force of arms: '"You are my horse, Pommers," Nigel whispered, and he laid his cheek against the straining head. "I know you, Pommers, and you know me, and with the help of Saint Paul we shall teach some other folk to know us both." '[1]

This episode strikingly reveals the autobiographic aspect of the hero and the novel which bears his name. The theme of ordeal, so important to all the characters and to Nigel in particular, appears also in the events they take part in. Using the incantatory power that English prose can draw from rhythms and sounds, the story begins with a description of the arrival of the Black Death in England:

> In the month of July 1348, between the feasts of St. Benedict and of St. Swithin, a strange thing came upon England, for out of the east there drifted a monstrous cloud, purple and piled, heavy with evil, climbing slowly up the hushed heaven. In the shadow of that strange cloud the leaves drooped in the trees, the birds ceased their calling, and the cattle and the sheep gathered cowering under the hedges. A gloom fell upon all the land, and men stood with their eyes upon the strange cloud and a heaviness upon their hearts. They crept into the churches, where the trembling people were blessed and shriven by the trembling priests. Outside no bird flew, and there came no rustling from the woods, nor any of the homely sounds of nature. All was still and nothing moved, save only the great cloud which rolled up and onward, with fold on fold from the black horizon. To the west was the light summer sky, to the east this brooding cloud-bank, creeping ever slowly across, until the last thin blue gleam faded away and the whole sweep of the heavens was one great leaden arch. Then the rain began to fall.[2]

Like this premonitory cloud, the beneficent results of the epidemic lead to a mystical interpretation of the pest. It is the same interpretation that we find later—only ten years later—applied to modern cataclysms, both in *The British Campaigns in Europe* and *His Last Bow*. One may see nothing in this coincidence except evidence of Conan Doyle's sensibility; but in the series of stories published in

[1] HIS., p. 452.   [2] *Ibid.*, p. 425.

1911 under the title of *The Last Galley* we can already trace a prophetic purpose that is more clearly stated in a letter to Greenhough Smith: 'I wonder if you saw the two sketches, *The Last Galley* and *The Passing of the Legions*, the one dealing with the British naval question in parable, the other with the abandonment of India question in the same way.'[1]

It matters very little that Conan Doyle's historical novels should have belonged to the somewhat old-fashioned aesthetic school of Walter Scott. His originality appears in the way he used a conventional form to achieve a poetic result. *Sir Nigel* completes the catharsis begun in *The White Company*. Conan Doyle has created a world of dreams rather than an historical one, and transferred something of his own spiritual make-up to the character of his hero. The heroes of both the novels of chivalry are autobiographical. Each of them in his different way expresses the underlying, essential Conan Doyle. They are two different stages of the same portrait, and the distance between them tells us something about the novelist's development. The character of Nigel Loring definitely portrays his inner self, and this novel allows us to see more plainly than before to what extent Conan Doyle was at variance with his own century.

[1] 14 May 1910 (C.D.B.A.).

Chapter 18

FROM NOVEL TO MAGAZINE SERIAL

The White Company was followed in 1893 by *The Refugees*, which appeared as a serial in *Harper's New Monthly Magazine*, and in a three-volume edition ('three-decker') published by Longmans Green & Co. at the same time. If one compares the two novels, one is immediately struck by the differences between them, and these not to the advantage of *The Refugees*, which shows a definite and surprising collapse into the domain of the magazine serial. It does not seem to have been written with Conan Doyle's usual care, although it is an important book. Conan Doyle here abandons the age of chivalry, which had inspired *The White Company* so successfully, and returned to the seventeenth century, in fact to his starting point—the year of the battle of Sedgemoor, 1685. He probably first had the idea for the book when he was writing *Micah Clarke*, and after he had started work on it, at the end of 1891, he wrote to his mother, implying that it was to be a sequel:

> ... Meanwhile I see my way to my American book and am almost ready to start. It will again be told by Michah Clarke. When he flies from England he goes to France in 1685, gets to the Court of Louis XIV, joins the Swiss guard, is mixed up in the Montespan and Maintenon intrigues, is present at the Revocation of the Edict of Nantes, finds himself in the Cevennes Country, shares the vicissitudes of a Huguenot family, gets in love with a girl; loses them, finds that they have fled to the Puritan settlements of America, follows them, picks up Saxon at sea under very strange circumstances, gets to Canada, is plunged into the French and Indian wars, makes his way with Saxon through the Iroquois country, and so to rejoin his friends in the States.[1]

This idea of a sequel to *Micah Clarke* was soon abandoned in favour of a complementary novel, presenting us with a vast panorama of the religious wars of the period (1685 was also the date of the Revocation of the Edict of Nantes). In *The White Company* he had already produced a page of history involving both France and England.

[1] Unpublished (C.D.B.A.).

Pleased with this formula, he now proposed to enlarge the field even more by putting English, French and Americans on the stage, and making us travel through two continents. Alas, the lavish décor and caste scarcely make up for the frigidity that is given off by this ambitious work. One does not know whether it is the writer's interest in his subject that is at fault or his ability to describe it. One gets the impression that it interested him less than the other books he was writing at the time, particularly the first Sherlock Holmes stories. But this frigidity may perhaps be attributed to the conditions in which he was working. His early historical novels, especially the second, had been composed in an atmosphere of contemplation and enthusiasm; and his evocation of history is perfumed and impregnated with the local atmosphere of Hampshire. Micah, Aylward and Nigel are his compatriots, and their adventures begin, or develop, close to the places where he was living at the time, a fact which may explain their solidity and vitality. It was different with *The Refugees*. The décor must have been planned as a whole in the abstract, and reconstructed from memories—very often of books he had read. Here is one of the factors which dehumanises *The Refugees* and leaves it rootless. It was also the work of a man without roots. The few years Conan Doyle had spent at Southsea had been decisive ones. He was living in his own house for the first time, practising his profession, making a home and publishing books which almost immediately brought him national fame as a writer. It was natural that his departure from Southsea, and the events associated with it, should have important repercussions on his inner and creative life. His sudden journey to Berlin in October 1890, his move to London the following winter, and the successive interruptions of a visit to Vienna, professional disappointment, and a long, serious illness, all created extremely unfavourable circumstances for a writer. After deciding to give up medicine for good during his convalescence, Conan Doyle became a professional writer, and with characteristic seriousness embarked on four or five projects simultaneously. The first was to go on with, and bring to a conclusion, the first series of Sherlock Holmes stories for *The Strand Magazine*. Next he wrote three novels: *The Parasite*, which was not published until 1894, *Beyond the City*, and *The Doings of Raffles Haw*, all three in their different ways making use of his impressions of a suburban life at Norwood, where he had just taken a house.

It was soon obvious that *The Refugees* would be a more ambitious venture, although Conan Doyle's ambitions for it were not purely literary. He had already shown a desire to honour Anglo-American friendship in the indirect form of a historical novel. And he wanted to appeal directly to American readers, as is clear from a letter written to Mary Doyle in January 1892:

> Dearest Mam,
> You will be glad to hear that I have done very well with the *Refugees*. I have now finished all the European part, bringing me down to page 260 or thereabouts—and another 150 pages on the other side of the water will bring it to an end. I am at present revising the French part for a day or two, before finally leaving it. I think it will do. There is less fun than in the other books, but there are more surprises to the reader, a more finished plot, and more passion. I take a young American, a man who has hardly ever seen a city, a man of the woods, shrewd, ready, and yet naive and innocent, and I manage to mix him up with the French court of Louis XIV, much as Scott mixes up Quentin Durward with the Court of Louis XI. He gets involved in it all in a very natural way, and bears himself very consistently. There are many chapters which I have never beaten, but on the other hand, there may be bits which the general reader may think slow, for, after all, when you get subjects like the priestly scheming which brought about the Revocation of the Edict of Nantes, and sent all my characters flying like leaves before a hurricane, it is difficult, however carefully one may try and draw the characters and the subtle arts and devices, to make the story keep up the active interest which so many readers demand. On the other hand this should be a new thing to Americans, and I shall be surprised if it does not fetch them. If I, a Britisher, could draw their early types so as to win their approval, I should be indeed proud, for by such international associations, nations are drawn together, and on the drawing together of these two nations depends the future of the world. I have a fine old New England Puritan seaman as a foil to the young New Yorker, so I have two distinct early American types, each conscientiously worked out. This book shall be my last for a while (save the little annual) . . .[1]

Memories of the different history-books he had read, some about the French court, some about Canada, were combined with the plot of the novel and made the book a somewhat unhomogeneous whole. Conan Doyle was aware of this. As he wrote in his preface to the 1901 edition: ' . . The book, as I am painfully aware, is really two books with the Atlantic rolling between them. This defect is inherent in my

[1] Unpublished (C.D.B.A.).

plan of showing the causes which led to the disruption as well as its consequences to individuals.' The formula need not have been a bad one. He used the same in *A Study in Scarlet*, and very skilfully later on in *The Valley of Fear*. But it here has the disadvantage of emphasising the discordance of tone and atmosphere. *The Refugees* was written with more haste than enthusiasm or decision. Conan Doyle succeeded in writing fifty pages of manuscript a week, but he made important changes in the original plan as he went on. At least he had no illusions about the final result. He wrote to his mother on 7 December 1891:

> . . . I have begun my new novel and did 50 pages this week. 'The Refugees', I call it, and I think the name good—short and a propos. I have determined not to introduce Micah, but to have entirely new material. The first half lies at the court of Louis—De Montespan, De Maintenon, love, intrigue, Huguenots, and so on, with an American element all through it. I hope to finish by February, when I may arrange for a little change. The book will be conscientious, respectable and dull . . .

He gave up all idea of re-introducing the characters from *Micah Clarke*, and threw himself into a diffuse and repetitive description of the court of Louis XIV. The suppression is the less to be regretted since it led to an interesting description of the Père du Chayla. It delighted Stevenson, who described the Jesuit martyr's career in *Travels with a Donkey*. He wrote to Conan Doyle on 23 August 1893:

> . . . Have read the *Refugees*; Condé and old P. Morat very good; Louis XIV and Louvois with the letter bag very rich. You have reached a trifle wide perhaps; too *many* celebrities? Though I was delighted to re-encounter my old friend Du Chayla. Old Morat is perhaps your high water mark; it is excellently human, cheerful and real. Do it again. Madame de Maintenon struck me as quite good. Have you any document for the decapitation? It sounds steepish. The devil of all that first part is that you see old Dumas; yet your Louis XIV is *distinctly good*. I am much interested with this book, which fulfils a good deal and promises more. Question: How far a Historical Novel should be wholly episodic? I incline to that view, with trembling. I shake hands with you on old Morat.[1]

Micah Clarke's disappearance also makes way for a certain Amos Green, who had been Amos White in the original draft. The novel

[1] The *Letters of Robert Louis Stevenson*, ed. Sidney Colvin, 1901, vol. II, p. 302.

begins with the arrival of this young American in Paris, where he is
welcomed by a Huguenot family consisting chiefly of two other
young people, Amory and Adèle de Catinat. As is usual in the historical novels, there are two interconnected plots, one private, the
other national. The latter is concerned with the disgrace of Madame
de Montespan, which Conan Doyle closely connects with the Revocation of the Edict of Nantes. An element suggesting the magazine
serial already appears in this tendency to explain history by secret,
underlying causes. The two plots become closely mingled in an
episode in which Conan Doyle follows Alexandre Dumas. He puts
Madame de Montespan and his Refugees in a situation reminiscent
of that of Milady and the Three Musketeers. Relying on facility
rather than inspiration, he adopted the rhythm of the serial story, and
broke all records for speed. ' . . . I remember that I once did 10,000
words of the "Refugees" in 24 hours,' he tells us. 'It was the part
when the Grand Monarch was between his two mistresses, and contains as sustained an effort as I have ever made . . .'[1]

But what can be said about his descriptions, scenes, pictures and
faithful reconstructions? It is all too plain that they are as exact and
lifeless as a museum of waxworks. We have come a long way from
the lively Hampshire characters. In the ambitious scene of the royal
levée of which Conan Doyle was very proud, we witness a disconcerting parade of mannequins, moving awkwardly and convention-
ally, talking with improbable verisimilitude. The poets let fall epigrams
and maxims, the ecclesiastics hatch plots, Louvois takes advantage of
the unambitious, and the favourites quarrel ceaselessly for the King's
love. This petrifaction even affects the imaginary characters, who owe
their existence to the needs of the plot.

At the same time the story fails to grip us. In the Hampshire novels,
in which historical events were connected with different power groups,
Conan Doyle succeeded in bringing to life the entire social structure
upon which historical developments depended. On the other hand, he
had neither the experience nor the sensibility to treat French history
in the manner of Vigny or Mérimée. What have Madame de Montespan's private adventures, Louis XIV's hesitations, or the ambition
of the Père La Chaise to do with the story of these two young Huguenots? Fascinated by his portrait gallery, Conan Doyle forgets that

---

[1] Draft for an interview, 1924, unpublished, The Humanities Research Centre,
University of Texas.

the first part of the book should have been a mere introduction; and so, although it is not devoid of action or dramatic interest, or even of psychological acuteness at times, it seems out of key with the rest of the novel.

The latter part describes the eventful odyssey of the refugees. Adèle, Amory and Amos embark on the *Golden Rod* whose captain is an old Puritan from Boston, called Ephraim Savage. During the crossing the ship is wrecked on an iceberg. Picked up by a French ship, the four castaways are taken to Quebec under close guard, but they manage to escape and decide to make for New England together. After sailing up the St. Lawrence, they find their way through the forest, along the shore of Lake Richelieu, in the direction of Lake Champlain. The country is invaded by bloodthirsty Iroquois Indians, and before reaching Fort Sainte-Marie the travellers meet Père Morat who has been tortured by them. At Fort Sainte-Marie they are welcomed by an old French aristocrat, Charles de La Noue, and his Indian wife Onega. The fort is soon afterwards besieged by Sioux Indians, who are repulsed after a bloody battle, but take with them Adèle and Amory as prisoners. Of course they are miraculously rescued at the very moment when they are about to die under atrocious torture. This is the subject of the second part. One might almost call it a 'scenario'; Westerns so often exploit this sort of plot. It is probably the rivalry of the cinema that has drained *The Refugees* of interest for modern readers. Yet in the second part of the book Conan Doyle has regained his narrative vigour, as well as his power to group together unusual, varied, living characters—such as the Indian chief, Brown Moose, Du Lhut the trapper, La Noue the eccentric old-fashioned aristocrat, and finally Morat the Jesuit.

Conan Doyle achieved one of the aims he had set himself: the book made a direct appeal to the American public. The second part of *The Refugees* is much closer to the traditional novel of the wilderness than any other of the English school. It is a bad historical novel but a good magazine serial, in which the author's brio has often been given free rein, while at other times it becomes crudely mechanical. The device of ending a chapter on a note of suspense is used seven times in the first part, as against only three in the second. Nor is the style of the beginning at all convincing. Conan Doyle found himself up against a problem he was unable to solve, in spite of his skill at pastiche. This was the question of how to make conversation in a foreign language—and an archaic form of it at that—seem realistic. The attempt was doomed to failure: the falsity of the style draws attention to the artificiality of the descriptions.

However the book was received fairly well by the critics, and should not have fallen from favour so soon. But it did not contribute to Conan Doyle's reputation as a historical novelist. From now on he gave up writing 'three-deckers', and any historical fiction he produced was more compact. From writing the Sherlock Holmes stories and an increasing number of others, he had grown to prefer a more malleable form.

*   *   *   *   *

Among the historical works in Conan Doyle's second manner, there is one that shows a return to the weaknesses of *The Refugees*. This is *Uncle Bernac*. The similarity is not apparent at first sight and needs to be substantiated. Both stories are based on French history, but there is nothing very surprising in that; Conan Doyle's novels are as often concerned with France as with England. But *The Refugees* and *Uncle Bernac* are of very different lengths and do not belong to the same period. Between the two came the *Exploits of Brigadier Gerard* and *Rodney Stone*, both much more successful and attractive books. Conan Doyle tried to make *Uncle Bernac* a sequel to *Rodney Stone* just as *The Refugees* was in a sense a pendant to *Micah Clarke*. With his usual attention to dates, he chose for both stories the year 1805, a year as significant in the history of both nations as 1356 (*Sir Nigel*) or 1685. *Rodney Stone* is a social history and describes the atmosphere of England just before the battle of Trafalgar. As for *Uncle Bernac*, it includes a study of life on the other side of the Channel and a description of the Camp of Boulogne.

Rodney Stone was almost the only book Conan Doyle was commissioned to write. It appeared in *The Queen* in 1897, but he had finished writing it by the winter of 1895. He wrote to his mother in September of that year: 'You will be glad to hear that I have finished my book . . . I think of calling it "Rodney Stone", A Reminiscence of the Ring. On the whole I am satisfied with it . . . I shall have a little rest now and I must then attack my Napoleonic study which is due for "The Queen" next year . . .' And in December, from

Cairo: 'I have begun my Napoleonic book and done two short chapters, but I can't tell whether it will do or not . . .'[1]

Uncle Bernac gave him a chance to put right a surprising omission. Neither in the first of the Napoleonic series, with its suggestive title *The Great Shadow*, nor in the exploits of Gerard, nor in *Rodney Stone*, had Conan Doyle ever given his readers a full-length portrait of Napoleon, as he had of Louis XIV. *Uncle Bernac* came out in *The Queen*, which is a woman's weekly; and we know that in spite of its frigidity and artificiality, the refined and elaborate atmosphere of the first part of *The Refugees* had found favour with feminine readers. Perhaps this may have settled the fate of Napoleon in the new story. We have seen that Conan Doyle attributed the weakness of his Franco-American novel to its division into two parts, rather than to the artificial treatment of some of the episodes. He was afterwards to pronounce an equally unfavourable judgement on *Uncle Bernac*, in spite of his efforts to give it unity. Writing to Mary Doyle about *A Duet*, he told her: ' . . . My inmost soul tells me that it is not a failure—the same inmost soul which tells me that *Girdlestone* and *Cloomber* and even *Uncle Bernac* are failures and must be suppressed if I can do them . . .'[2] The unity of *Uncle Bernac* is more apparent than real, and we find in it the same two heterogeneous elements that made up *The Refugees*—an adventure story coupled with spectacular descriptions. But in this case, instead of dividing the book into two distinct parts, they form a sort of counterpoint of chapters with eloquent titles. Some have a 'cloak-and-dagger' flavour: 'The Ruined Cottage', 'Men of the Night' or 'The Secret Passage'; while others are more retrospective: 'The Camp of Boulogne', 'The Man of Action' or 'The Reception of the Empress.'

The hero of *Uncle Bernac* is a young émigré called Louis de Laval, who had been brought up in England but is drawn back to France by his taste for danger, the glamour of Napoleon, and a desire to see his native land. As soon as he arrives he becomes involved against his will in a political conspiracy which forms the core of the plot. Uncle Bernac wants to dispossess him of his inheritance, and tries to compromise him in culpable schemes. The circumstances of the plot give Conan Doyle the opportunity to contrast the points of view of successive generations more emphatically than he has done elsewhere. Of course he always takes the side of the younger generation;

[1] (C.D.B.A.)   [2] N.d., *circa* 1899 (C.D.B.A.).

perhaps this is one reason among many for his popularity with young readers. To give body to the plot he decided to introduce a detective element, as he had done in *Rodney Stone*. He made use for the first time of the situation he was to use in *The Valley of Fear*: in order to unmask a plot, a detective insinuates himself among the conspirators, wins their confidence and is even made their leader. This does not prevent a very perceptible oscillation between the two elements mentioned above; and there is also a certain awkwardness in the way Conan Doyle presents us with famous figures from history, standing on their pedestals.

He has again made one of his characters act as intermediary, or museum guide, just as Catinat did in *The Refugees*, when he took us to Versailles and led us into the majestic presence of the Roi Soleil. In *Uncle Bernac* this task is performed by the famous Brigadier Gerard with truly professional volubility, but it is doubtful whether his performance makes any contribution to literature.

The result of this method is to make the reader feel like a slightly credulous sightseer, and leave him with a flat and conventional image of some historical personages. This concession to facile vulgarisation on Conan Doyle's part gave us a poor likeness of Louis XIV; Napoleon's is more successful. For one thing he is better known, so that Conan Doyle does not feel the need to emphasise his outlines. For another, Napoleon belongs to the nineteenth century, and we do not get the impression that the writer is divided from the image he is contemplating by an insuperable gulf. Bernard Shaw's play about Napoleon, *The Man of Destiny*, had its first performances only a few weeks before *Uncle Bernac* was published. It is evident that Conan Doyle has understood Napoleon better than he did Louis XIV; his sources were less romantic and better assimilated. He uses a historian's method—he refers to it as 'Taine's method' elsewhere—and, after absorbing his notes, he succeeds in presenting us with a scene which, in spite of almost excessive documentation, has an undeniable ring of truth:

> The room into which we passed was of considerable size, but was furnished with extreme simplicity. It was papered a silvery-grey colour, with a sky-blue ceiling, in the centre of which was the imperial eagle in gold, holding a thunderbolt. In spite of the warm weather, a large fire was burning at one side, and the air was heavy with heat and the aromatic smell of aloes. In the middle of the room was a large oval

table covered with a green cloth and littered with a number of letters and papers. A raised writing desk was at one side of the table, and behind it, in a green Morocco chair with curved arms there sat the Emperor. A number of officials were standing round the walls, but he took no notice of them. In his hands he had a small penknife, with which he whittled the wooden knob at the end of his chair. He glanced up as we entered, and shook his head coldly at de Meneval.[1]

The fact remains that *Uncle Bernac* and *The Refugees* are not merely the weakest of Conan Doyle's historical writings, but they represent the reef on which his historical fiction foundered. In spite of their success, these books have had hardly any literary influence. They merely echo the permanent taste for the exotic and for documentation, which is satisfied more easily by the commercial cinema than by literature today. But this must not lead us to condemn the other historical novels; on the contrary, *Micah Clarke*, *The White Company* and *Sir Nigel* show us how successfully the writer's personal inspiration was embodied in them.

[1] NAP., p. 97.

Chapter 19

PROFESSOR CHALLENGER

The Lost World alone, and the series of stories that followed it, would have been enough to assure Conan Doyle's literary reputation. They are stories based on scientific imagination, and spring from the same source of inspiration as the detective-stories, which also exploit the wonders of science, as we have seen. But science fiction and the detective-story develop in opposite directions. In the latter there is a problem to be solved, and the circumstances of the plot produce the train of reasoning. In the former, on the contrary, the plot or narrative develops out of a train of reasoning or a hypothesis; the interest lies in illuminating the rational process or justifying the hypothesis. The atmosphere of science fiction had appeared in Conan Doyle's work before the Professor Challenger cycle. It impregnates certain stories, some of them tinged with occultism: for instance *Lot No. 249*, written in 1894. One might also instance *Playing with Fire* (1900), *The Leather Funnel* (1903) and *The Silver Mirror* (1908). It would however be going too far to see these stories as forerunners of *The Lost World*. Not until 1912 does Conan Doyle emerge as one of Jules Verne's most talented disciples. There is something of the detective story in *The Lost World*, but it is also linked to the historical novels: Conan Doyle's evocation of prehistoric times clearly shows the fascination that the past had for him.

We make the acquaintance of the eccentric, dictatorial Professor Challenger right at the beginning of the book. He has returned from a journey to Amazonia, and claims to have come within range of a 'lost world' where certain species of prehistoric animals still exist. Confronted by the amused incredulity of his colleagues, Challenger organises an expedition consisting of Professor Summerlee (his most fiery opponent), Lord John Roxton the explorer, and a young journalist called Malone, who is the narrator of the adventure. After a rather long voyage and a several days march into the South American interior, the four men arrive in sight of the 'lost world'. It is a high table-land, completely cut off from the rest of the world by a precipice and a deep moat-like valley. The explorers cut down an enormous tree, and make an improvised bridge; but they have hardly reached the plateau when, as a result of the malevolence of one of the porters, the tree-trunk falls to the ground, leaving them imprisoned on the plateau like Robinson Crusoe on his island. They are 'in truth as far from any human aid as if they were in the moon'. The story does in fact roughly resemble the Robinson Crusoe myth, and there are two details of *The Lost World* which bring out its relationship with Defoe's novel. Challenger's plateau is not devoid of human life, any more than Crusoe's island is. Defoe's adventure with cannibals is matched by Conan Doyle's with the ape-men (representatives of the famous 'missing link'). In both cases the novelist profits from the occasion to introduce an episode of strategic importance. In both cases the explorers become allies and protectors of 'noble savages', who treat them as idols as a result. In *The Lost World* Challenger and his companions come to the rescue of a tribe of very primitive Indians, and with their help engage the ape-men in pitched battle. Their numerical inferiority is more than made up for by their superiority in arms and strategy, and the ape-men are ousted from the lost world. Conan Doyle is here symbolising the beginning of human life on the earth; but, like Defoe, he has also tried to demonstrate the absolute superiority of the white man.

The Lost World, which was written in 1911, seems to have been the result of reading, conversations and observations, all bearing witness to a new interest in paleontology. For instance, in 1909, soon after he had moved to Crowborough, he noticed the imprints of some fossils in a neighbouring quarry. He informed the British Museum, who sent an expert to examine them. ' . . . I have another expert of the British Museum coming on Monday,' he wrote to his mother, 'to advise me about the fossils we get from the quarry opposite. Huge lizard's tracks.' The same year, when cruising in the Aegean Sea, he thought he saw an animal 'like a young ichthyosaurus' and noted the incident in his autobiography. It was also at about this time that the Conan Doyles got to know Sir Edwin Ray Lankester, and *The Lost World* contains a half-serious, half-humorous allusion to the eminent zoologist.

In August 1912, Sir Edwin Ray Lankester wrote to Conan Doyle, acknowledging the reference and suggesting further episodes: 'I feel proud to have had a certain small share in its inception as you indicate by quoting the book on extinct animals in the start . . . How about introducing a gigantic snake sixty feet long? and a rabbit-like beast as big as an ox . . .'[1]

As for the high plateau of Amazonia, chosen by the novelist as the site for his lost world, it is not entirely fictitious, and although Conan Doyle never felt the need to justify his choice, it is generally agreed that it can be identified with Mount Roraima.

The ingenuity with which Conan Doyle exploits the wonders of prehistory does not perhaps sufficiently explain the interest to be got from *The Lost World*, and an attentive reader will find the story more than a skilful and original variation on the Robinson Crusoe theme. The concessions made to realism disguise without completely obliterating the fascinating dream-like atmosphere. The adventure develops like a nightmare, and poetry is generated in the process. In contrast to the first part of the narrative—a prosaic account of the organisation and departure of the expedition—the eighth and ninth chapters take us into the heart of the Amazonian forest and its dream landscape. We find here one of the longest descriptions of nature that Conan Doyle ever wrote, and there are several phrases which stress its oneiric quality: 'the effect was a dream of fairyland' for instance, and 'for a fairyland it was—the most wonderful that the imagination of a man could conceive'. The forest is the barrier between the real world and that of the imagination. Their journey through a verdant paradise of a thousand shades of green prepares the travellers for the featureless and unreal plain that confronts them: 'In front was an open plain, sloping slightly upwards and dotted with clumps of tree-ferns, the whole curving before us until it ended in a long, whale-backed ridge. This we reached about mid-day, only to find the shallow valley beyond rising once again into a gentle incline which led to a low, rounded sky-line.'[2]

The dreamlike quality of the descriptions is interrupted by the incidents accompanying the explorers' arrival at the end of their journey, but the twelfth chapter contains an episode whose hallucinatory power makes it the climax of the story. Malone, the narrator, has undertaken to make a solitary reconnaissance by moonlight. As he advances, the scenery becomes less and less real, until he reaches a black volcanic desert, more reminiscent of the *Voyage to the*

[1] (C.D.B.A.)
[2] CHA., p. 81.

Centre of the Earth than a terrestrial landscape. In this scene, peopled with monstrous Chinese shadows, Malone is oppressed by a heavy sense of danger, and is finally rooted to the earth by panic, as if in some endless nightmare:

> I remembered again the blood-slobbered face which we had seen in the glare of Lord John's torch, like some horrible vision from the deepest circle of Dante's hell. With my knees shaking beneath me, I stood and glared with starting eyes down the moonlit path which lay behind me. All was quiet as in a dream landscape. Silver clearings and the black patches of the bushes—nothing else could I see. Then from out of the silence, imminent and threatening, there came once more that low throaty croaking, far louder and closer than before. There could no longer be a doubt. Something was on my trail, and was closing in upon me every minute. I stood like a man paralysed, still staring at the ground which I had traversed. Then, suddenly, I saw it.[1]

Such passages as this show that it is impossible to exaggerate Conan Doyle's influence on writers of science fiction. As for the cinema, twenty years later the film of King Kong took over the story of *The Lost World* and seasoned it with primitive erotism. And in 1925 Harry Hoyt and Willis O'Brien brought Conan Doyle's book to the screen in a modified form, so as to give an opening for a little sentimental plot with the accent on its grand-guignol element. The result of this distortion was to suppress the humour of the story, by which Conan Doyle set great store, and which came from the inter-relationships between the four explorers.

Conan Doyle was careful not to sacrifice his characters to the sensationalism of the plot. In Challenger himself, he had enjoyed re-viving his memories of one of the professors of the Faculty of Medicine at Edinburgh, the physiologist William Rutherford. Challenger is the most dominant of the four, but Conan Doyle has had the bright idea of giving him Professor Summerlee as a partner. His role is to make the reader accept improbable events by letting his natural in-credulity gradually yield to the evidence. And the incessant quarrels between the two scientists, with their contradictory opinions, is an easy but effective source of comedy. Their lack of common sense is often accentuated by contrast with Roxton, who is the incarnation of the professional explorer, tough and intrepid. Was Conan Doyle perhaps paying indirect homage through this character to Roger

[1] CHA., p. 143.

Casement, then at the height of his popularity? This would seem to explain the allusions to Peruvian atrocities in the book:

> The exploits of the Red Chief, as they called him, had become legends among them, but the real facts, as far as I could learn them, were amazing enough. These were that Lord John had found himself some years before in that no-man's land which is formed by the half-defined frontiers between Peru, Brazil, and Colombia. In this great district the wild rubber tree flourishes, and has become, as in the Congo, a curse to the natives, which can only be compared to their forced labour under the Spaniards upon the old silver mines of Darien. A handful of villainous half-breeds dominated the country, armed such Indians as would support them, and turned the rest into slaves, terrorizing them with the most inhuman tortures in order to force them to gather the india-rubber, which was then floated down the river to Para. Lord John Roxton expostulated on behalf of the wretched victims, and received nothing but threats and insults for his pains.[1]

Casement's report on South American atrocities was not published until 1912, but the results of his investigations had been known since 1911, particularly by anyone like Conan Doyle who had been in touch with him. As for the fourth member of the expedition, Malone, he is a creation sparkling with humour and made very sympathetic by his combination of naïveté and courage. It is very possible that Conan Doyle indulged the whim of caricaturing some of his own youthful characteristics, such as his desire to be a war correspondent.

Finally one must bear in mind the special significance these characters had for Conan Doyle's youthful readers, and remember that the dedication of *The Lost World* reads as follows:

> I have wrought my simple plan,
> If I bring one hour of joy,
> To the boy who's half a man
> Or the man who's half a boy.

Children could easily identify themselves either with Malone or Roxton, and this all the more readily because they are contrasted with two other, older characters, who stand for the adult world and its mysterious and comic seriousness. From this point of view the unintelligible and solemn discussions between Challenger and Summerlee can be seen as comic, in the same way that they might be on the silent screen. Another circumstance contributes to Challenger's involuntary comicality. His accidental likeness to the king of the

[1] CHA., p. 63.

ape-men gives rise to scenes of pure farce, which compensate for the scenes of terror, and flavour this whole part of the story with innocent trickery. Conan Doyle sometimes found it hard to resist a little trickery himself and on one occasion had himself photographed, disguised as Professor Challenger, for a practical joke. The 'science fiction' of today is the posterity of this memorable story.

Conan Doyle wrote two more stories about Challenger, and in 1925 he figured in an apologia for spiritualism in novel form. In *The Land of Mist* the explorer finds himself in an unaccustomed situation. Usually the pioneer or defender of revolutionary theories, he now has to play the part of the incredulous rationalist. His unexpected capitulation in its own way represents Conan Doyle's spiritual development.

Apart from this novel, we meet Professor Challenger again in three stories with scientific themes: *The Disintegration Machine, When the World Screamed*, and *The Poison Belt*. The first is based on the theme of the apprentice sorcerer, and also modelled on popular farce (the robber robbed, the biter bit, etc.); it shows how a diabolical invention turns against the inventor. The second is more unusual; it describes an experiment devised by Challenger to discover whether the terrestrial globe is, as he maintains, by nature animal, and endowed with sensibility. *The Poison Belt* was written towards the end of 1912.

The scientific hypothesis serving as argument to the story concerns the nature of the ether—the cosmic element in which the heavenly bodies move. Like the ocean, it is traversed by currents and zones, which shift in relation to the stellar systems. The nature and property of these zones are unknown to us. Like a doomed ship sailing towards an iceberg, our earth approaches some interstellar current, is drawn into it and all life seems to become extinct. England is submerged, with other countries, by this cosmic tidal wave. Challenger determines to be the last witness of the great annihilation. He hastily gathers together reserves of oxygen and improvises an air-tight shelter, in which he and his wife and his friends of the Amazonian expedition all take refuge. We notice that Conan Doyle takes this opportunity of reminding us of his theory that death is a commonplace and painless affair:

> 'It won't be painful, George?'
> 'No more than laughing gas at the dentist's. Every time you have had it you have practically died.'

'But that is a pleasant sensation.'
'So may death be.'[1]

Outside Challenger's shelter, life gradually becomes extinct, and when the survivors think that the oxygen supply is on the point of being exhausted, they decide to open the windows to death. But nothing happens: the earth has crossed the poison belt, Challenger and his companions are safe and sound, although they are very probably the only surviving members of the human race. This is the most interesting part of the story. How will the survivors adapt themselves to their solitude? Unfortunately for the reader the story takes a sudden turn: the poison has only had a soporific effect, the apocalypse is nothing but a temporary stupor, life returns. Just as a cinema film can be stopped for a moment and then start mechanically again, everyone begins again exactly where they left off the day before: golfers go on with their game, a nurse goes on pushing her perambulator, harvesters repeat their automatic movements. So that instead of dealing with the theme of a small group of survivors after the cataclysm, Conan Doyle has chosen to describe the rebirth following a period of universal unconsciousness. And this rebirth corresponds almost exactly to the spiritualistic conception of life in the next world, a doctrine which he seems to have been on the point of accepting: that it is a replica of life on earth.

While the heroes of his historical novels expressed certain emotional or sensitive aspects of Conan Doyle's personality, Challenger —like Sherlock Holmes—is a manifestation of his intellectual side. But whereas Sherlock Holmes rationalises and explains the world in ever more logical terms, Challenger explores the domain of the marvellous, without attempting to understand it. The hero of *The Maracot Deep* can be considered as one of Challenger's reincarnations. The characters of this story are grouped like those in *The Lost World*, and have similar roles given them; the sub-title of the book is 'The Lost World under the Sea.' All we have to do is substitute Maracot for Challenger, Scanlan for Roxton, and Headley for Malone. As for Summerlee, he has no counterpart in this story, one of the last Conan Doyle wrote. Its theme is submarine exploration. Maracot has had a diving-bell constructed, and he and his two friends take their places inside it. As the result of a broken cable, the three explorers descend into an abyss nearly 10,000 yards deep. Resigned

[1] CHA., p. 246.

to imminent death, they are however delivered from their prison by men who have ascended from a city built on the floor of the ocean. They are descendants of the people of Atlantis, who had succeeded in escaping from the catastrophe several thousand years earlier. They had built a shelter, and their civilisation had survived and adapted itself to new conditions. The story of the three earth-dwellers' adventures ends with a description of the way of life and civilisation of Atlantis, reminiscent of modern utopias. Huxley's famous *Brave New World* was only written four years after *The Maracot Deep*, and there are several remarkable similarities between the two books.

Two races differing widely in physical appearance and function make up the civilisation of Atlantis. The rulers are small, dark and Negroid in type, while the subordinate race, or workers, are large, fair and athletic. Clothes on the other hand are the same for all: tunic, belt and boots for men, and three sorts of dresses for women. The special conditions under which this society has had to live have made certain technical improvements absolutely necessary. The delicate problem of nutrition has been solved by chemistry, and such products as flour, tea, coffee or wine are entirely synthetic. Nuclear energy has been known for a long time, but the hopes of exploiting it have so far been unfulfilled. Television plays a much appreciated part in education and the spread of news. It is even associated with telepathy, so that the people of Atlantis can express their thoughts in visual as well as auditory form. Through television the explorers from earth are able to learn about the past history of this people, although ignorant of their language. Some other inventions however are unknown to them, and the three shipwrecked men teach them how to make wireless receivers. By means of balloons filled with an extremely light gas, a link with the earth is established, and the three inhabitants of our world return home. The novel ends with a somewhat mystical episode: the adventure of the Lord of the Dark Face. Next door to the city of Atlantis there is a world of monstrous and occult creatures. Here we meet a gigantic caterpillar armed with a death ray; here too there exists a curious form of intelligent life that is partly organic and partly gaseous. The Lord of the Dark Face, who appears in this macabre setting, is the reincarnation of Baal, the terrible god of the Phoenicians, ancestors of the people of Atlantis; he tells them that they will soon be exterminated, and that the danger can only be averted by a man capable of subjugating him by will-power alone. Maracot is momentarily visited by messianic power, and exorcises the demon, who is destroyed somewhat after the manner of the vampire in *Dracula*.

Such is the original, gripping and perhaps unjustly neglected story with which Conan Doyle took leave of his public.

Beginning with historical novels in the school of Walter Scott, he was writing forty years later in an apparently very different vein, but producing what was in reality a modern incarnation of the romantic novel—science fiction. It would be hard to find a writer whose development is so well-defined yet is based on so permanent a tradition. And if novelists are to be credited with an influence on literature, the debt of the modern adventure-story to Conan Doyle must be great indeed.

Chapter 20

THE WRITER AND HIS ROLE

Both as a Victorian writer and a doctor, Conan Doyle showed a conscientious desire to be of service to his fellow-men. Where literature was concerned, this attitude, this broadly democratic, moral and Protestant vision, led to the somewhat awkward and vague concept of 'interest' as the object of every work of art:

> All methods and schools, romance and realism, symbolism and naturalism, have the one object in view—to interest. They are all good so far as they attain that, and all useless when they cease to do so. The weary workers or the more weary idlers turn to the writer and demand to have their thoughts drawn away from themselves and the routine of their own lives. Within the bounds of morality all methods are legitimate by which we can effect this. Every school is right in claiming that it is justified, and every school is wrong when it tries to prove that its rival is unjustified. You are right to make your book adventurous, you are right to make it theological, you are right to make it informative or controversial or idyllic, or humorous or grave or what you will, but you *must* make it interesting. That is essential—all the rest is detail. There is nothing inconsistent in the same writer using every method in turn, so long as he can in each hold his reader and take his thoughts from his own selfish interests.
>
> But there comes the obvious retort, 'You say "interesting"—interesting to *whom*?' The difficulty is not really a great one. The higher and more permanent work has always been interesting to all. The work which is the cult of a clique, too precious for general use, must be wanting in some quality. We know cases where obscurity of style has retarded the recognition of really great writers—but obscurity of style is not a virtue, and they were great in spite of it. Take the most honoured names in our literature, Scott, Thackeray, Dickens, Reade, Poe, they do not interest one or other social stratum, but they appeal equally to all educated readers.[1]

This profession of pragmatism reveals his evident intolerance of the 'isms' that had appeared in nineteenth-century discussions of creative writing, and, even more, of what he considered the 'degenerate'

[1] Preface to the Author's Edition, 1903.

tendencies shown by modern art in its search for autonomous forms of expression. We find these explicitly condemned in his unpublished journal:

> One of the singular characteristics of the present age is a wave of artistic and intellectual insanity breaking out in various forms in various places. If it stops where it is it will only be a curious phenomenon. If it is a spreading movement it will be the beginning of vast human changes. It attracted Max Nordau's attention when he wrote 'Degeneration'. But look at the strides it has taken since. It is the difference between queerness and madness, between Preraphaelites and the Post impressionists, between Wagner's operas and Electra or between French symbolists and the Italian Futurists. Nietzsche's philosophy in a purely mental way is symptomatic of what I mean. It is openly founded in lunacy for the poor fellow died raving. One should put one's shoulder to the door and keep out insanity all one can. It threatens to submerge us. It is something akin to the grotesque Byzantine art which pushed out the splendid classical styles—but it is more insane than anything Byzantine. Perhaps in art as in history a sort of French Revolution is due from time to time, odious in itself and yet inaugurating a new and better era formed rather as a reaction against it than as a consequence of it. There is no need for it for surely there is plenty of scope for originality without going over the border of reason. That is why Tennyson seems to me so great. He was strong, original, and always sane. If his head was among the stars, his feet were on the ground . . .[1]

Nor must we forget the resolute realism Conan Doyle showed when speaking of the relation between a work of art and the public. 'Schools' were reduced to 'methods', if not to 'recipes'. The idea of 'interest' and its corollaries seems to compare a work of art to merchandise or consumer's goods. Besides assuming that this analogy was legitimate, Conan Doyle simplified the question considerably by equating the general public with 'educated' or 'cultured' readers. No doubt, at the time he was writing, the public was less susceptible of subdivision than it had been before 1850, or would be again about 1920; but we find clear evidence, in the press for example, that there were several distinct publics in England at the time. Conan Doyle's conclusions, and their social applications, differ very little from those of Gissing in *New Grub Street.* One of the objects of this novel was to denounce the abuses caused by this treatment of literature in terms of economics.

[1] Journal for July 1912, unpublished (C.D.B.A.).

Like Gissing, Conan Doyle never hesitated to remind his fellow-writers to respect their professional honour. And he also tried to define the nature of that 'appetite for reading' referred to by the character Milvain:

> ... And still critics are found to write: 'The book is interesting, but we confess that we are unable to say what useful purpose it serves.' As if interest were not in itself the essential purpose! Ask the sleepless man worn with insomnia, the watcher beside the sick-bed, the man of business whose very sanity depends upon getting his thoughts out of one weary groove, the tired student, the woman whose only escape from an endless sordid life is that one window of imagination which leads out into the enchanted country—ask all these if interest serves any useful purpose. The life of a writer of fiction has its own troubles, the weary waiting for ideas, the blank reaction when they have been used, worst of all the despair when the thought which had seemed so bright and new goes dull and dark in the telling. But surely he has in return some claim to hope that if he can but interest his readers he fulfils the chief claim of man in leaving others a little happier than he found them.[1]

Here we have a criterion as definite as De Quincey's classic distinction between the literature of power and the literature of knowledge. Fictional literature certainly has value as social therapy, but its mission is neither to instruct nor to edify. It is to produce dreams, to be 'that one window of imagination which leads out into the enchanted country'. Here we find Conan Doyle coming closer to Ruskin and aestheticism than is generally supposed. Although they refer to different experiences, the notions 'beautiful' and 'interesting' are equally subjective. Both imply a spiritual aim. But whereas the former alludes to the purely passive inward state caused by contemplating a beautiful object, the other implies dynamic participation, transference rather than abolition of the power to adapt to reality. As for the essential core of Conan Doyle's view, his emphasis on the hygienic value of fiction or poetry, it is surprisingly similar to that held by Walter Pater in 1889. When Pater wrote that 'the end of life is not action but contemplation'[2] he was not necessarily thinking of the mystic vision of the Pre-Raphaelites. And he went on to say: 'Not to teach lessons, or enforce rules, or even to stimulate us to noble ends; but to withdraw the thoughts for a little while from the mere machinery of life, to fix them with appropriate emotions on the

---

[1] Preface to the Author's Edition, 1903.
[2] W. Pater, *Appreciations, with an Essay on Style*.

spectacle of those great facts in man's existence which no machinery effects . . . To witness this spectacle with appropriate emotions is the aim of all culture.[1]

Carlyle's disciple would certainly not have gone so far as to write or say that contemplation was the end of life, but much more probably that 'the end of life is not contemplation but action'. However, where the principle of literary autonomy was concerned, he was in agreement with Pater and contemporary opinion. It is true that he spoke prudently of the 'moral limits' which a novelist should not transgress. Does this mean that Conan Doyle censored his own work with particular strictness and care? He certainly gave spontaneous support to Victorian conventions, and his preferences and tastes were largely guided by them. His favourite writers may not have been models of chastity but a certain decorum pervaded their work.

The aestheticists naturally aimed at the sublime, the metaphysical; Conan Doyle, on the other hand, made reality the raw material of his prose narratives. But it seems probable from his vaguely defined ideal of romantic inspiration combined with realistic treatment[2] that the object of both quests is the same: to reveal the presence of the marvellous. In this sense, the historical novels and the detective cycle are complementary, just as they are in their temporal aspect. That is to say that Conan Doyle was equally concerned in both to explain or reconstruct some event, and describe it in strictly spatio-temporal and positive terms; and that whether he was dealing with a complex situation whose mechanism Holmes studied, or with historical material, the passage of time seems to be completely automatic. Exploration of time was treated as an adventure comparable to exploration of space, and Conan Doyle's mind was so constructed as to see spiritualistic experiments within the framework of a threefold attempt at understanding: past events being the domain of the historian, current events the domain of the investigator, and the future the domain of the scientific magician or medium. Once reality had been reconstructed, how was its unexpectedly marvellous character to be expressed? By strictly dramatic means: action, movement, plot in the historical novels for example. Thus the novelist is a sort of conjurer or creator of marvels; he understands reality and also the

[1] W. Pater, *Appreciations, with an Essay on Style.*
[2] 'The ideal novel would be one which was romantically conceived and realistically treated.' Journal for July 1912.

magic which can summon up a fresh and unexpected image from it. Some of Conan Doyle's spontaneous remarks express this view. When Stanley Weyman sent him the first volume of his *Under the Red Robe*, obviously inspired by *The Refugees*, Conan Doyle's comment was typically generous: 'I think the first chapter to be the most dramatic opening of any historical novel I know.'[1]

It was only with the Challenger cycle that Conan Doyle began quite simply adding what was conceivable to what was real, thus adopting a frankly romantic attitude to the adventure story.

It was not by pure chance that Conan Doyle became one of the spokesmen for his generation. As we have seen, he belonged to the class of men who so completely identify themselves with the community that they feel an almost personal responsibility for it, whether they hold official positions or not. This feeling naturally affected his literary judgements and the opinions he expressed about his fellow writers. He shared the Victorians' admiration for all that was grand and monumental, and these were the qualities that first struck him in the works of the writers or thinkers on whom he more or less consciously modelled himself: Gibbon, Scott and Macaulay. This admiration accounts for the curious feeling of guilt aroused in him by the most memorable part of his own achievement. But he was also, and above all, the man who could say: 'The best literature is always the unconscious literature—the literature which takes no thought of grace or style or the right word, but comes in a deep strong stream from a human soul. He wrote as the bird sings, because he had a God given power, and it was a pleasure—the highest pleasure—for him to exercise it.'[2]

Why did he not judge his own work by the criteria he defined so felicitously: inspiration, facility, grace? Victorianism and the medieval myths which had always had so strong a hold over him took pride of place in the moral structure of his personality. No one went to meet difficulties as he did, nor took such delight in effort, either out of simple physical elation or as a result of a spiritual faith founded on the virtue of accepting a challenge, on self-discipline and the concept of moral progress for the whole species. He seemed to want to turn a

---

[1] Letter to Stanley Weyman, 18 February 1894, unpublished (C.D.B.A.).

[2] He was speaking of Robert Burns. Extract from a lecture given on 23 March 1901 at the Balmoral Hotel, Edinburgh, before the Edinburgh Burns Club. The text was published in a leaflet entitled *The Immortal Memory*, by Mitchell and Sons, Edinburgh, 1901.

blind eye to the evidence of his own gifts, and preferred to draw attention instead to his workmanlike industriousness, even when he was still on the threshold of his literary career.

Honest, meticulous, hard-working: that was the image of himself he tried to convey whenever he consented to be interviewed or pose for his photograph. The compensatory role played by Sherlock Holmes as his double may for this reason have been indispensable to him. At all events his work—the whole body of it—tranquilly defies the pedantry of unfavourable criticism. Always more generous to others than to himself, Conan Doyle was able to recognise the value or interest of works very different from his own. A sexually modest man, he defended George Moore; a 'middle-brow', he loved George Meredith and often went to see him. In 1890 he thanked Richard Le Galienne for publishing the first critical study of the novelist in his lifetime, and in 1888 he tried to add lustre to Meredith's reputation with a lecture given at Portsmouth.

Behind the writer stood the knight-errant: without being pledged to fight for any particular cause, Conan Doyle believed that a man of letters should practice the virtues he attributed to medieval chivalry. Though he did not formulate this idea in so many words, it emerges from the sum-total of his reflections and judgements. 'The public knows a writer by his or her work, but there is another point of view which authors must take. They are a profession, a noble profession, and they honour those members of it who conform to the highest traditions of that profession.'[1]

The Holmes cycle gave contemporary readers a flattering and possibly misleading picture of the contemporary social scene. Sherlock Holmes has certainly done more than is often realised to maintain the myth of a golden age in England. This flattering and reassuring picture did contain some elements of truth. It is representative, in that in reflects the ideology of the most important and powerful section of the population; and it depicts society in a way that brings out the relationships and tensions between the classes.

With the first of the historical novels, *Micah Clarke*, we are again shown a developing society. Conan Doyle lets us see it from inside, and understand how it works. Behind his account of the vicissitudes of Monmouth's rebellion we can make out the way in which the 'true country', temporarily defeated at the battle of Sedgemoor, finally

---

[1] 'Mrs. Humphrey Ward at the Authors' Club', *The Queen*, 25 May 1901.

triumphs over the 'legal country', which no longer represents it. The reader identifies himself with the hero—a Walter Scott hero—and thus with the 'true country'. For Micah has been intentionally made one of the typical lower middle-class latitudinarians of the latter part of the seventeenth century, a class from which the numerous and powerful provincial middle-classes of the nineteenth century derived their power. In the novels of chivalry that followed *Micah Clarke*, Conan Doyle deserted 'bourgeois realism' and took to 'critical realism', to use Lukacs's expressions.[1]

What Lukacs has to say about Thackeray, and the relation between *Henry Esmond* and the work of the English realists of the eighteenth century, clearly reveals the difference between Conan Doyle and Scott. Taking, or pretending to take, Scott as his model, Conan Doyle has portrayed a society whose ideological connection with the public of the nineties is very different to that between the world of *Ivanhoe*, for example, and English society in 1819. As with *Henry Esmond*, the relationship is implicitly satirical. We must remember that for Conan Doyle the second half of the fourteenth century marked the apogee of English power. Unless this view is quite senseless, it shows that Conan Doyle's conception of national power was not based on economic, military or even imperial considerations. How is it possible to maintain that England was more powerful in 1366 than in 1891? Only in so far as she can be seen to have had greater national unity—it is a somewhat Carlylian view—unity of class, community of effort and interest, omnipotence of religious faith. And in *The White Company*, Conan Doyle is faithful to the theories of the historian of the French Revolution, and presents us with the salutary example of a France divided against herself and given over to the Jacqueries. With Manichean simplicity, he reduces the social virtues to terms of national feeling combined with racial idealism, if not with religious fanaticism (even the heroes of the novels of chivalry resemble Micah Clarke in this respect).

Conan Doyle's development towards critical realism can be seen in all his historical novels up to the collection of stories called *The Last Galley*. We notice it particularly in *The Refugees*, whose plot depends on the Revocation of the Edict of Nantes and the disastrous results it had for France. Although Conan Doyle never stressed the political implications of his novels, there is a noticeable parallel

[1] *The Historical Novel*, 1962.

between *The Refugees* and *Micah Clarke*. Perhaps his interest in the status of religious minorities was connected with his feelings about Home Rule.

As for *Rodney Stone*, it contains an implicit condemnation of 'degenerate' dandyism, which he associated with futurism in art, as against 'healthy' dandyism, in other words the national trend represented by some of Nelson's most brilliant contemporaries.

The historical novel could not produce an awakening of the national conscience by its unaided efforts: this forseeable conclusion was borne in on Conan Doyle's mind the day after the publication of *Sir Nigel*. The comments that greeted this novel in 1906 reminded him of those with which *The White Company* had been received. For the second time the critics warmly praised the dramatic interest of the book and the talent of the narrator. But most of them gave merely perfunctory acknowledgement to the detailed historical and social background, and failed to understand the moral and political message. The Challenger cycle which, with *The Lost World*, initiated the final phase of Conan Doyle's literary activity, represented a form of renunciation on his part.

The general curve of his work thus follows the trend of his psychological and spiritual evolution: his inability to come to terms with the age in which he lived is shown in a tendency to diverge from contemporary reality in his work. He was destined to become a romantic. And who could have guessed that the young Southsea doctor would one day be the apostle of a world crusade?

As Conan Doyle would have wished, some of his historical novels have become classics outside England, particularly in the United States. As for Sherlock Holmes, a civilisation pledged to ever speedier scientific progress sees him as the symbol of its own attitude. The reason for this is that, beneath their diverse forms and subjects, Sir Arthur Conan Doyle's works are derived from the same source of epic inspiration as nourished England's greatest prose writers.

BIBLIOGRAPHY
BIOGRAPHICAL ARCHIVES
GENERAL SOURCES
INDEX

BIBLIOGRAPHY

Works by Sir Arthur Conan Doyle

The reader should consult Locke, H.: *A Bibliographical Catalogue of the Writings of Sir Arthur Conan Doyle, 1879–1928* (1928, 84 pp.), which it is neither possible nor necessary to reproduce here. However, since it stops at 1928 and contains a certain number of gaps, a supplementary bibliography is given below. Locke's *Catalogue* is divided into five sections: 'Contributions to Magazines' (pp. 11–18), 'Pamphlets' (pp. 19–21), 'Plays' (p. 22), 'Prefaces' (p. 23), 'Published Works' (pp. 24–79), this last section corresponding to the list printed in *The Cambridge Bibliography of English Literature*, vol. III, pp. 542–3. This supplement adopts Locke's classification.

I

London Society (Locke, p. 11), Christmas Numbers.
1881. *The Little Square Box.*
1883. *The Silver Hatchet.*
1885. *The Parson of Jackman's Gulch.*

Chamber's Journal (Locke, p. 11).
1895, Jan. *The Recollections of Captain Wilkie.*

The Nineteenth Century (Locke, p. 11).
1901, March. *Reply to Col. Lonsdale Hale on Home Defense* (see Col. Lonsdale Hale, *Sham versus Real Home Defence* in the preceding number, for February).

Harper's Magazine (Locke, p. 12).
1892, Sept. *Lot No. 249* (reprinted in *Round the Red Lamp*, 1894, cf. Locke, p. 41).

The Idler Magazine (Locke, p. 12).
1892, July. *The Glamour of the Arctic* (reprinted in *McClure, vide infra*, March 1894).
1892, March. *De Profundis* (reprinted in *McClure*, Nov. 1894 and in *The Last Galley*, 1911, cf. Locke, p. 60).
1892, Dec. *The Los Amigos Fiasco* (reprinted in *Round the Red Lamp*, 1894, cf. Locke, p. 41).

1893, Jan. *My first Book: Juvenilia*. (This article was the cause of Stevenson's famous letter to Conan Doyle of 9 September 1894; it was reprinted in *McClure*, August 1894.)

1893, Nov. *The Case of Lady Sannox* (reprinted in *Round the Red Lamp*, 1894, cf. Locke, p. 41).

1894, April. *The Doctors of Hoyland* (reprinted in *McClure*, Aug. 1894 and *Round the Red Lamp*, cf. Locke, p. 41).

1894, July. *Sweethearts* (reprinted in *McClure*, Oct. 1894).

The Strand Magazine (Locke, p. 13).
1891, March. *The Voice of Science*.

The following must be added to the list of eighteen magazines given by Locke:

The National Review.
1890, Jan. *The Methods of R. L. Stevenson in Fiction.*

Temple Bar.
1891, Feb. *Our Midnight Visitor.*

McClure's Magazine (New York).
1894, Dec. *A Foreign Office Romance* (reprinted in *The Green Flag*).
1897, May. *The Governor of St. Kitts* (reprinted in *The Conan Doyle Stories*, (*vide infra*), 'Tales of Pirates').
1897, July. *The Two Barks* (reprinted in Murray's edition under the title: *The Dealings of Captain Sharkey with Stephen Craddock*).
1897, Aug. *The Voyage of Copley Banks* (reprinted in Murray's edition.)

Young Man.
1894, Jan. *An Alpine Walk* (reprinted in *The Strand Magazine*, Dec. 1894 and *McClure*, March 1895).

Great Thoughts.
1894, May, June. *On Books.*

Sunlight Year Book.
1898. *The New Catacomb* (reprinted in *The Green Flag*, 1900, cf. Locke, p. 50).

Cosmopolitan (New York).
1895, Sept. *Tempted by the Devil.*
1898, Dec. *The Retirement of Signor Lambert.*

The Bookman.
1899, July. *Multiple Reviewing.*

Munsey's Magazine (New York).
1900, March. *My Favourite Novelist and His Best Book*.

The Irish Times.
1954, 13–22 September. *The Wild Geese, The Story of the Irish Brigades in France*. MS. dating from the end of 1897 or beginning of 1898. (On the back of the original Conan Doyle has written in pencil his poem *The Old Gray Fox*, published in 1898 in *Songs of Action*.)

III

Locke is inexact and incomplete here. The following should be differentiated:

1. Plays performed and published:
1893. *Jane Annie, or The Good Conduct Prize*. A Comic Opera by J. M. Barrie and A. Conan Doyle. Music by Ernest Ford. First performance: 13 May, Savoy Theatre. Published by Chappell and Co.
1894. *A Story of Waterloo*, adaptation of *A Straggler of Fifteen* (*Round the Red Lamp*, 1894, cf. Locke, p. 41). Produced and acted by Henry Irving. First performance, Prince's Theatre, Bristol, 21 September. Published by Samuel French Ltd., 1907.
1901. *Sherlock Holmes* (adaptation by W. Gillette and A. Conan Doyle). First performance, 9 September, Lyceum Theatre. Published by Samuel French, 1922.
1912. *The Speckled Band*. Numerous performances at the Adelphi Theatre; revived in 1921 at the St. James's, with Lyn Harding and H. A. Saintsbury. Published by Samuel French Ltd., 1912.

2. Plays performed but not published:
1895. *A Question of Diplomacy* (adaptation of one of the stories in *Round the Red Lamp*, cf. Locke, p. 41).
1899. *Halves* (or *Brothers*). First performance, 10 April, Her Majesty's Theatre, Aberdeen. Afterwards at the Garrick Theatre.
1903. *A Duet* (adaptation of the story of the same title).
1909. *The Fires of Fate* (adaptation of *The Tragedy of the Korosko*). Lewis Waller created the part of Colonel Egerton at the Lyric Theatre in June. Performed later that summer at the Shakespeare Theatre, Liverpool.
1910. *The House of Temperley* (after *Rodney Stone*). First performance, 11 February at the Adelphi Theatre. Played before the King on 14 February.
1910. *Brigadier Gerard*. Part created by Lewis Waller.
1912. *The Pot of Caviare* (adaptation of the story of the same title published in *The Strand Magazine*, 1908).

1921. *The Crown Diamond: An Evening with Sherlock Holmes*. At the Coliseum. Adapted in *The Adventure of the Mazarin Stone* (*The Strand Magazine*, Oct. 1921).

3. Unpublished texts of plays never performed:
Vide infra (unpublished sources).

IV

To Locke's list the following must be added:

1907. *The Construction and Reconstruction of the Human Body* by E. Sandow, with a foreword by Sir A. C. Doyle.

1909. *Great Britain and the Congo* by E. D. Morel, with an introduction by Sir A. C. Doyle.

1912. *Divorce and Morality* by C. S. Bremner, with a preface by Sir A. C. Doyle.

1914. '*G. H. Darby*', *Captain of the Wyrley Gang*, by G. A. Atkinson, with prefaces by Sir. A. C. Doyle.

1920. *Life after Death* by J. M. Wilson, Canon of Worcester, with replies by A. C. Doyle.

1924. *Phantoms of the Dawn* by V. C. Tweedale, with a foreword by Sir A. C. Doyle.

V

Before 1887 (Locke, p. 24), the following must be added:

1886. *Dreamland and Ghostland: an Original Collection of Tales and Warnings from the Borderland of Substance and Shadow*, 3 vol. (ed. G. Redway). Vol. I of this anthology includes: *J. Habakuk Jephson's Statement*, and Vol. III: *The Great Keinplatz Experiment, The Mystery of Sasassa Valley, The Captain of the Polestar, John Barrington Cowles*.

After 1928 (Locke, p. 79), the following must be added:

1929. *Our African Winter*, Hodder and Stoughton.
      The Roman Catholic Church, Psychic Press.
1930. *The Edge of the Unknown*, John Murray.
1928. The Complete Works, John Murray's edition: *The Complete Sherlock Holmes Short Stories*.
1929. *The Complete Sherlock Holmes Long Stories*.
1929. *The Conan Doyle Stories*.
1931. *The Conan Doyle Historical Romances*, vol. I.
1932. *The Conan Doyle Historical Romances*, vol. II.
1952. *The Professor Challenger Stories*.
1956. *The Complete Napoleonic Stories*.

BIOGRAPHICAL ARCHIVES

The catalogue compiled by Mr. Adrian Conan Doyle contains over fifty pages. A photographic reproduction of part of the archives will be found in *Sir Arthur Conan Doyle: Centenary, 1859–1959, some Aspects of his Works and Personality*, edited by Adrian M. Conan Doyle and P. Weil-Nordon, with a Biographical introduction by P. Weil-Nordon, London (John Murray), 1959.

The archives consist of:

1. Genealogical documents.

2. Mementos, albums and correspondence relating to Sir Arthur Conan Doyle's ancestors, as well as a certain number of works of art by them.

3. Mementos and correspondence concerning Sir Arthur; letters written or received by him.

4. The Conan Doyle Library (with the writer's own copies of his works and a unique copy of *The Great Boer War*).

5. Manuscripts of published and unpublished works. Among the latter:

Notes and interesting drafts for the published works.

Collections of more personal notes: 'Southsea Notebooks', 3 vols. 1885–1890; 'Diaries' (1915–1918); twenty-five exercise- and memorandum-books containing brief notes covering the period 1891–1928; two short stories; the MSS. of seven plays:

(*a*) 'Angels of Darkness', an adaptation of the American episodes in *A Study in Scarlet* with the following names among the Dramatis Personae: John Ferrier, A Gentile farmer of Utah; John Watson, M.D., San Francisco practitioner; Sir Montague Brown, Aristocratic English globe-trotter, but no Sherlock Holmes.

(*b*) 'Sir Charles Tregellis'.

(*c*) 'Admiral Denver'.

(*d*) 'Foreign Policy' (from which was adapted the story *A Foreign Office Romance* published in *The Green Flag* in 1900).

(*e*) 'Mrs Thompson'. (In 1924 Conan Doyle thought of getting this play produced and showed it to Sybil Thorndike.)

(*f*) 'The Stonor Case' (a first version of *The Speckled Band*).

(*g*) 'The Lift' (from which was adapted the story of the same name published in John Murray's edition, p. 864.)

6. Various, including a photocopy of *The Casement Petition*. (Source U.S.A. From the Clement Shorter sale, 1916).

GENERAL SOURCES

Historical and social documentation, history of ideas, critical interpretation, methodology, bibliography.

1 *The Dictionary of National Biography to 1900*, edited by Sir Leslie Stephen and Sir Sidney Lee, Oxford University Press, 22 vols.

Ditto. *The Twentieth Century*, Oxford University Press, 4 vols.
(*a*) Vol. I, 1901–1911, edited by Sir Sidney Lee (reprinted 1958).
(*b*) Vol. II, 1912–1921, edited by H. W. C. Davis and J. R. H. Weaver (reprinted 1947).
(*c*) Vol. III, 1922–1930, edited by J. R. H. Weaver (reprinted 1953).
(*d*) Vol. IV, 1931–1940, edited by L. G. Wickham Legg, 1949.

2 Halévy, E., *Histoire du Peuple Anglais au XIXe siècle*, Epilogue; vol. I. *Les Impérialistes au Pouvoir (1895–1905)*, Paris Hachette, 1926, vi + 420 pp;
vol II. *Vers la Democratie Sociale et vers la Guerre (1905–1914)*, Paris, Hachette, 1932, vi + 663 pp.

3 Trevelyan, G. M., *English Social History*, Longmans, 3rd ed., 1946, xii + 628 pp.

4 Trevelyan, G. M., *British History in the Nineteenth Century and After (1782–1919)*, Longmans, 2nd ed., 1948, xvi + 512 pp.

5 Trevelyan, G. M., *History of England*, Longmans, 3rd ed., 1947, xxii + 756 pp.

6 Touchard, J., *Histoire des Idées Politiques*, Paris, P.U.F. ('Themis'), 1959, 2 vols. 865 pp.

7 Young, G. M., *Victorian England, Portrait of an Age*, Oxford University Press, 1936, reprinted 1960 (Oxford Paperbacks), vii + 219 pp.

8 Lewis, R. and Maude, A., *The English Middle Classes*, Penguin, 1949, 256 pp. (Descriptive and not very scientific, although setting out to be an objective enquiry.)

9 Bridenne, J-J., *La Littérature Française d'Imagination Scientifique*, Paris, Dassonville, 1950, 294 pp. (A study of literary history concerned also with England).

10 Thomson, D., *England in the Nineteenth Century*, 1815–1914, Penguin, 1950, 251 pp.

11 Bennett, G. (Ed.), *The Concept of Empire from Burke to Attlee*,

1774–1947, A. & C. Black, 1953, xx + 434 pp. (On the political traditions and especially the history and principles of English imperialism; contains useful bibliographical material.)

12 Allen, W., *The English Novel*, Penguin, 1954, 376 pp.

13 Leclaire, L., *Le Roman Régionaliste dans les Iles Britanniques, 1800–1850*, Paris, Les Belles Lettres, 1954, 300 pp.

14 Tillyard, E. M. W., *The English Epic and its Background*, Chatto and Windus, 1954, x + 548 pp.

15 Wellek, R., and Warren, A., *Theory of Literature*, Jonathan Cape, 1953 (4th ed. 1955), 416 pp. (Contains some very interesting passages on the relations between science, religion and literature.)

16 Adams, W. S., *Edwardian Portraits*, Secker & Warburg, 1957, 228 pp.

17 Watt, I., *The Rise of the Novel*, Chatto & Windus, 1957, 319 pp.

18 Tillyard, E. M. W., *The Epic Strain in the English Novel*, Chatto & Windus, 1958, 208 pp.

19 Williams, R., *Culture and Society*, Chatto & Windus, 1958, x + 353 pp.

20 Allen, H. C., *The Anglo-American Relationship since 1783*, A. & C. Black, 1960, 247 pp.

21 Brock, W. R., *The Character of American History*, Macmillan, 1960, xii + 294 pp.

22 Lukacs, G., *La Signification Présente du Réalisme Critique*, Paris, Gallimard, 1960, 276 pp.

23 Lukacs, G., *The Historical Novel*, Merlin, 1962, 363 pp.

24 Bateson, F. W. (Ed.), *The Cambridge Bibliography of English Literature*, University Press, 4 vols. 1940.
Watson, G. (Ed.), *The Cambridge Bibliography of English Literature*, Supplement, University Press, 1957.

25 Sanders, C., *An Introduction to Research in English Literary History*, New York, Macmillan, 1952 (2nd ed. 1956), 423 pp. (A very useful work, and well worth consulting.)

Books and articles useful in the study of Sir Arthur Conan Doyle and his work.

26 1885. *Blackwood's Edinburgh Magazine*, April, no. 834, pp. 485–91, 'The Pictures of Richard Doyle'.

27 1892. *The Bookman*, May; R. Blathwayt, 'An Interview with Dr. Conan Doyle'.

28 1894. *The Young Man*, July; W. J. Dawdon, 'Arthur Conan Doyle, A Character Sketch'.

29 1895. Arthur Conan Doyle, *The Stark Munro Letters*, Longmans, Green & Co., 346 pp.

30 1901. Pond, J. B., *Eccentricities of Genius*, Chatto & Windus, xxvi + 564 pp.

31 1902. *The Bookman*, April; J. E. Hodder Williams, 'Sir Arthur Conan Doyle'.

32 1906. Bram Stoker, *Personal Reminiscences of Henry Irving*, Heinemann, xvii + 480 pp.

33 1907. Sir Arthur Conan Doyle, *Through the Magic Door*, Smith Elder & Co., 274 pp.

34 1912. *The Bookman*, November; A. St. John Adcock, 'Sir Arthur Conan Doyle'.

35 1914. McClure, S. S., *My Autobiography*, John Murray, 266 pp.

36 1915. Sladen, D., *Twenty Years of My Life*, Constable, xii + 365 pp.

37 1924. Sir Arthur Conan Doyle, *Memories and Adventures*, Hodder & Stoughton; 2nd ed., John Murray, 1930, 460 pp.

38 1929. Hammerton, J. A., *Barrie, The Story of a Genius*, Sampson, Low, Marston & Co., 344 pp.

39 ,, *A Mixed Grill, A Medley in Retrospect*, by the author of *A Garden of Peace*, Hutchinson, 288 pp.

40 ,, Davies, C. H., *Eugene Field's Creative Years*, New York, Doubleday, Page & Co., 339 pp.

41 1930. Villavieja, (Marquis de), *Life has been good*, Chatto & Windus, 336 pp.

42 ,, *The Spectator*, 12 July, obituary notice.

42 *bis* ,, *The New Statesman*, 12 July, obituary notice.

43 1931. Croxton, A., *Crowded Nights and Days, an unconventional pageant*, Sampson, Low, Marston & Co., xviii + 398 pp.

44 ,, Lamond, J., *Arthur Conan Doyle, a Memoir: with an Epilogue by Lady Conan Doyle*, John Murray, xiv + 310 pp.

45 1933. Walters, J. C., *Knight of the Pen*, 254 pp.

46 1934. Stannard, R., *With the Dictators of Fleet Street*, Hutchinson, 287 pp.

47 ,, Hamilton, C., *People Worth Talking About*, Hutchinson, 283 pp.

48 „ Hole, H., *Looking Life Over*, Ivor, Nicholson & Watson, 288 pp.

49 1937. Maxwell, W. B., *Time Gathered*, 357 pp.

50 1944. Arnold, J. B., *Giants in Dressing Gowns*, MacDonald, 176 pp.

51 1945. *John O'London's Weekly*, 1 June, M. Devereux 'With Bat and Pen'.

52 „ *The Cornhill Magazine*, Nos. 963 and 964; 'Richard Doyle'› by Peter Quennell.

53 „ Adrian M. Conan Doyle, *The True Conan Doyle, with a Preface by Sir Hubert Gough*, John Murray, 24 pp. (A biographical sketch in refutation of H. Pearson's pseudo-biography published by Methuen, 1943.)

54 1948. Hambourg, D., *Richard Doyle: His Life and Work*, Art & Technics Ltd., 96 pp.

55 1949. Carr, J. D., *The Life of Sir Arthur Conan Doyle*, John Murray, 362 pp.

56 1951. Phillpots, E., *From the Angle of 88*, Hutchinson, 128 pp.

57 1954. Trevelyan, G. M., *A Layman's Love of Letters* (The Clark Lectures, Cambridge), Longmans, 125 pp.

58 1959. Lochhead, M., *Young Victorians*, John Murray, xii + 240 pp.

59 „ Adrian M. Conan Doyle and P. Weil-Nordon (Ed.), *Sir Arthur Conan Doyle Centenary, 1859–1959*, John Murray, 136 pp. (illustrated commemorative album).

60 1960. *Journal of the Kansas Medical Society*, January (vol. LXI, No. 1); C. Frederic Kittle, 'Arthur Conan Doyle'.

The following works throw light on Sir Arthur Conan Doyle's (*a*) civic, (*b*) spiritualistic, and (*c*) literary activities respectively.

(*a*) *Civic Activities*

61 1900. *Macmillan's Magazine*, November; Fortescue, J. W., 'Our Army and its Critics'.

62 „ *The Cornhill Magazine*, December: Maude, F. N. (Lieutenant-Colonel), 'Reply to Conan Doyle'.

63 1901. *The Nineteenth Century*, February; Colonel Lonsdale Hall: 'Sham *versus* Real Home Defence'.

64 1905. St. John, (Sir Frederick), *Reminiscences of a Retired Diplomat*, Chapman & Hall, 307 pp.

65 1907. Sir Arthur Conan Doyle, *The Case of Mr. George Edalji*, Blake & Co. (A reprint of articles published in *The Daily Telegraph*.)

66 1910–1950. Roughead, W., *The Trial of Oscar Slater* (1st ed.); 4th ed. dedicated to Sir Arthur Conan Doyle, Hodge & Co., Ltd, 338 pp.

67 1920. Blücher, (Princess E.), *An English Wife in Berlin*, New York, E. P. Dutton & Co., xi + 336 pp.

68 1921. Irving, H. B., *Last Studies in Criminology*, W. Collins, Sons & Co., Ltd., 281 pp.

69 1951. Hunt, P., *Oscar Slater, The Great Suspect*, Carroll & Nicholson Ltd., 248 pp.

70 1955. Browne, D. G. & Tullett E. V., *Bernard Spilsbury: His Life and Cases*, Penguin, 408 pp.

71 „   Marquard, L., *The Story of South Africa*, Faber & Faber, 256 pp.

72 1956. MacColl, R., *Roger Casement: A New Judgement*, Hamish Hamilton, 328 pp.

73 1957. Patterson, S., *The Last Trek: A Study of the Boer People and the Afrikaner Nation*, Routledge, 345 pp.

74 1962. Compton Mackenzie, *On Moral Courage*, Collins, 255 pp.

(b) Spiritualistic Activities

75 1907. Myers, F. W. H., *Human Personality and its Survival After Bodily Death*, Longmans, Green & Co., xviii + 470 pp.

76 1920. Lodge, O., *The Survival of Man*, New York, vii + 379 pp.

77 1930. D. Arthur Jones, *The Life and Letters of Henry Arthur Jones*, Victor Gollancz, 448 pp.

78 1932. Ernst, B. M. L. and Carrington, H., *Houdini and Conan Doyle, The Story of a Strange Friendship*, New York, Albert and Charles Boni, Inc, 249 pp.

79 1948. Rhine, J. B., *The Reach of the Mind*, Faber & Faber; reprinted Penguin, 1954, 198 pp.

80 1951. Aron, R. (Ed.), *Mors et Vita* (Texts and documents), Paris, Plon, 291 pp.

81 1953. Broad, C. D., *Religion, Philosophy and Psychical Research*, Routledge, viii + 308 pp.

82 „   Flew, A. G. N., *A New Approach to Psychical Research*, Watts, viii + 161 pp.

83 „ Thurston, H., *Ghosts and Poltergeists*, Burns, Oates & Wash-bourne Ltd., 210 pp.

84 1954. Amadou, R., *La Parapsychologie*, Paris, Denoël. 369 pp.

85 „ Castellan, Y., *Le Spiritisme*, Paris, P.U.F. ('Que Sais-je?'), 126 pp.

86 1955. Castellan, Y., *La Métapsychique*, Paris, P.U.F. ('Que Sais-je?') 123 pp.

87 1957. Neuville, P., *Les Explorateurs de l'au-delà, les Médiums, leur Vie*, Paris, Robert Laffont, 247 pp.

88 „ Cooke, I. (Ed.), *The Return of Arthur Conan Doyle*, White Eagle Publishing Trust, xvii + 203 pp.

(c) Literary Activities

89 1892. Marbot, (Baron), *Memoirs* (translated by Arthur John Butler), Longmans, Green & Co., 2 vols., vii + 452 + 472 pp.

90 1896. *Warner's Library of Best Literature*, New York, vol. VIII, p. 4815, 'Arthur Conan Doyle'.

91 „ *The Windsor Magazine*, October; Maclauchlan, H.S., 'An Appreciation of Arthur Conan Doyle'.

92 1897. *The Canadian Magazine*, Toronto, October; D. C. Murray, 'My Contemporary in Fiction'.

93 1901. *The Twentieth Century*, May; R. Cromie 'Dr. Conan Doyle's Place in Modern Literature'.

94 „ Stevenson, R. L., *Letters to his Family and Friends*, selected and edited with notes and Introduction, by Sidney Colvin, Methuen & Co., 2 vol., xliv + 375 pp. and xiii + 389 pp.

95 1904. *The Quarterly Review*, July No. 399, Art. VII, 'The Novels of Sir Arthur Conan Doyle' (anonymous, attributed by me to Sir G. Prothero).

96 1913. A. C. Fox Davies (Ed.), *The Book of Public Speaking*, vol. I, xvi + 303 pp.

97 1923. A. St. John Adcock, *Gods of Modern Grub Street*, Sampson, Low, Marston & Co., viii + 327 pp.

98 1928. Locke, H., *A Bibliographical Catalogue of the Writings of Sir Arthur Conan Doyle, 1879–1928*, Tunbridge Wells, 1928, 84 pp. (Cf. my supplementary bibliography. This book includes invaluable indications of the way in which the novelist's various works were received.)

99 1929. *Evening News*, 16 August; J. B. Priestley, 'A Great Story Teller's Secret'.

100 1934. Grant Richards, *Author Hunting: Memories of Years Spent Mainly in Publishing*, with an Introduction by Alec Waugh, 1934. New edition 1960, The Unicorn Press, xix + 238 pp.

101 1938. Klinefelter, W., *Ex-Libris A. Conan Doyle*, Chicago, Black Cat Press.

102 1943. *John O'London's Weekly*, 27 August; L. A. G. Strong, 'What is a Short Story?'.

103 1947. *John Buchan by his Wife and Friends*, Hodder & Stoughton. (On p. 127 is an important letter from Buchan to his wife, dated 11 April 1893, about Conan Doyle's early works.)

104 1950. Bryant, A., *The Age of Elegance*, Collins; Penguin, 1958, 286 pp.

105 ,, *The Hampshire Chronicle*, 22 April, 'Conan Doyle and Hampshire'.

106 1955. Carrington, C., *Rudyard Kipling, His Life and Work*, Macmillan, xiv + 549 pp.

107 1956. Parkman, Francis, *France and England in North America*, A Selection, Edited with an Introduction and Notes by S. E. Morison, Faber & Faber, viii + 533 pp.

108 1957. Lewis, M., *The History of the British Navy*, Penguin, 288 pp.

109 1960. Morton Cohen, *Rider Haggard, His Life and Works*, Hutchinson, 327 pp.

Concerning Sherlock Holmes

110 1892. *The Bookman*, December, 'Dr. Joseph Bell on *The Adventures of Sherlock Holmes*'.

111 1908. *Collier's Weekly Magazine*, New York, 15 August, issue devoted to Sherlock Holmes.

112 1924. Locard, E., *Policiers de Roman et de Laboratoire*, Paris, Payot.

113 1928. Knox, R., *Essays in Satire*, Sheed & Ward, 2nd ed., 1954, x + 287 pp. (Contains an essay on Holmes written in 1911 for the Gryphon Club, Trinity College, and published in 1912 in the 'Oxford Blue Book'.)

114 1929. Messac, R., *Le 'Detective Novel' et l'influence de la Pensée Scientifique*, Paris, Champion, 675 pp.

115 1930. *Saturday Review of Literature*, New York, 2 August; Christopher Morley; 'In Memoriam: Sherlock Holmes'.

116 1932. Bell, H. W., *Sherlock Holmes and Dr. Watson: The Chronology of their Adventures*, Constable.

117 „ Blakeney, T. S., *Sherlock Holmes: Fact or Fiction?* John Murray, 134 pp.

118 1934. Bell, H. W. (Ed.), *Baker Street Studies*, Constable, 223 pp. (Contents: Dorothy Sayers, 'Holmes's College Career'; Helen Simpson, 'The Medical Career and Capacities of Dr J. H. Watson'; Vernon Rendall, 'The Limitations of Sherlock Holmes'; Vincent Starrett, 'The Singular Adventures of Martha Hudson'; Ronald A. Knox, 'The Mystery of Mycroft'; A. G. Macdonall, 'Mr. Moriarty'; S. C. Roberts, 'Sherlock Holmes and the Fair Sex'; H. W. Bell, 'The Date of The Sign of Four' and 'A Note on Dr. Watson's Wound').

119 „ Starrett, V., *The Private Life of Sherlock Holmes*, Ivor Nicholson & Watson, xi + 199 pp.

120 1935. Campbell, M., *Sherlock Holmes and Dr Watson, A Medical Digression*, Ash & Co. Ltd. (By the well-known English heart specialist.)

120A 1937. *Bulletin de la Société Jules Verne*, Paris, September, Cornelis Helling: 'Sherlock Holmes retrouvé dans Les Enfants du Capitaine Grant?' (A new light on the genesis of Sherlock Holmes.)

121 1939. *John O'London's Weekly*, 2 August; Lady Violet Bonham Carter: 'Characters I would like to meet: Sherlock Holmes's Boswell'.

122 „ *True Detective*, New York, December; Albert Ullman: 'Greater than Sherlock Holmes'.

123 1942. Haycraft, H., *Murder for Pleasure; The Life and Times of the Detective Story*, Peter Davies, 347 pp.

124 1946. Sayers, D., *Unpopular Opinions*, Gollancz, 190 pp.

125 1947. Warrack, G., *Sherlock Holmes and Music*, Faber & Faber, 56 pp.

126 1949. Pakington, H., *English Villages and Hamlets*, Batsford, xvi + 120 pp.

127 1951. Brend, G., *My Dear Holmes, A Study in Sherlock*, Allen & Unwin, 183 pp.

128 1951. *The Cornhill Magazine*, No. 987; James E. Holroyd: '221 B Baker Street?'

129 1953. Monod, S., *Dickens Romancier*, Paris, Hachette, 520 pp.

130 „ Roberts, S. C. *Holmes and Watson, A Miscellany*, O.U.P., 146 pp.

131 1954. *The Listener*, 14 January; Ridley M. R.: 'Sherlock Holmes and the Detective Story'. (1954 was the year of the centenary celebrations of Sherlock Holmes's birth.)

132 1956. Rhodes, H. T. F., *Alphonse Bertillon*, Harrap, 238 pp.

133 1957. O'Dea, T. F., *The Mormons*, C.U.P., xii + 290 pp.

134 1958. West, R. B., *Kingdom of the Saints*, Jonathan Cape.

135 „ Harrison, M., *In the Footsteps of Sherlock Holmes*, Cassell, xii + 292 pp.

136 „ Murch, A. E., *The Development of the Detective Novel*, Peter Owen, 272 pp.

137 1959. Holroyd, J. E., *Baker Street By-Ways*, Allen & Unwin, 158 pp.

138 „ Vigniel D., *Sherlock Holmes*. (Thesis for the Diploma of Advanced Studies of the University of Paris, 81 pp.; unpublished.)

139 1960. MacCleary, G. F., *On Detective Fiction and Other Things*, Hollis & Carter, 161 pp.

140 1961. *The Times Literary Supplement*, 23 June; A. Lejeune, 'Age of the Great Detective'.

141 „ *Punch*, 2 August; J. E. Hinder, 'Heartbeat in Baker Street'.

142 1962. Hardwick, M. and M., *The Sherlock Holmes Companion*, John Murray, ix + 232 pp.

143 „ *The Cornhill Magazine*, Winter 1962–3, No. 1034; Holroyd, J. E.: 'Baedeker and Baker Street'.

144 „ Baring-Gould, W. S., *Sherlock Holmes, A Biography of the World's First Consulting Detective*, Hart-Davis, 284 pp.

145 1964. Hardwick, M. and M., *The Man who was Sherlock Holmes*, John Murray, 92 pp.

INDEX

Sandow, E., 196
Sayers, Dorothy, 208
Scharlieb, Dr., 48
Schumacher, Dr. E. de, 71
Scott, C. P., 110
Scott, Admiral Sir Percy, 89
Scott, Robert, 198
Scott, Sir Walter, 3, 6, 15, 22, 225, 271,
   286-7, 297-9, 300, 302-3, 317, 320,
   336-7, 341, 343; *Ivanhoe*, 3, 298, 303,
   343; *Quentin Durward*, 320; *Rob Roy*,
   22
Seaman, Owen, 81
Shakespeare, 234, 239, 257, 264, 280;
   As You Like It, 186 n. 1; *Hamlet*,
   215-16, 269; *Macbeth*, 22, 264; *Mid-
   summer Night's Dream*, 209
Shannard (missionary in the Congo), 75
Sharp, Royden, 125-6
Sharp, Stephen, 205
Shaw, G. Bernard, xi, 15, 55, 66, 105,
   107, 110, 160, 185-6, 186 n. 1, 254; *The
   Man of Destiny*, 326; *Mrs. Warren's
   Profession*, 254
Shelley, Percy Bysshe, 249
Shepherd (missionary in the Congo), 75
Shorter, Clement, 105, 108-10
Sidgwick, Henry, 143
Sinclair, Upton, 105-6, 164, 187; *My
   Lifetime in Letters*, 106 n. 1
Sittig (cipher expert), 211
Sjoblom (missionary in the Congo), 75
Slater, Oscar, 114-15, 117, 127-38, 161,
   190-1, 275, 285
Smith, Captain (of the *Titanic*), 185
Smith, F. E. (afterwards 1st Earl of
   Birkenhead), 91, 98
Smith, George Joseph, 116
Smith, Greenhough, 203, 317
Smith, John Reginald, 56
Smith-Dorrien, General Sir Horace, 92-4,
   95 n.
Smollett, T., 225, 293
Socrates, 252
Sordet, General, 94
Spence, Edward, 198
Spencer, Herbert, 147
Spielmann, M. H., *History of Punch*, 13 n.
Spilsbury, Sir Bernard, 129 n., 137
Spinoza, B., 151
Spring Rice, Sir Cecil (afterwards 1st
   Baron Monteagle), 113
Stanbury, Captain, 155
Stanley, Lady Henrietta, 13
Stanley, John, 69
Stannard, R., *With the Dictators of Fleet
   Street*, 191
Starrett, Vincent, 277
Stead, William, 55-6, 58, 189, 232, 304;
   Methods of Barbarism, 56; *Shall I slay
   my Brother Boer?*, 56
Steele, Frederick D., 204
Stephen, Sir Herbert, 133, 135

Stephen, Sir Leslie, 104
Stevenson, R. L., 25, 33, 225, 228, 231,
   250, 321; *Correspondance*, 25, 321;
   Dr. Jekyll and Mr. Hyde, 217, 231, 241;
   The Dynamiter, 216, 228, 250-1; *The
   New Arabian Nights*, 228; *The Pavilion
   on the Links*, 228; *The Rajah's Diamond*,
   231; *Travels with a Donkey*, 321
Stewart, Balfour, 143
Stewart, J. I. M., 209
Steyn, Martinus, 49
Stoddart, 34
Stoker, Bram, *Dracula*, 336; *Personal
   Reminiscences of Henry Irving*, 39
Stokes, 70
Strauss, Richard, *Electra*, 338
Strutt, J., *Sports and Pastimes of the
   People of England*, 299 n. 2
Swedenborg, E., 149
Swinton, General, *Eyewitness*, 87
Sydenham, George, 1st Baron, 89, 110

Taine, H., 143, 326
Tchermak, 151
Tennyson, Alfred, Lord, 79, 143, 156,
   286, 304, 338
Thackeray, W. M., 5-6, 10-14, 33, 286,
   337, 343; *Henry Esmond*, 343; *The
   Kickleburys on the Rhine*, 11; *The
   Newcomes*, 11-13; *Our Street*, 11;
   Rebecca and Rowena, 11; *Snobs of
   England*, 10
Thesiger (British Consul in the Congo),
   75
Thiers, Adolphe, 14
Thomas, Sir Charles, 84
Thompson, Sir Henry, 56
Thomson, David, *England in the Nine-
   teenth Century*, 251
Thorne, Norman, 129 n.
Tillyard, E. M. W., 243, *The Epic Strain
   in the English Novel*, 243 n.
Toynbee, Arnold, 164
Trench, Detective-Lieut. J. J., 134-5
Trevelyan, G. M., 5 n. 2, 104; *British
   History in the Nineteenth Century and
   After*, 104; *History of England*, 304
Trevelyan, Sir George O., 110
Tullet, E. V. (and D. G. Browne), *Bernard
   Spilsbury, His Life and Cases*, 129 n.
Turner, Sir Alfred, 105, 110
Twain, Mark, *King Leopold's Soliloquy*,
   75
Tyrrell, Sir William, 112

Ure, Alexander, 131-2, 135

Vanbrugh, Sir John, *The Relapse*, 293
Vandervelde, Emile, 72
Van Dyck, A., 5, 190
Vermeersch, Father, 75-6, *La Question
   Congolaise*, 76